AMERICAN INDIAN CULTURE

Recent Titles in Cultures of the American Mosaic

Encyclopedia of Latino Culture: From Calaveras to Quinceañeras
Charles M. Tatum, Editor

AMERICAN INDIAN CULTURE

FROM COUNTING COUP TO WAMPUM

VOLUME ONE

Bruce E. Johansen, Editor

Cultures of the American Mosaic

An Imprint of ABC-CLIO, LLC
Santa Barbara, California • Denver, Colorado

Library of Congress Cataloging-in-Publication Data

American Indian culture : from counting coup to wampum / Bruce E. Johansen, editor.
    2 volumes – (Cultures of the American mosaic)
   Includes bibliographical references and index.
   ISBN 978-1-4408-2873-7 (alk. paper) – ISBN 978-1-4408-2874-4 (ebook) 1. Indians of North America–Social life and customs. I. Johansen, Bruce E. (Bruce Elliott), 1950-
   E98.S7A45 2015
   970.004'97–dc23   2015009534

ISBN: 978-1-4408-2873-7
EISBN: 978-1-4408-2874-4

19 18 17 16 15 1 2 3 4 5

This book is also available on the World Wide Web as an eBook.
Visit www.abc-clio.com for details.

Greenwood
An Imprint of ABC-CLIO, LLC

ABC-CLIO, LLC
130 Cremona Drive, P.O. Box 1911
Santa Barbara, California 93116-1911

This book is printed on acid-free paper ∞
Manufactured in the United States of America

CONTENTS

PREFACE

AMERICAN INDIAN CULTURE: FROM COUNTING COUP TO WAMPUM covers the broad roots of American Indian culture, including living traditions, rites of passage, folk culture, popular culture, subcultures, and other forms of shared expression. Non-Indians often believe there is a cohesive and shared culture among American Indians. While the broad culture shares general commonalities, rich variation exists within specific cultural expressions among different groups and regions. The essays in this work explore the commonalities and variations of cultural expression and provide readers with rich detail about the historical, regional, and ethnic/racial diversity within specific traditions. Essays cover history and origins; regional practices, traditions, and artifacts; and expressive forms in contemporary culture.

At about 300,000 words and filling two volumes, *American Indian Culture: From Counting Coup to Wampum* may seem quite lengthy, and, at first glance, comprehensive. However, anyone who knows how many thousands of books, articles, and other works have been published under the general rubric of Native American culture (past and present) will realize that this is only a brief swim in a sizable ocean.

Native American arts, for example, is a field that includes a wide array of genres, from ancient rock art to traditional painting, pottery, footwear, clothing, food-serving dishes, baskets, and boxes—all items used in everyday life, which have become media of artistic expression. The volumes excerpt an incredibly selective sampler of a very well-populated genre. To provide an idea of what's available, sample Dawn Reno's *Contemporary Native American Artists* (1995), which includes profiles of more than 1,000 visual artists of Native American ancestry. Gregory Schaaf's *American Indian Textiles* (2000) contains roughly 2,000 profiles of Native Americans who practice the weaving arts. Schaaf, who is director of the Center for Indigenous Arts & Cultures in Santa Fe, New Mexico, also has compiled *American Indian Jewelry III* (2013), a standard reference for the jewelers' trade that references more than 5,000 men and women in that field in two thick volumes, illustrated in full color. The "Music and Dance" section is equally varied. More precisely focused encyclopedias exist. See, for example, Elaine Keillor, Timothy Archambault, and John H. M. Kelly's *Encyclopedia of Native American Music in North America* (2013), with 449 pages.

This work is a compendium of a rich and enduring cultural past and present, richly illustrated with archival and contemporary images. It begins in Part 1 with a historical overview examining how many Native people lived in North America before sustained contact with Europeans, including the role of disease in depopulation and cultural destruction, concluding with demographic recovery (and revival of cultures) in the late 20th and early 21st centuries. The overview continues with profiles of Native nations, tribes, and other Native groups, including Alaska Native corporations; Apaches; California's plethora of Native peoples; Cherokees; Cheyennes; the Nez Perce; peoples of the Northwest Coast culture area; the Osage, Pequot, Ponca, and Pueblo cultural context; Seminole contemporary culture; the Utes; and Wyandot (Huron) economic culture. These are, of course, only a sampler of the more than 500 tribes and nations with whom the United States has treaty relationships (many others have survived, and some have gone largely extinct, without treaties).

The overview also includes several general historical considerations, such as the role of consensus in governance as a cultural value; guns, horses, and the fur trade's role in cultural change; and reflections on treaty diplomacy as an intercultural influence.

Part 2 offers essays on Cultural Forms, organized into the following topical sections: Arts; Family, Education, and Community; Food; Language and Literature; Media, Popular Culture, Sports, and Gaming; Music and Dance; Spirituality; and Transportation and Housing. Highlights are described in an introduction to each section. Several subjects (many of them new to the literature) receive Spotlight treatment, meaning the Spotlights provide more detailed information on an individual or topic related to the topic of the essay to which they are attached. Each essay includes a bibliography of important and useful print and electronic information resources, as well as cross-references to related entries in these volumes. The work concludes with a useful selected general bibliography and a detailed subject index.

The editor chose to focus on certain themes: the interface of tradition and change (understanding that traditions are not static) and continuity from the past, through a period of cultural repression, to revival in our time. The essays also concentrate on what makes certain peoples and individuals distinctive within the context of these themes. However, the tremendous variety of American Indian culture cannot be encompassed in just two volumes; it would take many more volumes to provide anything close to universality for 561 federally recognized tribes, bands, and nations. In addition, many individuals have distinguished themselves in cultural pursuits over the years. A complete account of all of this would require a large library.

American Indian Culture: From Counting Coup to Wampum may best be used by senior-level high school students, college undergraduates, and interested nonspecialist readers as an introduction to a large and rich field of study as well as a necessary corrective for many misunderstandings and stereotypes that have become embedded in general American society over many years. Readers will discover just how fundamentally their own lives have been influenced and enriched by Native American examples in our past, and by peoples with whom we live today. Be informed, and enjoy the journey.

Acknowledgments

Any book is a team sport, especially a large one that ranges over an expansive field of knowledge. Thanks are due to all the contributors, as well as our editors (most notably Kim Kennedy-White and John Wagner), for squeezing better work out of me. The University of Nebraska at Omaha interlibrary loan service has done yeoman service, as always. I am also indebted to the University of Nebraska at Omaha for allowing me partial relief from teaching duties (including what we used to call a sabbatical) to take this project to production during the fall of 2014. College of Communication, Fine Arts, and Media dean Gail Baker and School of Communication chair Hugh Reilly (who is one of our contributors) have been very helpful. Pat Keiffer, my wife, provided loving support, good food, and wise counsel as we worked our way through what became known around our house as "The Culture Monster."

INTRODUCTION

WHAT *IS* CULTURE? CULTURE PERVADES ALMOST EVERY ASPECT of human experience: economy, history, language, music, sports, food, housing, education, the arts, and spirituality, to name just some. "Culture" is thus one of those rubber words (another is "environment") that can mean many things. American Indian culture encompasses these aspects of human experience within and across the lives and societies of a great variety of groups and peoples native to the American continents. It is therefore important to begin this work by exploring the many definitions available for the word "culture" in an American Indian context.

Definitions of Culture

Culture may include the ways in which people wrest a living from their surroundings. The word itself comes from the Latin *cultura* (literally "cultivation"), as in "agriculture." Culture also refers to distinctive attributes of the knowledge of particular peoples ("Lakota culture," for example), or the shared practices, goals, and values of any group of people. Culture also has been defined in a broad sense as "shareable knowledge, practices, or technology that people use to adapt to an environment" (Dobbs, 2013, 53). "Culture" may also refer to human refinement or education; a person may be said to be "cultured." Such a person may be adept at creating or manipulating the arts and letters of a given language at a certain place and time, as a scholar or an artist.

So, for some Native American groups, "culture" includes tipis, arrowheads, and jingle dances. For others, particularly peoples of the Pacific Northwest, it more appropriately includes canoes, fish weirs, conical cedar hats, and "Indian ice cream." Culture also encompasses the ways people acquire, prepare, and consume food. Recovery of traditional food culture has developed on many reservations. The U.S. Agriculture Department gives grants for it.

Many things other than food may be cultivated, of course. Spirituality is part of culture, for example. American Indian spirituality often comprises creative combinations of Christian doctrines with Native traditions. English often does not contain the words required to describe how various Native peoples react with nature on a sacred level. A great many spiritual concepts have been Europeanized. The "Great Spirit," for example, is a monotheistic overlay upon cultures that usually did not recognize a single deity.

The ubiquity of culture, which pervades every aspect of collective and individual life, requires any reference work on American Indian culture to be highly selective about what it includes. For example, this work contains an essay on the cultural role of Haudenosaunee (Iroquois) women that is bound to provoke a question: Where are all the other women? Describing the women of more than 500 tribes and nations would require a book of its own (a thick one at that), thus the included essay invokes the Iroquois as an example of cultural attributes shared by many.

A people's explanation of its origins in a particular homeland is cultural; how a group describes its relations with nature and other human beings is cultural; the ceremonies and technology that developed over millennia related to the acquisition of food, shelter, and other necessities of daily life have cultural attributes—witness the First Salmon Ceremony, or the protocol of the buffalo hunt, or the rituals that accompany the raising of a Hidatsa earth lodge or a Haudenosaunee (Iroquois) longhouse. The longhouse in this case is a metaphor for a confederacy. How a people clothe themselves is an expression of culture. The artistry of daily life displays cultural attributes. What do the symbols on a "totem pole" mean? Every feather on certain types of headgear is a symbol, and symbols have cultural meaning. Pottery and baskets are more than vessels for cooking or carrying. They are receptacles of culture and artistry as well.

As the essays in these volumes indicate, Native cultures exhibit many surprising attributes. Some Native American cultural practices will strike many readers as very modern—for example, as regards sexual orientation, many American Indian attitudes toward gender fluidity (lesbian, gay, bisexual, transgender [or LGBT]) resemble a recent major change in attitudes among many non-Indians, as reflected even in decisions from the U.S. Supreme Court. Another surprise relates to the influence of Buffalo Bill's Wild West Show on pow wow formats (the "grand entry," for example, was invented by him in the 1880s). The vividness of Native American revival in the present, as people take charge of their own lives, appears in two entertaining essays that describe the role of "Indian humor" in modern Indian societies. Some essays deal with cultural misconceptions. For example, the "low man" on the totem pole usually has the highest status.

Other essays supply additional useful insights into American Indian culture. For example, in Plains warfare, touching an enemy ("counting coup") brought more valor than killing him. Some students at boarding schools took the English they learned there on the road as they took issue with the schools' assimilationist curricula in national magazines such as *Harper's* and *The Atlantic Monthly*. "Sleep on it" and "bury the hatchet" are figures of speech borrowed from Iroquois politics. A Cherokee (Sequoyah) was the first person in history to invent a written language on his own. Jay Silverheels (Tonto in *The Lone Ranger*) was also a labor organizer among Native American screen actors. The Pilgrims brought turkeys with them to Plymouth Rock. Wampum is most valuable among Native peoples for diplomacy and as a historical record, not as money, even though Harvard accepted wampum as payment of tuition during its earliest years. The richest group of people in the United States (per capita) in 1930 were the Osages in Oklahoma, due to their oil income.

Welcome to culture. Welcome to the tapestry of American Indian life.

The Politics of Naming

The right of naming is often assumed by the conqueror, but, as with culture of all kinds, this type of intercultural communication is never exclusively one-way. The title of this work—*American Indian Culture: From Counting Coup to Wampum*—refers to American Indians, but many of the people whose residence on the continents we now call "the Americas" object to that name on grounds that "Indian" recapitulates a mistaken assumption of Christopher Columbus that he was traveling to India. On the way, he bumped into a rather large obstacle that he did not expect to find. Thus, "American Indians" incorporates a problem of perspective. Millions of people had no problem finding their own homelands. "Native Americans" is often preferred, but even that assumes something of a European perspective because the continents have been named for an Italian mapmaker, Amerigo Vespucci (1454–1512).

In Canada, "First Nations" is used most often. "Indigenous" is also used, although the question then arises regarding how long a people must live in a place to become indigenous. That question was placed before American Indian author, historian, and activist Vine Deloria Jr. on a visit to Omaha in the early 1990s. He told a mainly "white" (another term with definitional problems) audience that a person is indigenous to a place where his or her ancestors are buried. This was suitable for a person who often said that although "race" has no validity as a biological concept, racism most surely exists in our culture.

Names used for various bands, tribes, nations, and confederacies of Native Americans can be confusing, often because they mix names that people used for themselves with those applied to them by immigrating Europeans. The word "Sioux," for example, was never used by the peoples to whom it has been applied by European immigrants. It is part of an archaic French word meaning "snake," or, by implication, "enemy." However, it is the only word that has been used in reference to the Dakotas, Nakotas, and Lakotas as a group, and it is used in this work in that sense. "Sioux" was sometimes also used in treaty language, as in "the Great Sioux Nation." Each of these confederacies, in turn, is made up of smaller subdivisions. The "Oglalas," for example, are one of seven groups within the Lakotas.

The "Iroquois" did not call themselves by that name. They were Haudenosaunee, the people of the longhouse, a confederacy of five nations (Mohawk, Oneida, Onondaga, Cayuga, and Seneca), which became six with the addition of the Tuscaroras during the early 18th century. Some names change over time. The Muckleshoots, for example, came to be known by that name only after treaties protecting their fishing rights were signed, a fact that provoked considerable legal confusion more than a century later during the legal battle to interpret and protect those rights. Courts at several levels took several decades to get the point that Muckleshoot rights were protected by treaties signed under other tribal names that included their ancestors.

The ethically diverse American culture often borrows "American Indian" names. Half the states borrow Native names, many of them Anglicized. Many cities, such as Omaha and Seattle, also bear such names. The Omahas (actually O'mo'hos) are a people. Seattle was a Duwamish and Suquamish leader (actually Sea'th'l), who did not want a city named for him because he believed that mentioning one's name after death prevented one's soul from finding peace. Perhaps his soul rested because the name was Anglicized. Native Americans are peoples of many cultures, and their names tell stories. For example, the editor of these volumes lives in Omaha on Blondo Street, named by someone who had no knowledge of French after an immigrant fur trader (Blondeau, most probably).

Cultural resurgence in Native America takes place in an atmosphere of historical perseverance. Alex White Plume, an Oglala Lakota, said:

> They tried extermination. They broke every single treaty they ever made with us. They took away our horses. They outlawed our language. Our ceremonies were forbidden. . . . Our holy leaders had to go underground for nearly a century. And yet our ceremonies survived. Our culture survived. (Fuller, 2012, 48)

Further Reading

Dobbs, David. "Restless Genes." *National Geographic*, January 2013, 44–57.

Fuller, Alexandra. "In the Shadow of Wounded Knee." *National Geographic*, August 2012, 30–67.

PART 1
OVERVIEW

POPULATION AND DEMOGRAPHICS

HOW MANY NATIVE PEOPLE IN 1491?

The number of people in a culture profoundly affects its complexity. Therefore, questions regarding the numbers of peoples who lived in the Americas prior to sustained contact with Europeans have provoked a lively debate. The size of Native populations at the first sustained contact with Europeans indicates not only the complexity of their cultures but also the scale of suffering during the holocaust that followed.

Estimates of hemispheric population at contact have ranged from 10 million to 110 million—a factor of 11. This debate involves two very different ways of looking at historical and archaeological evidence. One side in the population debate restricts itself to strict interpretation of the evidence at hand. Another point of view accepts the probability that observers (usually of European ancestry) recorded and gathered evidence from only a fraction of the phenomena that actually occurred in the Americas. Europeans have been attempting to estimate the number of Native peoples in the Americas nearly since Christopher Columbus made the first sustained contact with them.

The priest Bartolomé de Las Casas estimated that several million people lived on Hispaniola before Spanish guns and diseases killed nearly all of them. If 110 million people occupied the Americas in 1492 as Henry Dobyns (who died in 2009) has maintained, parts of the New World were as thickly populated as Europe and Asia. If estimates of 10 to 15 million are more accurate, many fewer died in the "encounter."

Estimates of Native American Populations

The fact that disease was a major cause of Native depopulation and cultural devastation is not at issue—both sides in this debate agree on the importance of disease. Disease ravaged Native Americans to such a degree that many early European immigrants (who at the time had no understanding of how pathogens spread disease) thought they had come to a land that had been emptied for them by their God. The debate is over the number of Native people who died.

The first systematic count was compiled during the early 20th century by James Mooney, who estimated that 1,153,000 people had lived in the land area now occupied by the United States when Columbus made landfall. Mooney calculated the 1907 Native population in the same area at 406,000. Dividing the country into regions, he calculated the percentage of population loss between 1492 and 1900 at between 61 percent (in the North Atlantic states) to 93 percent in California.

Following Mooney, the most widely followed population estimates were provided beginning in 1939 by A. L. Kroeber in his *Cultural and Natural Areas of Native North America*. By Kroeber's determination, only about 900,000 Native people had occupied North America north of Mexico before sustained European contact. According to Ann F. Ramenofsky, Kroeber did not consider disease as a factor in depopulation because he feared that such an emphasis would lead to an overestimation of precontact population sizes. One may speculate whether this was a case of deliberate scientific oversight or simple academic prudence, but the fact was that after nearly a half-century of authority for his conservative figures (a time when one could appear "radical" by arguing that in 1492 perhaps two million Native people occupied the area now occupied by the United States), a challenge was likely to arise.

Henry F. Dobyns, who did consider disease (some say he overemphasized it), stepped into that role along with others to initiate the modern debate. Dobyns estimated that about 16 million Native Americans lived in North America north of Mesoamerica, the area populated by the Aztecs and other Central American Native nations, at the time of Columbus's first voyage. Since population densities were much greater in Central America and along the Andes, an estimate of 16 million north of Mesoamerica indicates to Dobyns that 90 to 112 million Native people lived in the Americas before the year 1500, making some parts of the New World as densely populated at the time as many areas of Europe and Asia.

Dobyns's estimates of indigenous population at contact represented a radical departure from many earlier estimates, which depended, for the most part, on actual historical and archaeological evidence of Native populations, assuming

Aztec smallpox victims in the 16th century. Before the European invasion, Aztecs (or Mexicas) were more populous than any European nation. (Courtesy of the Peabody Museum of Archaeology and Ethnology, Harvard University, PM# 2004.24.29636)

that Euro-American scholars (and others, such as missionaries) were capable of counting Native people who had, in some cases, been dead for several centuries. Although anthropologists usually attribute the first attempt at measuring Native populations to Henry Schoolcraft (during the 1850s), Thomas Jefferson's *Notes on the State of Virginia* (published in several editions during the 1780s) contained an extensive (if fragmentary) Native American "census." Jefferson did not attempt to count the number of Native people inhabiting all of North America during his time—no one then even knew how large the continent might be, not to mention the number of people inhabiting it. Jefferson prudently settled for estimates of the Native nations bordering the early United States.

Disputes Regarding Research Methods

Defending his pre-Columbian population estimates, Dobyns argues that "absence of evidence does not mean absence of phenomenon," especially where written records are scanty, as in America before or just after sustained European contact (Dobyns, 1989, 286). Dobyns's position is that European epidemic diseases invaded a relatively disease-free environment in the Americas with amazing rapidity, first in Mesoamerica (via the Spanish), arriving in eastern North

America along Native trade routes long before English and French settlers arrived. The fact that Jacques Cartier observed the deaths of 50 Natives in the village of Stadacona in 1535 indicates to Dobyns that many more may have died in other villages that Cartier never saw. Given the lack of evidence, conclusions must be drawn from what little remains, according to Dobyns (1989), who extends his ideas to other continents as well: "Lack of Chinese records of influenza does not necessarily mean that the Chinese did not suffer from influenza; an epidemic could have gone unrecorded, or records of it may not have survived" (p. 296).

Critics of Dobyns's estimates assert that little information exists about pre-1500 population levels and that he misused evidence to sustain his argument for widespread 16th-century epidemics. To the critics of Dobyns, the fact that 50 Native people were recorded as dying at Stadacona means just that: 50 Natives died, no more, no fewer. To Dobyns (1989), however, such arguments "minimize Native American population magnitude and social structural complexity" (p. 289).

While Dean Snow and Kim M. Lanphear, both strident critics of Dobyns, maintain that buffer zones between populations may have impeded the spread of disease, Dobyns replies that the practice of trade, war, diplomacy, and other demographic movements obliterated such buffer zones and aided in the spread of disease. Snow and Lanphear also assert that the sparseness of Native populations in North America itself impeded the spread of disease, a point of view that does not account for the speed with which smallpox and other infections spread once history recorded them as having reached a particular area.

Dobyns not only denies that buffer zones existed but also maintains that smallpox was only the most virulent of several diseases to devastate New World populations. The others, roughly in descending order of deadliness, included measles, influenza, bubonic plague, diphtheria, typhus, cholera, and scarlet fever. According to Dobyns,

> The frontier of European/Euro-American settlement in North America was not a zone of interaction between people of European background and vacant land, nor was it a region where initial farm colonization achieved any "higher" use of the land as measured in human population density. It was actually an interethnic frontier of biological, social, and economic interchange between Native Americans and Europeans and/or Euroamericans. (Dobyns, 1983, 43)

The most important point to Snow and Lanphear, however, is "where one puts the burden of proof in this argument, or, for that matter, in any argument of this kind. . . . We cannot allow ourselves to be tricked into assuming the burden of disproving assertions for which there is no evidence" (Snow and Lanphear, 1989, 299).

Given the evidence they have in hand, however, even Snow and Lanphear acknowledge that between two-thirds and 98 percent of the Native peoples inhabiting areas of the northeastern United States died in epidemics between roughly 1600 and 1650. The Western Abenakis, for example, are said to have declined from 12,000 to 250 (98 percent), the Massachusetts (including the Narragansetts) from 44,000 to 6,400 (86 percent), the Mohawks from 8,100 to 2,000 (75 percent), and the Eastern Abenakis from 13,800 to 3,000 (78 percent) (Snow and Lanphear, 1988, 24). Given the number of people killed and the lengthy period during which they died, the world has probably not again seen such continuous human misery over such a large area.

Regardless of the dispute regarding population size and density before the devastation of European diseases, it is rather widely agreed that Native populations in North America bottomed at about half a million in the early 20th century, and they have been increasing since. For the United States, statistics contained in the 1990 Census indicated that roughly two million people listed themselves as Native American, a figure that nearly doubled in the 2000 U.S. Census. Such a measure may not be as precise as it sounds, because the Census allows people to categorize themselves racially. Also, for the first time, the 2000 Census was designed to allow people to report more than one ethnicity, a major source of the numerical increase for Native Americans.

See Also PART 1: OVERVIEW: POPULATION AND DEMOGRAPHICS: Disease, Depopulation, and Cultural Destruction; **PART 2: CULTURAL FORMS: FOOD:** Agriculture/Spotlight: Corn and Culture

Further Reading

Dobyns, Henry F. "Estimating Aboriginal American Population." *Current Anthropology* 7 (October 1966): 395–412.

Dobyns, Henry F. "More Methodological Perspectives on Historical Demography." *Ethnohistory* 36:3 (Summer 1989): 286.

Dobyns, Henry F. *Their Number Became Thinned.* Knoxville: University of Tennessee Press, 1983.

Henige, David P. *Numbers from Nowhere: The American Indian Contact Population Debate.* Norman: University of Oklahoma Press, 1998.

Johansen, Bruce E. "What Was the Population Density of the Native Peoples of America Prior to Sustained Contact with Europeans?" *The American Mosaic: The American Indian Experience.* ABC-CLIO, 2010. Web. Sept. 1, 2010. http://americanindian2.abc-clio.com/.

Las Casas, Bartolomé de. *The Devastation of the Indies.* New York: Seabury Press, [1542] 1974.

Mann, Charles C. "1491: America Before Columbus Was More Sophisticated and More Populous Than We Have Ever Thought—and a More Livable Place Than Europe." *The Atlantic Monthly*, March 2002, 41–53.

Mooney, James. "The Aboriginal Population of North America North of Mexico." Edited by J. R. Swanton. Smithsonian Miscellaneous Collections 80. Washington, DC: Smithsonian Institution, 1928.

Mooney, James. "Population." In F. W. Hodge, ed. *Handbook of American Indians North of Mexico. Bureau of American Ethnology Bulletin* 30, no. 2. Washington, DC: Smithsonian Institution, 1910, 28–87.

Ramenofsky, Ann F. *Vectors of Death: The Archeology of European Contact.* Albuquerque: University of New Mexico Press, 1987.

Snow, Dean R., and Kim M. Lanphear. "European Contact and Indian Depopulation in the Northeast: The Timing of the First Epidemics." *Ethnohistory* 35, no. 1 (Winter 1988): 15–33.

Snow, Dean R., and Kim M. Lanphear. "'More Methodological Perspectives': A Rejoinder to Dobyns." *Ethnohistory* 36, no. 3 (Summer 1989): 299–304.

DISEASE, DEPOPULATION, AND CULTURAL DESTRUCTION

Spanish chronicler Bernal Diaz del Castillo stood atop a great temple in the Aztec capital of Tenochtitlan and described causeways eight paces wide, teeming with thousands of Aztecs, crossing lakes and channels dotted by convoys of canoes. Spanish soldiers who had been to Rome or Constantinople told Diaz that "for convenience, regularity and population, they have never seen the like" (McDowell, 1980, 753). The comparisons of life among the Aztecs with what the Spanish knew of Europe acquire some substance as one realizes that, in 1492, the British Isles were home to only about five million people, while Spain's population has been estimated at eight millon. Even almost three centuries later, at the time of the American Revolution, the largest cities along the Eastern Seaboard of the new United States—Boston, New York, and Philadelphia—housed no more than roughly 50,000 people each. The Aztec metropolis is estimated to have contained 250,000 people at a time when Rome, Seville, and Paris housed about 150,000 each.

Descriptions of Native Populations and Their Demise

Within a decade of Hernan Cortés's first visit, Tenochtitlan and its culture was a ruin. Ten years after the Aztec ruler Moctezuma had hailed Cortés with gifts of flowers and gold (and had paid for such hospitality with his life), epidemics of smallpox and other diseases carried by the conquistadors had killed at least half the Aztecs. One of the Aztec chroniclers who survived described racking coughs and burning, painful sores.

The imported plague and cultural destruction followed the Spanish conquest as it spread in roughly concentric circles from the islands of Hispaniola and Cuba to the mainland of present-day Mexico. Bartolomé de Las Casas, the Roman Catholic priest who questioned Spanish treatment of the Natives, said that when the first visitors found it, Hispaniola was a beehive of people. Within 30 years of Cortés's arrival in Mexico, the Native population had fallen from about 25 million to roughly 6 million, according to "high-count" estimates. After Spanish authorities set limits on money wagers in the New World, soldiers in Panama were said to have made bets with Indian lives instead. Native people who were not killed outright by disease died slowly as slaves under the conquerors' lash.

Las Casas, who had arrived in the New World 10 years after Columbus, described one form of human servitude, pearl diving: "It is impossible to continue for long diving into the cold water and holding the breath for minutes at a time . . . sun rise to sun set, day after day. They die spitting blood . . . looking like sea wolves or monsters of another species" (Las Casas, [1542] 1974, 15). Other conquistadors disemboweled Native children. According to Las Casas, "They cut them to pieces as if dealing with sheep in a slaughterhouse. They laid bets as to who, with one stroke of a sword, could cut off his head or spill his entrails with a single stroke of the pike" (Las Casas, [1542] 1974, 43).

Fearing the Sight of the Honeybee

A century later, entering North America, the Puritans often wondered why the lands on which they settled, which otherwise seemed so bountiful, had been emptied of their Native American inhabitants. Four years before the *Mayflower* landed, a plague of smallpox had swept through Native villages along the coast of the area that the immigrants renamed New England. The disease may have been brought ashore by visiting European fishermen, who had been exploiting the rich coastal banks for many years. John Winthrop admired abandoned Native cornfields and declared that God had emptied the land for his fellow voyagers as an act of divine providence. As Native peoples died, complex cultures disintegrated.

As European immigrants spread westward, Native peoples learned to fear the sight of the honeybee. These "English flies" usually colonized areas about a hundred miles in advance of the frontier, and the first sight of them came to be regarded as a harbinger of death. The virulence of the plagues from Europe may be difficult to comprehend in our time. Even in Europe, where immunities had developed to many of the most serious diseases, one in seven people died in many smallpox epidemics. Half the children born in Europe during Columbus's life never reached the age of 15. Life expectancy on both sides of the Atlantic averaged 35 years as Europeans made sustained contact with the Americas.

Smallpox destroyed peoples and their cultures, including language and memory, which conduct cultures between generations. The incubation period for smallpox is two weeks, enough time for a person carrying it to mingle with many others (on a ship, for example) before the illness becomes obvious. Smallpox ravaged tribes in parts of Texas so often that no generation was left without memories, or scars: 1674–1675, 1688–1689, 1739, about 1746, 1750, 1759, 1763, 1766, 1778, 1801–1802, 1816, 1839–1840, 1861–1862, and 1864. Indians in present-day Oklahoma were immunized against smallpox in 1865, but another epidemic in New Mexico devastated the Mescalero Apaches in 1877. By 1882–1883, vaccination stemmed another possible epidemic among the Mescaleros. In addition to smallpox, epidemics of whooping cough, malaria, and influenza reduced Native populations, a devastating blow to languages and other attributes of culture that relied on human memory for transmission between generations.

Smallpox devastated the Pawnees along the Republican River so badly that their culture was forced to change as death overwhelmed their ability to cope. John Dougherty, an Indian agent at Cantonment Leavenworth, wrote that the Pawnees

> were dying so fast and taken down at once in such large numbers, that they had ceased to bury their dead, whose bodies were to be seen, in every direction, laying about in the river, lodged on the sandbars, in the hog weeds around their villages, and in their corn cashes [caches]; mothers again were dragged off by hungry dogs into the prairie. (Dougherty, 1831, n.p.)

When English explorer George Vancouver sailed into Puget Sound in 1793, he met Indian people with pockmarked faces and found human bones and skulls scattered along the beach, grim reminders of an earlier epidemic. Such scenes were repeated coast to coast in North America during the surge of European and European American exploration and settlement.

Cultural Consequences of Disease

Small tribes, devastated by diseases, combined with others to maintain some semblance of cultural identity. Disease affected the practice of war, as reductions in population made captives more valuable as adoptees. Torture and cannibalism of enemies declined in the face of epidemics. Human life was too valuable to waste. Traditional practices that had been used in the past to combat illness did not work against smallpox and other imported diseases, but Native people knew no alternatives. A Comanche treatment for smallpox in 1816 was described by David Burnett:

> The patients were strictly confined to their lodges, excluded from the [outdoor] air, and almost suffocated with heat. In many instances, while under the maddening influence of the disease, exasperated by a severe paroxysm of symptomatic fever, they would rush to the water and plunge beneath it. The remedy was invariably fatal. (Burnett, 1851, 234)

As populations declined, cultures became less complex; languages lost words. Especially in oral cultures, a declining population beset by disease and assimilative pressures destroyed cultural knowledge. The peoples' memories were the "libraries" of the cultures.

Epidemics of smallpox, measles, bubonic plague, influenza, typhus, scarlet fever, and many other European diseases sharply curtailed Native Americans' economic productivity, generating hunger and famine. Birthrates fell, and many survivors allayed their losses with alcoholic beverages, further reducing Native societies' vibrancy and economic productivity. Societies that had been constructed on kinship ties dissolved as large parts of many families were wiped out. Survivors faced the world without family elders' help, while traditional Native healing practices were found to be useless against European-imported pathogens. The ravages of disease undermined the traditional authority of Native American healers, who found their practices useless.

The arrival of European pathogens affected Native American tribes and nations differently, depending on the economic conduct of their lives. Sedentary groups were hit the hardest, while migratory groups (such as the Cheyennes after about 1800) suffered less intensely, at least at first, because they moved from place to place, leaving their wastes (which drew disease-carrying flies and other insects) behind. Migratory peoples also left behind water that they might have contaminated, usually exchanging it for fresh supplies. The Cheyennes were quite conscious of water contamination and always set up camp so that their horses drank and defecated downstream from human occupants. The Cheyennes consciously fought the spread of disease by breaking camp often and scattering into small family groups, so that one infected family would not bring disease to an entire band.

While the worst of the bubonic plague killed one in three Europeans, continuing waves of epidemics nearly obliterated many Native American societies and economies within a few years of Europeans' arrival in any given area.

Plagues of various pathogens—smallpox, influenza, measles, and others—took nearly all of the Western Abenakis and at least half the Mohawks. A disease frontier spread across North America about a generation before European American settlers, traders, and miners reached a given area.

Recent Surprises in the Amazon Valley

Modern archaeology regularly provides surprises, unsettling any attempt to determine pre-1492 population estimates with precision. For example, researchers working in the Amazon River basin during 2003 discovered a 15-square-mile region at the headwaters of the Upper Xingu River that contained at least 19 villages of 2,500 to 55,000 people each, spaced at regular intervals of between one and two miles, connected by wide roads, surrounded by evidence of intense agriculture. This discovery upended long-held assumptions that the rainforest was a pristine wilderness before its first visits by Europeans, as well as assumptions that the environment of the area could not support sophisticated civilizations.

For many years, archaeologists had argued with considerable conviction that the soil of the Amazon Valley was too poor to support large populations. The ancient residents intensively cultivated cassava, which grows well in poor soil. Recent researchers, including some descendants of pre-Columbian Native peoples who lived in the area, found evidence of densely settled, well-organized communities with roads, moats, and bridges. Some of the area's precisely designed roads were more than 50 yards wide. The people of the area cleared large areas of the rainforest to plant orchards; they preserved other areas as sources of wood, medicinal plants, and animals.

Michael J. Heckenberger, lead author of an article in *Science*, said that the ancestors of the Kuikuro people in the Amazon basin had a "complex and sophisticated" civilization with a population of many thousands before 1492. People were not organized into cities but into varied patterns of small, tightly integrated settlements. The extent of the road network is unknown at this time. "Here we present clear evidence of large, regional social formations (circa 1250 to 1650 C.E.) and their substantive influence on the landscape," wrote Heckenberger and colleagues (Heckenberger et al., 2003, 1710). "This is an incredibly important indicator of a complex society," said Susanna Hecht, a geographer at Stanford University's Center for Advanced Study in the Behavioral Sciences. "The extent of population density and landscape domestication is extraordinary" (Stokstad, 2003, 1645).

Heckenberger said, according to an Associated Press account, that the Amazon people moved huge amounts of dirt to build roads and plazas. At one place, there is evidence that they even built a bridge spanning a major river. The people also altered the natural forest, planting and maintaining orchards and agricultural fields, and the effects of this stewardship can still be seen today. Diseases such as smallpox and measles, brought to the New World by European explorers, probably killed most of the population along the Amazon, he said. By the time scientists began studying the indigenous people, the population was sparse. As a result, some researchers assumed that the same pattern had been common prior to European exploration. Heckenberger's assertions have been questioned, however, by Betty J. Meggers of the Smithsonian Institution's National Museum of Natural History, who asserted in *Science* with several colleagues that this study says little about population density in the Amazon Valley because the site is peripheral to the rainforest.

Thus the debate over indigenous population density in antiquity continues.

See Also PART 1: OVERVIEW: POPULATION AND DEMOGRAPHICS: How Many Native People in 1491?; **NATIONS, TRIBES, AND OTHER NATIVE GROUPS:** Apache Culture; California's Plethora of Native Peoples; Cherokee Political and Legal Culture; Cheyenne Cultural Context; Nez Perce; Northwest Coast Culture Area; Osage Economic Culture; Pequot Cultural Context; Ponca Culture; Pueblo Cultural Context; Ute Culture; Wyandot (Huron) Economic Culture; **GENERAL HISTORICAL CONSIDERATIONS:** Guns and Cultural Change; **PART 2: CULTURAL FORMS: Arts:** Cultural Appropriation: Questions and Issues; **FAMILY, EDUCATION, AND COMMUNITY:** Education: Acculturalization and Boarding Schools; Spotlight: Reindigenization; Restorative Justice; **FOOD:** Food Sovereignty; **LANGUAGE AND LITERATURE:** Humor, as Cultural Attribute; Language Recovery in Indigenous North America

Further Reading

Borah, Woodrow. "The Historical Demography of Aboriginal and Colonial America: An Attempt at Perspective." In William M. Denevan, ed. *The Native American Population of the Americas in 1492*. Madison: University of Wisconsin Press, 1976, 13–34.

Burnett, David G. "The Comanches and Other Tribes of Texas and the Policy to Be Pursued Respecting Them." In Henry R. Schoolcraft, ed. *Historical and Statistical Information Respecting the History and Prospects of the Indian Tribes of the United States*. Philadelphia: Lippincott, Granbo, 1851.

Cook, Sherburne F., and Leslie B. Simpson. *The Population of Central Mexico in the Sixteenth Century. Ibero-Americana*. Berkeley: University of California Press, 1948.

Dougherty to William Clark (October 29, 1831), James Jackson to Lewis Cass (March 16, 1832). H. Doc. 190 22nd Congress. 1st Session. Unpaginated.

Ewers, John C. *Plains Indian History and Culture: Essays in Continuity and Change*. Norman: University of Oklahoma Press, 1997.

Heckenberger, Michael J., Afukaka Kuikuro, Urissapá Tabata Kuikuro, J. Christian Russell, Morgan Schmidt, Carlos Fausto, and Bruna Franchetto. "Amazonia 1492: Pristine Forest or Cultural Parkland?" *Science* 301 (September 19, 2003): 1710.

Kroeber, A. L. *Cultural and Natural Areas of Native North America*. University of California Publications in American Archeology and Ethnology 38. Berkeley: University of California, 1939.

Las Casas, Bartolomé de. *The Devastation of the Indies*. New York: Seabury Press, [1542] 1974.

Mann, Charles C. "1491: America Before Columbus Was More Sophisticated and More Populous Than We Have Ever Thought—and a More Livable Place Than Europe." *The Atlantic Monthly*, March 2002, 41–53.

McDowell, Bart. "The Aztecs." *National Geographic* 158 (December 1980): 753.

Meggers, Betty J., Eduardo S. Brondizio, Michael J. Heckenberger, Carlos Fausto, and Bruna Franchetto. "Revisiting Amazonia Circa 1492." Letter to the editor. *Science* 302 (December 19, 2003): 2067.

Portilla, Miguel Leon. *The Broken Spears: The Aztec Account of the Conquest of Mexico*. Boston: Beacon Press, 1962.

Recer, Paul. "Evidence Found of Arctic Hunters Living in Siberia Near New World 30,000 Years Ago." Associated Press, January 2, 2004.

Recer, Paul. "Researchers Find Evidence of Sophisticated, Pre-Columbian Civilization in the Amazon Basin." Associated Press, September 19, 2003.

Stannard, David E. *American Holocaust: The Conquest of the New World*. New York: Oxford University Press, 1992.

Stokstad, Erik. "Amazon Archaeology: 'Pristine' Forest Teemed with People." *Science* 301 (September 19, 2003): 1645.

Wright, Ronald. *Stolen Continents: The Americas Through Indian Eyes Since 1492*. Boston: Houghton Mifflin, 1992.

CULTURAL GENOCIDE

Assertions have been made that today's Native Americans are survivors of a holocaust with losses, disease, and violence that impact every aspect of Indian life. Such an assertion runs into intellectual rough weather from some historians, however, who contend that in international law, "genocide" is taken to mean systematic and deliberate destruction (e.g., with forethought, a condition often called "malice" in law) of a racial, political, or cultural group. Destruction and eviction from homelands of Native Americans by European immigrants seeking their land and resources has been said not to legally qualify as "genocide" within the rubric of laws framed under European standards because the people who performed the deed were not coordinated under an enunciated policy.

Even lacking a singular, stated motive, however, the historical outcome has been much the same. The combination of effects (disease, displacement, killings in wars or murders) caused eradication of peoples, land bases, and cultures.

Even deliberate legislative acts (such as the Indian Removal Act signed in 1830 by President Andrew Jackson) were justified at the time as legal shields enacted for the Indians' own good. Even after whole peoples were displaced and significant proportions died on removals (a quarter of the Cherokees on the Trail of Tears, for example), peoples reconstructed cultures in their new homes.

This begs a question, however, because even the Nazi genocide of the Jews did not eradicate Judaism. The Removal Act was written to sound as if Indians had a choice, but on the ground they usually were moved out at bayonet point. The Indian people who remained in their homelands did so by evading the dragnet. Squatters often took Indian lands without legal right; if they fought back, indigenous landholders were killed or evicted. In this manner, the Creek nation lost 22 million acres in Alabama and Georgia.

America and Nazi Genocide

The genesis of Nazi genocide policy may lie at least in part with the holocaust of American Indians. The Yale historian Timothy Snyder, in *Bloodlands*, describes how Adolf Hitler attributed the genesis of Nazi concentration and death camps to the U.S. expansion westward in the 19th century. "The East was the Nazi Manifest Destiny," Snyder wrote. Hitler phrased it as *lebensraum*— literally, in German, living room, or territory into which to expand. In Hitler's view, "in the East, a similar process will repeat itself for a second time, as in the conquest of America" (Snyder, 2010, 160).

As Hitler imagined the future, Germany would deal with the Slavs much as the North Americans had dealt with the Indians. He once proclaimed that the Volga River, in Russia, would become Germany's Mississippi. Hitler also said that the world's proven indifference to the fate of the Apaches gave him "confidence that he would get away with it" (Gopnik, 2012, 115).

A Cultural Dimension of Genocide

Raphael Lemkin, an attorney, proposed a cultural dimension of genocide in 1933. The idea was considered as part of the 1948 United Nations Convention on Genocide, but dropped. The United Nations Declaration on the Rights of Indigenous Peoples included the idea in a 1994 draft but did not define it. The draft, one of few that have attempted to define this idea on an official level, read:

> Indigenous peoples have the collective and individual right not to be subjected to ethnocide and cultural genocide, including prevention of and redress for:

(a) Any action which has the aim or effect of depriving them of their integrity as distinct peoples, or of their cultural values or ethnic identities;

(b) Any action which has the aim or effect of dispossessing them of their lands, territories or resources;

(c) Any form of population transfer which has the aim or effect of violating or undermining any of their rights;

(d) Any form of assimilation or integration by other cultures or ways of life imposed on them by legislative, administrative or other measures;

(e) Any form of propaganda directed against them.

In 2007 the idea surfaced again (as "ethnocide"), but it was omitted from the final document.

"Kill the Indian, Save the Man"

The idea of cultural genocide has been defined as much broader than the diminishment of culture that results from the physical eradication of a population. People may survive physically, but with their culture removed, as when boarding schools in the United States during the 19th century proposed to "Kill the Indian and save the man"—that is, kill the culture and recast the Indians as culturally European. This type of change has been examined in a religious context, as in George E. Tinker's *Missionary Conquest: The Gospel and Native American Cultural Genocide,* in which he examines the cases of Junipero Serra (the Franciscan whose mission to California Natives has made him a candidate for sainthood); John Eliot (renowned Puritan missionary to Massachusetts Indians); Pierre-Jean De Smet (Jesuit missionary to the Indians of the Midwest); and Henry Benjamin Whipple (engineered the U.S. government's theft of the Black Hills from the Sioux).

During 2007, a member of the Canadian Parliament said that that nation's Ministry of Indian Affairs had committed "cultural genocide" when it destroyed documents describing treatment of First Nations members. Some observers have even extended the idea of cultural genocide to the usage by non-Natives of traditional American Indian points of view regarding nature.

Debate over whether or not what happened to Native Americans facing European immigration qualifies as genocide comes from books such as *American Holocaust* (1992) by David Stannard or, more recently, Brendan C. Lindsay's *Murder State: California's Native American Genocide, 1846–1873* (2012). The latter argues that the enslavement, rape, and murder of thousands of Native people in California was legitimized at every level of state government. Those

Native people who resisted were branded as violent savages, "'red devils' who were constantly lurking and ready to pounce" (Lindsay, 2012, 121).

In the meantime, Anglo-American immigrants were shooting Native Americans to death for sport in San Diego. The *Chico Weekly Courant* (September 15, 1866) advised distribution of strychnine-laced watermelons to Indians all over the Pacific Coast. During 1856, "a group of men turned on a Native American on the street and stoned him to death, apparently without direct provocation and for sport" (Lindsay, 2012, 152).

A reduction in population results, *ipso facto*, in a reduction of culture, especially for oral cultures in which human memory is the repository of knowledge. Ways of doing, making, and believing die along with the people. Every person carries a library of culture in his or her head. Complexity of language is reduced. Culture erodes with each death. Between 1848 and 1860, the ratio of Native to non-Native population in California changed from 10:1 (150,000 to 15,000) to more than 1:10 (35,000 to 380,000) (Lindsay, 2012, 128). Events during these years included the forty-niner gold rush and the war with Mexico.

Whites killed with impunity in California because between 1850 and 1872 the California legal code did not allow Indians and blacks to bear witness against Anglo-Americans in court. Thus, a murder or rape of an Indian did not exist in the legal system unless a white man testified against another European American man, a very rare event. Lindsay makes a case that this and other organized, state-level actions comprised genocide under international law. Lindsay wrote:

> [This law] shielded individual miners from crimes even more horrendous than rape or murder of just a few people. In fact rape was just one of the despicable recreational activities miners engaged in. Others . . . [used] Native Americans and their villages as target practice. At other times, rape was mixed with murder, arson, and thievery, leading to extermination of entire communities. (Lindsay, 2012, 221)

Elsewhere, cultural destruction continued apace. Following the Custer battle (1876), the U.S. Army swarmed Sioux country, devastating it militarily and culturally, even as private hunters were obliterating the buffalo, its economic base. Lacking an economic base, Native American cultures disintegrated. The Army attacked villages along the Powder River, Slim Buttes, along the Red Fork of the Powder River, and Muddy Creek and destroyed Indian possessions including clothing, food, tools, and personal belongings.

See Also PART 2: CULTURAL FORMS: Arts: Cultural Appropriation: Questions and Issues/Spotlight: Paleontology and Appropriation; **FAMILY, EDUCATION, AND**

COMMUNITY: Education: Acculturalization and Boarding Schools; Native American Graves Protection and Repatriation Act (NAGPRA) (1990); Spotlight: Reindigenization; Restorative Justice; FOOD: Food Sovereignty; LANGUAGE AND LITERATURE: Humor, as Cultural Attribute; Language Recovery in Indigenous North America

Further Reading

Barrera, Jorge. "'Genocide' Target of Fed Cover-up." *Edmonton Sun*, April 25, 2007, n.p.

French, Laurence Armand. *Native American Justice*. Chicago: Burnham, 2003.

Gopnik, Adam. "Faces, Places, Spaces: The Renaissance of Geographic History." *The New Yorker*, October 29 and November 5, 2012, 108.

Hedren, Paul L. *After Custer: Loss and Transformation in Sioux Country*. Norman: University of Oklahoma Press, 2011.

Kershaw, Ian, *Hitler: A Biography*. New York: W. W. Norton, 2008.

Lindsay, Brendan C. *Murder State: California's Native American Genocide, 1846–1873*. Lincoln: University of Nebraska Press, 2012.

Nelson, Melissa K. *Original Instructions: Indigenous Teachings for a Sustainable Future*. Rochester, VT: Bear, 2008.

Powell, Peter J. *Sweet Medicine: The Continuing Role of the Sacred Arrows, the Sun Dance, and the Sacred Buffalo Hat in Northern Cheyenne History*. 2 vols. Norman: University of Oklahoma Press, 1969.

Snyder, Timothy. *Bloodlands: Europe between Hitler and Stalin*. New York: Basic Books, 2010.

Taylor, Bron. "Earthen Spirituality or Cultural Genocide?: Radical Environmentalism's Appropriation of Native American Spirituality." *Religion* 27, no. 2 (April, 1997): 183–215.

Tinker, George E. *Missionary Conquest: The Gospel and Native American Cultural Genocide*. Philadelphia: Fortress Press/Google eBook, 1993.

Yellow Horse, Maria Brave Heart, and L. M. DeBruyn. "The Historical Trauma Response Among Natives and Its Relationship with Substance Abuse: A Lakota Illustration." *Journal of Psychoactive Drugs* 35, no. 1 (January–March 2003): 7–13.

TODAY'S NATIVE AMERICAN DEMOGRAPHICS

Native Americans are now the fastest growing racial group in the United States, according to the 2010 U.S. Census. These numbers reflect both a real increase in population and a change in the ways that the Census classifies people who declare more than one racial heritage. American Indians and Alaska Natives are probably more likely than members of other racial groups to have multiple heritages. The Census Bureau, reporting on the 2010 count, said that 44 percent of American Indians and Alaska Natives (2.3 million people) reported more than one race, a 39 percent increase in 10 years, much more than could be accounted for by natural increase.

Susan Stewart Medicine Horse, a Crow, and manager of the Chief Plenty Coups State Park stands in front of the chief's house on the park site September 14, 2004, in Pryor, Montana. (AP Photo/Billings Gazette, David Grubbs)

Native populations in the United States bottomed at about half a million in the early 20th century and have been increasing since. The 1990 U.S. Census indicated that roughly 2 million people listed themselves as Native American, a figure that nearly doubled in the 2000 Census. In 2000, for the first time, the Census allowed people to report more than one racial or ethnic heritage. In 2010, 5.2 million people (1.7 percent of the U.S. population) classified themselves as Native American or Alaska Native alone, or in combination with other groups. This population comprised about 1.1 million families in 2012. The total population grew by 27 percent in a decade. The number who reported being Native American or Alaska Native alone grew by 18 percent to 2.9 million. The U.S. population as a whole increased by 9.7 percent during the same period.

Twenty-two percent of American Indians and Alaska Natives lived in American Indian areas or Alaska Native Village Statistical Areas in 2010. These American Indian areas include tribal-designated statistical areas, state and federal American Indian reservations, and state-designated American Indian statistical areas, according to the Census. More than three-quarters (78 percent) of the people who classified themselves as Native American or Alaska Native lived outside of reservations in 2010. Reservations themselves—often allotted to non-Indians—often have minority American Indian populations. The Nez Perce reservation in Idaho, for example, reported more than 18,000 people, of whom only about 2,000 were Nez Perce. This is not atypical. The Census reported, however, that most areas with higher proportions of Native Americans tended to be closer to reservations and trust lands, especially throughout Oklahoma and the West.

Most American Indians (alone or mixed) lived in 10 states: California, Oklahoma, Arizona, Texas, New York, New Mexico, Washington, North Carolina, Florida, and Michigan. Texas, North Carolina, and Florida grew 46 percent, 40 percent, and 38 percent, respectively. The largest number who identified as American Indian were Cherokees (819,000 people), while Navajos were the largest group listing American Indian and no other categories (287,000). Three quarters of Blackfeet listed other races or ethnic groups, the highest percentage. The largest Alaska Native groups, alone or mixed, were Yup'iks (34,000) and Inupiats (33,000). The Yup'iks were the largest group alone (29,000).

Fourteen U.S. states reported more than 100,000 American Indian and Alaska Native residents, alone or mixed, in 2012: California, Oklahoma, Arizona, Texas, New Mexico, Washington, New York, North Carolina, Florida, Alaska, Michigan, Oregon, Colorado, and Minnesota. The proportion of Alaska's people who reported American Indian and Alaska Native heritage, alone or mixed, in 2012 was 19.6 percent, the highest of any state, followed by Oklahoma (13.4 percent), New Mexico (10.4 percent), South Dakota (10.0 percent), and Montana (8.1 percent).

The median household income of American Indian and Alaska Native households declaring only one ethnic or racial heritage in 2012 was $35,310, compared to $51,371 nationally. The percentage living in poverty as defined by the U.S. government was 29.1 percent, compared to 15.9 percent nationally.

See Also PART 1: OVERVIEW: POPULATION AND DEMOGRAPHICS: How Many Native People in 1491?; **PART 2: CULTURAL FORMS: FAMILY, EDUCATION, AND COMMUNITY:** Spotlight: Education Revival: A Muckleshoot Case Study; LANGUAGE AND LITERATURE: Language Reclamation: Eastern Tribes; Language Recovery in Indigenous North America

Further Reading
"2010 Census Shows Nearly Half of American Indians and Alaska Natives Report Multiple Races. U.S. Census." *U.S. Census Newsroom.* January 25, 2012. http://www.census.gov/newsroom/releases/archives/2010_census/cb12-cn06.html.

2012 American Community Survey. *U.S. Census.* http://factfinder2.census.gov/bkmk/table/1.0/en/ACS/12_1YR/S0201/0100000US.04000/popgroup~009.

NATIONS, TRIBES, AND OTHER NATIVE GROUPS

ALASKA NATIVE CORPORATIONS

Unlike Native peoples in the "lower 48," Alaska Native peoples had no treaties. As treaties were often negotiated during the 19th century to clear the way for railroads and non-Native immigration, Alaska Native corporations created a legal path for resource exploitation, notably North Slope oil (discovered in 1968) and the Trans-Alaska Pipeline from the North Slope to Valdez. The Alaska Native Claims Settlement Act of 1971 also was a response to Native activism seeking economic self-determination.

Under this act, 40 million acres were allocated to 12 regional and 220 village corporations (a 13th was created later representing Alaska Natives living out of state). Alaska Native people and their descendants born before 1971 each were given 100 shares in their member corporations. The Natives' shares cannot be sold or traded and thus have no market value. Shares can be passed down to family members and provide dividends, which vary according to the income of the corporations. Shareholders also may be entitled to benefit from social programs.

Some village corporations have since merged; by 2010, according to the Alaska Division of Banking and Securities, there were 198 of them. In 1986, Congress provided Alaska Native corporations with access to the Small Business Administration's "8(a)" disadvantaged business program. These benefits later were extended to permission to win no-bid contracts (in any amount) and

Tara Sweeney, an Inupiat Eskimo who supports Arctic oil drilling, lobbying the U.S. Congress in 2002. (AP Photo/Kenneth Lambert)

ownership of several subsidiaries that are not allowed to other businesses under the "8(a)" program.

Later, the U.S. Senate Subcommittee on Contracting Oversight found that these special preferences have sometimes been abused, provoking criticism of Alaska Native corporations by other businesses. According to some analysts American Indian shareholders did not see improvements or increased opportunities. In some instances, non-Native workers benefited more.

Congressional hearings and newspaper investigations followed, describing how the 75,000 Native shareholders often had been short-changed. Robert O'Harrow Jr. wrote in the *Washington Post*, for example (2010), that some 75,000 original Alaska Native shareholders were promised a stake in the new corporations. These corporations received exemptions and $29 billion in federal contracts while not fulfilling their promises to shareholders. The Senate Subcommittee on Contract Oversight calculated that ANC contract awards increased from $508.4 million in 2000 to $5.2 billion in 2008. Yet many shareholders remained poor. Much of the money was being paid to non-Native contractors outside Alaska.

While the top 10 percent of the Alaska Native corporations have been financially successful, many of these have been involved in extractive resource and natural resource industries and continue to prosper. For example, the Arctic Slope Regional Corporation's primary funds came from gas and oil leases, and in 2012 the NANA Regional Corporation produced $170 million.

See Also PART 2: CULTURAL FORMS: FAMILY, EDUCATION, AND COMMUNITY: Climate Change and Native Peoples/Spotlight: Climate Change and Alaska Natives

Further Reading

Grabell, Michael, and Jennifer LaFleur. "What Are Alaska Native Corporations?" *ProPublica*, December 15, 2010. http://www.propublica.org/article/what-are-alaska-native -corporations.

Howard, Morgan. "Despite Challenges, Alaska Native Groups Must Build New Businesses." *Alaska Dispatch*, December 21, 2013. http://www.alaskadispatch.com/article /20131221/despite-challenges-alaska-native-groups-must-build-new-businesses.

O'Harrow, Robert, Jr. "For Many with Stake in Alaska Native Corporations, Promise of Better Life Remains Unfulfilled." *Washington Post*, September 30, 2010. http://www .washingtonpost.com/wp-dyn/content/article/2010/09/29/AR2010092906318.html.

APACHE CULTURE

Like the Navajos, the Apaches, part of the Athapascan linguistic family, moved into the present-day U.S. Southwest and northwestern Mexico between roughly 1400 and 1525 CE. While the Navajos became sedentary, however, the Apaches adopted a nomadic life in the harsh, dry climate of the area. The Apaches separated into a number of bands that had only occasional contact with one another, although they shared a language, culture, and economic practices. Each band—Mescaleros, Chiricahuas, Jicarillas, Mimbreños, and others—had its own hunting grounds. A band was composed of a number of extended families who cooperated in economic pursuits. Scarcity of resources promoted cooperation and sharing within the various Apache bands.

The Apaches were able to survive under harsh conditions in the deserts of southeast Arizona, southwest New Mexico, and the present-day Mexican states of Sonora and Chihuahua. Unlike the Plains tribes, who relied on buffalo, the Apaches had no single staple food and could not be forced from their traditional homes and lifeways by its extermination. When necessity called, an Apache would not shrink from eating desert vegetation, pack rats, and lizards.

Some of the Apaches' band names are Spanish for various cultural activities: Jicarilla, for example, means "little basket," and Mesceleros means "mescal makers," because they ate it. The word "Apache" is probably a Spanish adaptation of the Zuni *apachú*, meaning "enemy." The Apaches, like the Navajos, called themselves Diné, meaning "the people." Jicarillas and Mescaleros occasionally traded with the Pueblos of the Rio Grande Valley, exchanging their hides, skins, and sometimes captives for Pueblo corn, tobacco, and cotton. More often, however, the Apache bands raided the sedentary Pueblo towns, earning the Zunis' name for "enemy."

Apache Political and Legal Culture

Apache society was centered around groups of two to six matrilocal extended families, a unit sometimes called a *gota*. Members of the *gota* lived together, and members of the different households cooperated in the pursuit of game and raising of crops. A *gota* was usually led by a headman who assumed his status over several years by general consensus of the extended families in the *gota*. The headman in some cases inherited the title of "true chief." He would not retain the position, however, unless he displayed leadership. If no qualified headman was raised through inheritance, a consensus would form in favor of another leader who would be informally "elected" by members of the *gota*. Headmen were invariably male, but women exercised influence as political advisers, and it was their society and kinship lineages that maintained the Apaches' matrilineal society.

A headman could wield considerable influence, but only if the people in the extended families he led were willing to follow his advice, which could include detailed lectures on how to hunt, the techniques of agriculture, and who should work with whom. He also coordinated labor for foraging and hunting, advised parties engaged in disputes, and was sought out for advice regarding spousal choices. At times, the wife of a chief would become, in effect, a subchief. As a chief aged, he was not only charged with maintaining exemplary behavior but also with identifying young men who might become leaders in the future. He was expected to tutor younger men in the responsibilities of leadership. A chief was also charged with aiding the poor, often by coordinating distribution of donations from more affluent members of the *gota*. If two or more *gotas* engaged in conflict, their headmen were charged with resolving the dispute.

Each Apache was a member not only of a *gota* but also one of 62 matrilineal clans that overlapped the individual settlements. Members of one's clan (and, in some cases, others identified as being close to it) helped one another in survival tasks and usually did not intermarry. Such a system resembles that of many peoples in the Eastern Woodlands (Cherokees, Wyandots, and Iroquois, for example). Even the ways in which Apaches raised up chiefs generally recalls the system of the Iroquois, under which a person could "inherit" a title (from membership in a clan, not head to head); other Iroquois sachems were named to office by the Grand Council solely on the basis of their leadership qualities.

Unlike the Iroquois and Wyandots, however, the Apaches did not maintain a formal political structure beyond the local level.

Among some Apaches magic (or the fear of becoming the target of sorcery) was called into service as a social-control device, especially in the case of conflict between members of different kin groups. Social control was also maintained by positive means; a person who behaved according to socially cohesive norms was said to have access to one or more of several forms of "power," which insulated the person from misfortune and calamity. "Power" in several forms (Wind Power, Mountain Lion Power, and Fire Power are three examples) could be acquired by anyone who displayed the proper behavior, but such acquisition was expensive in terms of goods, time, and energy. A person who was acquiring a given power learned it from a shaman who already had it, a procedure requiring hundreds of hours of tutoring for which the supplicant paid in horses, food, or other goods. Shamans usually were said to have acquired one or more forms of power through dreams or visions, followed by exhaustive attention to a corpus of chants and prayers. This was no small task. Acquisition of Black-tailed Deer Power required memorization of nearly 60 chants, each containing 20 or more half-hour verses. Less than letter-perfect performance was said to insult the power.

The Apaches and Spanish Horse Culture

The Apaches first crossed paths with the Spanish during 1599, when they joined in the defense of the Acoma Pueblo against troops led by Juan de Oñate. Soon after that, the Apaches greatly enhanced their diet, mobility, and hunting range by raiding Spanish settlements and missions for cattle, mules, and horses. The Apache economic culture was enriched as prospects for raiding improved through the adoption of Spanish horses. The Spanish tried to maintain a monopoly on the use of horses, but the Apaches refused to abide by their rules. By the 1630s, Pueblos escaping from Spanish missions sometimes took refuge with Apaches, often taking sizable numbers of Spanish horses with them. The Spanish retaliated by capturing Apaches and selling them as slaves, most of whom were compelled to work in Spanish mines. Any Apache was game for enslavement, even those who presented themselves at Spanish settlements to trade. Some Apache Christian converts also were sold into slavery by the Spanish.

The Apaches adapted Spanish horse culture, including riding gear, to their needs. The number and sizes of raiding parties increased to such a degree that by the 1660s a large number of Spanish settlers were leaving the area rather than risk Apache raids. In 1673, the Spanish government outlawed slavery of the Apaches, but the colonists in their country ignored the edict. The Apaches, in the meantime, stole almost every horse belonging to the Spanish garrison at Santa Fe. By the late 17th century, raiding had become the Apaches' main economic livelihood. Some raiding parties included several hundred warriors. By the 1750s, many Spanish mines, military posts, and ranches in Sonora had been abandoned in the face of Apache assaults. In 1776, the Spanish government created a special military force, the Commandancy General of the Interior Provinces, in an attempt to stop the Apaches.

Spanish efforts to subdue the Apaches continued until 1821 with Mexican independence, whereupon the Mexicans became the Apaches' raiding targets. The road along the Rio Grande between Valverde and El Paso was called *Jornada del Muerte*—"journey of the dead." The United States took on the Apaches when it assumed control of Arizona and New Mexico in 1848. Apaches earned a reputation for being hard to catch because they knew the lay of the land, had become superb horsemen, and had bred small, muscular horses that could outrun anything mounted by the Spanish, Mexicans, or North American immigrants.

The Apaches Resist Colonization

The Apache resistance to the U.S. Army lasted nearly four decades and produced a number of legendary warriors, among them Geronimo (1825–1909) and Mangas Coloradas (c. 1791–1863). While Geronimo was not a hereditary chief, his reputation among the Apaches increased due to his bravery and prowess in battle. In 1858, Mexicans killed Geronimo's wife, mother, and three children, causing him to dislike Mexicans intensely and mount campaigns against them for revenge. In Apache culture, Geronimo also was a respected medicine man. The Spanish feared him so much that Geronimo's Spanish name was derived from their cries for mercy to Saint Jerome (the Catholic saint of lost causes) when they heard his Apaches were near. Geronimo's Apache name (Goyathlay) meant "He who yawns." Both his parents had been Spanish captives.

The man the Spanish would come to call Geronimo was born along the upper Gila River, very likely on the Arizona side of the New Mexico–Arizona border. Taklishim, his father, was a Chiricahua as was his mother, Juana, although she had been a captive among the Mexicans during childhood. In his youth, Geronimo served under the Chiricahua leader, Cochise, and Mangas Coloradas, a Mimbreño.

Due to incessant Apache raiding on Mexican settlements, officials in the state of Chihuahua, Mexico, put a $100 bounty on Apache scalps regardless of gender or age. Although initial relations with Americans were friendly, things changed rapidly. In 1837, a group of trappers invited the Mimbreños to a great feast at Santa Rita, then began to slaughter them for their scalps. To retaliate,

Mangas Coloradas and his men killed most of the miners and trappers and raided nearby settlements.

After decades of guerrilla war in the United States and Mexico, Geronimo surrendered at Canyon de los Embudos in northern Mexico on March 25, 1886. Following their forceful subjugation by the U.S. Army, the Apaches were assigned cultural assimilation—agriculture, Christianity, and "civilizing" education. With a few exceptions, most Apaches resisted these forms of cultural subjugation, and most of the programs of the early reservation era failed miserably. In the early years, the Apache reservations, like most in the West, had no economic activity to speak of. A sizable number of Apaches left their assigned reservations in the face of starvation. By 1914, nearly 90 percent of the Jicarillas were afflicted with tuberculosis, and their death rate was so high that the Bureau of Indian Affairs (BIA) predicted they would be extinct within a few years.

In the 1920s, however, some of the Apaches established herds of sheep with BIA assistance, and hospitals were built to treat the tuberculosis epidemic. Most of the Apache bands began to recover slowly. Several Apaches also developed cattle herding. By 1942, every Mescalero family had been provided with a wooden house built with lumber that had been harvested and processed on their own land. In 1948, a group of Mescaleros answered a call to fight forest fires; within a few years, they were steadily employed and became known as the now-famous "Red Hats," more than 200 men who made a specialty of parachuting into blazing forests throughout the American West. In the 1960s, the Mescaleros began plans to enhance tourism; a number of Apaches also earned their livings as cowboys.

Apaches Today

By the late 20th century, Apache reservations were scattered across Arizona, with one Apache settlement in Oklahoma. Most of the reservations are small, with a few hundred residents, but two of them, Fort Apache and San Carlos, east of Phoenix, hold sizable land areas. Fort Apache ranges over 1,664,972 acres with a population of 10,500; San Carlos has 1,854,000 acres and also about 10,500 residents. Many people living at Fort Apache have successfully ranched cattle since government programs introduced them in the early 1930s; the tribe maintains a 15,000-head cattle herd. The Fort Apache Timber Company harvests from some of the 800,000 acres of ponderosa pine on the reservation. Stumpage revenues were adding $5 million a year to the tribal budget in the mid-1990s. McDonnell-Douglas Company also subcontracts with Apache Aerospace Company for prefabricated helicopter parts. Apaches operate several roadside markets, grocery stores, and gas stations for an increasing tourist trade drawn, in part, to the reservation's Sunrise Ski Resort. The San Carlos reservation hosts an industrial park as well as a tribally owned sawmill.

See Also PART 2: CULTURAL FORMS: ARTS: Clothing; **FAMILY, EDUCATION, AND COMMUNITY:** Civic and Military Societies; Wedding Customs; Women in Native American Cultures; **LANGUAGE AND LITERATURE:** Language Recovery in Indigenous North America; **TRANSPORTATION AND HOUSING:** Tipi

Further Reading

Baldwin, Gordon C. *The Warrior Apaches*. Tucson: University of Arizona Press, 1965.

Debo, Angie. *Geronimo: The Man, His Time, His Place*. Norman: University of Oklahoma Press, 1976.

Dobyns, Henry. *The Apache People*. Phoenix: Indian Tribal Series, 1971.

Tiller, Veronica E. Velarde. *The Jicarilla Apache Tribe: A History, 1846–1970*. Lincoln: University of Nebraska Press, 1983.

Worcester, Donald A. *The Apaches: Eagles of the Southwest*. Norman: University of Oklahoma Press, 1979.

CALIFORNIA'S PLETHORA OF NATIVE PEOPLES

Precontact

Before the arrival of European colonists (the Spanish from the south, then Anglo-Americans from the east), California was home to hundreds of Native American nations, tribes, and bands. Native populations in the area were among the densest in the Americas. During more than four centuries, enslaved by the Spanish missions, decimated (and worse) by the Anglo-American gold rush, Native Americans have struggled to survive and adapt, but also have taken part in today's cultural and economic revival.

California Indians spoke more than 100 languages comprising 300 dialects before contact, a period dating to at least 17,000 years before the present. Archaeologists have identifed at least 500 groups of 50 to 500 members each. Because the climate was moderate and food usually abundant, roughly one-third of Native peoples in the present-day United States probably lived in what we now know as California. Most were hunter-gatherers of several animals and food and medicinal plants, although they generally did not practice organized agriculture. Acorns were a staple in some areas, along with fish, shellfish, antelope, elk, deer, and plants that included sage seed and buckeye.

Cultures were varied and complex. Many tribes in the northwestern part of the area carried on a rich spiritual life, including a world-renewal ceremony

View of an Indian Rancheria (probably Maidu), Yuba City, California, 1852. (Corbis)

each autumn sponsored by the affluent men in each community, held to avert natural disasters such as floods, failure of food crops and salmon runs, or earth-quakes. The Pomos were notable as basket makers whose coiled and twine type baskets were some of the most elaborate in North America, a tradition that continues today. Kuksu dances that assure renewal of plant and animal foods also continue today. Most villages as large as 1,000 people were governed lo-cally. Alliances were rare. Residents on Southern California offshore islands developed sophisticated canoes called *tomols* that were carved by a guild of specialists and that could carry a dozen people and several hundred pounds of trade goods.

Arrival of the Spanish

The Spanish *conquista* included missions that were coercive labor camps under a religious patina, organized to supply the colonizers. The Indians understood who was doing what to whom, and they periodically rebelled, escaping the disease-ridden labor camps. More than 80,000 were baptized in the Catholic Church, and several thousand of them became fugitives. Several padres also were assassinated by the Indians they subjugated. Three of them were poisoned at Mission San Miguel in 1801 alone. One Yokut man tried to stone a padre to death. In the meantime, feral hogs that had escaped the missions destroyed large parts of the free Indians' acorns as epidemics that had started in the missions swept over the countryside.

Use of indigenous languages (and refusal to communicate in Spanish), as well as the practice of Native religious ceremonies, dreams, and dances were additional realms in which Indians managed to register dissent. Women often found themselves at the forefront of this resistance. While some of them aborted their progeny so that their sons and daughters would not have to live in the world of mission slavery, others instigated local revolts provoked by priests' rapes and beatings.

The rape of a chief's wife at the San Gabriel mission united several groups of Native people from the Pacific Coast to the Sierra Nevada whose plans were thwarted by the Spanish military. In the San Diego area, Spanish abuse of Native women provoked a major revolt there during 1775. Eight hundred Indians from more than 70 rancherias, aided by several thousand others outside the Spanish subjugation system, burned the San Diego mission after Spanish soldiers had raped several Native women. Father Luis Jayme, who had warned of the retaliation, was killed, his body "found naked, bruised, and disfigured at the bottom of a dry creek" (Bouvier, 2001, 140).

Priests who beat Native women sometimes died as their Native cooks decanted something extra into their soup. In 1812, for example, Father Jose Pedro Panto died from poisoning at the San Diego mission. His cook, Nazario, later confessed to slipping powdered *cuchasquelaai* into the priest's food after he engaged in excessive floggings.

The U.S. Incursion

During the mid-1800s, hundreds of thousands of gold-hungry Anglo-Americans invaded California, which had just been annexed from Mexico by the United States. The miners often worked for large corporations; the popular image of solitary miners panning for gold on their own is mainly historical fiction. The miners blasted mountains and polluted lakes and streams as they massacred, raped, and enslaved the people who lived there. Filmed on location throughout Northern California, the film *Gold, Greed & Genocide* includes statements by California tribal elders, other leaders, and members of families whose descendants survived the onslaught. Local historians and scholars have also examined the ecological destruction of gold mining in California.

Native American population fell by about 90 percent during the 19th century, from at least 200,000 to less than 15,000, mainly due to imported epidemics. Brendan C. Lindsay's *Murder State: California's Native American Genocide, 1846–1873* (2012) provides vivid descriptions of the human toll during the early years of the Anglo-American incursion in the second half of the 19th century when mass genocide was carried out in California: "The murder, rape, and enslavement of thousands of Native people were legitimatized . . . at every level of California government. . . . Those Native people who resisted were branded as violent savages, 'red devils' who were constantly lurking and ready to pounce" (Lindsay, 2012, 121).

In the meantime, Anglo-American immigrants were shooting Native Americans to death for sport in San Diego. The *Chico Weekly Courant* (September 15, 1866) advised distribution of strychnine-laced watermelons to Indians "all over the Pacific Coast" (Lindsay, 2012, 320).

A reduction in population results, *ipso facto*, in a reduction of culture, especially for oral cultures in which human memory is the repository of knowledge. Ways of doing, making, and believing die along with the people. Every person carries a library of culture in his or her head. Complexity of language is reduced. Culture erodes with each death. Between 1848 and 1860, the ratio of Native to non-Native population in California changed from 10:1 (150,000 to 15,000) to more than 1:10 (35,000 to 380,000). Events during these years included the forty-niner gold rush and the war with Mexico.

Whites killed with impunity in California because between 1850 and 1872 the California legal code did not allow Indians and blacks to bear witness against Anglo-Americans in court. Thus, a murder or rape of an Indian did not exist in the legal system unless a white man testified against another European-American man, a very rare event. Lindsay makes a case that this and other organized, state-level actions comprised genocide under international law. Lindsay wrote:

> [This law] shielded individual miners from crimes even more horrendous than rape or murder of just a few people. In fact, rape was just one of the despicable recreational activities miners engaged in. Others . . . [used] Native Americans and their villages as target practice. At other times, rape was mixed with murder, arson, and thievery, leading to extermination of entire communities. (Lindsay, 2012, 221)

By the late 19th century, Native peoples in Southern California were adapting to the new order of life, in some cases hiring lawyers to assert their rights, as a rising tide of non-Native immigration inundated their homelands. By 1903, the Cupenos were resisting forced removal to the Pala reservation, as immigrants flooded their San Jose Valley. Many arrived at Pala to find only tents, hastily erected, many of which quickly became houses of tears.

By the middle 1950s, the Bureau of Indian Affairs began plans to end services for California Indians (as in the rest of the United States) under a policy of termination. In California, dispossession and transfer of authority to the state was legislated as part of the Rancheria Act of 1958, which allowed distribution of remaining communal lands to individuals, opening the way for their sale to non-Indians. This change was dressed up as an enhancement of individual freedom and independence, with promises of repairs to broken-down housing, pot-holed roads, shaky bridges, and water projects that were only rarely realized. Between 1958 and 1970, 23 small reservations (rancherias) were terminated. Native recipients of land grants, who often lacked cash, were legally obligated to pay property taxes. All health, education, and social services ended, requiring more cash payments. Many who were unable to pay lost their land, which usually was auctioned off to non-Indians. People were more impoverished than ever. Later this policy was reversed, and communal land holding and the communities it supports were revived.

California Tribes Today

California as of 2014 had more Indian tribes (109) than any other U.S. state, with 78 more having filed for federal recognition. More Native Americans live in California than in any other U.S. state, rural and urban, and this population is characterized by immense diversity, with many people who are native to the area, and many others who have moved to the area from outside.

California also is notable in the history of American Indian activism as the staging ground of the Alcatraz Island occupation in 1969. The wave of activism energized reservation development throughout the state for decades afterward, helping to provoke an economic and cultural revival. California also became a national leader in Native American studies as an academic pursuit, most notably through the University of California at Los Angeles American Indian Studies Center and its many published books, as well as the *American Indian Culture and Research Journal*.

California in 2014 had more than 60 Native American casinos, generating about $7 billion a year in revenues, about a quarter of the $28 billion in revenues nationally, a spur to other forms of economic development, as well as cultural revival.

See Also PART 1: OVERVIEW: POPULATION AND DEMOGRAPHICS: Cultural Genocide; **PART 2: CULTURAL FORMS: ARTS:** Spotlight: Culture Bearers; Luna, James; **FAMILY, EDUCATION, AND COMMUNITY:** Urban American Indians; **SPIRITUALITY:** Ghost Dance; Sweat Lodge

Further Reading

Bouvier, Virginia Marie. *Women and the Conquest of California, 1542–1840.* Tucson: University of Arizona Press, 2001.

Duncan, Dalina, and Pratap Chatterjee. *Gold, Greed & Genocide: The Untold Tragedy of the California Gold Rush.* Video recording, 2003.

Golla, Victor. *California Indian Languages.* Berkeley: University of California Press, 2011.

Heizer, Robert F., ed. *Volume 8: California.* In *Handbook of North American Indians.* Washington, DC: Smithsonian Institution, 1978.

Lightfoot, Kent G., and Otis Parrish. *California Indians and Their Environment: An Introduction.* Berkeley: University of California Press, 2009.

Lindsay, Brendan C. *Murder State: California's Native American Genocide, 1846–1873.* Lincoln: University of Nebraska Press, 2012.

CHEROKEE POLITICAL AND LEGAL CULTURE

The Cherokees, who called themselves Ani-Yunwiya ("the real people" or "the principal people"), were organized in settlements scattered in fertile bottomlands among the craggy peaks of the Great Smoky Mountains. In the early 18th century, the Cherokee nation comprised 60 villages in five regions, with each village controlling its own affairs. The Cherokees took public opinion so seriously that they usually split their villages when they became too large to permit each adult a voice in council, so the number of villages varied over time.

Villages sent delegates to a national council only in times of national emergency. Cherokee villages averaged 300 to 400 persons each; at about 500 people, a village usually split in two. In Cherokee society, each adult was regarded as an equal in matters of politics. Leadership titles were few and informal, so when Europeans sought "kings" or "chiefs" with whom to negotiate treaties, they usually did not understand that a single person could not compel the allegiance or obedience of others. The Cherokees made a conscious effort to keep government to a minimum in the belief that personal freedom would be enhanced.

According to John Phillip Reid (1976), the town council was the closest semblance to a permanent government body and was based on consensus. Women were equal to men in the debates that led to consensus. However, women's rights to speak in council were restricted to certain delegates according to clan. Men did most of the talking.

A Cherokee headman belonged to a specific clan; he was assisted by a second from the same clan. When a change of leadership was called for, clan elders agreed with the village community as a whole on a successor. Often, the second was groomed for the position. While some European commentators of the time held that the Cherokees and neighboring Native American nations were without government or law, Reid writes that the Cherokees had a national law within their kinship system.

Cherokee Clans

As among the Iroquois, each Cherokee was a member of a matrilineal clan: Wolf, Deer, Bird, Blue, Red Paint, Wild Potato, or Twisters. The clans formed an intervillage kinship system, which linked them in peaceful coexistence. As with many other confederacies, a clan system among the Cherokees bound the individual villages together. A man or woman outside his or her own village knew that members of the same clan would be awaiting them in other villages to provide hospitality and other support. The clan system cemented the confederacy, giving it a strength and enduring quality that prevented a high degree of local autonomy from degenerating into anarchy. In village councils, each clan caucused before decisions were reached by consensus in a general session.

As they had among the Iroquois before the organization of Deganawidah's confederacy, the Cherokee clans had a judicial function. They avenged crimes against their members. If a member of one clan killed a member of another, a life was owed. The power of this sanction was so strong that, when combined with many other aspects of Cherokee society that restrained violence, the resulting murder rate was insignificant. In Cherokee society, a decent person was one who sought consensus, agreed with the majority, and avoided physical conflict. People who were antisocial by these standards faced ridicule, gossip, and eventual ostracism from the community.

George Milliken Johnson, a surgeon who lived with the Cherokees during the middle of the 18th century, observed that they were unacquainted with subjugation as coercive power was not part of their culture. Another observer of the Cherokees commented at about the same time: "It is by native politeness alone . . . that the chiefs bind the hearts of their subjects, and carry them wherever they will" (Grinde and Johansen, 1991, 34–35).

Cherokee, Iroquois, and Wyandot Political Similarities

Some similarities between the political systems of the Cherokees, Iroquois, and Wyandots (Hurons) probably were not accidental, since all three groups were linked by common ancestry. Floyd G. Loundsbury, a linguist, traced the Iroquois and Cherokee linguistic base to a shared language that split between 3,500 and 3,800 years ago (Fenton and Gulick, 1958, 3). It is believed that the Cherokees migrated southeastward from the Ohio Valley, where they had shared the basics of their language with both the Iroquois and the Wyandots, with some movement taking place as late as 1700. About that time, some of the Tuscaroras moved from an area near Cherokee country to become the sixth nation of the Iroquois.

Like the Iroquois, the Cherokees frowned on excessive concentration of material wealth, although class distinctions did exist. Henry Timberlake speculated that the Cherokees buried valuables with the dead to prevent development of a class structure based on inherited wealth, to make "merit the sole means of acquiring power, honour and riches" (Grinde and Johansen, 1991, 34–35). According to Timberlake's account, the Cherokees maintained a ceremony to provide for the poor. During a special dance, each warrior was called on to recount the taking of his first scalp. During the ceremony, anyone with something to spare heaped the goods on a blanket or animal skin that had been placed on the ground. Afterward, the collection was divided among the poor of the community, with a share reserved for the musicians who had provided entertainment during the ceremony.

Cherokee Councils and Rituals

When council meetings were held, a large proportion of the men, women, and children of a village (as many as 500 people) would gather in the council house; each clan sat together, facing the "beloved old men." The council held no coercive power. According to Duane Champagne, important matters were discussed in the council as a whole, after which the clans caucused individually so that everyone could speak and reach a consensus. Each clan reported its consensus to the village council as it was reached. The council as a whole could adopt a consensus from those of the various clans, or not. If not, there was no binding national consensus and each clan or group of individuals acted on its own.

Cherokee council meetings could last for several days, even weeks. Debate was usually quiet, with participants trying to avoid direct conflict with other residents of the village. Speeches and debate continued until a consensus was reached. While most of the speechmaking was done by men, women often were active behind the scenes. In addition to the matrilineal nature of the clans, home life was matrilocal among the Cherokees of the Smoky Mountains.

Cherokee political and social ritual displayed a striking affection for the number seven. Not only were there seven clans and seven members in the inner council, but the council house had seven sides (one for each clan). The Great New Moon Feast (the Cherokee New Year, held in the autumn) was preceded by seven days of hunting, as seven prominent men were selected to organize the feast, and seven honorable women were picked to prepare it. At dawn on the day of the feast, seven ears of corn (and bits of other crops) were offered to a perpetual fire in the council house. After a sacred dance by the women, the priest-chief led participants to a river that had been scattered with medicinal leaves, where people bathed seven times so that they would be purified and restored. In the evening, the people of the settlement shared a communal banquet.

The Great New Moon Feast opened the most important ritual occasion in Cherokee life, a rite of interpersonal healing. The dates of the ritual were set by the priest-chief and inner council of "beloved men." Seven days before the ritual began, seven men went out to hunt; as the men hunted, seven women selected by the priest-chief and his assistants danced in the village. Seven men were appointed to clean the council house as all village officials fasted. On the seventh day of this ritual, the men who had been cleaning the council house extinguished the central, ceremonial fire of the settlement, after which all families doused their own blazes. The women of each household then relit home fires from a rekindled central blaze. The people then followed the priest to the river and immersed themselves seven times, stripping away their old clothes, as the current swept them downstream. The expressed aim of the entire ritual was renewal of village unity and eradication of anger among villagers that might otherwise have been directed at each other.

The fact that the most important peacemaking rituals of the year were held during the council's meeting was probably not accidental. The participation of the entire village in a mass exercise emphasizing unity and eradication of bad feelings allowed the people to get through an otherwise tense time without undue animosity. After the unity ritual ended, the hunters returned with fresh game, signaling the transition from a season of political debate and ritual to the part of the Cherokees' annual cycle when the emphasis was on provision of food and other essentials of daily life.

See Also PART 1: OVERVIEW: General Historical Considerations: Guns and Cultural Change; **PART 2: CULTURAL FORMS: Arts:** Cultural Appropriation: Questions and Issues; Tattoos; **Family, Education, and Community:** Birthing Customs; Restorative Justice/Spotlight: Harmony Ethic, Cherokee; Wampum; Wedding Customs; **Language and Literature:** Hobson, Geary; Humor, as Cultural Attribute; Owens, Louis/Spotlight: Sequoyah; Silko, Leslie Marmon; **Media, Popular Culture, Sports, and Gaming:** LaCrosse: Cultural Context; Rogers, Will; Sixkiller, Alex (Sonny); Studi, Wes

Further Reading
Corkran, David H. *The Cherokee Frontier: Conflict and Survival, 1740–62.* Norman: University of Oklahoma Press, 1962.

Fenton, William N., and John Gulick. *Symposium on Cheokee and Iroquois Culture.* Bureau of American Ethnology Bulletin 180 (1958): 3. http://archive.org/stream/symposiumonchero00symp/symposiumonchero00symp_djvu.txt.

Gearing, Fred. *Priests and Warriors: Social Structures for Cherokee Politics in the Eighteenth Century.* Memoir 93, American Anthropological Association, 64:5, Part 2, October, 1962.

Grinde, Donald A., Jr., and Bruce E. Johansen. *Exemplar of Liberty: Native America and the Evolution of Democracy.* Los Angeles: UCLA American Indian Studies Center, 1991.

Kupferer, Harriet J. *Ancient Drums, Other Moccasins: Native North American Cultural Adaptation.* Englewood Cliffs, NJ: Prentice-Hall, 1988.

McKee, Jesse O., and Jon A. Schlenker. *The Choctaws: Cultural Evolution of a Native American Tribe.* Jackson: University Press of Mississippi, 1980.

Mooney, James. *Myths of the Cherokee.* In J. W. Powell, *Nineteenth Annual Report*, Bureau of American Ethnology. Washington, DC: Smithsonian Institution, 1897–1898, Part I.

Perdue, Theda. *Slavery and the Evolution of Cherokee Society.* Knoxville: University of Tennessee Press, 1979.

Reid, John Phillip. *A Better Kind of Hatchet: Law, Trade and Diplomacy in the Cherokee Nation During the Early Years of European Contact.* University Park: The Pennsylvania State University Press, 1976.

Reid, John Phillip. *A Law of the Blood: The Primitive Law of the Cherokee Nation.* New York: New York University Press, 1970.

CHEYENNE CULTURAL CONTEXT

Before they lived on the Great Plains of North America, the Cheyennes resided south and southwest of Lake Superior, using a combination of horticulture, gathering, and small game to feed themselves. Growing seasons were short, making harvests unreliable. The amount of corn they could grow, for example, varied by latitude; the farther south a band lived, the more reliant it was on corn. Cheyennes and other Native peoples in this area often farmed in river valleys, where the presence of trees added to the richness of the soil and made it easier to work. They sought sandy soils over clay because this type of earth was easiest to work. Some of the trees were girdled to kill them and let sunshine through. Gardens often were built in terraces at different elevations on river banks. Lower terraces might be flooded in wet years, or the higher ones might die of drought in dry years.

Before the arrival of horses from the Spanish colonies to the south beginning about 1600, life for the Cheyennes often was stark. People's belongings were restricted to the bulk that they could move on an A-shaped travois pulled by a dog or a human being. After the diffusion of horses, tipis became larger, because horses could carry poles up to 30 feet long between summer and winter camps. A person's wealth came to be counted in horses. The Cheyennes, like the Sioux, moved westward in advance of the Euro-American frontier to the high plains of Wyoming and Montana.

While Cheyenne life lost its agricultural focus (a traditional domain of women), the influence of women did not wane in the society as a whole. According to Anne S. Straus, women in Cheyenne society had always been the stable core of domestic life who pulled in the "reins of the Four Directions." Cheyenne women who lived in the same camp gathered and prepared food in common, tanned, sewed, beaded, and quilled together. Cheyenne women literally kept the home fires burning. Women had quilling societies similar to the military societies of the men, where, according to Straus, they celebrated their achievements in solidarity.

Cheyenne Political Culture

The Cheyennes maintained a powerful central government that united the nation's various bands, as well as kin-based groups. At the head of this organization was the Council of Forty-four, on which civil chiefs served 10-year terms. After serving a 10-year term, a Cheyenne chief appointed his own successor, usually from within his own band, but never his own son. The Cheyennes built this and other checks into their system to prevent the rise of a hereditary ruling class. A chief also could not appoint himself to a new term, although he could be "held in the lodge," or reappointed at a future date by another retiring chief. The Council of Forty-four was led by five priest-chiefs. The five "sacred chiefs" remained on the council, with the consent of the rest of its members, after they had completed their ordinary 10-year terms. The leader of the five, who was called Sweet Medicine Chief, acted as a religious intermediary between the Cheyennes and their creator. He was said to represent Sweet Medicine, the Cheyenne culture hero, who filled a role something like that of Deganawidah among the Iroquois. The four subchiefs, whose names evoked ritual spiritual personages, acted as the head chief's assistants.

Cheyenne oral history holds that Sweet Medicine gave the people a sacred bundle of four arrows (probably about the year 1775), a symbol of a code of laws believed to have been handed down from Ma?he?o, the Creator or Supreme Being. The Cheyennes' acceptance of the sacred bundle formed a covenant; the Cheyennes believed that they would prosper if they adhered to the laws of the sacred bundle. Later, the prophet Erect Horns brought to the people the sacred buffalo hat and the sun dance. The buffalo hat (sometimes called the "holy hat") was said to ensure the survival and well-being of the group, while the Sun Dance ensured world renewal.

The number four occurs time and again in Cheyenne social relations, religion, and government, similar to the number seven among the Cherokees; the Council of Forty-four carried this tradition. Anthropologists refer to the

Cheyenne social system as "religiously integrated." Membership on the council was drawn from the 10 traditional Cheyenne bands, but membership in a band was voluntary, not a factor of kinship ties, as among the Iroquois and Wyandots. While kinship ties did not define membership in a band or representation on the council, they still played an important role in day-to-day Cheyenne politics and economic activity. When a man addressed the council, the other members assumed he was speaking on behalf of his extended family. The Council of Forty-four appointed one of the Cheyenne soldier societies to manage the annual buffalo hunt, the premiere economic activity. The 10 traditional bands and affiliated kinship groups managed their own economic resources, including the redistribution of food to feed people such as orphans, the elderly, and the poor, who could not provide for themselves.

Members of the Council of Forty-four were male. One description of a Cheyenne chief's demeanor sounds remarkably similar to the behavior that was expected of Iroquois sachems under their Great Law of Peace:

> A chief must be brave in war, generous in disposition, liberal in temper, deliberate in making up his mind, and of good judgment. A good chief gave his whole heart and his whole mind to the work of helping his people, and strives for their welfare with an earnestness and a devotion rarely equalled by other rulers of men. Such thought for his fellows was not without its influence on the man himself. After a time, the spirit of goodwill which animated him became reflected in his countenance, so that, as he grew old, such a chief came to have a most benevolent and kindly expression. Yet, though simple, honest, generous, tender-hearted, and often merry and jolly, when occasion demanded, he could be stern, severe, and inflexible of purpose. Such men, once known, commanded general respect and admiration. (Hoebel, 1954, 155)

Generosity was a key attribute of a Cheyenne leader, because he was charged with caring for widows and orphans. A chief also was called on to resolve disputes, so people who were good at mediation were usually chosen over those who were not. A chief would strive to resolve a dispute so that it would not disrupt the camp. In the most serious disputes, the entire council acted to mediate.

The Council of Forty-four engaged in lengthy debates whenever it needed to make major policy decisions or adjudicate a serious crime. By custom, each speaker was allowed to discourse until he finished, without interruption, followed by a period of silent reflection to consider his remarks before the next speaker began. Arguing or exchange of angry words was considered to be extremely bad form in the council. After they reached a decision by consensus, the chiefs sent out riders mounted on horseback to announce it. Each chief then returned home to explain the council's actions, which sometimes were changed if large numbers of people disagreed.

Each 10 years, a new council was installed amid feasting and celebration; leaders whose records were esteemed often were asked to serve a second term, even if they were not among the five head chiefs. While all the chiefs were men, women served in influential advisory roles. As with many other Native nations, the general tenor of the society, including political decision making, was set by women. While men did most of the speaking in the council, they could not act without the general consent of the women. Harriet J. Kupferer has called the Cheyennes' governmental system "a type of representative democracy," a description that has been extended to the Iroquois and several other Native nations, especially in the Eastern Woodlands.

Cheyenne Military Societies

Cheyenne military societies served as police, as well as organizers of war parties. Six such societies were called Fox, Elk, Shield, Bowstring, Dog, and Northern Crazy Dogs. These societies maintained order during communal hunts and ceremonial rituals. Discipline meted out by the military societies was swift and unequivocal, especially when a transgression involved jumping the gun during buffalo hunts, when the coordinated action of everyone in the group was held to be sacrosanct. An elderly Cheyenne, Stump Horn, gave an account in 1935 in which Shield Soldiers found two young men who had started the buffalo hunt before the rest of the people, as described by anthropologist E. Adamson Hoebel (1954):

> A Shield Soldier chief gave the signal to his men. They paid no attention to the buffalo, but charged in a long line on the two violators of the rules. Little Old Man [a Shield Soldier] shouted out for everyone to whip them: "Those who fail or hesitate shall get a good beating themselves." The first men to reach the spot shot and killed the horses from under the hunters. As each soldier reached the miscreants, he slashed them with his riding whip. Then some seized the guns of the two and smashed them. (151)

The military societies of the Cheyennes were open to all men in the nation. All of these societies grew out of the horse culture of the plains. As a civil function, the military societies often carried out the council's orders. As the periods of peace dwindled with the onset of the Euro-American invasion, the police societies evolved into war societies, which assumed much of the authority of the Council of Forty-four.

Cheyenne Legal Culture

A Cheyenne who murdered another Cheyenne was not killed, but ostracized and considered impure. The murderer was banished, and for seven years no Cheyenne was allowed to give him aid or assistance. A murderer was usually left to fend for himself on the open plains. In some cases, the murderer was allowed to petition for readmittance to the community by bearing a sacred and symbolic gift to the family of the victim. The gift was a sign from the murderer that he would accept the rules of Cheyenne society. If the family and the Council of Forty-four accepted the gift, the murderer was allowed to return.

The Cheyennes also practiced a form of religious asylum. Anyone being pursued for a crime (even the most serious, such as horse theft or murder) could take shelter in the home of the priest-chief who held the holy hat. Once inside the hat keeper's lodge, the miscreant would be given free passage out of Cheyenne territory. When the Cheyennes were moving, without fixed lodgings, this power was exercised by the wife of the hat keeper, who could declare asylum by embracing a person who was being pursued on a criminal charge.

Guns, Horses, Disease, and Trade

With the coming of Europeans and their horses and guns, Cheyenne culture changed radically. Within a few decades, the Cheyennes had moved to a new home on the western high plains of North America and adopted the horse in a new style of life based on buffalo hunting, as well as remnants of their previous horticultural tradition. This change occurred gradually during the 18th century. In the process, the Cheyennes also found themselves ideally situated for long-distance trade between peoples to their north, such as the Mandans and Arikaras (who acquired guns in Canada), and long-time occupants of the plains, such as the Apaches and Comanches, who had been among the first to develop economic activities based on the horse. At this time, the Cheyennes also adapted the tipi, which could be transported on a travois attached to a horse; tipis also could be assembled and disassembled quickly.

At first, trade with the advancing whites brought prosperity to the Cheyennes. Horses, called *sunka wakan*, "mysterious dogs," by the Sioux, extended the range of their buffalo hunts and made moving camps much easier. Guns aided hunting but raised the level of violence in warfare. By the early 19th century, however, disease, especially smallpox, was devastating Cheyenne society and economy. The Cheyennes concluded a treaty with the United States in 1825 at Teton River, after which the nation split. The Southern Cheyennes

migrated to the Arkansas River area of Colorado, while the Northern Cheyennes settled in southeastern Montana. By the mid-18th century, the economies of both were crumbling under assault by disease and settlement pressure.
In 1864, Black Kettle's band of Cheyennes was massacred at Sand Creek. Many
survivors of the first massacre were killed by troops under George Armstrong
Custer at Washita in 1868, during which time the Cheyennes were living as
prescribed by the Medicine Lodge Treaty of 1867. Survivors combined with
the Arapaho on 81,167 acres spread across eight counties of rolling hills in
northwest and north central Oklahoma.

The Northern Cheyennes were among the last of the Plains tribes to be
subjugated by the U.S. Army, after their active participation in the Battle of the
Little Bighorn (1876). The Northern Cheyennes were compelled to move to
Oklahoma at the conclusion of the Plains Indian wars, where illness and lack
of a sustainable economic base caused a large number to die. During the late
1870s, survivors of forced exile decided to return to Montana on their own and
endured a long march with the Army in pursuit. Fewer than 100 Northern
Cheyennes survived to establish their lives and economies in Montana in 1884.
By 1885, with the buffalo nearly extinct, the Cheyennes were confined to a
reservation with virtually no economic base. The ravages of disease continued
into well into the 20th century. For several decades after that, the government
ignored the survivors.

The Cheyennes in the Late 20th Century

In 1934, the Northern Cheyennes organized under the Indian Reorganiza-
tion Act, and New Deal programs provided some employment. The Southern
Cheyennes' slow recovery from near annihilation began with tribal reorgani-
zation in 1937. By the late 1980s, the Oklahoma Cheyennes and Arapahos
owned two small gaming facilities and three smoke shops. Tribal infrastructure
also has benefited from oil and gas revenues. By the early 1960s, energy companies also were signing leases with the Cheyennes in an attempt to get the
rights to 55 billion tons of low-sulfur coal that lies under the 450,000 acres
of Cheyenne land. In 1972, CONSOL, an energy company, made a grab for
power that would have placed more than two-thirds of the Cheyenne reservation in the hands of mining companies with the right to strip-mine coal.
Cheyennes then rebelled to reclaim their sovereignty and right to a clean
environment.

In the late 20th century, livestock grazing was a major source of employment on the Northern Cheyenne reservation. The tribe has begun a concerted
effort to purchase non-Indian land on the reservation and transfer it to tribal

members in sizes sufficient to sustain cattle ranching. Ranchers on the reservation run an estimated 12,000 to 15,000 head of cattle annually.

See Also PART 2: CULTURAL FORMS: ARTS: Spotlight: Paleontology and Appropriation; **FAMILY, EDUCATION, AND COMMUNITY:** Buffalo (Bison) Culture; Gift-Giving; Trade, Cultural Attributes; **LANGUAGE AND LITERATURE:** Humor, as Cultural Attribute/ Spotlight: Humor: Today's Reservation Jibes; Language Recovery in Indigenous North America; **MEDIA, POPULAR CULTURE, SPORTS, AND GAMING:** Eyre, Chris; West, W. Richard; **MUSIC AND DANCE:** Musical Instrumentation, Traditional and Modern; Sun Dance; **SPIRITUALITY:** Peyote; Thunderbird; Vision Quest

Further Reading

Champagne, Duane. *American Indian Societies: Strategies and Conditions of Political and Cultural Survival.* Cambridge, MA: Cultural Survival, 1989.

Grinnell, George Bird. *The Cheyenne Indians: Their History and Ways of Life.* New York: Cooper Square, [1923] 1962.

Hennepin, Louis. *Description of Louisiana.* Minneapolis: University of Minnesota Press, 1938.

Hoebel, E. Adamson. *The Law of Primitive Man.* Cambridge, MA: Harvard University Press, 1954.

Hoebel, Edward A. *The Cheyennes: Indians of the Great Plains.* New York: Holt, Rinehart, and Winston, 1960.

Kupferer, Harriet J. *Ancient Drums, Other Moccasins: Native North American Cultural Adaptation.* Englewood Cliffs, NJ: Prentice-Hall, 1988.

Lewin, Julius, and E. A. Hoebel. *The Cheyenne Way: Conflict and Case Law in Primitive Jurisprudence.* Norman: University of Oklahoma Press, 1941.

McNickle, D'Arcy. *They Came Here First: The Epic of the American Indian.* New York: Harper & Row, 1975.

Moore, John H. *The Cheyenne.* Oxford: Blackwell, 1997.

Straus, Anne S. "Northern Cheyenne Kinship Reconsidered." In Raymond J. DeMallie and Alfonso Ortiz, eds. *North American Indian Anthropology: Essays on Society and Culture.* Norman: University of Oklahoma Press, 1993, 147–171.

Tiller, Veronica E. Velarde, ed. *Tiller's Guide to Indian Country: Economic Profiles of American Indian Reservations.* Albuquerque: BowArrow, 1994.

NEZ PERCE

"Nez Perce" is French for "pierced nose," although the Nez Perce (who call themselves *Nimi'ipu,* meaning "The People") did not traditionally pierce their noses. The mistaken reference may have been to the Chinooks of the lower Columbia River, who did use nose ornaments. The Nez Perce also call themselves *Iceye¢ yenm mama¢ yac,* "children of Coyote," from their origin story.

The Nez Perce migrated between semipermanent villages in winter and summer camps, following food sources. Since they live along rivers, the Nez Perce have fished for several species (including salmon) for many centuries. Fishing is also an important part of their ceremonial life. In addition to salmon and other fish, the Nez Perce utilized mountain goats, moose, bear, deer, elk, birds, and other small game. Traditional plant foods included pine nuts, wild onions, bitterroot bark, camas bulbs, and many types of berries.

The Nez Perce homeland traditionally included about 17 million acres in present-day Oregon, Washington, Idaho, and Montana, centering in the valleys on either side of present-day Idaho's Snake, Clearwater, and Salmon Rivers. The people's ancestors etched more than 100 pictographs in the Snake River's Hells Canyon, which is laced by rapids at a depth greater than that of the better-known Grand Canyon. Today this canyon forms part of the border between Idaho and Oregon; the Nez Perce lived on both sides. More than 70 village sites along the Snake River and its tributaries have been carbon-dated to about 11,000 years before the present. At least 300 village sites have been identified. In 1800, more than 100 villages were home to 50 to 600 people each, a total population estimated in 1805 at about 12,000. This population declined to about 2,000 late in the same century, due to epidemic diseases, conflict with immigrants, and destruction of Nez Perce culture.

Traditional Nez Perce believe in spirits they call *weyekins* (wie-a-kins) that provide protection, including a guardian spirit that a girl or boy acquires between ages 12 and 15 on a vision quest. The *weyekin* are said to protect the individual throughout life.

Within a decade of Lewis and Clark's visit in 1805, the Nez Perce became part of immigrant trading networks, contributing to a period of prosperity in the first half of the 19th century before the arrival of mass migration, disease, and railroads. As Anglo-American immigrants arrived in the 19th century, territorial governor Isaac Stevens, who negotiated treaties acquiring land for the United States (seeking also to clear the right of way for railroads), in 1855 pressured the Nez Perce to abandon their homeland and move to the Umatilla reservation in Oregon, where they would have lived with the Cayuse, Umatilla, and Walla Walla peoples. The Nez Perce opposed the plan so strenuously that Stevens agreed to another plan whereby they remained on some of their own land but gave up 13 million acres of it to the U.S. government.

The Nez Perce became steadfast U.S. allies as immigrants moved into the Pacific Northwest in the face of opposition from Great Britain. They even rescued a body of U.S. troops in 1858. Nevertheless, the United States signed a treaty with Nez Perce "treaty commissioners" who did not represent the nation.

The treaty ceded the Nez Perce's Wallowa Valley to the United States, opening it for settlement.

The Long March

During the 1870s gold was discovered on Nez Perce land, and they were again pressured to move from their home valleys where the Snake and Clearwater rivers converge, later the sites of Lewiston and Clarkston. The Nez Perce split into two factions, one of which accepted assignment to a reservation. The other refused. The result, for those who refused, was the "Long March." Joseph the Elder died in 1871, passing the leadership of his Nez Perce band to Hinmaton Yalatik, "Thunder Rolling over the Mountains" (1841–1904), whom English-speakers at first called Young Joseph and later Chief Joseph. Like his father, Young Joseph refused to surrender to reservation life. The Nez Perce in Joseph's band stayed in the valley, tending their large herds of prized horses, as European American immigrants moved in around them, sparking several violent incidents.

As Young Joseph assumed leadership of his Nez Perce band, government emissaries continued to press the Nez Perce to move to a reservation where they would be allocated far too little land to run the blue Appaloosas that the Nez Perce used for hunting and war. Under pressure from the United States, during 1871 Joseph and his band signed the last treaty negotiated by any Native nation with the United States. Under the terms of the treaty, the Nez Perce agreed to move to Lapwai, Idaho. As the logistics of the move were being worked out, settlers stole hundreds of Nez Perce horses. A renegade band of young Nez Perce led by young Wahlitis, whose father had been murdered by whites two years earlier, retaliated by killing 18 settlers. The Army was brought in to arrest the "hostiles." Instead of surrendering, the entire band of about 800 men, women, and children decamped and marched into the mountains.

During the next several months, the vastly outnumbered Nez Perce led U.S. Army troops on a 1,000-mile trek through some of the most rugged country on the continent, north into Canada, then south again. Joseph, with at most 200 warriors, fought over a dozen engagements with four U.S. Army columns, evading capture every time. On one occasion, in a night raid, the Nez Perce made off with the pursuing Army's pack animals. At other times, the Nez Perce so skillfully evaded Army pincer movements that the two closing columns ran into each other without capturing a single "hostile." The Army did inflict casualties on the Nez Perce at other times. Eighty-nine were killed in one battle, 50 of them women and children. Despite the deaths, the Nez Perce continued to fight.

Chief Joseph of the Nez Perce. (Library of Congress)

Through the Bitterroot Mountains and the present-day Yellowstone National Park, to the headwaters of the Missouri, then to the Bear Paw Mountains, Joseph's band fought a rear-guard action with unquestioned brilliance.
At one point, the Indians were harbored briefly in Canada by Sitting Bull's
refugees, who also had been exiled from their homelands. Exhausted, the
Nez Perce surrendered on October 5, 1877, at Eagle Creek, roughly 30 miles
south of the Canadian border. Many of the Nez Perce were starving. Several
also were maimed and blind. Joseph handed his rifle to General Miles and said
he was

> tired of fighting. . . . My people ask me for food, and I have none to give.
> It is cold, and we have no blankets, no wood. My people are starving to
> death. Where is my little daughter? I do not know. Perhaps, even now, she
> is freezing to death. Hear me, my chiefs. I have fought, but from where the
> sun now stands, Joseph will fight no more forever. (Johansen and Grinde,
> 1997, 189)

Chief Joseph then drew his blanket over his face and walked into the Army camp, a prisoner. Of roughly 800 Nez Perce who began the Long March, about half (87 men, 184 women, and 147 children) surrendered to the U.S. Army at its end. After the surrender, Joseph and his band were marched to Indian Territory (later Oklahoma), where another 150 died.

In 1879, Chief Joseph appealed to Congress (speaking in person to a full chamber) to let his people return home. "It has always been the pride of the Nez Perce that they were the friends of the white men," he began, recounting how the Indians helped support the first few immigrants. "There was room enough for all to live in peace, and they [Joseph's ancestors] were learning many things from the white men that appeared to be good. . . . Soon [we] found that the white men were growing rich very fast, and were greedy to possess everything the Indian had." He recalled how his father had refused to sign a treaty with Washington territorial governor Isaac Stevens: "I will not sign your paper. . . . You go where you please, so do I; you are not a child; I am no child; I can think for myself. . . . Take away your paper. I will not sign it" (Nabokov, 1991, 130–131). Joseph said that the Nez Perce had given too much, and that they had only gone to war when the immigrants forced them off their cherished homeland.

The War Department refused Chief Joseph's request to let his people resettle in their homeland. Instead, they were imprisoned at Fort Leavenworth, Kansas, where many who had survived the Long March died of malaria. Years later, roughly seven-score survivors were finally allowed to return to the Northwest—some to Lapwai, Idaho, and others to the Colville reservation in eastern Washington. The Nez Perce were provided no supplies as they arrived at the onset of winter. They experienced profound suffering. Lieutenant Wood, who had witnessed Chief Joseph's surrender speech and later wrote a narrative of the Nez Perce's Long March, said: "I think that, in his long career, Joesph cannot accuse the Government of the United States of one single act of justice" (Johansen and Grinde, 1997, 190). Joseph died at Colville in 1904, his heart still yearning to go home to the land where he had buried his father.

By 1895 the Nez Perce reservation was being allotted and opened to non-Indian settlement, as much remaining land was lost. Lost land due to the inability to pay taxes reduced landholdings further over several decades.

The Nez Perce Today

Today, the Nez Perce Indian Reservation is located in central Idaho, in Nez Perce, Idaho, Perce, Lewis, and Clearwater counties, including the towns of Lapwai, Kamiah, Winchester, Craigmont, Culdesac, Ahsahka Spalding, Stites, and Orofino. Nez Perce enrollment was 2,251 in 1969; Nez Perce population was 3,250 in 1994. Reservation population was 18,437 in the 2010 Census, of which about 2,000 were Nez Perce. The total tribal roll in 2010 was 3,513. The Joseph Band of Nez Perce continues to reside on the Colville reservation in north central Washington State. In 2013, the Nez Perce reservation comprised 770,453 acres, of which 385,227 acres were used as cropland, 261,954 acres for grazing, and 100,159 acres as forest.

In 2013, the fighting spirit of the Nez Perce again was marshaled by transport through their lands of huge loads destined for Alberta's tar-sands fields. On August 5, 2013, more than 200 Nez Perce intercepted a convoy of trucks destined for the oil-sands fields of Alberta, forming a blockade that was broken up by police, who arrested 30 people, including the Executive Committee chair, Silas Whitman, and six members of the tribe's Executive Council.

"The development of American corporate society has always been—and it's true throughout the world—on the backs of those who are oppressed, repressed or depressed," Silas Whitman told the *New York Times*. "We couldn't turn the cheek anymore." After their meeting, the Nez Perce leaders decided to face arrest as a group (Johnson, 2013). Whitman, 72 years of age at the time, was one of several Nez Perce arrested at the barricade as police dismantled it. The blockade lasted four nights.

The protests paid off. In September 2013, the Forest Service closed the Nez Perce route to "mega-loads," effective immediately, and required consultation with the tribe in the future.

See Also PART 2: CULTURAL FORMS: ARTS: Moccasins; **MEDIA, POPULAR CULTURE, SPORTS, AND GAMING;** Spencer, Chaske; **SPIRITUALITY:** Seven Drums (Dreamer) Spirituality; **TRANSPORTATION AND HOUSING:** Tipi

Further Reading
Beal, Merrill D. *"I Will Fight No More Forever": Chief Joseph and the Nez Perce War.* Seattle: University of Washington Press, 1963.

Bial, Raymond. *The Nez Perce.* New York: Benchmark Books, 2002.

Johansen, Bruce E., and Donald A. Grinde Jr. *The Encyclopedia of Native American Biography.* New York: Henry Holt, 1997.

Johnson, Kirk. "Fight over Energy Finds a New Front in a Corner of Idaho." *New York Times,* September 25, 2013. http://www.nytimes.com/2013/09/26/us/fight-over-energy-finds-a-new-front-in-a-corner-of-idaho.html.

Josephy, Alvin M. *The Nez Perce Indians and the Opening of the Northwest.* New Haven, CT: Yale University Press, 1964.

Nabokov, Peter. *Native American Testimony.* New York: Viking, 1991.

Nerburn, Kent. *Chief Joseph & the Flight of the Nez Perce: The Untold Story of an American Tragedy.* New York: Harper, 2005.

Nez Perce Tribal Government Website. http://www.nezperce.org/. Accessed August 25, 2014.

"Nez Perce Victory: U.S. Forest Service Forbids Mega-Loads Along Highway 12." *Indian Country Today Media Network.* September 20, 2013. http://indiancountrytoday -medianetwork.com/2013/09/20/nez-perce-victory-us-forest-service-forbids-mega-loads -along-highway-12-151372. Accessed August 25, 2014.

NORTHWEST COAST CULTURE AREA

The peoples of the Northwest Coast—who occupied parts of western Washington and Oregon, the west coast of Vancouver Island, the coasts of British Columbia, and the Alaska Panhandle—harvested mainly fish and sea mammals. Among the Makahs, the word for "fish" is the same as the word for "food." The ocean and forests along the Northwest Coast were so abundant and so skillfully exploited by the Northwest Coast peoples that most were able, during the summer, to dry enough food to last the winter. On this basis, the coastal peoples created a rich culture that generated enough surplus goods to base ceremonial rituals on gifting.

The Northwest Coast peoples also traded with several of their neighbors. The region drained by the Columbia River was a native crossroads, mainly north to south and vice versa along the entire coast; the language of the Chinooks was reduced to an elementary form as a trading medium that spread from Alaska to California. The Chinooks merged with the Chehalis in the mid-18th century and quit using their language, which survived for many years afterward only in the simplified form used for trading.

The Bounty of the Land and Sea

Instead of pottery, the Northwest Coast peoples created exquisite baskets and wooden bowls, which they filled with the bounty of the forests and the sea. The land and sea teemed with fish and game—several kinds of salmon and shellfish, white-tailed deer, mountain goat, black bear, porcupine, marmot, snowshoe rabbit, and others. Some hunters ranged inland from the coast to hunt brown bear, moose, bighorn sheep, and caribou. Along the coast, sea otters, hair seals, and other coastal mammals were hunted. Northwest Coast peoples also gathered wild berries of many varieties, as well as wild rice, wild celery, rhubarb, and many roots and stems. The Saskatoon berry, which they harvested, contains three times as much iron as prunes and raisins.

From the Chicklisets in the north to the Makahs on the coast of Washington, southward to the Hupas on the present-day northern California coast, the

A Makah whaler carried a large harpoon in this E. S. Curtis photograph, probably taken early in the 20th century. (Historic Print & Map Company)

Northwest Coast peoples lived on the natural produce of the land and took sturdy whaling canoes to sea; in times of war, which occurred with a frequency and intensity that usually surpassed the wars of most peoples in North America, the canoes could be used for raiding and to capture slaves from neighboring Native nations.

Maria Parker Pascua described Makah whaling:

> Several canoes leave Ozette together and reach the feeding grounds a few miles offshore before dawn. The harpooners' wives lie still in their long-houses, a bodily prayer that the whale will also be docile. A yew-wood harpoon is not thrown, but pushed into a whale's shoulder behind the flipper. This does not kill the whale, but the wound and inflated sealskin buoys attached to a hundred-foot-long harpoon line slow it down. Then the men begin singing to the whale to encourage it to swim toward shore. When the whale slows, a crewman may leap on its back to kill it with a lance. Then

another crewman dives and threads its mouth closed with cedar-bark rope so water will not fill the whale's stomach. The singing continues all the way back to Ozette. (Pascua, 1991, 41)

When the English first encountered them in 1778, European diseases were just beginning to affect a group of peoples who had built a dense population in a network of relatively large villages among the fjords of western Vancouver Island. Skillful use of abundant fish runs and timber resources encouraged a density of population known in only few areas of North America outside of the areas dominated by the Aztecs and Mayas. Each year, millions of salmon migrated past their villages, on their way from the ocean to their spawning grounds at the headwaters of hundreds of rivers and streams. Northwest Coast villages usually did not communicate with one another on a regular basis because they often were separated by nearly impassable mountains. While the villages evolved distinct languages, their cultures shared many characteristics. Occasionally, nearby villages (which often communicated by sea) were grouped in loose confederacies, but no political authority existed that united all of the coast peoples.

Housing, Labor, and Class Structure

Northwest Coast peoples built large, substantial houses for extended families from massive beams harvested from the tall timber of the coast. The lodges averaged roughly 15 yards by 40 yards in floor area; some were larger. Rank and status permeated nearly every facet of their lives—even dictating what portion of a house a given person occupied. The class system was hereditary as well. Most Northwest Coast peoples recognized three classes that seemed as imperishable as the red cedar from which they constructed their lodges: nobility, commoners, and slaves. The nobility included chiefs and their closest relatives; the eldest son was the family head. He, his family, and a few associates lived in the rear right-hand corner of the house, abutted by people of lower status. These people were said to be "under the arm" of the chief. The next highest ranking chief, usually a younger brother of the head chief, invariably occupied the rear left-hand corner of the house with his family. He, too, had a number of people "under the arm." The other two corners were occupied by lesser chiefs' families.

The space between the corners of a family longhouse, along the walls, was used by commoners' families and a few junior-ranking nobility. They were called "tenants," while the nobility in the corners reserved the right to ownership of the house. Commoners could move from one house to another at will, and since they often performed arduous but necessary skilled labor (such as carpentry or whaling), chiefs competed to retain the best workers. The most successful chiefs were affectionate and generous toward the common families who chose to live in their lodges. Slaves had no designated lodgings or rights; they were captured in raids of other peoples along the coast, and sometimes they were traded for other slaves or goods. A noble in one village could be captured and sold into slavery in another. The captive's relatives might then mount a counter-raid to free him.

Northwest Coast cultural economies were complex. Labor was organized by class, sex, age, and status. A man caught doing what was regarded as woman's work (or vice versa) would be ridiculed. House building, canoe making, carving, making tools and weapons, trading, hunting, and fishing were regarded as strictly men's work. Preparing food, cleaning, weaving, gathering wild foods, and drying fish were regarded as women's work. Some tasks, including rearing children, were regarded as joint labor for both men and women. Leaders performed no menial tasks.

Professions were strictly delineated. Song making was a profession; for example, in several villages song makers organized as a group to make music available for marriages, deaths, and other ceremonial occasions. Anyone could go to the society and buy a song, or, if he was not satisfied with what was on hand, he could have one created to order.

The Potlatch

A family gained class standing or rank in many Northwest Coast cultures based on the ceremonial value of its crests, as well as on the number of potlatches it initiated. A crest acquired value when a member of the owning family displayed it during a potlatch. Crests were given names that signified their value in potlatch terms, such as "Two coppers facing one another," or "A stack of blankets gun high."

Before contact with Europeans, the Tlingits used only slaves and coppers at potlatches. The slaves were usually acquired on raids of the Salish peoples living along Puget Sound. Slaves to be used as potlatch commodities (they could be killed, freed, or given away) usually were acquired for that purpose. Tlingits, for example, did not use their household slaves as potlatch gifts. Often, a potlatch would climax with the freeing of slaves bought or captured for that purpose. During the 20th century, slaves and coppers were replaced by other objects, such as money and wool blankets. The objects stockpiled as potlatch goods are never used in the secular Tlingit economy.

The lavishness of potlatch giveaways reflects a society able to produce goods in excess of everyday needs; great numbers of slaves were killed or freed, many valuable coppers were thrown into the sea. Many blankets were torn into small squares to give away as keepsakes of the occasion at which they were presented. In addition, enormous amounts of food were consumed at potlatches. Custom required that more food be prepared than would be necessary for the feast. Most potlatches lasted four days, with a great deal of feasting, speechmaking, singing, and dancing, as well as gift-giving. A potlatch among the Tlingits might also include a fish-oil drinking contest. Following the introduction of European whiskey and other hard liquors, some potlatches degenerated into drunken orgies punctuated by fistfights.

As the potlatch progressed, the value of gifts usually rose. After the rival chiefs had given away valuable cedar boxes and other expensive items, one chief might sacrifice a slave with a special club called a "slave killer." The "giving" chief might then hurl the scalp of the dead slave at his rival. A potlatch might climax with the giving and destruction of large copper plates that served as currency of very high denominations, in the thousands of dollars each if converted into U.S. currency.

Like most other aspects of life among Northwest Coast peoples, the potlatch was carried out with time-honored formality. Part of the ritual included shouting rehearsed insults, during which one chief goaded others to give away ever more precious objects, such as the fabled canoes that were carved out of huge tree trunks and used to hunt whales. Some of the insults were personal, such as this one recorded in William Brandon's *Book of Indians*: "Do you know what you will be like? You will be like an old dog, and you will spread your legs before me when I get excited. You did so when I broke the great coppers 'Cloud,' and 'Making Ashamed,' my great property. . . . This I throw in your face" (Brandon, 1961, 267).

Woodworking

Forest-dwelling Pacific Coast peoples became expert woodworkers, creating many functional items for the home, such as trays used for serving food. The tray was similar in design to a very small canoe; individual trays were about one foot long. Larger trays, three to four feet, were used to serve food during ceremonies. Wealthier people had polished, decorated bowls, some containing designs of shells or sea otter teeth on their edges. Yew, alder, or maple knots were used for making bowls that held fish oil. Spoons and wooden ladles used for serving food also were carved. Cedar, a very versatile straight-grained wood that has become relatively scarce and expensive today, was central to Muckleshoot traditional woodworking culture. Children were introduced to the characteristics of cedar because their future depended on knowing its use.

Before contact with manufactured items imported by people of European descent, tools were made by hand. Sharp-edged stones were used for scraping, cutting, and chipping. Rocks, bones, or animal horns were used as wedges and adzes. Cedar bark made good twine and pine-tree pitch was used as a glue or sealer. Yew and vine maple were used for the tools that required durability. A variety of woods were used to make tool handles, wedges, bows, canoe paddles, and eating utensils. Digging sticks pointed at one end to which a horn or antler was attached also were created from many types of wood. Cedar logs could be split with wood, stone, bone, or horns. Hammers of stone were used to drive wedges into wood. Adzes with stone blades and wooden handles wrapped in twine were made of wild cherry bark or cedar bark twine. Shells were sharpened and set in wooden handles for carving. Drills were fashioned with sharpened edges that included sharp pieces of stone attached to a stick. Wet sand, sandstone rocks, and sand-coated string were used in carving and shaping stone, bones, and horns.

Northwest Coast bentwood boxes combined fine art with everyday function. These square cedar boxes had wooden handles through the tops of their rims. The boxes were so tight and durable that they could be used as pots to boil water. They were assembled without sawing or cutting. Instead, the soft wood was steamed until it was pliable enough to bend, then laced together. A section was cut in the corners of the box so that adjacent boards would meet each other squarely. The bottom of the box was grooved and fitted without lacing. Boxes varied in size depending on whether they were used in homes or in canoes. Many of them were elaborately decorated and carved. Some of these masterful boxes have become part of museum displays around the world and have lasted for centuries.

Early Contact with Europeans

The first brief European contact with the Northwest Coast peoples was provided by Vitus Bering, a Dane sailing from Siberia in search of the strait that now bears his name. A few years after that, Juan de Fuca sailed through the strait between the Olympic Peninsula and Vancouver Island, where he left his name. Bering made only the slightest encounter with Native peoples (on Kayak Island) before his ship, the *St. Peter*, was wrecked on an island between Siberia and Alaska during his return trip. Bering died on that island, but most of his crew survived, eating the flesh of sea otters as they rebuilt the ship. The crew took some of the otters' sleek pelts home with them to Europe. Within a few years, those otter skins ignited a commercial stampede to the Northwest Coast in search of the biggest fur discovery since the beaver.

The first European to cross the continent from east to west, Alexander Mackenzie (1796), said that European diseases were killing the people of the northern forests "as the fire consumes the dry grass of the fields" (Brandon, 1961, 269). In the meantime, the life-sustaining whales and caribou and other sea and land animals were being hunted nearly to extinction by immigrants in some areas of the Northwest. Freebooting Russian *promyshleniki* killed whatever they could find, from giant (six feet claw to claw) Bering Sea king crabs, to beached seals. The freebooters also slaughtered the Native Aleuts, whom they described as artistic, mild, polite, and hospitable. The Russians' words seemed to echo those of Columbus nearly three centuries earlier, as he spoke of the Indians' hospitality, and of how easily they might be enslaved. By 1799, 90 percent of the Aleuts had been killed.

Among the Native people of the Northwest Coast, the Russians became known as the most ruthless of colonizers. Their demands for tribute in furs were met by armed resistance by the Tlingits, to whom the Russians' British and American colonial competitors happily supplied firearms and even cannon. In 1802, Tlingit war parties, long practiced in internecine warfare up and down the coast, struck at Russian settlements. A large force of Tlingits descended on the Russian colony of New Archangel on Sitka Island, burned most of the structures in the town, and made off with 4,000 sea-otter pelts as they killed 20 Russians and 120 Aleuts. The Tlingits held the position for two years, until Russian warships shelled it in 1804. The next year, the Tlingits resumed their insurgency, attacking the Russian settlement of Yakutat, killing 22 Russians. In 1806, roughly 2,000 Native warriors assembled near Sitka in 400 boats. The Russians, warned of the new attack, decided to throw a large feast, which defused the planned assault. Nevertheless, the Russian settlements faced regular guerrilla raids by smaller Native bands for years afterward.

The search for a reliable food supply to provision their growing settlements brought the Russians to the California coast shortly after 1800, where they imitated the Spanish missions by establishing farming settlements that used coerced Native labor. Landing at Bodega Bay in 1812, 95 Russians and 80 Aleuts founded Fort Ross. The location was appealing because of rocky islands offshore from which the Russians also could hunt sea otters for their prized pelts. At the fort, the Russians established vineyards, orchards, and fields of grain. The Russians ordered the fields tended by labor drafted from local Pomo Indians. As the demand for labor rose from fewer than 100 people to more than 250, the Pomos rebelled, burning fields, killing stock, and running from Russian conscription squads. In the meantime, diseases introduced by the Russians were killing Pomos in large numbers.

Before 1900, among the Inuit of the Canadian North trade with the Russians and English brought the "summer drunk," during which men, having been paid for their furs, spent the short summer feeding their money back to the traders in exchange for hard liquor. In the traditional way of life, summer had been a time of hunting and gathering, and storing provisions for the long, hard winter. Coming off their summer drunks with no supplies, the Inuit men and their families died in large numbers during the winter. In 1888, a revenue ship docked at St. Lawrence Island, at the southern aperture of the Bering Strait, to find the entire population of three settlements, 400 people of both sexes and all ages, dead of starvation.

See Also PART 2: CULTURAL FORMS: ARTS: American Indian Arts and Crafts Fairs; Silverwork; Totem Poles; **FOOD:** Food and Culture: North Pacific Coast; **LANGUAGE AND LITERATURE:** Humor, as Cultural Attribute; **SPIRITUALITY:** The Shakers (Pacific Northwest); Thanksgiving; Thunderbird; **TRANSPORTATION AND HOUSING:** Longhouses (Pacific Northwest)

Further Reading

Brandon, William. *Book of Indians.* New York: American Heritage, 1961.

Drucker, Philip. *Cultures of the North Pacific Coast.* San Francisco: Chandler, 1965.

Drucker, Philip. *Indians of the Northwest Coast.* New York: McGraw-Hill, 1955.

Drucker, Philip. *The Native Brotherhoods: Modern Intertribal Organization on the Northwest Coast.* Washington, DC: Government Printing Office, 1958.

Drucker, Philip. "The Northern and Central Nootkan Tribes." *Bureau of American Ethnology Bulletin* No. 144. Washington, DC: Smithsonian Institution, 1951.

Gibson, Arrell Morgan. *The American Indian: Prehistory to Present.* Lexington, MA: D. C. Heath, 1980.

Gunther, Erna. *Indian Life on the Northwest Coast of North America.* Chicago: University of Chicago Press, 1972.

Maxwell, James A. *America's Fascinating Indian Heritage.* Pleasantville, NY: Readers Digest, 1978.

Oberg, Kalervo. *The Social Economy of the Tlinget Indians.* Seattle: University of Washington Press, 1973.

Pascua, Maria Parker. "Ozette: A Makah Village in 1491." *National Geographic,* October, 1991, pp. 38–53.

Wilson, Duff. *Images, Stone, B.C.: Thirty Centuries of Northwest Coast Indian Sculpture.* Seattle: University of Washington Press, 1975.

OSAGE ECONOMIC CULTURE

The Osages (a French rendering of Wazhazhe, Washashe, or Was-has-he, "people of the water") may have originated on the Virginia piedmont. By the time European immigrants met them, the Osages had migrated into the Ohio

Valley. Gradually, the Osages followed the course of the Ohio westward and southward to its confluence with the Mississippi, then to the Mississippi's confluence with the Missouri River, near present-day St. Louis. By 1673, as they were acquiring horses, the Osages moved to present-day western Missouri, adjacent to the buffalo plains to their west.

When the first French explorers reached them in 1673, the Osages were making a reasonably abundant living from hunting deer, prairie chicken, turkey, skunk, and buffalo, and also growing corn, pumpkins and other squashes, beans, and potatoes. Walnuts, pecans, acorns, and other nuts and berries gathered from the forests supplemented the Osage diet. The Osages used dogs for transportation until they acquired horses.

First Contact: The French and Anglo-Americans

French traders arrived early in the 18th century, integrating the Osages into the European cash economy. Guns, eating utensils, pots and pans, and whiskey became part of Osage culture and daily life. The Osages took up trading with some degree of fervor, for a time selling captured enemies into slavery through French and Spanish markets.

Following the Louisiana Purchase in 1803, the United States replaced France as the Osages' main non-Indian influence. Beginning in 1808, the Osages took part in a number of treaty negotiations in which they ceded claims to most of present-day Missouri, northern Arkansas, northeast and north-central Kansas, and large portions of northern Oklahoma. Oklahoma, then called "Indian Territory," was set aside by the government for the use of many Native peoples who were being "removed" from eastward, particularly the Five Civilized Tribes of the Southeast. The Osages were pressured from one reservation to another by a flood of immigrants, first from western Missouri to eastern Kansas, finally to a tract of land in northeastern Indian Territory.

With the Osages being squeezed treaty by treaty out of their aboriginal land, the U.S. government finally decided in 1825 to designate a permanent strip of land for their villages. The first Osage reservation occupied a southern strip of land in the present-day state of Kansas. In 1825, the Great and Little Osages relinquished claim to all lands in the state of Missouri and Arkansas territory for a 20-year annuity of $7,000 per annum, plus 600 head of cattle, 1,000 domestic fowl, 600 hogs, 10 yoke of oxen, and 6 carts, plus farming utensils and the services of a blacksmith. Land was set aside for the Osages "beginning due east of White Hair's village, and 25 miles west of the western boundary line of the state of Missouri, fronting on a north and south line, as to leave 10 miles north, and 40 miles south, of said beginning, and extending west to the width of 50 miles" (Congressional Record, 1877).

Another treaty was signed with the Osages at Fort Gibson, "west of Arkansas," in 1839, containing land cessions of all land claimed under the treaties of 1808 and 1825, except for explicit exceptions. The Osages were to be paid an annuity of $20,000 a year for 20 years, $12,000 in cash, and $8,000 in goods, stock, provisions, or money "as the President may direct." Provisions included a grist mill and sawmill, a grist miller, two blacksmiths, and two assistants, plus 1,000 cows and calves, 2,000 breeding hogs, 1,000 ploughs, 1,000 sets of horse gear, 1,000 axes, and 1,000 hoes.

For a time, the Osages engaged in prosperous trade with the Comanches, offering blankets, guns, powder, and lead (bought or traded from Anglo merchants) in exchange for mules and other items. The Osages became adept as middlemen. In 1847, for example, they bartered $24,000 worth of trade goods for mules that later were sold for $60,000. In the meantime, Osages returned to their reservation in Kansas to find their homelands invaded by belligerent non-Indian squatters. By 1870, the government sought the sale of the Osages' land and their removal to Indian Territory. By the middle of 1872, nearly 4,000 Osages and 12,000 horses had moved there. For a few more years the Osages tried to wrest subsistence from their traditional spring and fall buffalo hunts, with diminishing success. In 1874, the Osages sold traders 10,800 buffalo robes valued at $60,000. Within a generation, the buffalo were nearly extinct.

A New Homeland in the Cherokee Outlet

The Osages lived on the Kansas reservation for 60 years, but a growing number of squatters pressured the government to have them removed from prime farmland. Additionally, the U.S. government had another problem that could be solved by moving the Osages. The Cherokee tribe was not using a strip of land along the Kansas border called the Cherokee Outlet, which had been set aside as a corridor to the Plains for buffalo hunting. The U.S. government sought to effectively block the Cherokees' path to the Plains to counter their support for the Confederate Army during the Civil War.

The new Osage reservation occupied all of the roughly 1.5 million acres comprising Osage County in north-central Oklahoma, adjacent to the Kansas border, an area that varies from woods to open plains and grasslands. Osage County, which is roughly the size of Delaware, is the largest county in Oklahoma and the only one created explicitly to correspond to the boundaries of an Indian reservation. The county was created because the Osages feared that Oklahoma statehood might crimp their ability to control their own affairs.

The land was purchased in 1871 by the Osages from the Cherokees, part of Osage ancestral land that had been ceded in 1825 in a treaty with the U.S.

government. In 1865, arrangements were made for the Osages to buy the land and sell their 8 million acres of treaty lands in Kansas, two-fifths of which were sold for $1.25 per acre. The government then advanced $300,000 to the Osages and sold the land for $1.1 million, keeping the funds for the "civilization" of other Native nations. An inquiry by the Court of Claims, presented in the *Congressional Record*, March 9, 1877, found that the treaty had been presented to a hastily convened "council" of full bloods who could not read the 16-page typewritten document that was presented for their approval. The treaty was rushed through the approval process, aided by interpreters, in three hours.

Congressional records indicate that the Osages fought several proposals or attempts to abolish their tribal government early in the 20th century. As early as 1874 and 1875, they also protested to Congress establishment of a territorial government that would have had powers superior to those of the Indian nations in the territory. Just a few decades later in a new century, the Osages would discover just how far greed could drive individuals. Land-hungry squatters and disreputable government agents had been only an indication of times to come. Then came oil and the hundreds of white people who were attracted by its scent of wealth.

Osage Oil and Traditional Culture

Oil was first discovered under Osage land in Oklahoma (then Indian Territory, before statehood) in small amounts as early as 1896, but the first well drilled in that year was a dry hole. The first successful drilling began a year later in 1897. More than 300 oil wells had been drilled by 1904, as production increased with the demands of industry and a growing national fleet of automobiles. The Osages found themselves sitting on one of the richest oil fields in the United States just as the internal combustion engine was becoming a major form of transportation in America. The discovery of oil disrupted Osage culture at the same time that the traditional council structure was used to maintain collective control of the resource.

In 1920, oil royalties amounted to an average of $40,000 per family on the Osage reservation; newspapers featured stories about Osages who "built elaborate homes but spent nights in traditional teepees, and . . . [purchased] costly automobiles that they were unable to drive" (Baird, 1972, 1). Many Osages spent their money quickly and foolishly as every imaginable stripe of huckster and easy-money man converged on the newly rich Osage "oil barons."

By 1929, as the oil boom reached its peak, each of the roughly 2,200 enrolled Osages had received an average of about $100,000 in oil royalties. Actual income was based on ownership of "headrights," which could be inherited. A number of lawyers, appointed as guardians of "incompetent" Osage "wards," cheated the Indians of their oil income. Pawhuska, Oklahoma, the capital of the Osage Nation, hosted traffic jams in the early 1920s that resembled those in much larger cities. Oil income continued for several decades after the booming 1920s, but at a diminished rate. For a time, the Osages became the richest people, per capita, in the world.

These oil and mineral rights brought unprecedented wealth to the Osages. In 1880, an Osage received $10.50 per year from the tribe's common fund. In 1900, the amount was $200 per year. In 1920, that yearly amount jumped to $8,090 (per headright, not per household). By 1923, two years after increasing numbers of Osages were murdered, a headright was bringing in $12,440 per year, equivalent to more than $980,000 per year in 1998 dollars.

By 1939, more than 500 million barrels had been taken from lands of the Osage Nation. Osage leases and royalties from oil and gas by the 1990s generated between $10 million and $25 million per year, as the price of oil fluctuated from $12 to $25 per barrel. The reservation's grasslands also supported about 150,000 head of cattle.

What emerges from this history is an irony; in the case of the Osages, allotment legislation, originally meant to break up collective tribal identity, culture, and rights in favor of individual landholding and Anglo-Saxon–style property rights, was used at a key juncture in a culturally collective manner to maintain Osage control of oil and other mineral rights. The Osages in effect used U.S. law to maintain the collective ownership that they deemed proper for their culture, even as non-Indian corporations tried to break it up.

The legal key to collective control was insertion of a clause to that effect into the legislation passed in 1906 that initiated allotment for the Osages. At every turn, the Osage tribal government has protected its rights to manage oil production for the common good of the nation, even as private interests and internal tribal factions have tried to assail it. Through several decades, the Osages have used legal resources to lobby Congress to use its plenary power vis-à-vis Native nations to maintain its right to manage the nation's natural resources.

Teresa Trumbly Lamsam and Bruce E. Johansen

See Also PART 2: CULTURAL FORMS: ARTS: Tattoos; **LANGUAGE AND LITERATURE:** Language Recovery in Indigenous North America

Further Reading

"Annual Summary of Production and Pipeline Runs, Oklahoma and Kansas, for the Year 1939." *Petroleum Statistical Guide*, p. 11, cited in *U.S. v. Stanolind* (1940).

Baird, W. David. *The Osage People.* Phoenix: Indian Tribal Series, 1972.

Congressional Record. 44th Congress, 2d Session, Ex. Doc. No. 186. Committee on Indian Affairs, March 9, 1877.

Glasscock, C. B. *Then Came Oil: The Story of the Last Frontier.* Indianapolis: Bobbs-Merrill, 1938.

Hogan, Lawrence J. *The Osage Indian Murders.* Frederick, MD: Amlex, 1998.

Miner, Craig H. *The Corporation and the Indian: Tribal Sovereignty and Indian Civilization in Indian Territory, 1867–1907.* Columbia: University of Missouri Press, 1989.

"Osage Civilization Fund." Hearing on Joint Resolution No. 67. Committee on Indian Affairs, House of Representatives. Washington, DC: Government Printing Office, 1909.

Tiller, Veronica E. Velarde. *Tiller's Guide to Indian Country: Economic Profiles of American Indian Reservations.* Albuquerque: BowArrow, 1996.

PEQUOT CULTURAL CONTEXT

One of the first Native American nations to come into contact with English colonists in the area later called New England, the Pequots assembled an alliance of Native peoples in 1636 and then tried to push the Puritans into the sea. Due in part to the Puritans' Native allies, the attempt failed, as the Pequots were nearly exterminated in the Pequot War of 1636–1637, and much of their language, economy, and other cultural attributes vanished. Late in the 20th century, however, the remnants of the Pequots reassembled on a small plot of land in Connecticut with a massive cash infusion supplied by the largest Native American gambling operation in the United States.

Before they were slaughtered in the Pequot War, the Pequots were some of the most affluent Native Americans to do business with the early English immigrants. "Pequot" is derived from the Algonquian word *pekawatawog* or *pequttoog* meaning "destroyers" ("Pequot History," 1997). The Pequots and the Mohegans originated as a single group that migrated to eastern Connecticut from the upper Hudson River Valley in New York, probably the vicinity of Lake Champlain, sometime around 1500. At the time of their first contact with Europeans, the Pequots occupied southeastern Connecticut from the Nehantic River eastward to the present-day border with Rhode Island. The Pequots were no larger in numbers than the peoples surrounding them, but they were more highly organized, with strong central authority exercised by a council led by a grand sachem. Their organized nature provided the Pequots a considerable military advantage over their neighbors before the intervention of English immigrants.

Pequot Cultural History

The economic culture of the Pequots, who lived in sedentary villages, was based on cultivation of corn and other crops, as well as hunting and fishing. They grew several kinds of squashes as well as corn, beans, Jerusalem artichokes, and tobacco. The Pequots hunted white-tailed deer, bear, raccoon, opossum, gray squirrel, gray fox, and other land animals, as well as geese, turkeys, and loon. They fished for Atlantic sturgeon, striped bass, and skate, as well as other fish and shellfish. The Pequots also made use of wild fruits and berries, such as strawberries, blueberries, blackberries, walnuts, acorns, and butternuts. As was common through most of the Northeast, women performed most cultivation (except that men grew tobacco).

Precontact Pequot villages usually were inhabited seasonally. Crops were planted, tended, and harvested at locations along the coast during the summer; during the winter, many Pequot bands moved inland and subsisted mainly by hunting and gathering. Houses were constructed of woven mats (made by women) that could be easily erected, dismantled, and moved. If the Mohegans are included, the Pequots probably numbered around 6,000 in 1620. After a major smallpox epidemic during the winter of 1633–1634 and the departure of the Mohegans, about 3,000 Pequots remained by the middle 1630s. Fewer than half are believed to have survived the Pequot War of 1636 and 1637.

Between 1616 and 1619, before large-scale contact and trade with Europeans, the Pequots were devastated by imported diseases, including bubonic plague and smallpox, as well as hepatitis A. Another plague, mainly smallpox, swept the area in 1633. Between 55 percent and 95 percent of area populations were killed, with consequent destruction of the Pequot culture base. A likely population of 12,000 to 15,000 Pequots was reduced to about 3,000 by these plagues. According to historian William Cronon, the most likely cause of the 1616 epidemic in New England was chickenpox, which was not deadly to most Europeans. Among Native Americans, chickenpox killed so many people that the few who survived could not bury the dead. The spread of disease broke down social and economic organization among most Native peoples. Many were weakened and could not carry out the tasks of hunting and planting corn. The cycle continued as they were weak when the next infection arrived.

Facing a growing European American presence spreading from the Boston area by about 1635, the Pequots split into two factions. Opponents of the English colonists, led by Sassacus, at one point, limited its trade to the Dutch. Another faction, led by Uncas, allied with the British colonists, often fighting with the English against dissident Pequots and other Native peoples. They were known at the time as the Mohegans.

Massacre at Mystic

About 400 Pequots died in the burning of their main fort at Mystic, Connecticut, as flames turned the thatch fort into an inferno, frying many of them alive as they tried to escape. The Pequot War, during which the massacre occurred, began during the summer of 1636 when a Boston trader, John Oldham, was killed as the western Niantics captured his boat near Block Island. Richard Mather, in a sermon delivered in Boston, denounced the Pequots as the "accursed seeds of Canaan," in effect imagining the confrontation in Connecticut as a holy war by the Puritans against the forces of evil.

With these fiery words urging them to action, Massachusetts, without bothering to consult the colonists in Connecticut, sent a punitive expedition of 90 men under the command of John Endicott to Block Island in August with orders to kill every man and take the women and children prisoner. The English soldiers managed to kill 14 Niantics and an undetermined number of dogs before they escaped into the woods and then burned the village and crops. Endicott then loaded his men back into the boats and sailed over to Fort Saybrook to add some additional soldiers for the second part of his mission—a visit to the Pequot village at the mouth of the Thames river to demand 1,000 fathoms of wampum for the death of Oldham and several Pequot children as hostages.

The Pequots were furious. During the winter they plotted revenge and sent war belts to the Narragansetts and Mohegans asking their help in a war against the English. However, because of their past actions, the Pequots had few friends, and the English found it fairly easy to isolate them. Early in 1637, Sassacus ordered a series of raids against the Connecticut settlements to retaliate for Endicott's raid of the previous summer. Two hundred warriors attacked Wethersfield on April 12 and killed nine colonists (six men and three women). Other victims were 20 cows and a horse. Taking two teenage girls hostage, the war party loaded their loot into canoes and went home on the Connecticut River. Passing the fort at Saybrook, they taunted the garrison by waving the bloody clothes of their victims. The colonists lost 30 people in these raids, and in May the General Court at Hartford formally declared war.

A joint expedition of 90 English and 70 Mohegan warriors under Uncas assembled near Hartford to attack the main Pequot fort at Mystic. Commanded by Captain John Mason, an experienced soldier, this tiny army departed on what seemed a suicide mission. Passing down the Connecticut River, it stopped at Fort Saybrook to add a few soldiers and then proceeded up the coast only to discover the Pequots waiting for them at Mystic.

When Mason reached the Narragansett villages, 200 warriors joined his ranks, and he received their permission to travel overland through Narragansett territory for a surprise attack on Mystic from the rear. With his force now numbering more than 400 men, Mason left the Narragansett villages and moved west across the hills of western Rhode Island. The English and their allies arrived at Mystic undetected because the Pequot warriors who usually would have been defending Mystic were absent. Lulled into a sense of false security by the sight of what had earlier seemed to them like a retreat by Mason's men, the Pequots had formed a war party to raid settlements near Hartford.

The Pequots had gathered at Mystic for an annual Green Corn Dance ceremony. As the colonists and their allies surrounded the fort and set it aflame, the trapped Pequots who sought to escape the flames met the business end of Puritan muskets at point-blank range. Witnesses left descriptions of Pequot flesh sizzling as the strings on their bows melted in a holocaust of roaring fire.

A few Pequot bowmen stood their ground amidst the flames, until their bows singed and they fell backward into the fire, their flesh sizzling like bacon on a hot griddle. The English, Dutch, and their Indian allies held their noses against the stench of burning flesh. The entire roaring inferno burned itself out less than an hour after the torching had begun. During that hour, at least 400 Pequots died.

> Those Pequot not burned to death were killed when they tried to escape. Following Mason's orders, the Narragansett and Mohegan finished any Pequot the English missed but were aghast when the English indiscriminately slaughtered Pequot women and children. Their grim work completed, Mason made a hasty retreat (actually, a headlong rush) to his boats waiting at a rendezvous on the Thames. Sassacus' village was only five miles away, and his warriors were in hot pursuit. Hartford declared June 15th as a day of prayer and thanksgiving for the "victory" at Mystic. ("Pequot History," 1997)

The colonists then declared the Pequots extinct. The purported extinction of the Pequots has been one bit of Connecticut folklore that has made its way into some important precincts of American letters. Alexis de Toqueville, passing though the area as a tourist, missed several remnants of the Pequot Nation when he declared them extinct during 1833. He also declared extinct all of the Native peoples who had once inhabited New England (including, by name, the Narragansetts and Mohicans, as well as the Pequots). In *Moby Dick*, published in 1851, Herman Melville explains that the *Pequod*, Captain Ahab's doomed ship, was named after a New England Indian tribe that the narrator believes to be extinct. Melville also missed the scattered remnants that had survived the Puritans' war of extermination.

While a few Puritans remonstrated regarding the violence, many (Bradford included) soon placed the massacre in the category of God's necessary business, along with all sorts of other things, from smallpox epidemics to late frosts and early freezes.

The Aftermath of the Pequot War

The outcome of the Pequot War during the summer of 1636 devastated Native cultures and radically altered the demographic balance in New England. Before it, the English colonists were a tiny minority. Afterward, the immigrants held a slight majority. The terms of the peace treaty signed after the Pequot War systematically dismembered the Pequots as a people. After the Pequot War most captured warriors were executed, and the English sold the remainder as slaves to the West Indies. Some of the women and children were distributed as "servants" to colonial households in New England. Some of the survivors also were divided as slaves among the Indians who had supported the Puritans: 80 to Uncas and the Mohegans; 80 to Miantonomo and the Narragansetts, 20 to Ninigret and the Niantics. No Pequots were thereafter allowed to inhabit their traditional lands. The name "Pequot" was to be expunged; survivors were instructed to take the names of the Native nations to which they had been given.

Pequots who escaped the inferno at Mystic separated into small bands and tried to escape, but Puritan soldiers tracked them with the aid of Mohegan and Narragansett allies. After the war, the Pequot population probably fell below 1,000. Remnants of the Pequot nation settled on a 2,000-acre reservation near the Mystic River in 1655. Surviving Pequots became influential in the regional fur trade, particularly of beaver. Through the early 18th century, most surviving Pequots continued traditional subsistence patterns as best they could; some adopted European farming techniques, raising pigs and other livestock. The Mohegans treated their Pequots so badly that by 1655 the English were forced to remove them. Two reservations were established for the Pequots in 1666 and 1683. By 1762 there were only 140 Pequots; their population decline continued to a low point of 66 in the 1910 census.

In 1855, the state of Connecticut auctioned off about 90 percent of the Pequot reservation, as the population there declined due to diseases and lack of economic opportunity. Proceeds from land sales were invested and paid for tribal welfare, depleting their account over the years; by 1940, the tribal credit balance stood at less than $3,000. As the balance fell, so did the amount of accrued interest, forcing the Pequots to erode their capital base still more. By the 1940s, the size of the reservation was down to 214 acres and the number of Native American residents down to one extended family.

Modern Economic and Cultural Recovery

In the 1970s, the Pequots followed the legal example of the Passamaquoddy and Penobscots of Maine, who had been able to regain lost land (along with some funding for economic development) by proving violation of the federal Non-Intercourse acts. Several federal laws, passed first in 1790, forbade state taking of Indian land without federal approval, as a device to prevent fraud. The laws, which had been ignored for almost two centuries after that, were the basis of legal action by which the Mashantucket Pequots regained 1,600 acres of land, mostly by repurchase, along with a $900,000 economic development fund that was part of an out-of-court settlement.

The Native American population of the Pequot reservation increased to about 200 by 1980, as a number of enterprises drew economic development to the area, involving agriculture, harvesting maple syrup, timber sales, and a greenhouse project. One of those businesses was a bingo hall that developed into the Foxwoods Casino, the largest Native American gaming operation in the United States, which lies within a 100-mile radius of 25 million people along the New York–Boston urban strip. Increasing prosperity among the Mashantucket Pequots had spurred a large number of applications for tribal enrollment by about 1990, as proceeds from gambling were used to recover cultural knowledge, including language and history.

See Also PART 2: CULTURAL FORMS: LANGUAGE AND LITERATURE: Figures of Speech, Native American Origins/Spotlight: Names from Native Cultures; MEDIA, POPULAR CULTURE, SPORTS, AND GAMING: Gambling; Museums; MUSIC AND DANCE: Litefoot (Gary Paul Davis); Native American Music Awards & Association (NAMAA)

Further Reading

Barry, Ellen. "Recognition Is a Contentious Process: James P. Lynch, Who Debunks Tribes, Says He Was Shocked to Find the Pequots' Proof of Ancestry So Tenuous." *Boston Globe*, December 12, 2000. http://www.citizensalliance.org/links/pages/news/National%20News/Connecticut.htm.

Covey, Cyclone. *The Gentle Radical: A Biography of Roger Williams.* New York: Macmillan, 1966.

Cronon, William. *Changes in the Land: Indians, Colonists, and the Ecology of New England.* New York: Hill and Wang, 1983.

Eisler, Kim Isaac. *Revenge of the Pequots: How a Small Native American Tribe Created the World's Most Profitable Casino.* New York: Simon & Schuster, 2001.

Hauptman, Laurence M., and James D. Wherry. *The Pequots in Southern New England.* Norman: University of Oklahoma Press, 1990.

"Pequot History." 1997. http://www.dickshovel.com/peq.html. Accessed August 25, 2014.

PONCA CULTURE

The Poncas are of the Degiha division of the Siouan language family, which also includes the Omaha, Osage, Kansa, and Quapaw languages and is further related to the Chiwere division, which includes the Iowa, Oto, and Missouri languages. In language and customs the Poncas are mostly akin to the Omahas, whom they separated from some time between 1390 and 1700 after moving into present-day northeast Nebraska from southern Ohio.

The proximity with the Omahas presents a major problem in identifying traditions specific to the Poncas because the Omahas are often representatives of the group. Since much of Ponca political and legal traditions in past literature may actually be Omaha, careful review is necessary to identify what truly are Ponca political and legal traditions.

Legal, Moral, and Social Rules

The Poncas possessed a strict set of moral and social rules. Ponca elder Peter LeClaire (1947) offered the following moral laws as told to him by both northern and southern Ponca elders: (1) Have one god; (2) do not kill one another; (3) do not steal from one another; (4) be kind to one another; (5) do not talk about each other; (6) do not be stingy; and (7) have respect for the sacred pipe. Almost all government and law was based on family relations or kinship; family clans were central in Ponca governance. Social rules were both tribal and clan based. Individual violations of specific laws of the Poncas often were enforced by the victim or their relatives, as was common among Plains Native nations. The punishment of an adulterer was left to the injured husband who might kill, scalp, or cut off the hair of a man whom he caught with his wife. A wife could kill another woman with whom her husband eloped. Occasionally, Ponca women also went to war and became braves, whereas Omaha women did not.

Killing as a form of capital punishment or in warfare was not considered murder. When murder was committed, retaliation was left to the relatives of the murdered individual and was often swift due to the belief that "the spirit of a murdered person will haunt the people, and when the tribe is on the hunt, will cause the wind to blow in such a direction as to betray the hunters" (Fletcher and La Flesche, 1911, 216). Religious sanctions acted as a powerful deterrent to illegal acts.

Ponca law required that property belong to families, individuals, or the nation as a whole. Community buildings and land belonged to the nation. Individual property might include a man's gun and clothes. People had to ask to use the individual property of others, and stealing was not tolerated. Families owned their tents or houses. If a family member left, he lost his rights to the house. If a man left his wife, she kept the tipi. If she ran off with another man, he kept it. Divorce was simple in Ponca society. If a couple did not get along, they just split up. The children might go with their mother, her mother, or their father's mother. Should the father be unwilling, the wife could not take the children with her. Each could remarry.

In terms of clan politics and law, each clan was responsible for a certain duty. One clan might take care of military matters, another of religious duties, while another took charge of hunting or the harvest. The political structure of the Ponca clans was hereditary and patrilineal. An individual's position in Ponca society depended upon his or her position in their family, their family's position in the clan, and the clan's position in the nation. Certain clans outranked certain others socially and had special rights and prerogatives not possessed by others. The terms *clan*, *band*, and *gente* have been used synonymously throughout past literature. The Poncas, like the Omahas, were divided into two moieties or half-nations: the earth and the sky. The Poncas had seven clans until the mid-1800s when the Wa-ge-ziga or Whitemen's Sons Clan became the eighth.

The Poncas also obtained horses after settling on the Niobrara River sometime between 1725 and 1750, which led the Poncas to extend both their hunting and trade territories throughout the 18th and 19th centuries. Archaeological findings at the Ponca Fort site, located west of the Niobrara's entry into the Missouri River, identify that the Ponca trade with other tribes was both extensive and lucrative. Pottery, stone mauls, mealing slabs and mullers, bone knives, hoes, tubes, shaft wrenches and picks, catlinite pipes and disks, twined mats, and strip bark in rolls have been found at the Ponca Fort site from tribes as far away as the southeastern United States. Corn was a basic article of trade, and although the Poncas raised corn, they often preferred to trade robes and meat to the Omahas for corn.

Camps, Clans, and Buffalo Hunts

A traditional Ponca camp is called *Hu-thu-gah*. It is round with the entrance in the east. Each of the bands has duties in the camp. From the entrance, left to right, the *Wazaze* or *Wahja-ta* (snake or Osage) guard the entrance and are expert trackers. Touching snakes is taboo to members of this clan. The *Nikapasna* (skull or bald head) know all about the human head and how it should be dressed. The *Dixida* (blood) or *Te-xa-da* perform magic, and when the camp is getting short of meat, they get their bows and arrows out and make believe they are shooting animals, saying, "I'll shoot this fat one." The band in the center is the *Wasabe, Washabe*, or *Wahshaba*. The principal chief of the Poncas was always selected from this clan, and its members are forbidden to touch the head of an animal because they belong to the head clan. The *Maka* or *Miki* (medicine) know all about medicines, and members are the best herbalists among the Poncas.

The clan heads and their subchiefs enforced the laws of the clan and settled conflicts within the clan. Conflicts between members of different clans often were settled by the council of seven, which was made up of the first-order chiefs and the principal chief. Intragroup loyalty and cooperation required that even the clan heads must follow Ponca law. Clan heads and subchiefs must be (1) good to the old; (2) good to orphans; and (3) good to the needy. Any violation could mean shame to the clan and removal as clan head. Although the Poncas have had no female chiefs during the time they have been known to historians writing in English, Ponca oral history indicates that women were not barred from becoming chiefs. Often they were women with great supernatural power, medicine women, to whom the Poncas looked for leadership in times of uncertainty due to unknown causes, such as an extended drought.

The summer buffalo hunt was one instance in which Ponca law predominated because all the clans were together for an extended period of time and a successful hunt was essential to the survival of the nation. The *Washabe* and the *Maka* clans "were given charge of the communal buffalo hunt—the direction of the journey, the making of the camp, and preservation of order. From these two camps the two main chiefs must come" (Fletcher and La Flesche, 1911, 48). The Omahas had one hunt leader rather than two, and the Nikapasnas were responsible for the supervision of all hunting of deer. The leaders were in complete charge of the hunt and maintained discipline through the hunt police or Buffalo-police. "Those selected to be hunt police were the bravest warriors of some clan but not the whole tribe . . . the bravest of some other clan served at another time." The hunt police "were chosen from those who had the right to wear the 'Crow', a decoration possessed by those men who more than once had achieved war honors of the first three grades" (Fletcher and La Flesche, 1911, 441; Skinner, 1915, 794–795).

Fletcher and La Flesche (1911, 439–440) identified the Poncas' six grades of honor: (1) to strike an unwounded man; (2) the first to strike a fallen enemy; (3) the second to strike a fallen enemy; (4) to kill a man; (5) to take a scalp; (6) to capture horses from the enemy. When the Poncas were not on the hunt, responsibility and rules continued to be enforced by one or two Buffalo-police appointed by the head of each clan. These Buffalo-police did not have to achieve the war honors necessary to wear the "Crow," but personal leadership and character were important factors in becoming Buffalo-police. The

Buffalo-police could be very severe in their punishments, even to the point of killing the offender. Ponca justice was directed more at preserving order than social revenge. Conformity, not revenge was sought, and immediately after a promise to conform was secured from the perpetrator, steps were taken to reincorporate him or her into the society once more. For example, after the Buffalo-police had whipped a man for violating the rule against individual hunting during the communal bison hunt, they would give him gifts so that "his heart would not be bad" (Howard, 1965, 96).

The main functions of the Buffalo-police were (1) to regulate the communal hunt; (2) to regulate ceremonies; (3) to settle disputes, punish offenders, and preserve order in the camp; and (4) to regulate war parties and restrain them at inopportune times. Being a clan head, subchief, or member of the Buffalo-police in a small, highly interrelated nation such as the Poncas was not easy, for right or wrong, the actions of these political and legal positions were liable to earn the ill will not only of the persons directly involved, but of the clansmen of all those persons as well. In conclusion, the well-being of the group was always a major influence on the implementation of the Ponca political and legal traditions. A Ponca elder reported in 1979: "Not like the white people who put their laws in large, heavy books and forget them. We Ponca carry our laws in our hearts, where we never live a day without them" (Elders' oral discussion, 1979).

Average annual corn production in the early 1860s was 5,000 bushels, and in 1865 and 1866, the Ponca had such good crops that they gave corn to the Yankton Sioux. Grasshoppers destroyed the crops in 1867, 1868, and 1869. A drought in 1870 forced the Poncas to combine with the Pawnees to hunt buffalo, but the Brule Sioux were on the range and the Poncas brought no meat home. Agent reports in the 1870s describe the Poncas as destitute, starving, and living on wild potatoes and rations hauled in from Fort Randall and the Yankton agency. Agency records from 1876 state that the Poncas had taken up farming as their main economic endeavor and were requesting a new school so that their children could learn the trades of whites.

Ponca Removal, Return, and Revival

Another factor in the study of Ponca traditions was the U.S. government's removal of the Poncas from Nebraska to Oklahoma in the summer of 1877. The government removed the Poncas because of the continual attacks by the Brule Sioux, which played havoc with the Ponca economy. Clan head Standing Bear and 66 fellow Poncas returned to Nebraska during the winter of 1877–1878 where they were arrested and incarcerated in Omaha, Nebraska, by General

George Crook. This act led to the famous *Standing Bear v. Crook* case and Judge Elmer Dundy's landmark ruling that found whites and Indians to both be entitled to constitutional protection. Consequently, since that time there have been two Ponca tribes, the southern Poncas in Oklahoma and the northern Poncas in Nebraska, both adjusting and assimilating to their geographic and cultural surroundings. Farming among both the northern and southern Poncas increased with the allotment period but decreased as more and more allotted land was obtained by white people.

Fred LeRoy and Jerry Stubben

See Also PART 2: CULTURAL FORMS: FAMILY, EDUCATION, AND COMMUNITY: Civic and Military Societies; **LANGUAGE AND LITERATURE:** Spotlight: Humor: Today's Reservation Jibes; **MUSIC AND DANCE:** Pow Wows; **SPIRITUALITY:** Peyote

Further Reading

Connelley, William E. "Notes on the Early Indian Occupancy of the Great Plains." Collections. *Kansas State Historical Society* (1915–1918), vol. 14.

Dorsey, J. O. "Migrations of the Siouan Tribes." *American Naturalist* 20, no. 3 (1886): n.p.

Dorsey, J. O. "Omaha Sociology." *Third Annual Report of the Bureau of American Ethnology*. Smithsonian Institution Bureau of Ethnology. Washington, DC, 1884.

Dorsey, J. O. "Siouan Sociology." *Fifteenth Annual Report, Bureau of American Ethnology*. Washington, DC: Smithsonian Institution, 1893–1894 (1897).

Dorsey, J. O. "A Study of Siouan Cults." *Eleventh Annual Report, Bureau of American Ethnology*. Washington, DC: Smithsonian Institution, 1889–1890 [1894].

Elders' oral discussion. Stubben's Discount Store, Niobrara, Nebraska, 1979.

Fletcher, Alice C. "Tribal Structure: A Study of the Omaha and Cognate Tribes." *Putnam Anniversary Volume*. Anthropological Essays. New York, 1909.

Fletcher, A. C., and F. La Flesche. "The Omaha Tribe." *Twenty-Seventh Annual Report of the Bureau of Ethnology*. Washington, DC: Smithsonian Institution, 1911.

Howard, James H. *The Ponca Tribe*. Smithsonian Institution Bureau of American Ethnology. Bulletin 195. Washington, DC: Smithsonian Institution, 1965.

Jablow, Joseph. *Ponca Indians: Ethnohistory of the Ponca with Reference to Their Claim of Certain Lands. A Report for the Department of Justice, Lands Division, Indian Claims Section.* New York: Garland, 1974.

Le Claire, Peter. "Ponca History: Letter Written on Tribal History by Ponca Indian." August, 26, 1947. Niobrara, Nebraska. In J. H. Howard. *The Ponca Tribe*. Oral interview with tribal elder Peter Le Claire.

LeRoy, Fred. Chair, Northern Ponca Tribe of Nebraska. Oral history and personal research on Ponca tribal sites, 1986.

Ponca Census. *Census Roll of the Poncas Tribe Taken at the Poncas' Camp, July 6, 1860 by I. Shaw Gregory, U.S. Special Agent.* Niobrara, Nebraska.

Province, J. H. "The Underlying Sanctions of Plains Indian Culture." In Fred Eggan, ed. *Social Anthropology of North American Tribes.* Chicago: University of Chicago Press, 1937, 341–374.

Skinner, Alanson. "Ponca Society and Dances." *Anthropological Papers of the American Museum of Natural History*, vol. 11, part 9 (1915): 679–801.

Wishart, David J. *An Unspeakable Sadness—The Dispossession of the Nebraska Indians.* Lincoln: University of Nebraska Press, 1994.

Wood, Raymond W. "Historical and Archeological Evidence for Arikira Visits to the Central Plains." *Plains Anthropologist* 4 (1955): 27–39.

Yerington Paiute Tribe. *Introduction to Tribal Government.* Yerington, NV: Yerington Paiute Tribe, 1985.

PUEBLO CULTURAL CONTEXT

The twenty-one Pueblo communities clustering in the highlands rising from the Rio Grande Valley have been located in this region for at least 15,000 years, according to archaeological findings. The Pueblos themselves say they have lived in this region from time immemorial. Nineteen Pueblo settlements are located on or near the river, and two, Taos and Picuris, are nestled in the highlands of present-day Taos County in the northernmost part of New Mexico.

According to Pueblo historian Joe S. Sando,

> At the time of the infamous European Inquisition of 1100 to 1200, the Pueblos had long since been living in peaceful, settled communities. . . . When England and France were in the throes of the Hundred Years' War (1337–1453), the Pueblos were raising corn, squash, beans, and many other varieties of foods, in villages where each individual had a place in work and worship, and society served the needs of the people. (1992, 21)

Chaco Canyon, a major center of Pueblo settlement, was ideally suited for irrigation using floodwater runoff. The area had abundant sandstone, which is used in building by the Pueblo peoples. The higher elevations had pine forests that could be used for construction materials and fuel. Game was plentiful.

The "Ancient Ones"

The Pueblos' ancestors were called Anasazi (the Ancient Ones) by the Navajos, who migrated into the area from the north and west at about 1000 CE. The Anasazi began building their characteristic canyon-rim homes in the area by about the year 700.

Precipitation was scarce, with most of it arriving in brief heavy bursts during summer thunderstorms. To utilize this irregular rainfall, the Anasazi built irrigation systems consisting of dams, canals, and reservoirs. One Anasazi dam, unearthed by archaeologists in 1967, was at least 120 feet long, 20 feet wide, and 7 feet high. The irrigation systems often were built at the bases of steep cliffs to gather water striking them during storms. Water was stored in reservoirs near Anasazi towns. The Spanish (later, Mexicans and North Americans) adopted Pueblo methods to cope with agriculture in a near-desert environment. Some of the Pueblos' original irrigation canals were still in use in the late 20th century.

The ancestors of the Pueblos had adapted to survive on little water, but when the rains nearly completely ceased for at least half a century (roughly 1150 to 1200 CE), the Pueblos' culture suffered. The effects of the drought were not evenly spread across Pueblo country; some areas, such as the Red Rock Plateau, saw an increase in rainfall between 1200 and 1260 CE and were repopulated. The highlands became more habitable than lower elevations during this time, due to greater rainfall; settlers in the Red Rock Plateau may have been refugees from lower elevations, which were still suffering intense drought. Renewed drought enveloped the entire area about 1270 CE and forced abandonment even of highland settlements, where resident populations had depleted scanty groundwater supplies.

The Pueblos were the inventors of adobe construction, which has been adopted widely in the U.S. Southwest and northern Mexico because of its compatibility with the area's climate, which includes large variations in temperature not only from season to season but often also from day to night. Adobe conserves warm air in winter and cool air in summer unlike any other building material.

The Pueblos' staple food was (and remains) corn, which is still grown in irrigated fields. In ancient times, cornmeal and corn pollen also were major trade items. The Pueblos probably engaged in widespread trade before contact with the Spanish in 1539 CE. Items of Aztec manufacture have been found in the Rio Grande Valley, along with seashells from the Pacific Coast. The Pueblos also maintained mines of highly prized turquoise that were used in trade, and they were exporters of salt to surrounding Native peoples. From earliest times, the Pueblos hunted small game (such as rabbits), as well as an occasional elk and deer. Some of the Pueblos also joined in buffalo-hunting expeditions north and east of the Rio Grande Valley. To this day, some of the Pueblos include a Buffalo Dance in their ceremonies.

While the peoples of the various pueblos spent most of their lives at home, they did meet in hunting expeditions, at trade fairs, and on travels to gather piñon nuts and salt. In times of famine and drought, Pueblos who had surpluses shared or traded to alleviate shortages.

Society and Government

While the Pueblos used similar architecture, spoke related languages, and observed a similar ceremonial cycle, each village was autonomous in government and law, although for several centuries they communicated with one another through an all-pueblo council. The governing structures of the various pueblos are similar, a mixture of precontact systems and structures imposed by the Spanish beginning in 1598.

While few Native American cultures observed the separation between church and state that distinguishes U.S. law, the Pueblos are especially notable for meshing religious and secular life. According to legal scholar Sharon O'Brien (1989), "Pueblo spiritual life was not just a part of life, but was life itself." In the Pueblo belief system, the spirit of nature infuses everything. As O'Brien described it,

> Nature and God are one. Humankind's task is to maintain a harmonious relationship with nature. An intricate system of dances and celebrations reinforces the Pueblos' quest for this oneness with God and Nature. The Pueblos give thanks and prayer for all aspects of their lives; the rain that falls, the crops that grow, the game they hunt, their good life, and their fellow human beings. (1989, 27)

Pueblo societies tend to be close-knit, with a strong emphasis on community life and welfare of the group. In most Pueblo communities, a person is a member of a clan and one or two moieties that govern daily life. The clans are responsible for maintaining interpersonal harmony. Most children are initiated into katsina (kachina) or kiva societies. In addition, most Pueblos also have specialized societies for curing (medicine), hunting, and war. The Clowns, who have important roles in many ceremonies, also have their own society.

Most pueblos are governed by one or two priests (if two, each serves half the year, alternating). In some pueblos, the position is hereditary, whereas in others the leader is selected by a council of elders. The leadership position is a lifetime appointment. The priest is the head, in title, of all the societies in the community, but he can only counsel and not compel obedience. He is charged with guiding the community toward decision by consensus and with affirming the decision once it is made. Traditionally, a community provides for the leaders' daily needs so that their attention may be directed toward spirituality and governance.

In several pueblos, the leader is also assisted by a civil assistant and two war captains who look after the day-to-day practical needs of the people, including the care of livestock, the planting cycle, irrigation system maintenance, and construction. These positions are made by annual appointment by the priest (who is sometimes called a *cacique*, after Spanish usage). The appointees are expected to serve without monetary compensation as a service to their people. The assistants also often adjudicate disputes between individuals and, when necessary, provide for the defense of the pueblo from outside attack. The council of elders in most pueblos also assists the priest in adjudicating disputes, addressing antisocial behavior, and making laws for the community. Usually, the elders debate a measure until consensus is reached.

Many pueblos also have the position of governor, instituted during Spanish colonization. According to Pueblo historian Joe S. Sando:

> The office of pueblo governor . . . shows the unique character of this great people. This office, originally designed for Spanish domination, was converted by the Pueblos into an effective bulwark against intrusion by foreigners. The governor, in effect, protected the spiritual leaders. Thus were their human values preserved. The governor is responsible, under the cacique, for all tribal business of the modern world. He is the liaison with the outside business and economic world. (1992, 14)

In the 20th century, the Pueblos' traditional governance system adapted to the requirements of U.S. Indian policy. By 1990, six pueblos (Isleta, Pojoaque, Santa Clara, Zuni, Laguna, and San Ildefonso) selected their governors and councils by secret ballot.

Cultural Adaptation to European Contact

Following first contact with the Spanish during the Coronado expedition of 1539 and 1540, continuing through establishment of U.S. administration in their homeland in 1848, the Pueblos adapted to changes in their economies and cultures made necessary by the immigration of Europeans. The Spanish greatly influenced Pueblo religious life through the introduction of Catholicism and enhanced the Pueblo diet with the introduction of wheat and wheat flour, while the Spanish adopted corn. At the same time, most notably in the Pueblo Revolt of 1680, the Pueblos have demanded (and often achieved) a measure of self-determination. The Pueblos resisted subjugation on Spanish missions and struggled to maintain their traditional culture and economy, modified to accept Spanish religious, cultural, and economic influences.

Unable to wrest wealth from the land themselves, the Spanish colonists of New Mexico squeezed the Pueblos harshly for produce and labor. Spanish priests railed against the Pueblos' "devil worship," and from time to time whipped some of the Pueblos' most respected elders (sometimes to death) in public displays. All of this fired resentment among the Native people. Fifty years after the first colonization, in 1650, the Pueblos joined with their ancient enemies the Apaches in an effort to drive the Spanish out. This first revolt failed.

Thirty years later, however, in 1680, a coalition of Pueblos unified by the war captain Popé raised a furious revolt that killed a quarter of the settlers, trashed the Spanish churches, and sent the surviving colonists down the Rio Grande to El Paso Norte, leaving behind almost everything they owned. The governor summed up the situation: "Today they [the Pueblos] are very happy without religion, or Spaniards" (Johansen and Maestas, 1983, 47).

Popé's policies after the rout of the Spanish proved too zealous for most Pueblos. He took on the airs of a petty tyrant and forbade his people to use anything that the Spanish had brought in, including new crops. Most of Popé's edicts regarding crops were ignored. Popé even ordered the execution of some of his reputed enemies, after which the Pueblo confederacy that had expelled the Spanish broke into two camps, one favoring Popé, the other opposing him. Popé was deposed but then restored in 1688, shortly before he died. Four Spanish attempts at reconquest in eight years combined with a plague of European diseases and the existing civil war to depopulate the Pueblos' villages after Popé's death. In 1692, the Spanish returned to stay, until the United States ousted them in 1848.

After the U.S. takeover, settlers began to usurp Pueblo land, an effort that was bitterly fought and that eventually stopped during the early 20th century after adoption of the Pueblo Lands Act.

The Cash and Credit Economy

In much of Pueblo country, the transition from a traditional economy to one based on cash and credit did not take place until the 1920s and 1930s. By that time, many of the pueblos were being enveloped by the Albuquerque–Santa Fe urban area, making the traditional economy based on the raising of corn (and sheep, in some areas) largely untenable. Unemployment in many of the pueblos rose to 50 to 70 percent in the 1920s and remained little changed for several decades after that. Many Pueblo young people migrated to the urban areas for education and jobs. By the 1990s, only the westernmost pueblos (Acoma, Laguna, and Zuni) were significantly involved in sheep raising. Cattle are still raised in most of the pueblos, and corn is still raised for both sustenance and ceremonies. Some of the pueblos have established bingo halls that draw a non-Indian customer base, while others host substantial numbers of skilled craftspeople who make many items, from pottery to silver jewelry. An increasing number of Pueblos are self-employed as building contractors, architects, photographers, and graphic artists, among other trades and professions.

A number of enterprises have been established in the pueblos. One of the more notable has been Laguna Industries, which by the early 1990s received more than $72 million in federal and private contracts, including one $10.8 million contract to assemble mobile communication centers for the U.S. Army.

In 1990, 55,776 Pueblos were listed in the U.S. Census; Pueblo landholdings at the same time totaled 419,430 acres. The term "Pueblo" today encompasses about 75,000 people speaking six mutually unintelligible languages and occupying about 30 villages, who share a sense of cultural similarity.

See Also PART 2: CULTURAL FORMS: Arts: Navajo Weaving; Pottery/Spotlight Biography I: Martinez, Maria Montoya and Spotlight Biography II: Nampeyo; Rock Art; Silverwork; **Family, Education, and Community:** Funerary Customs; Gift-Giving; Sexual Orientation; Wedding Customs; **Food:** Agriculture; **Language and Literature:** Humor, as Cultural Attribute; Language Recovery in Indigenous North America; Ortiz, Simon J.; Silko, Leslie Marmon; **Spirituality:** Katsinas/Spotlight: Kiva; **Transportation and housing:** Hogan, Navajo; Pueblo Architecture

Further Reading

Dozier, Edward P. *The Pueblo Indians of North America.* New York: Holt, Rinehart, and Winston, 1970.

Johansen, Bruce E., and Roberto F. Maestas. *El Pueblo: The Gallegos Family's American Journey. 1503–1980.* New York: Monthly Review Press, 1983.

Knaut, Andrew L. *The Pueblo Revolt of 1680: Conquest and Resistance in Seventeenth-Century New Mexico.* Norman: University of Oklahoma Press, 1985.

Longacre, William A., ed. *Reconstructing Prehistoric Pueblo Societies.* Albuquerque: University of New Mexico Press, 1970.

O'Brien, Sharon. *American Indian Tribal Governments.* Norman: University of Oklahoma Press, 1989.

Ortiz, Alfonso. "The Dynamics of Pueblo Cultural Survival." In Raymond J. DeMaille and Alfonso Ortiz, eds. *North American Indian Anthropology: Essays on Society and Culture.* Norman: University of Oklahoma Press, 1993, n.p.

Ortiz, Alfonso, ed. *New Perspectives on the Pueblos.* Albuquerque: University of New Mexico Press, 1972.

Sando, Joe S. *Pueblo Nations: Eight Centuries of Pueblo Indian History.* Santa Fe: Clear Light, 1992.

Silverberg, Robert. *The Pueblo Revolt.* New York: Weybright and Talley, 1970.

Upham, Steadman. *Politics and Power: A Social and Economic History of the Western Pueblo.* New York: Academic Press, 1982.

SEMINOLE CONTEMPORARY CULTURE

The Seminoles' ancestors were chased by an army under the command of Andrew Jackson from present-day Georgia into Florida during the early 19th century, when the area was still claimed by Spain. The Seminoles hid in the Everglades for nearly half a century, resisting repeated attempts at subjugation by the U.S. Army as Jackson's presidency came and went, and as the other four of the "Five Civilized Tribes" (Cherokees, Creeks, Chickasaws, and Choctaws) were removed to Indian Territory, now Oklahoma.

Until the mid-20th century, some of the Seminoles lived nearly isolated in the Everglades. When Seminole land claims were settled, the traditional Seminoles refused to take part, insisting that land cannot be bought and sold under the Creator's law. They insisted on their right to occupy the land that had belonged to their ancestors under natural law, not U.S. civil law.

A Struggle to Maintain Tradition

For nearly a hundred years after the Seminole wars ended in the mid-19th century, the surviving Seminoles were left more or less alone because immigrants regarded the Everglades as hostile and nearly impenetrable. In the mid-20th century, however, roads and canals with picturesque names like Alligator Alley began to pierce the "wild" Everglades. Many of the Seminoles settled a land claim stemming from 1842 by agreeing to move to designated reservations. One such group (there are five Seminole reservations) became known as the Seminole Tribe of Florida, Inc., a body known to patrons of Everglades "Jungle" tours, alligator wrestling, and gambling. This "recognized" Seminole tribe opened the first Indian bingo halls in the late 1970s and has since figured in several major lawsuits defining the legal status of Indian gaming.

The traditional Seminoles point to the 1842 agreement, which was signed by President James Polk, as evidence that they have a right to live on the land like everyone else. In the middle 1950s, however, as the federal government pressed the Seminoles to accept reservation land in exchange for extinguishment claims to five million acres of southwest Florida, the traditionals refused to participate because, said Seminole leader Bobby Billie, "We don't sell the land; we don't buy the land, and we don't say a person can own the land, because it doesn't belong to man. It belongs to the Creator" (Johansen, 1996, 45).

For many years, the traditional Seminoles had lived largely by hunting and trading, almost unknown to other Floridians, wishing to be left alone. As long as their land was held to be without value as defined by mainstream capitalism, the traditional Seminoles were allowed to live outside the dominant culture. As the 20th

Seminoles posed in Monroe Station, Florida, c. 1935. (Library of Congress)

century passed its midpoint, however, the tendrils of asphalt, the wakes of power-boats, and the attention of county governments breached their cherished solitude.

When the federal government prepared to pay off Seminole land claims with $16 million in the late 1970s and early 1980s, the traditionals engaged legal help from the Indian Law Resource Center to make sure they would not get any of it. The request was lodged by Guy Osceola, a descendant of the famous Seminole chief of the same family name who led resistance during conflicts with the U.S. Army in the early 19th century. The ILRC persuaded Congress to overrule the state of Florida and regard the traditional Seminoles as a separate group.

Anglo-American Remakes of the Seminole Image

The traditional Seminoles also detest attempts to memorialize their ancestors in Anglo-American fashion. In 1995, a number of traditional Seminoles protested the unveiling of a life-size bronze statue of Seminole medicine man Sam

Jones, who also fought in the Seminole wars, at Florida's Tree Tops Park. Bobby Billie told the Fort Lauderdale *Sun-Sentinel* that a statue of a holy man is sacrilegious. The Seminole Tribe of Florida, Inc. had paid $15,000 of the statue's $60,000 cost.

The villages of the traditional Seminoles contrast sharply with the garish development that characterizes the Seminole Tribe, Inc.'s reservation near Hollywood, Florida, which straddles State Route 441 amidst discount smoke shops, a tourist attraction called the Magical Indian Village, and the facade of the original Seminole Bingo. Tribal chair James Billie operates his own tourist attraction, Camp Billie Safari, where, according to an article in the magazine *South Florida*, tourists to the Everglades can ride in a swamp buggy and stay in a chickee (traditional house).

An alligator wrestling arena with a wet bar has been added recently to the camp. It was Billie who came up with the idea of bingo in the 1970s. He calls it "the best thing that ever happened to the Seminoles," and "sweet revenge" on the Seminoles' conquerors. The money is all the sweeter, says Billie, because the federal and state governments cannot tax it. With Billie in the lead, the Seminole Tribe of Florida, Inc. also has negotiated a royalty on the sales of sports clothing marketed by Florida State University. Instead of rejecting the Seminole mascot as a stereotype, Billie decided to get in on the fiscal action. Since bingo was introduced in 1979, the Seminoles' annual income has risen from $1 million to $40 million a year.

Seminole Tradition vs. Building Codes

Today's traditional Seminoles have been likened to descendants of the "unconquered Seminoles" of Florida schoolbook cliché. The distance between schoolbook cliché and present-day reality can be measured in time (a century and a half) and in space (several million acres). In 1996, the assimilative weapon of choice against one small village of the surviving traditional Seminole community, who were down to their last five acres of land (to which they did not even hold title), was a county electrical and plumbing code. Collier County, which includes Naples, Florida, was attempting to disperse one of the last surviving traditional Seminole settlements because their chickee dwellings (which are designed with four cypress poles and a thatched roof of palmetto fronds) do not conform to late-20th-century Anglo-American regulations for plumbing and electrical wiring. At least two children were removed from traditional Seminole villages by county officials on grounds that their parents' homes were "substandard"—this, despite the fact that the Seminoles' lodgings are adapted to the area's endemic heat and humidity, with open-sided buildings, deep eaves, raised floors, and thatch roofs that allowed the air to circulate above and below.

As some Seminoles raised casinos and wet bars and joined the cash economy, a number of traditionals continued to live in small villages of traditional chickee huts. Because they had refused to deal with the federal government, the traditional Seminoles had no treaty, no reservation status, and no protection from the body of federal law that defines Native American communities' semisovereign status. Because these Seminoles had held to their traditional law and culture, the U.S. legal system had defined them out of existence. The present-day traditional Seminole villagers live on land owned by Pacific Land Company, which is leased to them at $1 a year. Many of the Seminoles work in the vast agricultural fields that surround their settlement.

Bobby Billie reacted to the eviction threat by becoming one of the main organizers of a 750-mile environmental protest walk from the Everglades to Florida's state capitol in Tallahassee. Along the way, the walkers visited with Mexican farm workers who are constantly exposed to pesticides in central Florida, poor people who live near large phosphate mines, and others who are fighting development of a major landfill near Newberry. They made a point of visiting burning sugarcane fields and pulp mills, as well as portions of the Ocala National Forest that serve as a bombing range for the U.S. Navy. About 30 people walked all or most of the 750 miles as others came and went. The statewide walk was organized by the Florida Coalition for Peace and Justice, based in Gainesville. Walkers included local residents, a number of traditional Seminoles, and other people from such countries as Venezuela, Mexico, and Belgium. Walkers averaged 18 miles on foot a day, with an occasional day off to rest.

Along the way, Billie and his co-walkers held press conferences and issued statements summarizing the environmental destruction they had been witnessing:

> You cannot overpower the Creator's law. You are part of the creation. I'm telling you to stop destroying his creation. You are part of the creation, and you are destroying yourselves—which means your [children, and their] kids, and their grand kids beyond the future. You are not thinking about them. . . . I know you white people who look like a human being. I am asking you to act like human beings and do the right thing for generations yet to come. . . . [Y]ou call yourselves human beings, but I don't think so. (Johansen, 1996, 46)

During the nearly two months that the Walk for the Earth traversed Florida, the Seminoles' situation provided a unifying issue for environmentalists in Florida, many of whom admit that they are fragmented, out-lobbied, and shamelessly outspent by the allies of development in state politics. Still, despite numbers that ranged up to 200 people at a time, the marchers for the Earth met a lonely welcome at the end of their walk.

Julie Hauserman, columnist for the Tallahassee *Democrat*, wrote: "No cheering crowds greeted Bobby Billie as he walked up Monroe Street toward the Old Capitol." Billie and 200 others who took part in the Walk for the Earth seemed hardly noticed by the thousands of people who milled along the street in mid-April as part of the annual Springtime Tallahassee celebration (Johansen, 1996, 46). Legislators in the Florida statehouse, where Billie had arrived with a petition for the governor, seemed even less concerned. The petition called for an end to pollution, unrestrained development, and corporate control of resources, especially Florida wilderness areas. It pointed out that the greatest impact of pollution falls on the poor, many of whom, like the traditional Seminoles, are members of minority groups.

Bobby Billie arrived home again after the Walk for the Earth to his family's hamlet of chickee huts near Immokalee, in the Everglades roughly 30 miles northeast of Naples, to catch up on the battle of the building code. Contrary to the impressions of some people who have never lived in them, the Seminoles' traditional houses are quite sturdy; many of them are said by their occupants to have withstood hurricanes.

As they defend their right to live in chickees, the traditional Seminoles have adapted other aspects of late 20th-century U.S. society, economy, and culture. Many of the chickees now have electricity; some have computers, telephones, and fax machines, all now enlisted in the effort to maintain their small island of personal and communal sovereignty. They are adamant that change should be accommodated on their own terms. English is spoken side by side with Seminole in the settlements; some Seminoles drive trucks and drink soda pop, but they also maintain schools in their villages in a conscious effort to maintain their language and culture. While the best-known traditional village is Bobby Billie's settlement of about 30 people on five acres near Immokalee, other traditional settlements nestle in the Everglades near Naples and Tampa, as well as along the Tamiami Trail across the Everglades.

"They are trying to take the last things that are part of our lifestyle," said Danny Billie of the struggle to retain traditional chickee dwellings. "What's happening to us is a continuation of what happened five hundred years ago when Europeans arrived," Billie told the Fort Lauderdale *Sun-Sentinel* (Johansen, 1996, 46).

In early September 1996, amid a growing chorus of protest from Indians and non-Indians across the United States, the Collier County Commission relented and allowed the traditional Seminoles to live in their own chickee huts without harassment. In addition to gathering substantial public and media support, the Seminoles had gained legal support as well from two lawsuits designed to protect their religious rights. In addition, the Pacific Land Company had given the land to its original owners, including the Seminoles, who now had an ownership stake for the first time.

See Also PART 2: CULTURAL FORMS: ARTS: Tattoos; LANGUAGE AND LITERATURE: Language Recovery in Indigenous North America/Spotlight: Indigenous Language Institute; MEDIA, POPULAR CULTURE, SPORTS, AND GAMING: Gambling; MUSIC AND DANCE: Native American Music Awards & Association (NAMAA)

Further Reading

Johansen, Bruce E. "The Right to One's Own Home: The Seminole Chickee Sustains Despite County Codes." *Native Americas* 18, no. 3 (Fall 1996): 44–47.

Nabokov, Peter, and Robert Easton. *Native American Architecture*. New York: Oxford University Press, 1989.

UTE CULTURE

The Utes, after whom the state of Utah is named, called themselves Nuu-ci (or Noochew, spelled variously), meaning "people." Until late in the 19th century, however, many of the people who came to be called Utes carried on a nomadic life within the area that became Colorado. Large parts of their homeland (a large area roughly from today's Taos, New Mexico, to the Great Salt Lake, to Denver, or about 225,000 square miles) was parceled out to immigrating Anglo-Americans about 1905, following passage of the Allotment Act.

Precontact Ute Culture

Before contact, the Utes' economic culture was based on hunting elk, deer, and other animals in the mountains and foraging in their home valleys. They ate just about anything that was available—bison and mountain sheep, rabbits, antelope, waterfowl, fish, piñon nuts, and mecal, as well as elk and deer. In hard years, crickets and grasshoppers were gathered in organized drives. Fishing was well developed in precontact times, making use of mountain streams and lakes with a sophisticated array of weirs, harpoons, and traps. A skilled fisherman could even harvest fish by hand. Fish were dried and smoked, and thus preserved for winter use. Utes also dried the meat of several animals for storage.

The Utes shared a common cultural identity, but they were never unified politically, instead constituting a large number of autonomous bands. Clifford Duncan, a Ute himself, wrote that a few activities involved interfamily cooperation and listed 11 bands (groups of families) by name and locality. Utes governed themselves informally at the family and band level, forming alliances as necessary for hunting and self-defense. Utes' leaders arose in bands and families based on situational needs, such as an antelope or bison hunt. Families followed a seasonal round of migration based largely on availability of food, forming larger encampments in fall and winter, but dividing into small family units in summer. The Utes adopted housing styles suited to the environment and season: Plains-style buffalo-hide tipis in winter, and Great Basin–style wickiups (a frame of wooden poles covered with reeds and brush) in summer.

Ute spiritual life included a bisexual figure often called Manitou (Anglicized in the Canadian province named Manitoba) that resembled that of some Plains peoples. Like the Diné (Navajos), they revered the east (associated with the advent of the rising sun) as the source of all life. In a morning rising ritual, Utes faced the rising sun and "poured" its warmth over their bodies. Spirituality was a personal matter, with no hierarchy, although shamans were consulted in times of illness and affliction. Dreams were believed to carry spiritual messages. Like many Plains peoples, young Utes sought visions in solitary quests, often associating them with a spirit animal. Illness was believed to follow violation of social norms (taboos), provoking disharmony with nature. The sweat lodge was used for purification and was identified as Earth's womb. The wealthy were buried with their possessions (even favorite horses in some cases). Burial of possessions was supported by a belief that handling the deceased's worldly goods could make a living person ill (with "ghost sickness").

Arrival of the Spanish

Following contact with the Spanish before 1776, the Utes acquired horses and became suppliers of them to neighboring Native American peoples. They also traded Paiute slaves to the Spanish, aided by the fact that the Paiutes at the time had no horses. Possession of horses also allowed the Utes to adopt the Plains tipi (which was too large to be transported without them) and to amass other forms of property. Horses allowed the Utes to expand their trading and hunting ranges. The Utes also adopted guns from the Spanish before the Paiutes, giving them another advantage. Quickly, the Utes became sewn into the trading economy, acquiring, first from the Spanish (and later the immigrants from the United States), such things as brass tacks, thimbles, Chinese tea, brown sugar, coffee, gunpowder, lead, and flints.

The Utes prospered briefly as they became major fur traders during the 19th century, supplying the Spanish (later Mexicans) in Santa Fe and other towns with skillfully tooled leather, of which deerskins were most prized. Utes also created intricate cradleboards with buckskin covers that were remarkable for their artistry. Some Utes generally did not use pottery (much of their environment did not provide the proper clays). Baskets, such as their signature *Kanosh*, were lined with pitch and used for cooking and water storage. If the materials were at hand, however, some Utes did use pottery.

The U.S. Incursion

In the Mexican-American War that ended in 1848, the Utes sided with the invading United States, only to lose nearly all of their land and their economic base to this second, larger wave of immigrants. Their vital water supplies also were diverted to white ranchers as their lands were seized.

The Mormons arrived in the Ute homeland in large numbers during March 1849. The Utes quickly realized that they could be driven off their lands by this new incursion. The Mormons trained some of their people in the Utes' language to negotiate. At the same time, the Mormons built a fort on the site of present-day Provo. An Indian who was accused of stealing a shirt was killed, disemboweled, and disposed of in the Provo River. Old Elk, the Utes' principal war chief, who was opposed to Mormon settlement, then became ill with measles, raising suspicion among the Utes that the immigrants were spreading disease deliberately.

A brief conflict ensued, in which Old Elk and many other Utes were killed or died of exposure to the cold. Old Elk's head was severed and presented for a $100 bounty. After that, the Mormons asserted their dominance over the Utes' best lands. A decade later, hostilities erupted again, led this time by Black Hawk. After several battles, by the middle 1860s the Mormons had strengthened their position. Several gold rushes on Colorado's Front Range at about the same time brought waves of immigration to that area as well, taking Ute lands.

Treaties were negotiated (in 1863, 1868, 1873, and 1880), then violated, especially after gold strikes on treaty lands. Between 1863 and 1905, 10 delegations of Utes traveled to Washington, D.C., to meet with U.S. officials, including presidents Abraham Lincoln (in 1863) and Ulysses S. Grant (in 1872). They met with Indian Bureau and Department of the Interior officials, and testified to congressional committees. At the same time immigration (backed by the Allotment Act in 1905) was destroying the Ute land base and, with it, their populations and culture. Some bands of Utes nearly went extinct.

By the early 20th century, some bands lived in tents trying as best they could to get enough temporary work or food to stay alive. A picture emerged in U.S. mass media of the Utes as desperate nomads scratching for survival on the most basic level. Ironically, the immigrants who took control of allotted land found that very little of it was suitable for European American forms of agriculture. Most of them had gone broke by 1912. However, much of the Utes' prime hunting land had been seized by white ranchers, so the Indians were destitute, reliant on government rations. Utes who tried to farm were short on cash. Anglos also were competing with them for scarce water. Failure to pay irrigation assessments caused many Utes to lose what land had remained in their hands after allotment. Thus a program designed to establish Utes (and many other American Indians) as farmers ended up costing them their land. By the 1930s, most Utes were living on government rations of salt and beans and whatever else they could find.

The Utes Today

The Utes numbered about 30,000 in 2000. Today, the Ute Mountain Utes, with about 1,700 members, live on a 600,000-acre reservation in southern Colorado, having received $6 million as a land-claims settlement in 1950. Life expectancy in the early 1990s was about 38 years, and half lived in poverty, with unemployment of almost 60 percent.

The Southern Utes have succeeded in adapting to the modern economy, however. They husbanded modest resources with economic development and took control of their own energy resources from the Bureau of Indian Affairs in 1982, including major natural gas assets in the San Juan basin. They also negotiated a compact with the state of Colorado that allowed a successful casino. By 2003, the Southern Utes owned about $1.5 billion in assets and had created more jobs than they had tribal members.

See Also PART 2: CULTURAL FORMS: FAMILY, EDUCATION, AND COMMUNITY: Wedding Customs; **SPIRITUALITY:** Ghost Dance

Further Reading

Duncan, Clifford. "The Northern Utes of Utah." In Forrest S. Cuch, ed. *A History of Utah's Native Americans.* Salt Lake City: Utah State Division of Indian Affairs, 2000, 166–224.

Martineau, LaVan. *The Southern Paiutes.* Las Vegas: KC, 1992.

Reyher, Kan. *Antione Robidoux and Fort Uncompahgre.* Montrose, CO: Western Reflections, 2002.

Thompson, Jonathan. "The Ute Paradox." *High Country News,* July 19, 2010, 14–22.

WYANDOT (HURON) ECONOMIC CULTURE

The name "Huron" was given by the French to the first Wyandot (or Wendat) people whom they met. Examining the men's hairstyles, the French compared them to the bristles on the forehead of a boar (*hure*, in French, means "boar's head"), a reference that some Wyandots have found to be distastefully racist. The Wyandots' (or Wendats') own name meant "dwellers on a peninsula," or "island people." Traditionally, the Wyandots occupied land near the eastern edge of Georgian Bay, part of Lake Huron.

A Mixed Economy in an Abundant Environment

The settlements of the Wyandots tended to cluster in a region that had access to abundant fish, waterfowl, and game, as well as arable farmland. The Wyandots were among the northernmost peoples in North America to be capable of growing corn. They produced surpluses of the grain for trading with Native peoples in more northerly and more desolate country that was incapable of productive agriculture. Principal game hunted by the Wyandots included bear, beaver, and deer. Major fisheries included pike, trout, and sturgeon. The Wyandots fished with traps and nets, as well as hooks and sinkers. They also fished through lake ice during the winter. Fish were fried or smoked for storage.

Wyandot agriculture was practiced with an eye toward late freezes and early frosts. Fields were usually planted a few hundred feet above valley bottoms to avoid cold air that pooled in low areas. Corn was planted on small hillocks that also reduced the possibility that the corn would be damaged by freezing. The corn used by the Wyandots matured in only 100 days, just quickly enough for the short growing season in the area. Planting in hillocks also reduced hillside erosion.

In the early 1600s, before contact with Europeans, the Wyandots' mixed economy and abundant environment is said to have supported between 20,000 and 30,000 people, most of whom lived in villages with ready access to streams. Water access was important for transportation, including trade, as well as for sandy soils near streams that were suitable for growing corn. Among the Wyandots, labor was divided generally by gender, in a manner similar to that of the Iroquois: women farmed, kept the hearth, and raised the young, while men hunted and engaged in trade, diplomacy, and government, going to war when necessary. While women tilled the fields, men cleared them; women also gathered many species of wild berries, nuts, and roots, concentrating on these if harvests failed. Men and women took part together in late-winter hunts, with men bringing down the game as women butchered and dressed it. Men also were the major builders of multifamily longhouses, as well as the palisades around many Wyandot villages, which served as protection against attack. Men also manufactured tools and weapons.

Wyandot Trading Networks

The Wyandots carried on extensive trade with their Native American neighbors, importing luxury goods from the south, such as wampum, raccoon skin robes, and tobacco. Copper and buffalo robes were imported from the west, and furs from the north. Because the Wyandots lived in relatively close quarters, game near their settlements became increasingly hard to find, so northern trading partners also traded meat for corn.

European trade goods reached the Wyandots before their first encounter with the French in 1609. The Wyandots were quickly incorporated into the European fur trade. Beaver were quickly hunted to extinction by about 1630 in Wyandot country, as the Wyandots acquired trade goods of European (mainly French) manufacture. Lacking beaver of their own, the Wyandots acquired skill as middlemen, especially with several Algonquin hunting groups, as they brokered furs between several Native peoples and the French. Surplus corn continued to enable the Wyandots to purchase other peoples' fur harvests.

The Wyandots also brokered European goods between the French and several Native peoples who supplied them with beaver and other skins, including lynx, fox, moose, otter, badger, and muskrat. The Wyandots' perception of the French as a source of trade goods is reflected in their early name for them, "The Iron People." Trade relationships made the Wyandots allies of (and heavily dependent on) the French, who were colonizing the Saint Lawrence Valley.

Between 1634 and 1640, roughly half of the Wyandots' population was killed by a series of epidemics, mostly smallpox and influenza. By unhappy coincidence, the Jesuits chose the same years for a concerted thrust into Wyandot country, bringing accusations that their witchcraft had caused the plague. Some of the Jesuits felt threatened, but they were not hurt because to do so would have threatened trading relationships with the French, particularly the fur trade, which was becoming the Wyandots' main economic activity. Trade was interrupted only rarely by the waves of epidemics. The number of beaver pelts exported to France actually increased between 1634 and 1640.

The paths of epidemics—vectors of disease—often followed trade routes. The smallpox epidemic of 1539 started in New England before it spread to the Saint Lawrence Valley, where it was picked up by Wyandots who had gathered to trade at Quebec and Three Rivers. The traders transported the pathogens to their families along with trade goods. Within a few weeks, Algonquins were dying so rapidly that the living were unable to bury them. Many bodies were eaten by hungry dogs.

By 1640, the Wyandots' economy was nearly totally dependent on trade with the French. At the same time, as they were weakened by disease, the Wyandots found themelves facing waves of raids by the Iroquois (principally Mohawks and Senecas), who were seeking to capture the Wyandots' share of the fur trade. The Mohawks had been exposed to European trade goods earlier than the Wyandots and may have been looking for furs to finance trade. The Wyandots' location at the center of several trade routes also made them an appetizing point of attack at a time when demand was rising for beaver pelts, and the available supply was declining.

Cultures in Conflict

For nearly a decade, the Mohawks and Senecas harassed the Wyandots. The Wyandots, fearing Iroquois attacks, sometimes curtailed their trade with the French in the 1640s. Between 1647 and 1650, a final Iroquois drive swept over the Wyandots' homeland, provoking the dissolution of their confederacy, as well as usupation of the Wyandots' share of the fur trade by the Senecas and Mohawks. The added furs seem to have been a secondary interest of the Iroquois; their main motive may have been the destruction of the Wyandots as a functioning society and culture. Iroquois pressure against the Wyandots continued for several years after the conclusion of the "Beaver Wars," as Wyandot refugees sought new homes throughout the Great Lakes region and Saint Lawrence Valley. Many of the Wyandot refugees experienced acute hunger, and a sizable number starved during this diaspora. Some Wyandots became so hungry that they ate human excrement; others exhumed dead bodies and ate them. This was done in desperation and with great shame, because cannibalism is directly contrary to Wyandot belief and custom.

Scattered communities of Wyandots gradually revived traditional economies after the hungry years of the 1650s. Many Wyandots settled in or near European communities (including Jesuit missions). Even those who became somewhat Christianized and Europeanized continued to live in longhouses during these years. They continued to hunt and trap as much as possible, and to practice slash and burn agriculture.

A number of Wyandot refugees were adopted after the Beaver Wars by their enemies, the Iroquois, who, true to their own traditions, socialized agreeable Wyandot prisoners into the various Haudenosaunee families and clans. The Iroquois were also replenishing their societies, which had been hard hit by disease and the casualties of continual war.

See Also PART 2: CULTURAL FORMS: FAMILY, EDUCATION, AND COMMUNITY: Restorative Justice/Spotlight: Reciprocity; **FOOD:** Agriculture; LANGUAGE AND LITERATURE: Language Reclamation: Eastern Tribes; Oratory and Oral Culture; SPIRITUALITY: Kateri Tekakwitha (Mohawk)

Further Reading

Clarke, P. D. *Origin and Traditional History of the Wyandotts*. Toronto: Hunter, Rose, 1870.

Heidenreich, Conrad E. *Huronia: A History and Geography of the Huron Indians, 1600–1650*. Toronto: McClelland and Stewart, 1971.

Tooker, Elisabeth. "The Iroquois Defeat of the Huron: A Review of Causes." *Pennsylvania Archaeology* 33, no. 1–2 (1963): 115–123.

Trigger, Bruce G. *Children of the Aataentsic: A History of the Huron People*. 2 vols. Montreal: McGill–Queen's University Press, 1976.

Trigger, Bruce G. *The Huron: Farmers of the North*. New York: Holt, Rinehart, and Winston, 1969.

GENERAL HISTORICAL CONSIDERATIONS

CONSENSUS IN GOVERNANCE AS A CULTURAL VALUE

Coming from societies based on hierarchy, early European explorers and immigrants came to America seeking kings and queens and princes. What they sought they believed they had found, for a time. Quickly, however, they began to sense a difference: the people they were calling "kings" had few trappings that distinguished them from the people they "ruled," in most Native societies. They only rarely sat at the top of a class hierarchy with the pomp of European rulers. More importantly, Indian "kings" usually did not rule. Rather, they led, by mechanisms of consensus and public opinion that Europeans often found admirable.

Increasingly, Native societies in America came to serve the transplanted Europeans, including some of the United States' most influential founders, as a counterpoint to the European order. They found in the Native polities the values that the seminal documents of the time celebrated—life, liberty, happiness, a model of government by consensus, with citizens enjoying rights due them as human beings. The fact that Native peoples in America were able to govern themselves in this way provided advocates of alternatives to monarchy with practical ammunition for a philosophy of government based on the rights of the individual, which they believed had worked, did work, and would work for them in America. This is not to say they sought to replicate Native polities among societies in America descended from Europeans. The new Americans were too practical to believe that a society steeped in European cultural traditions could be turned on its head so swiftly and easily. They chose instead to borrow, to shape what they had with what they saw before them, to create a new order that included aspects of both worlds. They may be faulted in our time for failing to borrow certain aspects of Native American societies, such as important political and social roles for women.

Native American Confederacies

All along the Atlantic Seaboard, Native American nations had formed confederacies by the time they encountered European immigrants, from the Creeks, which Hector Saint John de Crevecoeur called a "federated republic," to the Cherokees and Choctaws, to the Iroquois and the Wyandots (Hurons) in the Saint Lawrence Valley, as well as the Penacook federation of New England, among many others. The Illinois Confederacy, the "Three Fires" of the Chippewas, Ottawas, and Pottawatomis, the Wapenaki Confederacy, the Powhatan Confederacies, and the tripartate Miamis also were members of confederations.

Each of these Native confederacies developed a variation on a common theme of counselor democracy. Most were remarkably similar in broad outline. By the late 18th century, as resentment against England's taxation flared into open rebellion along the Atlantic Seaboard, the colonists displayed widespread knowledge of Native governmental systems. Thomas Jefferson, Benjamin Franklin, and others along the length of the coast observed governmental systems that shared many similarities.

Colonists arriving in eastern North America encountered variations of a confederacy model, usually operating by methods of consensus that were unfamiliar to people who had been living in societies usually governed by queens, princes, and kings. The best-known of these consensual governments was the Haudenosaunee (Iroquois Confederacy), which occupied a prominent position in the diplomacy of the early colonies.

The Importance of the Iroquois Confederacy

Observations of Indian governments showed a remarkable similarity all along the Atlantic Seaboard. Everywhere they looked, immigrant observers found confederacies of Native nations, loosely governed by the kind of respect for individual liberty that European savants had established only in theory, or as relics of a distant European Golden Age. Indian languages, customs, and material artifacts varied widely, but their form of government, perhaps best characterized as counselor democracy, seemed to be nearly everywhere.

The ideas and political systems of the Iroquois and other confederations were so appealing that 300 years ago while he was still in England, William Penn described the functioning of the Iroquois Confederacy in glowing terms.

> Every King hath his council, and that consists of all the old and wise men of his nation. . . . Nothing is undertaken, be it war, peace, the selling of land or traffick [*sic*], without advising with them; and which is more, with the young men also. . . . The kings move by the breath of their people. It is the Indian custom to deliberate. . . . I have never seen more natural sagacity. ("William Penn," 1982, 2:452–453)

Penn described the Native confederacies of eastern North America as political societies with sachemships inherited through the female side. Penn also was familiar with the Condolence Ceremony of the Iroquois that was crucial for an understanding of their confederacy. He stated that when someone kills a woman, the wampum is doubled due to her ability to bear children. In 1697, after lengthy personal exposure to American Indian forms of government, Penn proposed a "Plan for a Union of the Colonies in America."

The Iroquois system was the best-known to the colonists in large part because of the Haudenosaunee's pivotal position in diplomacy not only between the English and French but also among other Native confederacies. Called the Iroquois by the French and the Five (later Six) Nations by the English, the Haudenosaunee controlled the only relatively level land pass between the English colonies on the Atlantic Seaboard and the French settlements in the Saint Lawrence Valley, later the route of the Erie Canal.

Without authority to command, Iroquois and other Native American political leaders honed their persuasive abilities, especially their speaking skills. In his *History of the Five Nations* (1727), Cadwallader Colden attributed the Iroquois' skill at oratory to the republican nature of their government. Colden described the intense study that the Iroquois applied to the arts of oral persuasion, to acquisition of grace and manners before councils of their peers. Benjamin Franklin compared the decorum of Native American councils to the rowdy nature of debate in British public forums, including the House of Commons. This difference in debating customs persists to our day.

Each Iroquois nation has its own council, which sends delegates to a central council, much as each state in the United States has its own legislature, as well as senators and representatives who travel to the central seat of government in Washington, D.C. When representatives of the Iroquois nations meet at Onondaga, they form two groups: the Elder Brothers (Mohawks and Senecas) and the Younger Brothers (Cayugas and Oneidas). The Onondagas are the fire-keepers.

The Iroquois built certain ways of doing business into their Great Law to prevent anger and frayed tempers. For example, an important measure may not be decided the same day it is introduced to allow time for passions to cool. Important decisions must take at least two days to allow leaders to "sleep on it" and not to react too quickly. The Great Law may be amended just as one adds beams to the rafters of an Iroquois longhouse. The Great Tree of Peace is regarded as a living organization. Its roots and branches are said to grow to incorporate other peoples.

The Iroquois also are linked to each other by their clan system, which ties each person to family members in every other nation of the federation. If a Mohawk of the Turtle Clan has to travel, he will be hosted by Turtles in every other Iroquois nation.

Rules and Roles for Leaders

A leader is instructed to be a mentor for the people at all times. Political leaders must strive to maintain peace within the league. A chief may be "dehorned" (impeached) if he engages in violent behavior of any kind. Even the brandishing of a weapon may bring sanction. The traditional headdress of an Iroquois leader (an emblem of office) includes deer antlers, which are said to have been "knocked off" if the sachem has been impeached. Chiefs of the Iroquois League are instructed to take criticism honestly, and that their skin should be seven spans thick to absorb the criticism of the people they represent in public councils. Political leaders also are instructed to think of the coming generations in all of their actions.

Sachems are not allowed to name their own successors, nor may they carry their titles to the grave. The Great Law provides a ceremony to remove the "antlers" of authority from a dying chief. The Great Law also provides for the removal from office of sachems who can no longer adequately function in office, a measure remarkably similar to a constitutional amendment adopted in the United States during the late 20th century providing for the removal of an incapacitated president. The Great Law of Peace also includes provisions guaranteeing freedom of religion and the right of redress before the Grand Council. It also forbids unauthorized entry of homes, one of several measures that sounds familiar to U.S. citizens through the Bill of Rights.

In some ways, the Grand Council operates like the U.S. House of Representatives and Senate with their conference committees. As it was designed by Deganawidah, the Peacemaker (founder of the confederacy with his spokesman Hiawatha), debating protocol begins with the elder brothers, the Mohawks and Senecas. After debate by the Keepers of the Eastern Door (Mohawks) and the Keepers of the Western Door (Senecas), the question is then thrown across the fire to the Oneida and Cayuga statesmen (the younger brothers) for discussion in much the same manner. Once consensus is achieved among the Oneidas and the Cayugas, the discussion is then given back to the Senecas and Mohawks for confirmation. Next, the question is laid before the Onondagas for their decision.

At this stage, the Onondagas have a power similar to judicial review; they may raise objections to the proposed measure if it is believed inconsistent with the Great Law. Essentially, the legislature can rewrite the proposed law on the spot so that it can be in accord with the constitution of the Iroquois. When the Onondagas reach consensus, Tadadaho asks Honowireton (an Onondaga sachem who presides over debates between the delegations) to confirm the decision. Finally, Honowireton or Tadadaho gives the decision of the Onondagas to the Mohawks and the Senecas so that the policy may be announced to the Grand Council as its will.

Benjamin Franklin and the Lancaster Treaty Council (1744)

If the U.S. government's structure closely resembles that of the Iroquois Confederacy in some respects, how did the founders observe the Native model? The historical trail begins in 1744, as Pennsylvania officials met with Iroquois sachems in council at Lancaster. Canassatego, an Onondaga sachem, advised the Pennsylvania officials on Iroquois concepts of unity. Canassatego and other Iroquois sachems were advocating unified British management of trade at the time. While the Iroquois preferred English manufactured products to those produced in France, the fact that each colony maintained its own trading practices and policies created confusion and conflict.

> Our wise forefathers established Union and Amity between the Five Nations. This has made us formidable; this has given us great Weight and Authority with our neighboring Nations. We are a powerful Confederacy; and by your observing the same methods our wise forefathers have taken, you will acquire such Strength and power. Therefore whatever befalls you, never fall out with one another. (Van Doren and Boyd, 1938, 75)

Using Iroquois examples of unity, Franklin sought to shame the reluctant colonists into some form of union in 1751:

> It would be a strange thing . . . if Six Nations of ignorant savages should be capable of forming such an union and be able to execute it in such a manner that it has subsisted for ages and appears indissoluble, and yet that a like

union should be impractical for ten or a dozen English colonies, to whom it is more necessary and must be more advantageous, and who cannot be supposed to want an equal understanding of their interest. (Smyth, 1905)

At the Albany Congress, the Iroquois leader Hendrick admonished the Americans to use Iroquois-style unity and to bring "as many into this covenant chain as you possibly can" (O'Callaghan, 1855, 6:869). With this admonition and his knowledge of the imagery and concepts of the Iroquois Great Law at hand, Franklin met with colonial and Iroquois delegates to create a plan of unity that combined the Iroquois and English systems. During these discussions, Hendrick openly criticized the colonists and hinted that the Iroquois would not ally with the English colonies unless a suitable form of unity was established among them. Hendrick asserted on July 9, 1754, "We wish [that] this . . . [tree] of friendship may grow up to a great height and then we shall be a powerful people." James DeLancey replied to Hendrick's speech using Iroquois metaphors: "I hope that by this present Union, we shall grow up to a great height and then we shall be as powerful and famous as you were of old" (O'Callaghan, 1855, 6:884).

Thomas Jefferson Observes Native Political Culture

Thomas Jefferson characterized the Native societies he knew in his *Notes on the State of Virginia*. This wording was inserted into the 1787 edition as the Constitutional Convention was meeting. Native Americans, wrote Jefferson, had never

> submitted themselves to any laws, any coercive power and shadow of government. Their only controls are their manners, and the moral sense of right and wrong. . . . An offence against these is punished by contempt, by exclusion from society, or, where the cause is serious, as that of murder, by the individuals whom it concerns. Imperfect as this species of control may seem, crimes are very rare among them. (Jefferson, 1955, 93)

Writing to Edward Carrington during 1787, Jefferson associated freedom of expression with happiness, citing American Indian societies as an example:

> The basis of our government being the opinion of the people, our very first object should be to keep that right; and were it left to me to decide whether we should have a government without newspapers or newspapers without a government, I should not hesitate for a moment to prefer the latter. . . . I am convinced that those societies [as the Indians] which live without government enjoy in their general mass an infinitely greater degree of happiness than those who live under European governments. (Boyd, 1950, 11:49)

To Jefferson, "without government" could not have meant without social order. He, Franklin, and Thomas Paine all knew Native American societies too well to argue that their members functioned without social cohesion, in the classic Noble Savage image, as autonomous wild men of the woods. It was clear that the Iroquois, for example, did not organize a confederacy with alliances spreading over much of northeastern North America "without government." They did it, however, with a non-European conception of government, one of which Jefferson, Paine, and Franklin were appreciative students who sought to factor "natural law" and "natural rights" into their designs for the United States during the revolutionary era.

See Also PART 1: OVERVIEW: NATIONS, TRIBES, AND OTHER NATIVE GROUPS: Apache Culture; Cherokee Political and Legal Culture; Cheyenne Cultural Context; Pueblo Cultural Context; **GENERAL HISTORICAL CONSIDERATIONS:** Treaty Diplomacy, Cultural Context; **PART 2: CULTURAL FORMS: FAMILY, EDUCATION, AND COMMUNITY:** Restorative Justice; **FOOD:** Agriculture/Spotlight: Corn and Culture; **LANGUAGE AND LITERATURE:** Erdrich, Louise; Humor, as Cultural Attribute; Oratory and Oral Culture; **MEDIA, POPULAR CULTURE, SPORTS, AND GAMING:** Rogers, Will

Further Reading

Boyd, Julian. "Dr. Franklin, Friend of the Indian." In Ray Lokken Jr., ed. *Meet Dr. Franklin.* Philadelphia: Franklin Institute, 1981, 244–245.

Boyd, Julian P., ed. *The Papers of Thomas Jefferson.* Vol. 11. Princeton, NJ: Princeton University Press, 1950 to present.

Colden, Cadwallader. *The History of the Five Nations Depending on the Province of New York in America.* Ithaca, NY: Cornell University Press, [1727, 1747] 1958.

Crevecoeur, Hector Saint John de. *Journey into Northern Pennsylvania and the State of New York.* Ann Arbor: University of Michigan Press, [1801, in French] 1964.

Ford, Paul L., ed. *The Writings of Thomas Jefferson.* Vol. 3. New York: J. P. Putnam's Sons, 1892–1899.

Grinde, Donald A., Jr., and Bruce E. Johansen. *Exemplar of Liberty: Native America and the Evolution of Democracy.* Los Angeles: UCLA American Indian Studies Center, 1991.

Jefferson, Thomas. *Notes on the State of Virginia.* Edited by Willam Peden. Chapel Hill: University of North Carolina Press, [1784] 1955.

Johansen, Bruce E. *Forgotten Founders: How the Iroquois Helped Shape Democracy.* Boston: Harvard Common Press, 1987.

Labaree, Leonard W., ed. *The Papers of Benjamin Franklin.* Vol. 4. New Haven, CT: Yale University Press, 1950 to present.

"Mr. Penn's Plan for a Union of the Colonies in America, February 8, 1697." In E. B. O'Callaghan, ed. *Documents Relative to the Colonial History of New York.* Vol. 4. Albany: Weed, Parsons, 1853–1887.

O'Callaghan, Edmund Bailey, ed. *Documents Relative to the Colonial History of New York.* Vols. 4, 6. Albany: Weed, Parsons, 1853–1887.

Smyth, Albert H., ed. *The Writings of Benjamin Franklin*. Vol. 3. New York: Macmillan, 1905–1907.

Van Doren, Carl, and Julian P. Boyd, eds. *Indian Treaties Printed by Benjamin Franklin 1736–1762*. Philadelphia: Historical Society of Pennsylvania, 1938.

"William Penn to the Society of Free Traders, August 16, 1683." In Richard S. and Mary M. Dunn, eds. *The Papers of William Penn*. Vol. 2. Philadelphia: University of Pennsylvania Press, 1982.

THE FUR TRADE AND CULTURAL CHANGE

Across much of North America, Native Americans initially became part of the European cash economy—a primary conduit into Anglo-American culture generally—through the fur trade. The type of animal harvested varied (from beaver in the northeast to deer in the southeast, bear in the Rocky Mountains, and sea otters along the Alaskan coast, for example), but the economic system was largely the same. The fur trade flourished in most areas until the early to mid-19th century, after which it was curtailed by near extinction of some species, as well as changes in European fashion culture, especially in coats and headgear.

The Fur Trade Alters Native Cultures

The fur trade changed Native American culture in little more than a generation. Fur traders made better weapons such as guns, steel knives, traps, and iron arrowheads, making them available to Indians and thus changing the way they practiced their hunting traditions. Historian John Fahey described ways in which the fur traders encouraged Native Americans to hunt well beyond their own needs. Consequently, in some areas, the natural balance of wildlife and environment was negatively impacted.

During the fur trade, Native American men harvested most of the furs, while Native women prepared the skins for market. Native people also provided many goods and services that supported the fur trade, such as corn, maple sugar, wild rice, canoes, and snowshoes. The fur trade brought social as well as economic change to Native American societies. The number of men with more than one wife increased in some Plains cultures, for example, because an individual male hunter could employ more than one woman tanner. Historian Colin Calloway further outlined the effects of the fur trade, describing it as a Trojan horse in North America in which Native Americans were thrown into capitalism and competition for hunting grounds, pelts, and trade.

Englishmen trading furs with American Indians, engraved by William Faden, February 1777. (Library of Congress)

The Haudenosaunee (Iroquois) were pivotal in the regional fur trade, as well as in diplomacy. In exchange for furs, the Iroquois took trade goods such as iron needles, copper kettles, and knives. Traders with the Iroquois and other Native peoples soon learned to sell the Indians kettles of thinner metal, using an early form of planned obsolescence since they cost less to manufacture and wore out more quickly, increasing sales.

Epidemics, first of measles, then smallpox, reached Haudenosaunee country with the fur trade, peaking in 1634 and 1635. Societies and economies were stressed severely. The Mohawk population dropped from 7,740 to 2,830 within a matter of months. Firearms reached the Haudenosaunee within a generation following the advent of the fur trade. In 1639, the Dutch tried, without success, to outlaw the sale of guns to Indians. By 1648, however, Dutch merchants in Albany were enthusiastic participants in the firearm trade, in part because the use of guns increased Native Americans' productivity as harvesters of beaver and other fur-bearing animals.

By 1640, the Wyandots (whom the French called Hurons) and many other Native nations in eastern Canada and adjacent areas had become heavily dependent on the export of furs, mainly beaver. At the same time, increasing demands for European trade goods were creating new conflicts between various Native peoples, and deepening old enmities. According to Fahey (1974), whether intentionally or not, the fur trade forever changed Native American traditional life by contributing to the fast depletion of game and buffalo, documenting Native populations and lands, and opening up agricultural opportunities.

Drafting American Indians into Capitalism

According to David J. Wishart, a historian of the fur trade, the traders disrupted political hierarchies among community members by undermining the influence of those chiefs working against them. Finally, the fur traders "co-opted Indians in the destruction of their own resource base" (Wishart, 1994, 47). Native people became employees in a worldwide capitalistic enterprise that relaxed traditional inhibitions against overhunting. The beaver often was the first to disappear under intense hunting pressure because of its low reproduction rate.

In the late 20th century, historians and anthropologists debated how the fur trade changed Native Americans' relationships with animals and the natural world. Calvin Martin, a professor of history at Rutgers University, instigated debate with his publication of *Keepers of the Game* (1979), which argued that Native Americans abandoned their environmental ethics because they thought that animals were responsible for epidemic diseases ravishing human populations. Martin's argument virtually ignores the fact that Native Americans were being drawn into a capitalistic world economy. Martin also ignores diversity among Native cultures, as well as the fact that in many cases epidemic diseases reached Native populations after (not before) the fur trade reached its height. Native American oral and written histories refute Martin's idea. These histories accurately attribute imported diseases to human beings (usually European immigrants) rather than animals that were native to North America. Historian William Cronon argued that the fur trade was more complicated than simple exchanges of European and Indian goods. For the Native Americans, objects began to have prices and monetary worth. Previously, they had had little incentive to hunt for more than was needed.

The fur trade eroded Native peoples' traditional cultural inhibitions against the killing of animals above and beyond their own needs. In New England, beaver populations ceased to be commercially exploitable after 1660, but animals continued to be harvested in areas that had been reached in later years. By the 19th century, however, beaver populations had fallen below sustainable levels in most of North America. Fortunately for the beaver, European hat styles changed, sparing surviving stocks in North America from extinction.

The "Beaver Wars"

"Beaver Wars" has become a historical shorthand reference for the Haudenosaunee (Iroquois) campaign against the Wyandots (Hurons), which culminated in their defeat and assimilation by the Haudenosaunee about 1650. Like most wars, this one had more than one provocation. The most prominent reason for the antipathy leading to the war, however, was competition over diminishing stocks of beaver and other fur-bearing animals. The Haudenosaunee were aided immeasurably by their acquisition of European firearms, which the Wyandots at the time lacked for the most part. The Mohawks, situated near trading centers at Albany and Montreal, were among the first to acquire a stock of firearms; one French source estimated that they had close to 300 guns by 1643.

At the beginning of the 17th century, the Wyandots, who lived near Georgian Bay on Lake Huron, were a prosperous confederacy of 25,000 to 30,000 people, comparable to the Haudenosaunee. By 1642, the Wyandots had allied with the French and also entered an alliance with the Susquehannocks, south of the Iroquois. In 1642, 1645, and 1647, the Haudenosaunee tried to secure peace with the French, to no avail. After the third try, they decided to break the alliance.

By 1640, the Wyandots' culture and economy were nearly totally dependent on trade with the French. At the same time, as they were weakened by disease, the Wyandots found themselves facing waves of raids by the Iroquois (principally Mohawks and Senecas), who were seeking to capture the Wyandots' share of the fur trade. The Mohawks had been exposed to European trade goods earlier than the Wyandots and may have been looking for furs to trade. The Wyandots' location at the center of several trade routes also made them an appealing target at a time when demand was rising for beaver pelts, and the available supply was declining.

For nearly a decade, the Mohawks and Senecas harassed the Wyandots. Fearing Iroquois attacks, the Wyandots curtailed their trade with the French during the 1640s. Between 1647 and 1650, a final Iroquois drive swept over the Wyandots' homeland, provoking the dissolution of their confederacy, as well as usurpation of the Wyandots' share of the fur trade by the Senecas and Mohawks. Iroquois pressure against the Wyandots continued for several years after the conclusion of the Beaver Wars, as Wyandot refugees sought new homes throughout the Great Lakes region and Saint Lawrence Valley. Many of the Wyandot refugees experienced acute hunger, and a sizable number starved during this diaspora. Some Wyandots became so hungry that they ate human excrement; others dug up the bodies of the dead and ate them, a matter of desperation and great shame because cannibalism is directly contrary to Wyandot belief and custom.

Scattered communities of Wyandots gradually revived traditional economies after the hungry years of the 1650s. Many Wyandots settled in or near European communities (including Jesuit missions). Even those who became somewhat Christianized and Europeanized continued to live in longhouses during these years. They continued to hunt and trap as much as possible and to practice slash and burn agriculture.

A number of Wyandot refugees were adopted after the Beaver Wars by their former enemies, who, true to their own traditions, socialized Wyandot prisoners into the various Haudenosaunee families and clans. The Iroquois were also replenishing their societies, which had been hard hit by European diseases and the casualties of continual war.

See Also PART 1: OVERVIEW: NATIONS, TRIBES, AND OTHER NATIVE GROUPS: Pequot Cultural Context; Ute Culture; Wyandot (Huron) Economic Culture; GENERAL HISTORICAL CONSIDERATIONS: Guns and Cultural Change; **PART 2: CULTURAL FORMS:** FAMILY, EDUCATION, AND COMMUNITY: Buffalo (Bison) Culture/Spotlight: Buffalo Hunt Customs and Protocols; Funerary Customs; TRANSPORTATION AND HOUSING: Canoes and Culture: Eastern North America

Further Reading

Calloway, Colin. *The Western Abenakis of Vermont, 1600–1800: War, Migration, and the Survival of an Indian People.* Norman: University of Oklahoma Press, 1990.

Cronon, William. *Changes in the Land: Indians, Colonists, and the Ecology of New England.* New York: Hill and Wang, 1983.

Fahey, John. *The Flathead Indians.* Norman: University of Oklahoma Press, 1974.

Fahey, John. *The Kalispel Indians.* Norman: University of Oklahoma Press, 1986.

Martin, Calvin. *Keepers of the Game.* Berkeley: University of California Press, 1979.

Richter, Daniel K. *The Ordeal of the Longhouse: The Peoples of the Iroquois League in the Era of European Colonization.* Chapel Hill: University of North Carolina Press, 1992.

Snow, Dean. *The Iroquois.* London: Blackwell, 1994.

Trigger, Bruce G. *Children of the Aataentsic: A History of the Huron People.* Montreal: McGill–Queen's University Press, 1976.

Wishart, David J. *The Fur Trade and the American West, 1807–1840.* Lincoln: University of Nebraska Press, 1979.

Wishart, David J. *An Unspeakable Sadness: The Dispossession of the Nebraska Indians.* Lincoln: University of Nebraska Press, 1994.

GUNS AND CULTURAL CHANGE

The introduction of European firearms to Native American cultures wrought fundamental change. The advent of the horse, emerging from the Spanish colonies in what is now the southwestern United States, merged with the "gun frontier" (advancing westward across North America from the French and British colonies in the east) on the high plains before the year 1800 CE, fundamentally changing Native American ways of life generations before large numbers of immigrants arrived.

Native peoples acquired guns in trade shortly after British, French, and Dutch colonists arrived, and this proved to have a profound impact on the military power of both the colonizers and Indian tribes. Some historians argue that the introduction of the gun by Europeans was the single greatest factor in changing Native American culture.

Attempts to Regulate the Gun Trade

Guns often were subject to stringent regulation by colonists who often feared that, in Native American hands, they could become aids to resistance. However, Indians were well armed by gun merchants despite the laws from at least 1675. Firearms became a necessary tool of the fur trade that introduced the profit motive to many Native cultures as their members were introduced to the market economy.

With their noises, great speed, and powerful force, guns were sometimes venerated as magical when they first came into Native hands. Many Indians believed guns to be inhabited by spirits. Colonizers benefited economically from the gun trade with disastrous results for both land and bison. Once Indians came to depend on guns for hunting and warfare (and as traditional crafts associated with the manufacture of bows and arrows fell into disuse), nothing could be done without access to ammunition and gunsmiths supplied by European Americans. Guns became a tool of colonization even as colonial authorities sought to restrict their use. As early as 1648, Massachusetts law made it a crime to "directly or indirectly amend [or] repair . . . any gun . . . belonging to an Indian" (Riley, 2012, 1688). The same law forbade the sale of guns or gunpowder to Indians.

While the Spanish often strictly banned the sale or trade of guns to Indians, the French freely traded them for beaver and other pelts, along with iron kettles, knives, blankets, and many other goods. The British Hudson's Bay Company established a standard exchange rate: in 1742, 20 beaver pelts equaled one trade gun. The French in New Orleans also armed the Choctaws, Cherokees, and Natchez. Between 1710 and 1790, the aboriginals of the Plains engaged in an aboriginal arms race as flintlock rifles spread from the Great Lakes to Texas. By 1630 the Iroquois Confederacy owned enough guns to drive the Algonquins out of their territory. The French then answered the Algonquins' requests for guns of their own.

A specific type of firearm, widely called the "Northwest Indian trade gun," a single-barrel shotgun, was mass-produced for exchange with Indians. The flintlock (used in trading as early as 1620) became a prototype for the trade gun. French traders called it the fuse, fusil, or fuke; the English called it the London fusil or Carolina musket, the Hudson's Bay fuke, or the Mackinaw gun. These weapons were manufactured in London and Birmingham, and they were so prone to exploding and injuring their makers and users that their sellers were sometimes called blood merchants and their places of manufacture "blood houses."

Traditional weapons were used alongside imported guns; lances, war clubs, and bows and arrows sometimes were quicker and easier to use and maintain, even as guns supplied range and intimidating noise. "By the time a muzzle-loader was reloaded," wrote one observer, "the Indian could ride 300 yards and discharge 20 arrows." Breech-loading rifles were more efficient. By the late 19th century, "Sioux warriors were among the most renowned cavalrymen in the world" (Eddins, n.d.).

Guns as the Currency of Power

Guns became the currency of power, arraying one group against another and changing hunting, which had been part of a reciprocal relationship with nature, into a predatory pursuit for profit. Native nations and tribes with guns enjoyed a military advantage over those without them. Peoples with guns also were able to harvest a great many more animals for food and pelts than those without. Guns raised the intensity of violence in all forms of conflict. Intertribal discord that had been largely ceremonial (with the counting of coup and other rituals) became deadly. At the same time, the use of both horses and guns fundamentally changed the buffalo hunt on the Plains from basic sustenance to a campaign of near extermination that fed the transatlantic market economy. This change provoked a short, robust flash of prosperity that crashed just as quickly as buffalo were hunted out, and Indians were forced onto reservations as European American immigration surged across the continent between 1800 and 1900 CE. The gun also became a status symbol. Several U.S. presidents, among them Jackson, Polk, and Grant, gave pistols and rifles to Native leaders who visited them in Washington, D.C.

Buffalo Bill's Wild West Show, which began in 1883, recognized the role of the gun in transforming Native American cultures of the time, with its mock battles and sharpshooting, which went along with its horses, buffalo, and elk, ersatz cyclones and prairie fires. Today, the National Museum of the American Indian at the Smithsonian on the National Mall in Washington, D.C., recognizes the role of firearms with a wall of guns on display. Three glass cases are filled, one each with guns, Bibles, and government treaties, all demonstrating "how all three served as instruments of dispossession . . . [but also] instruments of resistance, resilience, and survival" (Cobb, 2005, 485).

See Also PART 1: OVERVIEW: POPULATION AND DEMOGRAPHICS: Disease, Depopulation, and Cultural Destruction; **NATIONS, TRIBES, AND OTHER NATIVE GROUPS:** Cheyenne Cultural Context; Osage Economic Culture; Ute Culture; **GENERAL HISTORICAL CONSIDERATIONS:** The Fur Trade and Cultural Change; **PART 2: CULTURAL FORMS: FAMILY, EDUCATION, AND COMMUNITY:** Buffalo (Bison) Culture/Spotlight: Buffalo Hunt Customs and Protocols; Civic and Military Societies/ Spotlight: Coup, Counting Coup; Trade, Cultural Attributes

Further Reading

Cobb, Amanda J. "The Museum of the American Indian as Cultural Sovereignty." *American Quarterly* 57, no. 2 (June 2005): 485–508.

Eddins, O. Ned. "The Northwest Indian Trade Gun." *The Fur Trapper.com*. http://www .thefurtrapper.com/trade_guns.htm. Accessed August 25, 2014.

Ewers, John C. *Plains Indian History and Culture: Essays on Continuity and Change*. Norman: University of Oklahoma Press, 1997.

Given, Brian J. *A Most Pernicious Thing: Gun Trading and Native Warfare in the Early Contact Period*. Ottawa: Carlton University Press, 1994.

Hansen, Charles E. *Northwest Guns*. Lincoln: University of Nebraska Press, 1956.

Isenberg, Andrew C. *The Destruction of the Bison: An Environmental History, 1750–1920*. Cambridge: Cambridge University Press, 2000.

Riley, Angela. "Indians and Guns." *The Georgetown Law Journal* 100 (2012): 1675–1745.

Russell, Carl P. *Guns of the Early Frontier*. Berkeley: University of California Press, 1962.

Schilz, Thomas, and Donald E. Worcester. "The Spread of Firearms Among the Indian Tribes on the Northern Frontier of New Spain." *American Indian Quarterly* 11, no. 1 (1987): 1–10.

Secoy, Frank Raymond. *Changing Military Patterns in the Great Plains*. Lincoln: University of Nebraska Press, 1953.

Taylor, Colin F. *Native American Weapons*. Norman: University of Oklahoma Press, 2005.

HORSES AND CULTURAL CHANGE

The Spanish conquistador Hernando de Soto brought the first horses to Native Americans during the 16th century, in Florida westward to the Mississippi River. Francisco Vásquez de Coronado found no gold in present-day Kansas when he sought the golden kingdom of Quivira, but he did leave horses behind.

Native nations did not date the arrival of the first horses in their midst, but their usefulness was quickly recognized, and they spread rapidly among the Kiowas, Arapahos, Shoshones, Cheyennes, Lakotas, and many others. With horses came cultural change—home territories grew, with the ability to transport heavy loads. Pasturage was required; anyone who has cared for horses quickly realizes that they come with a way of life. "Ownership of horses," wrote Kathleen Margaret Dugan, "gave power, strength, and superiority" (1985, 31).

Horses were a subject of awe: *shonka wakan*, in Lakota—"medicine dogs." The Blackfeet in Montana organized a horse medicine cult, which "invoked horse power through prayers, songs, and mimic dances, to cure several Indians who had been sickly that winter" (Ewers, 1997, 207). William Brandon wrote, "Above all, the new world of the horse brought time and temptation to dream. . . . The Plains had always been a place of dreams, but with horses they were more so. Something happens to a man when he gets on a horse, in a country [where] he can ride at a run forever" (1971).

Amazing Dogs

Before horses diffused into Indian country from Spanish settlements, the only beast of burden used by American Indians was the dog, which could pull small loads on a travois. Not surprisingly, horses were first greeted as a larger, stronger kind of dog. Native peoples who acquired horses usually affixed travois to them before learning to ride. A number of Native peoples gave horses names based on their earlier nouns for dogs: the Assiniboine called them *sho-a-thin-ga* and *thongatch-shonga*, both meaning "great dog." The Gros Ventres called horses *it-shou-ma-shunga*, meaning "red dog." The Blackfeet called them *ponokamita*, for "elk dog." The Crees called horses *mistatim*, meaning "big dog." The Sioux called their wonderful newly domesticated beasts *honk-a-wakan*, meaning "mystery dog" or "amazing dog."

Ethnohistorian Dean Snow described the diffusion of the horse through the Plains:

> The Shoshones adopted Spanish horses quickly, taking them north and east, introducing them to the Indian societies of the Great Plains. Algonquians such as the Blackfeet, Gros Ventres, and Arapahos, as well as some Crees and Ojibways, abandoned forest hunting and gathering to become mounted nomadic hunters on the Great Plains. . . . Later, the horticultural Cheyennes (Algonquians) entered the Plains as well, quickly becoming the quintessential American Indian nation in the eyes of many. (Snow, 1996, 193)

Horses diffused northward mainly after Spanish settlement began in New Mexico after 1600 CE, but some Native peoples, including the Pawnees, may have had access to them earlier than that. As early as the 1500s, some horses escaped Spanish herds in New Spain and bred wild in New Mexico and Texas. These were "Indian ponies," averaging less than 1,000 pounds in weight, smaller than modern-day riding horses. These agile, fast horses were interbred with larger animals acquired from Spanish (and later Anglo-American) herds. The Pawnees, especially, became known as horse traders on the Plains. These horses probably were traded to the Pawnees by Native horse merchants who tapped supplies in Mexico.

The herds that the Spanish built at Santa Fe following the Juan de Oñate expedition about 1600 CE supplied horses to many Native peoples in that area. During the 17th and early 18th centuries, horses spread rapidly among Native American peoples from the Apaches in present-day New Mexico (on one occasion, Apaches stole nearly every horse at the Santa Fe garrison). Horses became such an essential part of many North American Indian cultures that the Apaches, for example, incorporated them into their oral history as gifts of the gods. The horse completely changed the lifestyles of some Plains Indian nations who adapted their use to the hunting of buffalo and other animals.

Horses provided a brief flush of prosperity for many Plains Native peoples, before the disease and settlement frontiers reached them. The horse turned a subsistence lifestyle on the harsh High Plains of North America into a festival of ornamentation for a few decades. Prince Alexander Philipp Maximilian, a German aristocrat, naturalist, ethnographer, and explorer, described the Sioux in 1833: "Many of the Sioux are rich, and have twenty or more horses, which they obtained originally from the Spanish" (Roe, 1955, 90). Many Native nations on the Plains and adjacent Rocky Mountains became rich in horses. The various divisions of the Lakotas, Nakotas, and Dakotas, the Crows, and the Nez Perce were only a few examples. Some Native peoples, such as the Pawnees, enjoyed prosperity as horse traders.

The horse extended Native peoples' control over their environment. A Native group on foot was limited to a few miles a day, while with horses a camp could be moved 30 miles or more in the same period. A small party of warriors on horseback could cover 100 miles of rough country in a day or two. By 1659, Spanish reports indicate that the Apaches were stealing horses from them, despite their best efforts to keep the valuable animals out of Indian hands. At roughly the same time, the Apaches and Pueblos traded for horses; by shortly before 1700 CE, the Utes and Comanches had acquired mounts. After that, Native peoples' use of horses diffused across the continent. By 1750, the horse was recognized as far north as Montana as transportation and as a unit of barter.

Horses Shape Societies

When they provided the major form of land transportation in North America, horses were invested with considerable financial value. Hernan Cortés personally kept track of the Spaniards' stables as the Aztecs were conquered: "When anything happened to a horse, he does not fail to notice it," a Spanish observer said of Cortés. Once Spanish colonization of New Mexico began about 1600 CE, the immigrants were conscious of their monopoly on the horse as they sought to outlaw use of the animals by Native peoples.

Soon, many Native peoples' wealth was measured in horses. By roughly 1700 CE, the horse frontier had reached a line stretching roughly from present-day eastern Texas, northward through eastern Kansas and Nebraska, then northwest through Wyoming, Montana, Idaho, and Washington. Having acquired horses, a number of Native peoples migrated to the Plains because mounts made economic life, especially the buffalo hunt, more efficient. Some of these peoples were also being pressured westward by the European American settlement frontier. The various bands of the Sioux moved westward before widespread white contact, as did the O'ma'has, and many others. The introduction of horses accentuated the creation of class structures because wealthy families could more easily move their possessions with several horses. A wealthy man also could lend horses to poorer tribal members for a share of what they killed in the hunt.

Assimilation of horses into Plains Indian cultures also changed the conduct of warfare. The stealing (or, more euphemistically, "capture") of enemy horses provided an entirely new provocation for conflict. In fact, horse raids soon outnumbered any other single trigger of conflict. Raids were planned with military precision, even with group planning sessions and rough maps. John C. Ewers noted that similar to the World War II commando raids, horse raids were organized, small-scale military expeditions designed to capture horses with minimal losses. Horse thieves caught in the act could be killed. During the 19th century, more Indians probably died stealing horses than in raids for revenge.

Native Americans explored different ways of training horses. Unlike the English and Spanish, the Cheyennes, for example, did not usually "break" their horses. Instead, they "gentled" them. Boys who tended horses stroked them, talked to them, and played with them. An owner of a horse might sing to it or smoke a pipe and blow smoke in its face. At age 18 months, the horse would begin more intense training, but was still sung to, smoked over, and stroked with eagle-wing fans. Gradually, the horse was habituated to carrying a human being, saddle, and bridle. Horses meant for war or hunting were trained specifically in those skills.

The horse shaped Native peoples' behavior in many ways. One was the productivity of raiding, which acquired considerable status. By the early 19th century, raiding on horseback supplied the Apaches' major sustenance; the greatest fame a Crow could earn came when he was able to snatch a tethered horse from under the nose of an enemy. "What must certainly be considered a really remarkable feature in the Plains Indian horse culture is the almost phenomenal rapidity with which they mastered their early fears and developed into one of the two or three foremost equestrian peoples on earth," commented historian Frank Gilbert Roe.

The horse also changed some Native peoples' housing styles from fixed lodges to mobile tipis, and allowed the size of the average tipi to increase, because a horse could haul a tipi as large as 18 to 20 feet in diameter, much larger than a dog or a human being could carry. Some tipis weighed as much as 500 pounds and required three horses. The horse reduced economies of scale in hunting, especially of buffalo, making hunting parties smaller. The increased mobility brought by horses energized trade, as well as intertribal conflict, because ease of transport brought more contact between diverse peoples, friendly or not.

See Also PART 1: OVERVIEW: POPULATION AND DEMOGRAPHICS: Disease, Depopulation, and Cultural Destruction; **NATIONS, TRIBES, AND OTHER NATIVE GROUPS:** Apache Culture; Cheyenne Cultural Context; Nez Perce; Osage Economic Culture; Ponca Culture; Ute Culture; **GENERAL HISTORICAL CONSIDERATIONS:** Guns and Cultural Change; **PART 2: CULTURAL FORMS: FAMILY, EDUCATION, AND COMMUNITY:** Buffalo (Bison) Culture/Spotlight: Buffalo Hunt Customs and Protocols; Civic and Military Societies/Spotlight: Coup, Counting Coup; Funerary Customs; Trade, Cultural Attributes; Wedding Customs; Women in Native American Cultures; **LANGUAGE AND LITERATURE:** Spotlight: Humor: Today's Reservation Jibes; Owens, Louis/Spotlight: Sequoyah; Welch, James; **MEDIA, POPULAR CULTURE, SPORTS, AND GAMING:** Gambling; Silverheels, Jay; Thorpe, James; Wild West Shows and American Indian Cultural Clubs; **MUSIC AND DANCE:** PowWows; Sun Dance; **SPIRITUALITY:** Vision Quest; **TRANSPORTATION AND HOUSING:** Hogan, Navajo; Tipi

Further Reading

Anderson, Terry L. *Sovereign Nations or Reservations?: An Economic History of American Indians*. San Francisco: Pacific Research Institute for Public Policy, 1995.

Brandon, William. *The American Heritage Book of Indians*. New York: Dell, 1971.

Calloway, Colin. *New Worlds for All: Indians, Europeans, and the Remaking of Early America*. Baltimore: Johns Hopkins University Press, 1997.

Denhardt, Robert M. *The Horse of the Americas*. Norman: University of Oklahoma Press, 1975.

Dugan, Kathleen Margaret. *The Vision Quest of the Plains Indians: Its Spiritual Significance*. Lewiston, ID: Edwin Mellen Press, 1985.

Ewers, John C. *Plains Indian History and Culture: Essays on Continuity and Change*. Norman: University of Oklahoma Press, 1997.

Holder, Preston. *The Hoe and the Horse on the Plains.* Lincoln: University of Nebraska Press, 1970.

LeBounty, Andrew. "Technological Introductions and Social Change: European Technology on the Great Plains." *Nebraska Anthropologist* paper 39, January, 2008. http://digitalcommons.unl.edu/nebanthro/39.

Moore, John H. *The Cheyennes.* London: Blackwell, 1997.

Roe, Frank Gilbert. *The Indian and the Horse.* Norman: University of Oklahoma Press, 1955.

Saum, Lewis O. *The Indian and the Fur Trader.* Seattle: University of Washington Press, 1965.

Snow, Dean. "The First Americans and the Differentiation of Hunter-Gatherer Cultures." In Bruce G. Trigger and Wilcomb E. Washburn, eds. *The Cambridge History of the Native Peoples of the Americas.* Cambridge: Cambridge University Press, 1996, 125–199.

Wilson, H. Clyde. "An Inquiry into the Nature of the Plains Indian Cultural Development." *American Anthropologist* 65 (1963): 355–369.

Wissler, Clark. "The Influence of the Horse in the Development of Plains Culture." *American Anthropologist* 16 (1914): 1–25.

TREATY DIPLOMACY, CULTURAL CONTEXT

Between the mid-17th century and the end of the 19th century, the Haudenosaunee (Iroquois) negotiated more than 100 treaties with English (and later U.S.) representatives. Until about 1800 CE, most of these treaties were negotiated according to Haudenosaunee cultural protocol. By the mid-18th century, this protocol was well established as the "lingua franca" of diplomacy in eastern North America. According to this protocol, an alliance was adopted and maintained using certain cultural rituals.

Iroquois Diplomatic Protocols

Initial contacts between negotiating parties usually were made "at the edge of the forest," on neutral ground, where an agenda and a meeting place and time could be agreed upon. Following the "approach to the council fire," the place of negotiation, a Condolence Ceremony was recited to remember those who had died on both sides since the last meeting. A designated party kindled the council fire at the beginning of negotiations and covered it at the end. A council was called for a specific purpose (such as making peace) and could not be changed once convened. Representatives from both sides spoke in a specified order. No important actions were taken until at least one night had elapsed since the matter's introduction before the council. The passage of time was said to allow the various members of the council to attain unanimity—"one mind"—necessary for consensual solution of a problem.

Wampum belts or strings were exchanged when an important point was made or an agreement reached. Acceptance of a belt was taken to mean agreement on an issue. A belt also might be refused or thrown aside to indicate rejection of a proposal. Another metaphor that was used throughout many of the councils was that of the Covenant Chain, a symbol of alliance. If proceedings were going well and consensus was being reached on major issues, the chain (which was often characterized as being made of silver) was being "polished," or "shined." If agreement was not being reached, the chain was said to be "rusting."

During treaty negotiations, a speaker was generally allowed to complete a statement without interruption, according to Haudenosaunee protocol, which differs markedly with the cacophony of debate in European forums such as the British House of Commons. Often European representatives expressed consternation when carefully planned schedules were cast aside so that everyone (warriors as well as their leaders) could express an opinion on an important issue. Many treaties were attended by large parties of Iroquois, each of whom could, in theory, claim a right to speak.

The host of a treaty council was expected to supply tobacco for the common pipe, as well as refreshments (usually alcoholic in nature) to extinguish the sour taste of tobacco smoking. Gifts often were exchanged and great feasts held during the proceedings, which sometimes were attended by entire Haudenosaunee families. A treaty council could last several days even under the most agreeable of circumstances. If major obstacles were encountered in negotiations, a council could extend two weeks or longer, sometimes as long as a month.

A main treaty council often was accompanied by several smaller ones during which delegates with common interests met to discuss problems that concerned them. Usually, historical accounts record only the proceedings of the main body, leaving out the many important side conferences, which, in the diplomatic language of the time, were often said to have been held "in the bushes."

Treaty councils were conducted in a ritualistic manner to provide common points of understanding between representatives who otherwise were separated by barriers of language and cultural interpretation. The abilities of a good interpreter who was trusted by both sides (an example was Conrad Weiser in the mid-18th century) could greatly influence the course of negotiations. Whether they knew the Iroquois and Algonquian languages or not, Anglo-American negotiators had to be on speaking terms with the metaphors of Iroquois protocol, such as the council fire, condolence, the tree of peace, and many others.

Diplomacy, Kinship, and Reciprocity

Haudenosaunee treaty relations, including trading relationships, were characterized in terms of kinship, hospitality, and reciprocity, over and above commercial or diplomatic interests. The Dutch, in particular, seemed to be easily annoyed when they were forced to deal with trade relationships based on anything other than commerce. They, among other Europeans, seemed not to understand that, to the Iroquois, trade was conceived as part of a broader social relationship. The Mohawks seemed to resent the attitude of the Dutch negotiators, who saw negotiations as a commercial transaction. During September 1659, a party of Mohawks complained, "The Dutch, indeed, say we are brothers and are joined together with chains, but that lasts only as long as we have beavers. After that, we are no longer thought of, but much will depend on it [alliance] when we shall need each other" (Dennis, 1993, 171).

From the first sustained contact with Europeans, shortly after 1600, until the end of the French and Indian War (1763), the Haudenosaunee Confederacy utilized diplomacy to maintain a balance of power in northeastern North America between the colonizing British and French. This use of diplomacy and alliances to play one side off against the other reached its height shortly after 1700, during the period that Richard Aquila called the "Iroquois Restoration."

This period was followed by the alliance of most Haudenosaunee with the British and the eventual defeat of the French. By the 1740s, England's developing industrial base had become much better at supplying trade goods to the Haudenosaunee and other Native American peoples; the balance of alliance was shifting. According to Aquila, the Iroquois' power had declined dangerously by about 1700, requiring a concerted effort on the part of the Grand Council to minimize warfare and build peaceful relations with the Haudenosaunee's neighbors. By 1712, the Haudenosaunee's military resources amounted to only about 1,800 men. Disease as well as incessant warfare also caused declines in Haudenosaunee populations at about this time; major outbreaks of smallpox swept through the Iroquois in 1696 and 1717. At the same time, sizable numbers of dissenting Haudenosaunee, especially Mohawks, moved to Canada and cast their lots with the French.

Alcohol also was devastating the Iroquois at this time, a fact emphasized by the many requests for restrictions on the liquor trade by Haudenosaunee leaders at treaty councils and other meetings. Aquila wrote:

> Sachems complained that alcohol deprived the Iroquois people of their senses, was ruining their lives . . . and was used by traders to cheat them out of their furs and lands. The Iroquois were not exaggerating. The French priest Lafitau reported in 1718 that when the Iroquois and other Indians

became intoxicated they went completely berserk, screaming like madmen and smashing everything in their homes. (1983, 115)

After 1763, the Haudenosaunee were no longer able to play the French and the English against each other. Instead, the Iroquois faced pressure to ally with Native peoples to their west against the English. Many Senecas sided with Pontiac against the English in 1763 and 1764.

Today's Iroquois Passports

Today, some members of the Iroquois Grand Council travel the world on their own national passports. The passport states that it has been issued by the Grand Council of the League of the Haudenosaunee, and that "The Haudenosaunee continues as a sovereign people on the soil it has occupied on Turtle Island since time immemorial, and we extend friendship to all who recognize our constitutional government and who desire peaceful relations" (Hill, 1987, 12). The passports were first issued in 1977 to Haudenosaunee delegates who attended a meeting of the United Nations in Switzerland. Since then, the United States, Holland, Canada, Switzerland, France, Belgium, Germany, Denmark, Italy, Libya, Turkey, Australia, Great Britain, New Zealand, Iran, and Colombia have been among the nations that have recognized the Haudenosaunee documents. Even so, it takes a talented travel agent to get a visa on an Iroquois passport, because formal diplomatic relations often do not exist between the country recognizing the document and the Haudenosaunee Grand Council.

See Also PART 1: OVERVIEW: NATIONS, TRIBES, AND OTHER NATIVE GROUPS: Wyandot (Huron) Economic Culture; **GENERAL HISTORICAL CONSIDERATIONS:** Consensus in Governance as a Cultural Value; The Fur Trade and Cultural Change; **PART 2: CULTURAL FORMS: ARTS:** Silverwork; **FAMILY, EDUCATION, AND COMMUNITY:** Gift-Giving; Restorative Justice/Spotlight: Reciprocity; Trade, Cultural Attributes; Wampum; Women in Native American Cultures; **LANGUAGE AND LITERATURE:** Oratory and Oral Culture; **TRANSPORTATION AND HOUSING:** Canoe Culture, Pacific Northwest; Canoes and Culture: Eastern North America

Further Reading

Aquila, Richard. *The Iroquois Restoration: Iroquois Diplomacy on the Colonial Frontier, 1701–1754.* Detroit: Wayne State University Press, 1983.

Dennis, Matthew. *Cultivating a Landscape of Peace.* Ithaca, NY: Cornell University Press, 1993.

Hill, Richard. "Continuity of Haudenosaunee Government: Political Reality of the Grand Council." *Northeast Indian Quarterly* 4, no. 3 (Autumn, 1987), 10–14.

PART 2
CULTURAL FORMS

ARTS

Native American arts include a wide array of genres, from ancient rock art to traditional painting, pottery, footwear, clothing, food-serving dishes, baskets, and boxes—all items used in everyday life, which have become media of artistic expression. What follows is an incredibly selective sampler of a very well-populated genre. To provide an idea of what's available, sample Dawn Reno's *Contemporary Native American Artists* (1995), which includes profiles of more than 1,000 visual artists of Native American ancestry. Gregory Schaaf's *American Indian Textiles* (2000) contains roughly 2,000 profiles of Native Americans who practice the weaving arts. Schaaf, who is the director of the Center for Indigenous Arts & Cultures in Santa Fe, New Mexico, also has compiled *American Indian Jewelry III* (2013), a standard reference for the jewelers' trade that references more than 5,000 men and women in that field in two thick volumes, illustrated in full color.

The following entries summarize several types of artistic expression (ledger art, Navajo weaving, rock art, pottery, sandpainting, silverwork, tattoos, and totem poles) as well as profiles of three artists who work in very different styles (James Luna, R. C. Gorman, and Peter Jemison). The potter's art is represented by Spotlight biographies of Maria Montoya (1887–1980) and Nampeyo (ca. 1859–1942). A brief contextual profile also is supplied on the vital role of Native culture bearers.

A few words also are included on some of the better-known of several hundred American Indian arts and crafts fairs, along with a smattering of details

117

regarding clothing and moccasins, both of which combine the necessity of covering the body with a sense of sophisticated art. Legal context is provided by a profile of the Indian Arts and Crafts Act (1990), which is meant to prevent fakery and fraud in the creation and sale of American Indian artwork, protecting consumers and giving artists an opportunity to earn a livable income. Like many laws, however, it has not entirely prevented the local flea market from selling blue-painted rocks imported from Asian sweatshops as genuine New Mexico or Arizona turquoise.

Given its recent popularity among non-Indians, tattooing may seem contemporary, but it isn't. This form of adornment has been widely used by Native American peoples since antiquity to establish individual and collective identity, as well as to denote societal rank and accomplishments, such as heroism in battle. Tattoos sometimes have been associated with the acquisition of supernatural powers, or as representing an infusion of power from a specific species of animal.

The name "totem pole" is a misnomer, since these unique artworks usually do not display totems, "a creature or object that a person holds in great respect or religious awe" (Stewart, 1990, 7). The name has been so widely used, however, that it has become denotative. Originally, the poles stood as family heralds outside sturdy, pole-and-beam longhouses that opened on the water, greeting people arriving in canoes. The homes contained several related families in a culture based largely on rank and prestige. The poles described who lived in the houses, and where they ranked in society. Despite the assumptions of some Christian missionaries, totem poles are not religious shrines. People do not worship them. Nor are the poles considered sacred in a European religious sense. The history on a totem pole should be "read" top to bottom. The English aphorism "low man on the totem pole" has status reversed. Actually, the "last" image, on the bottom of the pole, usually carries the most prestige.

Working with silver, nearly unknown across North America before contact with Europeans, has become a means of artistic expression among Native Americans from coast to coast—Iroquois to Zuni pueblo. Silverwork has been adapted to items used in daily life, such as Navajo bowguards, bolo ties, belt buckles, and horse bridles. Silverwork often is ornamented with turquoise and sometimes other stones. Many Native American jewelers have earned international reputations, and their work is so good that it has become the target of mimics, fakes, and forgeries worldwide.

Further Reading

Reno, Dawn. *Contemporary Native American Artists*. Chicago: Alliance, 1995.

Schaaf, Gregory. *American Indian Textiles*. Santa Fe: The Center for Indigenous Arts & Cultures, 2000.

Stewart, Hilary. *Totem Poles*. Seattle: University of Washington Press, 1990.

AMERICAN INDIAN ARTS AND CRAFTS FAIRS

American Indian art fairs number in the hundreds, from side streets in tiny towns to the huge Southwest Indian Arts Fair, from cozy corners and secondhand bargains to Sotheby's, the international art auction house, which in 2013 held its first such event at which some items fetched several hundred thousand dollars.

Regional Variations

The Santa Fe Indian Market (New Mexico) is the best known. The flagship of American Indian arts and crafts fairs, the Santa Fe Indian Market, more than 90 years old, usually convenes during August around the city's plaza, but also involves a week-long celebration around the city "that includes dance, song, literature, and film," as well as marketing of arts and crafts. It is, in the words of the executive director of its sponsor, the Southwestern Association for Indian Arts, Inc. (SWAIA), "but a blink in the eye in the millennia of Native art traditions" (Bernstein, 2012, 18). The SWAIA also provides more than $100,000 per year in prize money for a market that is an arts and crafts show as well as a mercantile event.

The Santa Fe Indian Market is notable for its scale (more than 1,000 artists and 160 participating organizations) and the fact that many collectors return so often that they form personal relationships with artists and their extended families. Many families have been represented at the market for several generations. Many older artists take advantage of SWAIA programs to pass on their skills and cultural traditions through mentoring programs, some of which take place in partnership with the Smithsonian Institution's National Museum of the American Indian.

The market also has made an attempt to integrate presentation of Native American culture and history with buying and selling of artwork. "Indian Market is still very much led by the opportunity to purchase from the makers, but . . . [also] to enjoy and learn about the vast cultures and pageantry of America's Indigenous populations," wrote SWAIA's executive director Bruce Bernstein. "In a world beset by globalization, we celebrate peoples rooted in land and place" (Bernstein, 2012, 18).

The Southwest Indian Arts Fair at Tucson, Arizona, has been called southern Arizona's premier Indian art show and market, including more than 200 Native artists who create items such as Yaqui hand-carved masks, Tohono O'odham handwoven baskets, Navajo flutes, and Zapotec woven rugs, as well as Native music, frybread, and Indian tacos. The 19th year of this fair attracted about 7,000 people in February 2012.

The Arizona State Museum joined in an auction with the Friends of Hubbell Trading that raised scholarship funds for Hopi and Navajo college students. Called the best-kept secret in Arizona, the auction featured some 400 items and has benefited local communities with nearly $2 million.

Art fairs may be held as adjuncts of museums. Phoenix's Heard Museum convenes an annual Indian art fair every year that attracts national attention. The Museum of Man in San Diego, California, hosts an annual American Indian Art Market and Film Festival in Balboa Park during May, with three days of food, dancing, art exhibits, and crafts. The event combines aspects of an art show and pow wow with dancing, as well as

> all-day art demonstrations and collector-quality jewelry, pottery, Kachina carvings, basketry, beadwork, clothing, quilts, textiles, sculptures, masks, fetishes and paintings—contemporary and traditional. Dozens of American Indian artists . . . exhibit. Outdoor vendors . . . sell tamales, kettle corn, Indian fry bread and frozen lemonade. Contestants show off their native skills, from weaving rugs and making fry bread to butchering sheep. (Kragen, 2011)

Tiny Harbor Springs, Michigan, hosts an annual North American Indian Art Fair on its waterfront in midsummer. The National Park Service hosts an American Indian Art Show each June in the Petrified Forest National Park. Michigan State University College of Law presents an indoor American Indian Art Fair in midwinter, hosted by its Native American Law Students Association (NALSA). Arizona's fairs have been listed on the Internet.

Perhaps the most high-end art sales event to date was organized under the aegis of Sotheby's, the international auction house. New to the field, on May 22, 2013, Sotheby's held its first sale of "Arts of the American West," which brought in $3.8 million. A Northwest Coast wooden headdress sold for $425,000, and a Crow beaded hide war shirt fetched $341,000. Paiute and Pomo baskets sold for as much as $100,000.

See Also PART 1: OVERVIEW: NATIONS, TRIBES, AND OTHER NATIVE GROUPS: Pueblo Cultural Context; **PART 2: CULTURAL FORMS: ARTS:** Spotlight: Indian Arts and Crafts Act (1990); Clothing; Cultural Appropriation: Questions and Issues; Ledger Art; Navajo Weaving; Pottery; Sandpainting; Silverwork

Further Reading
Bernstein, Bruce. "Welcome to Market!" *Native Peoples Magazine*, July/August 2012, 18.

Kragen, Pam. "Indian Art Fair and Film Fest Return to Balboa Park." *U-T San Diego*, May 8, 2011. http://www.utsandiego.com/photos/2011/may/08/818618/http://www.utsandiego.com/news/2011/May/08/best-bet-indian-art-fair-and-film-fest-return-to/. Accessed August 26, 2014.

Krol, Debra Utacia. "Shopping for American Indian Art at Arizona's Art Festivals." October 18, 2013. http://www.arizonaguide.com/experience-and-share/featured-article /shopping-for-. Accessed August 26, 2014.

"The Southwest Indian Arts Fair, a Tucson Tradition." *Indian Country Today Media Network.* http://indiancountrytodaymedianetwork.com/photogallery/the-southwest -indian-arts-fair-a-tucson-tradition. Accessed August 26, 2014.

Spotlight

INDIAN ARTS AND CRAFTS ACT (1990)

With between $400 million and $800 million worth of American Indian jewelry and handicrafts selling per year in the United States by 2012 (according to the U.S. Department of Commerce), the Indian Arts and Crafts Act of 1990 (P.L. 101-644) has a broad purview, but the board charged with enforcing it has little money, making compliance largely voluntary. No exact figures exist, but trade groups estimate that half or more of Indian arts and crafts sold in the United States are counterfeit. Some artists refuse to allow photographs of what they create because graphic representations (especially on the Internet) enable fakery.

The U.S. federal government has sought to protect Native American arts and crafts for many years, beginning with the Indian Arts and Crafts Act of 1935, enacted while John Collier was President Franklin D. Roosevelt's Commissioner of Indian Affairs. This act was extended and refined under the Indian Arts and Crafts Act of 1990.

In the words of the Department of the Interior's official Internet site,

> The Indian Arts and Crafts Act of 1990 (P.L. 101-644) is a truth-in-advertising law that prohibits misrepresentation in marketing of Indian arts and crafts products within the United States. It is illegal to offer or display for sale, or sell any art or craft product in a manner that falsely suggests it is Indian produced, an Indian product, or the product of a particular Indian or Indian Tribe or Indian arts and crafts organization, resident within the United States.

The website notes that traditional arts and crafts that often have been copied by non-Indians include Indian-style jewelry, pottery, baskets, carved stone fetishes, woven rugs, katsina (kachina) dolls, and clothing. The act provides stiff penalties; first-time violators face criminal and civil penalties of a fine of up to $250,000 and a prison term of up to five years. Businesses face prosecution and penalties of up to $1,000,000. A Navajo jewelry sign means that it must be produced by enrolled Navajos.

The law directs customers who suspect fraudulent arts and crafts to first seek a refund. If a refund is not supplied, the customer should contact the Better Business Bureau, a local Chamber of Commerce, or a district attorney's office. Only if all other attempts at redress fail is a customer encouraged to contact the Indian Arts and Crafts Board with a written complaint. The Arts and Crafts Board places the burden on the consumer to ascertain whether artisans at individual pow wows, art fairs, or other events require compliance with the law.

In 2010, as part of the Tribal Law and Order Act, Congress made the law more stringent, a sign that even the tough-sounding 1990 law was not stopping fakes. Indian-style fetish animals might be mass-manufactured in the Philippines; ersatz turquoise may actually be plastic. Supposed silver may be pot metal.

The revised law allowed any federal law enforcement officer (Bureau of Indian Affairs, the National Parks Service, and U.S. Customs and Border Protection, expanding previous authority from the Federal Bureau of Investigation) to investigate violations. A Senate Committee on Indian Affairs report in 2008 found that although millions of dollars of fakes are sold annually, few have been prosecuted in federal court.

The 2010 amendments also linked fines and prison terms for convicted violators to the value of the arts and crafts being mimicked, which is designed to step up enforcement against small-time offenders. The steep nature of the penalties had been a deterrent against any except the largest violators. Even so, a violator faced up to a year in prison and a $25,000 fine for items worth less than $1,000. With so few prosecutions, however, the penalty structure remained largely symbolic. Zuni artist Nancy Westika, who makes fetish necklaces, expressed skepticism that the revisions will make a difference. In the past, she said, little has been done. "Every time somebody says that they're going to enforce it we say, 'Yeah, we'll see. We'll see.' Mostly it's just been talk" ("Congress Toughens," 2010). A private group, the Albuquerque-based Indian Arts and Crafts Association, also tries to enforce the law against fakes. "We don't want to tell people what to make or what to sell, but we want to make sure people represent it honestly," said Gail Chehak, executive director of the group.

Laws meant to protect authentic Native American arts and crafts have another sharp edge that raises objections from many Native people. Like blood quanta, they are yet another layer of government regulation of Native life, another reminder of the Great White Father's intrusion. The prominent Cherokee artist Jimmie Durham (who also has been active in the American Indian Movement) refuses to observe blood quanta and therefore is not enrolled as a tribal member. In addition, he refused to submit to regulation under the Indian Arts and Crafts Act and so, in 1992 (two years after the act became law), he faced cancellation of an art show at the American Indian Contemporary Arts Gallery in San Francisco for his noncompliance. Several artists refused certification. One of them, Eugene Pie, said: "No one has to prove anything. Black artists don't have to prove they're black. White artists don't have to prove they're white. I think the government still thinks we're possessions, that we're part of the National Park system, standing at the cabin door" (Porter, 2012, 80).

See Also PART 2: CULTURAL FORMS: ARTS: American Indian Arts and Crafts Fairs; Cultural Appropriation: Questions and Issues; Ledger Art; Navajo Weaving; Pottery; Sandpainting; Silverwork

Further Reading

"Congress Toughens Indian Arts and Crafts Act, Aimed at Halting Misrepresentation." Associated Press, September 18, 2010. http://www.foxnews.com/us/2010/09/18/congress-toughens-indian-arts-crafts-act-aimed-halting-misrepresentation/. Accessed August 26, 2014.

"The Indian Arts and Crafts Act of 1990." U.S. Department of the Interior. http://www.doi.gov/iacb/act.html. Accessed August 26, 2014.

Porter, Joy. *Land and Spirit in Native America*. Santa Barbara, CA: Praeger/ABC-CLIO, 2012.

CLOTHING

History and Origins

Each Native American nation, tribe, or band developed its own styles of clothing based on climate and what sorts of materials were available, which ranged from animal hides to cedar bark. Clothing has been created out of necessity for as long as Native Americans have lived in the Americas, perhaps tens of thousands of years. Members of a tribe or nation often could recognize each other's identities based on what they were wearing, and what an individual had attached to it.

Most clothing long has been made by women and designed for endurance. A person might wear the same piece of clothing for several years. Clothes became a record of a person's life as well. For example, a man whose clothing was adorned with several dozen (or even hundreds) of elk teeth told everyone of his prowess as a hunter—that is, until European factories were set up to manufacture fake elk teeth for sale, along with glass beads.

Regional Variations

Suede buckskins (usually, but not always, from deer or elk) were worn by many Native American peoples as jackets and pants. They were sewn with fringe, originally meant to help the garment to shed water, but later used mainly as fashion. Buckskin also has been worn by non-Indians over the years, including a number of 19th-century frontier personalities such as George Armstrong Custer, Calamity Jane, Davy Crockett, Wild Bill Hickok, Buffalo Bill Cody, and Annie Oakley. Buckskins may be adorned with beads or quills. They are durable and warm in outdoor conditions.

Beadwork was sewn into war shirts for good luck by many Apaches, who also worked them into saddle blankets, bags, and arrow quills. Other items of Apache clothing were borrowed from Mexican Native peoples, among them tunics and calico dresses. Apaches also borrowed clothing from their Kiowa neighbors, including feather headdresses. Woven blankets with intricate traditional patterns also were used as cloaks on the Northwest Coast.

Many Native men wore breechclouts (also called breechcloths), a piece of cloth or hide that could be draped in front and behind, tucked into a belt and attached to leather leggings. Some Plains tribes also wore war shirts that were ornamented with hair and beads. Women often wore skirts and leggings that varied in design tribe by tribe. Cheyenne women usually wore buckskin dresses. In colder weather, many peoples wore cloaks. Some adopted Inuit fur parkas, a style that also occasionally came into vogue among non-Indians.

Following the arrival of European American immigrants, Native American clothing changed as styles and materials evolved. Native styles also were mixed as Native peoples developed pan-Indian consciousness. Feather headdresses and buckskin, for example, were adopted in areas where people had not previously used them. In the Puget Sound area, for example, the Muckleshoot performance group, which had adopted the name Nesika Club (*Nesika* was Chinook trade jargon for "ours") during the 1930s, dropped its ancestors' clothing made from shredded cedar bark and nettle-cord twining for Plains headdresses and buckskin, which was what non-Indian audiences expected. Similar trends developed among the Iroquois in upstate New York at about the same time, where buckskin long had been used, but full-feathered headdresses had not. (Iroquois leaders' ceremonial headgear, the *gustowah*, does use feathers, but only a few at a time, with each feather having significance.)

Native peoples adopted aspects of European clothing into their own traditions, decorating cloth garments, for example, with traditional beadwork. The beads themselves often were imported from Europe and acquired as trade goods. Thus, combining designs and materials, Native peoples produced such items as beaded jackets, ribbon shirts, and woolen sweaters. Many Native peoples wore a combination of Native garments and European items, often using the traditional items as accents or as formal wear (often called "regalia") at pow wows and ceremonial events.

In precontact times, Coast Salish Native clothing was designed to compensate for rain and moisture. Capes were made from shredded cedar bark and nettle cord twining. Other clothing, made from cattails, also was efficient at shedding moisture. Cedar bark was used for clothing (as well as other purposes). Cedar clothing was functional, acclimated to the surroundings, and designed to clothe the wearer for many years. The bark was stripped into long sections, pounded to induce softness, and made into cone-shaped hats with a narrow top and wide brim that repelled rain and carried the water away from the head. Shirts and other garments to cover the entire body also were made from pounded cedar. Bark was even used for diapers. The making of hats and other clothing from cedar bark has been revived in recent years.

Considerable work was required to weave a cedar cape, a blanket or cape from the wool of a dog or a goat, or to tan hides. Old man's beard moss, which was disposable, was used for diapering babies. Variations on capes were used for fishing and hunting. Fishermen wore very little clothing; as they worked in the water, clothing inhibited movement. Women wore capes for work or special occasions. Utilitarian moccasins were used for travel over rough rocks and terrain.

Wayne Suttles and Barbara Lane, prominent ethnologists in the region, wrote that in warm weather, Coast Salish clothing often was minimal; before Europeans arrived bearing a sense of shame at showing genitalia, men sometimes wore cedar bark or animal hide breechclouts. Men sometimes went naked in public during warm weather. Women wore aprons or skirts of cedar bark. Animal fur was used for warmth, with mountain beaver fur for babies. Wool trade blankets had been available for decades by treaty times. For colder weather and ceremonial occasions, the skins of several animals were fashioned into robes for Puget Sound Salish peoples of both genders. According to an account in the *Handbook of North American Indians* by Suttles and Lane, "Bear skins with the fur intact were made into robes. Skins of beavers, raccoons, mountain beavers, sea otters . . . and even of birds were sewed together into robes" (1990, 491).

Suttles and Lane wrote that animal and bird skins were used to make caps worn during winter. Coastal peoples usually held their hair in place with a headband of fur, wool, or cedar bark. Hair was washed in a combination of plants to keep it healthy. A polished wooden comb about four inches wide with teeth two to three inches long also was used. Men and women wore dentalia and abalone shell earrings. Some people, usually the more affluent, also pierced the septum of the nose and inserted abalone ornaments.

Contemporary Forms

Native American clothing has proved very popular with many people in our time. Sales are thriving. Buckskins, for example, enjoyed a fashion vogue during the 1970s and are still sometimes worn in outdoor pursuits such as hunting and motorcycle riding. An Internet search ("Native American" + clothing) will garner hundreds of "hits" for commercial enterprises that sell Native-themed buckskins, sweaters, and other items. Some of the merchandise is Native-manufactured. Some of it is meant mainly for ceremonial use and should not be worn in every-day life; other items are street wear. Cowichan sweaters, for example, are woven from wool into Northwest Coast classic designs and sold to a wide variety of people. Much of the clothing, often of exquisite beauty, is made in Mexico, Central America, and South America.

Another Native article of clothing that has been widely adopted is the poncho, which began with peoples of the Andes in pre-Columbian times, designed for warmth and to shed moisture. Its simplest design is a single sheet of fabric with an opening for the head. Some ponchos have hoods and fasteners to close them in the rain, with spaces for the wearer's arms. Ponchos may be made of wool or yarn, and often are crocheted. Today ponchos also may be seen on high-fashion runways in Italy, France, and New York City, where their design, with its large exposed areas, lends itself to artistic design and use of a variety of colors.

Ponchos made of waterproof cloth were used by the U.S. Army on the Great Plains during the 1850s, and many also were widely used during the U.S. Civil War. They could double as bedrolls. These ponchos came into use again during the Spanish American War, World War I, and World War II, when troops encountered wet conditions. They also were modified to serve as roofs for makeshift one-man shelters on the battlefield. By the 1970s, lightweight nylon was being used for military ponchos. Ponchos are issued to troops today. They also have been adopted by hunters, campers, and first responders.

Traditional clothing manufacture is still practiced today. The George Gustav Heye Center of the Smithsonian's National Museum of the American Indian (New York City) hosted a show in September 2008, "Tradition, Change and Celebration in Native Women's Dresses," exhibiting 55 items designed from the 19th century to the present, showing continuity and innovation in styles across the present-day United States. The exhibition included the work of six living designers who used traditional sewing and beading techniques that are taught by cultural organizations in the Plains, Plateau, and Great Basin regions. The dresses were warm, tough, and meant to endure weather extremes, but stylish as well, adorned with porcupine quills, tin, shells, carved bone, coins, animal teeth, and a dazzling array of imported glass beads. Each dress was a personal statement that might require hundreds of hours to create.

See Also PART 1: OVERVIEW: Nations, Tribes, and Other Native Groups: Apache Culture; Northwest Coast Culture Area; **PART 2: CULTURAL FORMS: Arts:** American Indian Arts and Crafts Fairs; Cultural Appropriation: Questions and Issues;

Moccasins; **FAMILY, EDUCATION, AND COMMUNITY:** Buffalo (Bison) Culture; Education: Acculturalization and Boarding Schools; Sexual Orientation; Wedding Customs; **FOOD:** Food and Culture: North Pacific Coast; **LANGUAGE AND LITERATURE:** Eastman, Charles Alexander (Ohíye S'a); Figures of Speech, Native American Origins/Spotlight: Names from Native Cultures; Humor, as Cultural Attribute; **MUSIC AND DANCE:** Sun Dance; **SPIRITUALITY:** Seven Drums (Dreamer) Spirituality

Further Reading

Brasser, Theodore. *Native American Clothing: An Illustrated History*. Richmond Hill, Ontario: Firefly Books, 2009.

Gibby, Evard H. *Traditional Clothing of Native Americans*. Eden, UT: Eagles View, 2000.

Kearny, Cresson H. *Jungle Snafus . . . and Remedies*. Cave Junction, OR: Oregon Institute of Science and Medicine, 1996.

Koch, Ronald P. *Dress Clothing of the Plains Indians*. Norman: University of Oklahoma Press, 1990.

Marcy, Randolph B. (Capt.). *The Prairie Traveler*. Carlisle, MA: Applewood Books [1859] 1988.

Paterek, Josephine. *Encyclopedia of Native American Costume*. New York: W. W. Norton, 1996.

Suttles, Wayne, and Barbara Lane. "Southern Coast Salish." In Wayne Suttles, ed. *Handbook of North American Indians: Northwest Coast*. Vol. 7. In William C. Sturtevant, general ed. *Handbook of North American Indians*. Washington, DC: Smithsonian Institution, 1990, 485–502.

CULTURAL APPROPRIATION: QUESTIONS AND ISSUES

Who Is Native—and How Much?

The "Cherokee Princess" who has 1/32nd Native blood has become nearly a standing joke—and an ironic one, in living memory of some elders who hid their Indian blood rather than suffer vicious discrimination. David Treuer, an Ojibwe Indian from Leech Lake Reservation in northern Minnesota, noted in the *Washington Post* that regardless of how Indians classified themselves, their rights were automatically curtailed if they were classified as American Indian by the U.S. government. This included the rights to practice religion, travel, and pursue liberty and happiness within Indian culture.

This sort of persecution lasted through the 1940s, said Treuer, author of *Rez Life: An Indian's Journey Through Reservation Life* (2012): "to the extent that my grandfather, who couldn't have been mistaken for anything other than Indian, put down 'white' on his enlistment forms when he volunteered for the Army in

1943." During the 1960s and 1970s, however, Native cultures became attractive to whites who were ill at ease with their own way of life. Native people also took control of their own lives in important ways, as "activists helped force dormant treaty rights—such as hunting and fishing rights, exemption from some forms of taxation, and religious freedom—into court, where they were upheld" (Treuer, 2012). Forced acculturation came largely, but not entirely, to an end. The U.S. Census is ethnically self-identified; anyone can list as anything, or as a combination. Legal recognition requires a listing on a tribal roll.

What Is Spiritually Authentic—and by Whose Rules?

Joseph Medicine Crow, the Crow historian who authored *The Heart of Crow Country*, described the coming of "Wannabes" to his homeland: "Now, about ten years ago, this 'Wannabe Medicine Man' thing started coming up. Traditional Crows confronted them and we were told there was no law against it."

> "They're mean, sometimes dangerous, brazen, not at all like us regular Indians," Crow said. "These guys also write a lot of books: 'So and so on Indian religion.' . . . They either give themselves Indian names or become buddies with an Indian who they use as a front man and then charge hundreds, sometimes thousands, of dollars to Sun Dance or sweat lodges. It's terrible. Non-Indians are taking away our cultural activities." (Chapman, 2001, 20)

Elsewhere, whites began to steal the Sun Dance. One of them took the idea to Kentucky and started the White Buffalo Woman Strip Show. Suddenly, the Wannabes were charging thousands of dollars to people who wanted to fulfill fantasies that were not in any way connected to Oglala culture. By 1992, traditional Oglala were stopping busloads of New Agers led by phony medicine men who had invaded Bear Butte, a sacred vision quest site.

Cultural Borrowing vs. Appropriation

Non-Indian Americans have been borrowing Native American culture since they first arrived in North America, eating corn and fertilizing their gardens with fish heads, taking daily baths, and organizing a federal government that borrowed some of its attributes from the Haudenosaunee Confederacy as well as Greek city-states and England's Magna Carta. Half of the United States borrow their names in some measure from Indian languages, and when protesting colonists needed a metaphor for freedom vis-à-vis English tyranny they adopted a Mohawk disguise at the Boston Tea Party.

The people of the new United States borrowed liberally from Indian cultures. Few events of the revolutionary era have been engraved on America's popular memory like the Boston Tea Party. Nearly everyone, regardless of sophistication in matters American and revolutionary, knows that the patriots who dumped tea in Boston Harbor dressed as American Indians, specifically Mohawks. On why the tea dumpers chose this particular form of disguise, we are less fortunate. Judging by the dearth of commentary on the matter, one might conclude that it was chosen out of sheer convenience, as if Paul Revere and a gaggle of late 18th-century "party animals" had stopped by a costume shop on their way to the wharf and found the "Mohawk model" the only one available in quantity on short notice.

Boston's patriots were hardly so indiscriminate. The Tea Party was a form of symbolic protest—one step beyond random violence, one step short of organized, armed rebellion. The tea dumpers chose their symbols with utmost care. As the imported tea symbolized British tyranny and taxation, so the image of the Indian and the Mohawk disguise represented its antithesis: a "trademark" of an emerging American identity and a voice for liberty in a new land. The image of the Indian was figured into tea dumpers' disguises not only in Boston but also in cities the length of the Atlantic Seaboard. The tea parties were not spur-of-the-moment pranks but the culmination of a decade of colonial frustration with British authority. Likewise, the Mohawk symbol was not picked at random. It was used as a revolutionary symbol, counterposing the tea tax.

The image of the Indian (particularly the Mohawk) also appears at about the same time, in the same context, in revolutionary songs, slogans, and engravings. Paul Revere, whose "Midnight Rides" became legend in the hands of Longfellow, played a crucial role in forging this sense of identity, contributing to the revolutionary cause a set of remarkable engravings that cast as America's first national symbol an American Indian woman, long before Brother Jonathan or Uncle Sam came along.

"Playing Indian"

"Playing Indian is a persistent tradition in American culture, stretching from the very instant of the national big bang into an ever-expanding present and future," wrote Philip J. Deloria. "It is, however, a tradition with limitations. Not surprisingly, these cling tightly to the contours of power" (Deloria, 1998, 7). Through the Sons of St. Tammany to the Society of Red Men and the Improved Order of Red Men, Americans impersonated Indians as their diseases, alcohol, and armies subjugated them. While whites "played Indian," until the

Model Karlie Kloss was widely criticized for draping her otherwise semi-nude body in American Indian feathers and jewelry during a Victoria's Secret fashion show during November 2012, in New York City. (AP Photo/Evan Agostini/Invision)

20th century their governments and religious institutions stripped Native peoples of their own cultures through bans on Sun Dances and potlatches, religious indoctrination, and boarding schools.

Many colonial Americans viewed American society as a synthesis of Native American and European cultures. The Tammany Society, a classic example of the blending of the two cultures, was a broad-based popular movement that reinforced the founders' usage of symbols and ideological concepts indigenous to North America. The celebration of Tammany Day may have been an attempt to adapt May Day and other Old World holidays to the new American environment. Subsequently, when it inherited the patriotic mantle of the Sons of Liberty in Philadelphia, the Tammany Society espoused a philosophy that America was a unique synthesis of the best and noblest aspects of Europe and America. Building upon their own experiences with American Indians, founding fathers like James Madison and Thomas Jefferson used the Tammany Society and its membership to forge a new democratic party after the formation of the U.S. Constitution. Other founding fathers such as Benjamin Franklin, John Dickinson, and Benjamin Rush became influential members of the society.

To the Tammany Society, American Indians were more than a symbol of freedom. To members of the revolutionary generation, American Indians represented a wellspring of new ideas that freed Europeans from antiquated ideas of class and autocratic government that had so long existed in Europe. In the late 18th century, Tammany Society members from Georgia to Rhode Island to the Ohio River frequently consulted with American Indian leaders and sought to study American Indian languages and ideas. The society's members stressed concepts and values that founders such as Franklin and Jefferson found in Native societies—a weak executive (except in war), popular participation in government, and charity for the poor. Even James Madison was compelled to seek out the Iroquois and their council when he became disillusioned with the Articles of Confederation in 1784.

Although the early history of the Tammany Society is ambiguous, it appears that King Tammany, a Delaware chief friendly to William Penn, became a popular figure in the folklore of early Pennsylvania. The Tammany Society became an avenue for the expression of a regional American identity by the mid-18th century. The society's ability to synthesize American and European values and forge a new identity made it a potent force in creating a national identity as well.

The Society of Red Men organized as the Tammany Society, they used many of the same symbols and added military headquarters and protocols. Members assumed multiple identities, some with Native provenance, such as Black Wampum. "Like the Tammany organizations, the Red Men used Indian play to act out a story about their identity as Americans," Philip Deloria wrote. By the early 1830s, the flagship Philadelphia chapter of the Red Men dissolved. (Philadelphia also had been the center of the Tammany Society.) Soon thereafter, a new group organized in Baltimore, the Improved Order of Red Men, which practiced temperance, as well as an interest in patriotic aspects of American history. Their costumes combined Indian-style fringe with American flag motifs.

The combination of military style and Indian motifs also was used in the Boy Scouts of America (BSA) at the turn of the 19th to the 20th century. The Canadian author Ernest Thompson Seton, who resigned from the BSA in 1915 after having co-founded it (he was protesting the ascendancy of militarism), had written, "Most boys love to play Indian. They want to know all about the interesting things the Indians did that are possible for them to do" (Seton, 1903, 3). To this day, Scouts are organized in "patrols" and may become members of "The Order of the Arrow." Seton's original scouting program bestowed Indian titles on young men's groups, such as war chief, wampum chief, chief of the council fire. "Braves" earned awards by "counting coup." This penchant continued through a national "pow wow" highway of non-Indian hobbyists, the naming of sports teams for Indian mascots, and the naming of geographic features after ersatz cultural borrowings, including the ubiquitous and infamous "squaw." A magazine called *American Indian Hobbyist* followed the action.

The majority culture keeps remaking Native American reality in its own image. By 1972, for example, Chief Sea'th'l's often-rephrased "Farewell Speech" was called into the service of the new environmental movement with words he never had used. Embellishment of Sea'th'l's most famous speech occurred shortly after the modern advent of Earth Day in 1972. Ted Perry, a scriptwriter, put several phrases in the chief's mouth in the script of his 1972 film *Home*. Two examples: Sea'th'l never said "The earth is our mother" in those words. Nor did he discourse on the whites' slaughter of the buffalo. His people's culture was based on salmon, not buffalo. Nevertheless, Perry's paraphrased version of Sea'th'l's speech enjoyed wide circulation from the 1970s through the 1990s. Once again, Native American images were refashioned in a new ideological composite, reinventing history.

See Also PART 2: CULTURAL FORMS: ARTS: American Indian Arts and Crafts Fairs; Clothing; **FAMILY, EDUCATION, AND COMMUNITY:** Education: Acculturalization and Boarding Schools; **FOOD:** Foods and Medicines from Native American Cultures; **SPIRITUALITY:** "Great Spirit": Reality and Fantasy

Further Reading

Chapman, Serle. *We, the People: Of Earth and Elders, Volume II.* Missoula, MT: Mountain Press, 2001.

Deloria, Philip J. *Playing Indian.* New Haven, CT: Yale University Press, 1998.

Grinde, Donald, Jr., and Bruce E. Johansen. *Exemplar of Liberty: Native America and the Evolution of Democracy.* Los Angeles: UCLA American Indian Studies Center, 1991. http://www.ratical.org/many_worlds/6Nations/EoL/.

Seton, Ernest Thompson. *How to Play Indian: Directions for Organizing a Tribe of Boy Indians and Making Their Teepees in True Indian Style.* Philadelphia: Curtis, 1903.

Treuer, David. "Elizabeth Warren Says She's Native American. So She Is." *Washington Post*, May 6, 2012. http://www.washingtonpost.com/opinions/elizabeth-warren-says-shes -native-american-so-sheis/2012/05/04/gIQAn31z1T_story_1.html.

Spotlight

PALEONTOLOGY AND APPROPRIATION

History and Origins

The emergence of vertebrate paleontology as a scientific discipline can in part be attributed to large vertebrate fossils discovered on land inhabited by indigenous populations. Specifically, geographic locations in North America's continental interior, including many Indian reservations, are known to yield fossiliferous stratigraphic sequences. The Great Sioux Nation boundaries were initially defined in the 1851 Fort Laramie Treaty. The boundaries included land west of the Missouri River in South Dakota, north of the Platte River in western Nebraska, and east of the Powder River in Wyoming. Small areas in the southeast corner of Montana and southwest North Dakota also were included. On April 29, 1868, another treaty reaffirmed the borders of the Great Sioux Nation. Vertebrate fossils are yet another natural resource that was taken from subjugated peoples like the Sioux of the northern Great Plains of the United States.

Early accounts of American paleontology during the last quarter of the 19th century reveal a tendency to romanticize fossil hunting exploits ("Perilous Fossil Hunt," 1875; "Yale Expedition," 1871). Paleontologists may have been illegally trespassing while exploring and collecting fossils on Indian lands. They would portray themselves as reasonable scientists while often depicting Indians as ruthless savages. Personal letters of famed American paleontologists Edward D. Cope and Othniel Marsh reveal many cases of illegal dispossession of fossils located on Indian lands.

Most paleontologists agree that the first published material on Badlands fossils was written by a medical doctor in 1846. Fur traders working along the rivers of the interior Dakota portion of Nebraska Territory reported finding strange fossils. In 1849, John Evans was funded by and given authority by the U.S. Congress to explore the unknown areas of the Mauvais Terres (Badlands). In 1852, D. D. Owen published his findings in his *Report of a Geological Survey of Wisconsin, Iowa, and Minnesota; and Incidentally of a Portion of Nebraska Territory*. In Owen's survey of 1852, there is a chapter titled "Dr. Leidy's Memoir." Leidy gives credit to fossil hunters such as Joseph and Thaddeus Culbertson, D. D. Owen, and Hiram Prout. It is important to note that on September 17, 1851, the United States entered into a treaty with the Lakota that acknowledged that the Badlands belonged to the Indians. Yet, even then, the government-funded geological surveys were publishing reconnaissance information on Sioux country fossil resources. Furthermore, Joseph Leidy is considered the "Father of American Paleontology." Many of the fossil specimens Leidy used in his research were dispossessed from Lakota lands.

Exploitation of Fossils by Whites

Ferdinand V. Hayden was regarded as a premier surveyor of the western United States. In 1856 and 1857 Congress gave money to Hayden to explore Sioux country. Hayden would develop a keen eye for fossils situated on Sioux territory while surveying other geological resources. It has been suggested that Hayden took advantage of Sioux religious beliefs and feigned insanity to accumulate numerous fossils. Eventually, Hayden collected fossil specimens for paleontologist Joseph Leidy. Leidy would cite Dr. Hayden as the person who collected fossils weighing three to four tons from Mauvais Terres on the White River in 1866. In 1872, Hayden published his *Final Report of the United States Geological Survey of Nebraska and Portions of the Adjacent Territories*. Hayden described how the railroad companies assisted in hauling fossil freight for free.

Edward Drinker Cope (1840–1897) was considered a titan of early American paleontology. Cope was a noted naturalist who was based at the Philadelphia Academy of Science. He was promoted to a full professorship at the University of Pennsylvania in the fall of 1889 as the successor to Joseph Leidy (Wallace, 1999). Cope collected valuable fossils from Sioux reservations in the Dakotas in the 1890s. Indian agents helped Cope locate and remove fossils from the Cheyenne River Sioux and Standing Rock reservations. From the Cheyenne River Sioux Reservation Cope obtained and described a 3.5-foot skull of *Trachodon mirabilis* that was eventually displayed at the American Museum of Natural History (AMNH) in New York City. In a letter to his wife on July 16, 1892, Cope explained that he had collected 21 species of vertebrates from the Sioux reservation. In another letter, dated July 17, 1892, Cope described how Indian agent Major Lillibridge gave him preferential treatment and guided him to fossil localities. One of the fossil localities was a dinosaur bone bed 500 feet long by 50 feet wide and 30 feet high—a length 33 yards short of two football fields. Cope also violated Lakota religious beliefs as he collected bones in a manner that was taboo among the Lakotas.

Othniel Charles Marsh (1831–1899) was another pioneer of American paleontology. It would be safe to conclude that his fossil-collecting exploits helped build the foundation for the Peabody Museum of Yale University. Indeed, Marsh's wealthy uncle, George Peabody, for whom the museum is named, was known to fund paleontological collection expeditions. Many of the large vertebrate specimens O. C. Marsh collected for Yale came directly from Sioux lands.

The unfavorable state of Indian affairs in the West provoked the next big round of treaty talks between the United States and Sioux tribes. On April 29, 1868, another treaty was signed at Fort Laramie defining the Great Sioux Reservation. Marsh did not sit idly by during the ongoing negotiations. He approached the U.S. military and gained approval from William "Tecumseh" Sherman of the War Department for a free pass to all Army posts in the West. Marsh would utilize his political connections for several years as he expedited fossil collecting on Indian lands. The Union Pacific Railroad Company was also recruited to assist Marsh in the upcoming fossil expeditions.

In 1870, Marsh and Yale student volunteers began a series of fossil-collecting field trips through the northern Great Plains. On this particular trip, Yale University collected fossils from northwestern Nebraska Territory on land set aside as Sioux hunting territory. The expeditions incorporated military escorts from the U.S. Cavalry to ensure safety from bands of Sioux warriors. Pawnee scouts were also recruited and heavily depended upon to keep the team safe. This evidence suggests that Marsh's fossil expeditions were violations of the Fort Laramie Treaty of 1868, which defined Sioux lands and protected them against such intrusion. Fossils thus collected were shipped by railroad from a station near Fort McPherson, which is located near present-day North Platte, Nebraska.

In 1874, Marsh arrived at the Red Cloud Agency to collect fossils from land belonging to subjugated indigenous people. Military leaders at the agency suggested Marsh should hold council talks with Chief Red Cloud and other leaders. After numerous talks, Marsh became exacerbated and left the Red Cloud Agency in the middle of the night with U.S. Army personnel to collect fossils from a titanothere bone bed. In the meantime, Chief Red Cloud, an ever-shrewd leader, knew that the whites were going to collect fossils with or without tribal permission. Red Cloud called upon Marsh to inform Washington, D.C., about the rotten rations and subpar supplies at the agency when Marsh returned back East. What transpired in the next few years was a political firestorm about the maltreatment of Indians at the agencies.

Role of Museums and Universities

It is quite difficult to pinpoint exactly how many museums and universities were involved in dispossessing fossil resources from Sioux lands during the golden age of American paleontology. C. C. O'Harra, the first person to systematically collect for the South Dakota School of Mines (SDSM), wrote a concise history of early collection forays in the White River Badlands, which he published in 1920. O'Harra stated that besides the famous Marsh expeditions of the 1870s, Yale University hired collectors in the area in 1886, 1887, 1888, 1889, 1890, 1895, 1897, and 1898. Specifically, the collections amassed under Marsh during the years between 1886 and 1890 were conducted under the "auspices" of the United States Geological Survey (USGS) and shipped to the National Museum (the Smithsonian Institution).

Princeton University collected in the White River Badlands in 1882, 1890, 1893, and 1894. The Princeton expeditions were mostly headed by W. B. Scott. Princeton University was involved in collecting fossil mammals from Lakota reservations just shortly after the Wounded Knee Massacre of 1889.

William Berryman Scott's memoir provides a firsthand account of fossil collection on the Pine Ridge Reservation in 1882. The Princeton team was provided a military escort on orders of General Philip Sheridan (Scott, 1939). According to Scott, six infantrymen of the U.S. Army were to be under his command. Then, as now, it was illegal for a civilian to command troops. The U.S. Army thus became directly involved in dispossessing fossils from the Pine Ridge Reservation Indians under false and illegal orders. Not only that, but fossils collected at this time were shipped to the nearest railroad by wagons meant to haul food and supplies for the destitute Lakota. In 1985, almost a hundred years later, Yale Peabody Museum would acquire the Princeton University vertebrate fossil collection.

According to C. C. O'Harra, the University of Nebraska collected in or near the vicinity of Pine Ridge Reservation in 1892, 1894, 1895, 1897, 1905, 1907, 1908, and later. Professor E. H. Barbour was the top paleontologist working in the field for the University of Nebraska at that time. Barbour reported that the University of Nebraska had several cases of fossils collected from the Oligocene, Miocene, and other geologic formations from the badlands of Nebraska and South Dakota (Barbour, 1924).

Finally, the American Museum of Natural History (AMNH) entered the Great Sioux Nation area in 1892, 1893, 1894, 1897, 1903, 1906, 1908, 1911, 1912, 1913, 1914, and 1916. Like other museums, AMNH collected continuously from Indian lands for many decades. H. F. Osborn was the first vertebrate paleontologist from the New York City museum to lead expeditions on Lakota territory and/or reservation lands. AMNH collected an extraordinary amount of valuable fossil material. Fossil specimens were collected near the Wounded Knee Massacre site and other areas throughout the Pine Ridge Reservation.

The "Golden Age" of archaeology was built on paleontology resources dispossessed from Lakota lands. Leaders in the scientific field of paleontology may justify the actions of the Golden Age bone collectors as a necessary means to an end. Theories in biology, geology, geography, and other disciplines were influenced by the research based on dispossessed fossil material. Even so, significant ethical concerns must be addressed by the professors, museums, universities, and governments that have been implicated in this systematic plunder of indigenous natural resources.

Lawrence W. Bradley

See Also PART 2: CULTURAL FORMS: FAMILY, EDUCATION, AND COMMUNITY: Native American Graves Protection and Repatriation Act (NAGPRA) (1990)

Further Reading

Barbour, E. H. "A Preliminary Report on the Nebraska State Museum." *The Nebraska State Museum Bulletin* 1, no. 1 (December 1924): 1–19.

Bartlett, R. *Great Survey of the American West*. Norman: University of Oklahoma Press, 1962.

Dussais, A. "Science, Sovereignty, and the Sacred Text: Paleontological Resources and Native American Rights." *Maryland Law Review* 55 (1996): 84–159.

Hayden, F. V. *Final Report of the United States Geological Survey of Nebraska and Portions of the Adjacent Territories*. Washington, DC: Government Printing Office, 1872.

Kappler, C. J. *Laws and Treaties. Indian Affairs*. Vol. II. *(Treaties.)* Washington, DC: Government Printing Office, 1904.

Lanham, U. *The Bone Hunters*. New York: Columbia University Press, 1973.

Leidy, J. 1869. "The Extinct Mammalian Fauna of Dakota and Nebraska. Including an Account of Some Allied Forms from Other Localities, Together with a Synopsis of the

Mammalian Remains of North America." *Journal of the Academy of Natural Science Philadelphia* 7 (1869): 1–472.

Lindsay, C. "The Diary of Dr. Thomas G. Maghee." *Nebraska History Magazine* 12, no. 3 (July–September 1929): 252–263.

MacDonald, J. R. "The Miocene Fauna from the Wounded Knee Area of Western South Dakota." *Bulletin of the American Museum of Natural History* 125, no. 3 (1963): 140–238.

O'Harra, C. C. *The White River Badlands*. Rapid City, SD: South Dakota School of Mines, 1920.

Osborn, H. F. *Cope: Master Naturalist*. London: Oxford University Press, 1931.

Osborn, H. F. *The Titanotheres of Ancient Wyoming, Dakota, and Nebraska*. Vol. 1. Department of the Interior. U.S. Geological Survey. Monograph 55. Washington, DC: United States Government Printing Office, 1929.

Owen, D. D. *Report of a Geological Survey of Wisconsin, Iowa, and Minnesota; and Incidentally of a Portion of Nebraska Territory*. Philadelphia: Lippincott, Grambo, 1852.

"A Perilous Fossil Hunt." *New York Tribune,* Extra, no. 27. March 27, 1875: 46–51.

Prout, H. A. 1846. "Description of a Fossil Maxillary Bone of a Paleotherium, from Near White River." *American Journal of Science* 2, no. 2 (1846): 288–289.

Royce, C. C. *Indian Land Cession in the United States*. Washington, DC: Extract from the *Eighteenth Annual Report of the Bureau of American Ethnology*, 1900.

Schuchert, C., and C. M. LeVenne. *O. C. Marsh: Pioneer in Paleontology*. New Haven, CT: Yale University Press, 1940.

Scott, W. B. *Some Memories of a Paleontologist*. Princeton, NJ: Princeton University Press, 1939.

Wallace, D. R. *The Bonehunter's Revenge*. Boston: Houghton Mifflin, 1999.

"The Yale Expedition of 1870." *Harper's New Monthly Magazine* 257 (October 1871).

CULTURAL TOURISM

Some Native American peoples offer "cultural tourism" programs, during which outsiders may accompany individuals who act as "guides" in their everyday work or other activities. The Navajos, in particular, who often have been reticent to let non-Indians into their world, recently have allowed tourists to accompany sheepherders and weavers as a way of sharing culture and earning money. The offerings extend not only to herding and weaving but also to traditional dyeing, storytelling, cooking, and other pursuits. Cultural tourism programs have become very popular during the 21st century, but they are hardly a new idea. In a sense, Buffalo Bill's Wild West Show was one wildly successful venture in cultural tourism; Native American pow wows also long have had an educational function.

History and Origins

Herding was once a major Navajo way of life, having been introduced during the Spanish invasion about 1600. During the 1930s, however, most of their sheep were slaughtered during a U.S. government stock-reduction program meant to reduce soil erosion. Little thought was given to the fact that Navajos were being deprived of sustenance during the Great Depression. By the 1960s, only a few hundred of the Navajos' sturdy Churro sheep, which can survive a tough habitat, remained. The Churros formed the basis of a herding culture for more than 200 years, providing mutton as well as fleece with long fibers that worked well in blankets.

During the 1970s, a revival of sheepherding culture began, which includes a Sheep Is Life Festival each June, as well as Navajo Lifeway (Diné be Tina), a nonprofit group that promotes pastoral culture. By 2012, about 6,000 sheep were being herded. Cultural tourism was being agented by the Toadlena Trading Post in Toadlena, New Mexico, which also schedules time with Navajo weavers who sell rugs there.

A travel writer for the *New York Times*, Michael Benanav, accompanied Irene Bennalley, a herder, with her 800 sheep during the late spring of 2012, then described in the newspaper how cultural tourists camp out on the trail and cook their own food, paying $350 for three nights ($100 extra per night after that), or exchange labor for part of the fee. "It's like going to a Spartan Navajo dude ranch," Benanav wrote. "The sheep are like our parents," Bennalley told Benanav. "They feed us and give us comfort from the cold." The sheep also provided a rudimentary global positioning system. They keep together and find a way back to their pens after a day in open country. "I always tell my teenage granddaughter: 'Don't worry about getting lost out there. The sheep will lead you home,'" said Bennalley (Benanav, 2012, 10).

Regional Variations

Development of cultural tourism has sparked debates among Native peoples. For example, when the Cherokees of Oklahoma developed a cultural tourism program they were faced with deciding how to describe to non-Natives events in their history that were wrenching and devastating, such as the Trail of Tears (1838). They found an inherent tension between maintaining authenticity and maximizing economic return. Sometimes the raw nature of historical reality did not sit well with white audiences that were accustomed to a soft-pedaled history. They presented the historical facts accurately, therefore, but also emphasized that the Cherokees as a people had recovered their economic vibrancy and culture despite losing a quarter of their population during the forced migration. Today, with more than 200,000 members, the Cherokees are the second-largest Native nation within the United States (only the Navajos have more members).

During 2009, the American Indian Center at the University of North Carolina at Chapel Hill published an extensive handbook on *American Indian Cultural Tourism*, following a workshop on the subject on June 18–19 the same year. This project defined "cultural tourism" as attractions that draw visitors away from where they live to experience and gather information about new cultures.

The report included a wide range of activities under the term, including visits to museums or other exhibitions, either with the aid of a guide or docent, or self-directed; direct experience, such as immersion in a recreated village, or classes in dance, art, or other activities; performances, as participant or spectator, and "place marketing," described as collections of events and activities that attract people to particular places, such as festivals. The same report said that cultural tourism is best for local communities in which the residents can take ownership of projects, and tourists can learn about the reality of Native American life. The documentation of culture that is necessary for its presentation also aids preservation efforts.

In Oklahoma, the American Indian Cultural Center and Museum has combined efforts with several state-wide tourism offices and agencies (including the Oklahoma Tourism and Recreation Department and Oklahoma Travel Industry Association) to accentuate Native American cultural tourism through the Oklahoma Travel Industry Association. Oklahoma Indian efforts also have sought investment from private businesses for several projects, including an arts and crafts marketplace for Native artists in the state.

In Maine, the Four Directions Development Corporation (FDDC) has focused on events that bring audiences and buyers together with creators of local arts and crafts. The FDDC also planned "a virtual Wabanaki Trail" to assist in the location of Maine's Native communities and historical points of interest, as well as gas stations, restaurants, and shops. (The Wabanaki Confederacy includes several Native nations in Maine, Penobscot, Passamaquoddy, Mi'kmaq, and Maliseet.)

"We're interested in creating a Wabanaki Cultural Resort—a hotel with a cultural center—and we are interested in bringing awareness of the Wabanaki to the people here in Maine and in the Northeast and beyond," said FDDC executive director Susan Hammond, a citizen of the Penobscot Indian Nation. "Our market is actually worldwide. We know there is an interest in indigenous peoples and certainly in North American Indians, and we're trying to create our Wabanaki brand similar to the Northwest tribes around Seattle or even the

Southwest tribes. When you see their colors and art, you know where they're from. We want to do the same for the Wabanaki" (Toensing, 2012).

The FDDC in 2009 also obtained a grant from the U.S. Department of Housing and Urban Development to develop the Wabanaki Cultural Tourism Center, a world-class center that will assist Maine's tribes in creating opportunities for cultural tourism in their communities. Native artists and craftspeople who make baskets or create works of art in various mediums such as wood, beads, drawing, photography, jewelry, and so on would have outlets for their work.

A Native American Cultural Tourism Conference, May 9–11, 2012, was organized by the Institute of American Indian Arts' Center for Lifelong Education in Santa Fe, New Mexico, joined with the Moenkopi Legacy Inn and Suites and the Upper Village of Moenkopi (in Arizona). The 2012 conference (the eighth year of annual meetings on this subject) at the Moenkopi Legacy Inn and Suites in the Upper Village of Moenkopi, at the western gateway to the Hopi reservation, convened leaders in Native American cultural tourism from across the United States. Cherokee actor and film director Wes Studi was the event's keynote speaker. The conference provided tours, workshops, and hands-on opportunities and resources.

In South Dakota, the Crazy Horse Memorial and Mount Rushmore National Memorial have combined efforts to add cultural materials on Native American history and culture. Visitors also have been invited to the Pine Ridge (Oglala Lakota) Reservation to learn about the Oglala Lakota people of today.

New Mexico's 22 Indian tribes (19 pueblos and three other reservations) welcome visitors to many of their feast-day celebrations, with dances and rituals in brilliant attire. Some of the dances (Corn, Deer, and Buffalo) are usually public events. The ceremonial dresses that are worn by the dancers are more than just decorative, said one promotional website:

> The feathers, jewelry and beads all communicate part of the story. Every dance is considered a prayer, not a performance, and as such, outsiders are privileged to observe them. Drums beat with an insistent cadence and the air is filled with the fragrance of piñon smoke. Red chile ristras (strings) decorate many homes, with the chiles destined to add their distinct flavor to stews and sauces throughout the winter. The sights, sounds and smells of the pueblo celebrations are a feast for the senses. (Crow, 2011)

Arts and crafts (such as silver and turquoise jewelry, drums, pottery, weavings, carvings, and clothing) are offered for sale in many parts of New Mexico; Native food in several varieties also is available, including "bread baked in an *horno* (outdoor oven) or fry bread, best consumed on the spot, hot and honey-drizzled straight from the pan." In a pueblo, "Visitors are fascinated to see that pueblo life is a window to another world and time. Not relegated to history books or museums, this is a living culture that carries on the centuries-old traditions of their ancestors" (Crow, 2011). Many of the pueblos maintain visitors' centers and offer tours, but some ceremonies are private. Pueblos may be closed to the public on certain dates. Preparations in advance are advised. Tourists also are advised that they are visiting a people's home, so they should be respectful. Albuquerque's Indian Pueblo Cultural Center offers a calendar of feast days, as well as exhibits of arts and crafts from each pueblo or reservation.

See Also PART 2: CULTURAL FORMS: MEDIA, POPULAR CULTURE, SPORTS, AND GAMING: Wild West Shows and American Indian Cultural Clubs; **SPIRITUALITY:** Peyote; **TRANSPORTATION AND HOUSING:** Canoe Culture, Pacific Northwest; Hogan, Navajo

Further Reading

Benanav, Michael. "Cultured Traveler: Following a Navajo Sheep Herder." *New York Times*, July 29, 2012, Travel, 10.

Crow, Sharon. "Cultural Tourism: Native American Culture, Traditions and Heritage." November 17, 2011. http://culturaltourism-1.blogspot.com/2011/11/native-american-groups-have-inhabited.html. Accessed August 25, 2014.

"Four Directions Development Corporation: Investing in the Hopes and Dreams of Maine's Native People." http://www.fourdirectionsmaine.org/cultural-tourism-program. Accessed August 25, 2014.

A Handbook on American Indian Cultural Tourism in North Carolina. American Indian Center, University of North Carolina at Chapel Hill, August 2009.

"New Exhibits Promote Native American Cultural Tourism." March 12, 2010. Crazy Horse Memorial, South Dakota. http://crazyhorsememorial.org/755/new-exhibits-promote-native-american-cultural-tourism/. Accessed August 25, 2014.

"News Blurb: Native American Cultural Tourism Conference, Upper Village of Moenkopi, AZ, May 9–11, 2012." *Multicultural Marketing Resources.* May 9, 2012. www.iaia.edu/cle/events/ctw_home/. Accessed August 25, 2014.

Toensing, Gale Courey. "Maine Attraction: Ambitious Cultural Tourism Initiative Puts Wabanaki Nations on the Map." *Indian Country Today Media Network*, July 13, 2012. http://indiancountrytodaymedianetwork.com/2012/07/13/maine-attraction-ambitious-cultural-tourism-initiative-puts-wabanaki-nations-on-the-map-123188.

Spotlight

CULTURE BEARERS

Most Native American tribes and nations include people, often clan mothers, who, respected as transmitters of culture, pass on traditions to new generations.

Audrey Shenandoah-Gonwaiani, from the Onondaga Nation Clan, was such a person for more than 40 years before passing on in 2012. Her people selected her as the clan mother (*iakoiane* in the Mohawk dialect of the Iroquois language); she cared for her family, her nation, her cultural heritage, and her people's language. Gonwaiani, born and raised by her grandparents in the Onondaga culture, was the matriarch of her family of 10 children and her descendants.

Culture Bearers' Duties

An *iakoniane* has many duties during her lifetime, all of which Gonwaiani accepted without compromise. She had the duty of nominating the leadership from within her clan; the male leader (*roia:ne* or "chief"), his assistant (*rateron-tanonha*), and the two faith-keepers (male: *roterihonton*, female: *iakoterihon-ton*) who serve as spiritual advisors for the *roia:ne* and *iakoiane*. Her selections were then reviewed by her clan before being sanctioned by the Nation Council. Her nominations were inevitably wise ones and brought security and confidence to the Onondaga Nation.

The *iakoiane* had other duties. She was a peacemaker, serving as an arbitrator in disputes within the nation. She oversaw the use of the nation's natural resources as an extension of her relationship with Mother Earth. She was present at every one of the lunar rituals that mark the cycle of seasons among the Haudenosaunee. As a counselor she provided instruction in the meaning and dynamics of each ceremony; as a spiritual leader she worked with the nation to ensure the ceremonies were carried on across the decades.

Yet even as Gonwaiani was called to the people's service she was a devoted mother. As her international stature grew, requiring her to travel to distant places on behalf of the Haudenosaunee, she was always conscious of her personal family life first. She was a remarkable host for the many political gatherings at Onondaga, her presence as secretary for the nation steady and reassuring.

When the Haudenosaunee Confederacy was established hundreds of years ago Skennenrahowi, the messenger, created the position of *iakoiane* as an extension of natural law. He determined that the women, the lifegivers for all humanity, must have specific powers and freedoms to realize their status as the heart and soul of all nations. The first clan mother was Jikonsaseh and from her came the model for all others right to the present day. Just as Jikonsaseh (the Mother of Nations) was wise and loving, so was Gonwaiani. And when Jikonsaseh was strong and determined in defense of the people, so was Gonwaiani as she lived through the greatest changes in Haudenosaunee history. It was Gonwaiani's absolute conviction that the Haudenosaunee had teachings of utmost importance and in those instructions were the means by which human beings may survive on a changing earth. She lived those teachings every day of her life.

Culture bearers play a key role in recovering Native American cultural traditions. For example, on July 28, 2012, more than 500 people attended a Basket Welcoming Celebration honoring Ohlone artist and culture bearer Linda Yamane, with storytelling, dancing, and songs in the Oakland Museum of

California's outdoor gardens. She has replicated the first Ohlone baskets in almost 70 years. This was no ordinary basket; it was described in a newspaper account at the time as "Taking over three years to create, [with] 20,000 individual stitches and thousands of bird feathers . . . adorned with 1,200 red and white handcrafted Olivella shell beads" (Whitney, 2012). The Oakland Museum of California had given Yamane a commission in 2010 to create it for the Native American historical artifacts collection.

The Ohlone tribe's homeland is in the Alameda, Santa Cruz, Monterey, Contra Costa, Santa Clara, San Francisco, San Mateo, and San Benito counties of Northern California. Much of their culture had been lost beginning with the establishment of the Spanish missions, a diaspora that continued during and after the California gold rush after 1849. Beginning during the last half of the 20th century, a concerted effort was mounted by the Ohlone and other San Francisco Bay Area Native peoples to recover their traditions.

Pauline (Dimples) Murillo, a Cahuilla and Serrano elder and culture bearer in the California San Manuel Band of Serrano Mission Indians (in the San Bernardino Mountains foothills) was born February 3, 1934, on the San Manuel Reservation. By the time she passed away on January 21, 2011, at age 76, "Dimples" (with her husband of 58 years, George), was a mother of three, grandmother of eight, and great-grandmother of 19.

Cliff Trafzer, professor of history at the University of California–Riverside, identified Mrs. Murillo as an immensely important elder and a prominent voice in educating the public on Native American traditions and life. "They were way before their time," Trafzer said. "She would say, 'My mother and I always felt it was important that we tell our story, and not others—to get it right'" (Olson, 2011). She grew up on a reservation that lacked even basic necessities until the 1980s, and she was educated as a leader from the beginning by her mother, Martha Manuel Chacon, who often served as a spokeswoman for the tribe. Mother and daughter often visited local schools to work as culture bearers, passing on the tribe's heritage to young people, preserving their Serrano language and rituals, dedicated to the principle, "To never forget who you are or where you came from" ("Pauline," 2011). Murillo also helped develop an interactive Serrano-language CD-ROM.

The Cahuillas opened a bingo hall in 1986 and used its profits to capitalize casinos that made it wealthy. Murillo was proud of her roots and developed a successful business, becoming an inspiration to the youth, whom she called on to be proud of their heritage. In 2001, Murillo published a book titled *Living in Two Worlds,* which includes hundreds of family photographs that offer a view of life on the San Manuel Reservation. Her work continued in another book, *We Are Still Here Alive and in Spirit,* at the time of her death. Pauline and George also donated time and money to several hospitals (notably the Loma Linda University Medical Center) and schools, as well as, during 2009, to California State University–San Bernardino for an observatory that was named after the family. Her cradle dolls were notable at many craft fairs and pow wows.

Doug George-Kanentiio and Bruce E. Johansen

See Also PART 1: OVERVIEW: POPULATION AND DEMOGRAPHICS: Disease, Depopulation, and Cultural Destruction; Cultural Genocide; **PART 2: CULTURAL FORMS: ARTS:** Ledger Art; **FAMILY, EDUCATION, AND COMMUNITY:** Education: Acculturalization and Boarding Schools/Spotlight: Education Revival: A Muckleshoot Case Study; Spotlight: Reindigenization; **LANGUAGE AND LITERATURE:** Language Reclamation: Eastern Tribes; Language Recovery in Indigenous North America; **MEDIA, POPULAR CULTURE, SPORTS, AND GAMING:** Museums/Spotlight: National Museum of the American Indian (NMAI)

Further Reading

George-Kanentiio, Doug. "On the Passing of a Native Patriot: Onondaga Clanmother, 2012." Via email March 25, 2012.

Olson, David. "Pauline Murillo, 76, San Manuel Tribal Elder." *Riverside* (California) *Press-Enterprise*, January 26, 2011. http://www.pe.com/local-news/topics/topics-tribes -headlines/20110126-pauline-murillo-76-san-manuel-tribal-elder.ece. Accessed August 26, 2014.

"Pauline Murillo (Cahuilla/Serrano) Elder of the San Manuel Band of Serrano Mission Indians." http://www.sanmanuel-nsn.gov/press_releases/2011-03/2011-01-24%20 -%20Pauline%20Murillo%20Bio%20Final.pdf. Accessed August 26, 2014.

Whitney, Spencer. "Oakland Museum Honors Ohlone Basket Weaver and Culture." *Oakland North*, July 30, 2012. http://oaklandnorth.net/2012/07/30/oakland-museum -honors-ohlone-basket-weaver-and-culture/. Accessed August 26, 2014.

GORMAN, RUDOLPH CARL ("R.C.") (1931–2005)

Rudolph Carl ("R.C.") Gorman, a prominent Navajo (Diné) painter, was best known for lithographs, serigraphs, painted pottery, and sculptures of graceful female figures, as well as other paintings. Gorman's work featured fluid lines and bright colors. He also worked in sculpture, ceramics, and stone lithography. Gorman was also known for his defiance of artistic prudishness, which was reflected in the title of a cookbook (with drawings) that he authored: *Nudes and Foods: In Good Taste*. Gorman's most familiar paintings were reproduced by the millions on posters, coffee cups, and greeting cards. According to the Santa Fe *New Mexican*,

> Gorman carved new pathways for Indian artists, who, prior to the late 1960s, often were forced into unrealistic definitions by collectors—and by a market that relied upon a stereotype of stoic portraits and colorful dancers rooted in the Santa Fe Indian School style. "I paint what I see," Gorman once said. "I don't think. I don't have any message. I think it's so phony for artists to have this huge meaning. I don't." (Baker, 2007)

Gorman was a member of the Clauschii' (Red Bottom People) Clan and the *Dibé* lizhíní (Black Sheep People) Clan. He was born on July 26, 1931, in

R.C. Gorman at work. (Dave G. Houser/Corbis)

a traditional Navajo hogan near Chinle, Arizona, the oldest son of Carl Nelson Gorman. The elder Gorman, who was born in 1907, was a trader, artist, and rancher. He served during World War II as a Navajo code talker in the U.S. Marines. The younger Gorman's mother was Adella Katherine Brown, an accomplished Navajo weaver. Gorman was raised by both his mother and his maternal grandmother, Zonnie Maria Brown, in and near Black Mountain, Arizona, with five brothers and sisters. Early in life, his female relatives taught Gorman Navajo traditions, including songs, prayers, and respect for the land.

Gorman was something of a child prodigy. He began painting at the age of three, encouraged by his father, who also was a painter in experimental genres. Young Gorman first painted farm animals and local scenes, including the sheep that he tended in the Canyon de Chelly with his aunts. Some of his images also included automobiles, Mickey Mouse, and Shirley Temple.

Gorman quickly developed a style of his own that later would lead to his popular nickname in the media: "A Taos Original." Gorman's style inspired other visual artists to experiment with traditional forms in novel ways. Gorman often credited his inspiration to become a painter to encouragement by Jenny

Lind, a teacher at the Ganado Presbyterian Mission School, which had been founded by his mother and father.

Before he became a well-known painter, Gorman held a number of jobs, including technical illustrator at Douglas Aircraft. Gorman later attended Northern Arizona University (1950–1951 and 1955–1956), studying literature and art, but withdrew before he completed an undergraduate degree. Between 1951 and 1955, Gorman served in the U.S. Navy, part of that time in the Korean War. The Navajo Tribal Council gave him a scholarship in 1958 to study the art of Diego Rivera and Rufino Tamayo at Mexico City College, an experience that shaped Gorman's style for the rest of his life. Gorman moved to San Francisco during the early 1960s, where he studied art at San Francisco State University and worked in the Bay Area as a model. During 1968 Gorman moved to Taos, his home for the rest of his life, as his reputation grew.

Gorman's fame spread during the 1970s. In 1973, he was the only living artist exhibited in the "Masterworks of the American Indian" show held at the Metropolitan Museum in New York. A piece of his work was used on the cover of the exhibit catalog. By his death in 2005, Gorman's works had been collected and exhibited in more than 100 museums in the United States, Asia, and Europe. Before 1980, Gorman lived in his studio, but with fame came income that, in 1980, allowed him to build a $3 million mansion in El Prado, which he used to host legendary parties. At the same time, Gorman was noted for his generosity to local charities.

Gorman displayed his artistic skills in watercolors, etchings, acrylics, oils, paper casts, silkscreens, and stone lithographs, as he depicted highly stylized subjects, including landscapes, spiritual beings, animals, and people, many featuring important places in Navajoland, illustrating Navajo values. His famous female figures often were similar to his friends and relatives, shown large-breasted, often barefoot, in traditional dress, including the robes and blankets that are common in the Navajo homeland and the Rio Grande pueblos.

"I revere women. They are my greatest inspiration," Gorman told an interviewer in 1998. He continued:

> My first art effort in school was a drawing of a naked woman. I got a whipping from my teacher and from my mother. I am not obsessed with large women or even skinny women, but I do prefer to paint women. I'm attracted to them. And larger women, they fill up the paper more. There is more space to work with. My own aunts were large women. Maybe I am reflecting them. (Baker, 2007)

Gorman's grandmother appeared often in many of his earliest paintings.

As he aged, Gorman turned to writing as well as expanding his range in the visual arts. He wrote an autobiography; he also wrote about various styles of art and their history, as well as cooking, one of his lifelong loves. At home in his Taos studio, Gorman was known for creating an eccentric blend of styles in his mode of dress as well as his art. Some called it "bohemian." He favored headbands and custom-tailored Hawaiian shirts.

Gorman lived much of his adult life in El Prado, near Taos, doing business in his own venue, the R. C. Gorman Navajo Gallery of Taos, the first Indian-owned fine art display space when it opened in 1968. Gorman also had a stake in the Nizhoni Gallery of Albuquerque, which sold his publications and prints. Gorman enjoyed sharing the monetary profits of his work; he also donated his own library (more than 1,200 books and a large number of his own works of art) to Diné College to fulfill its guiding principle, *sa'ah naaghíí bik'eh hózhóón*, to help preserve Diné culture, language, and history. The College of Ganado and Northern Arizona University presented him with honorary doctorates. In 1986, as Harvard University recognized Gorman for his contributions to art and culture, San Francisco mayor Dianne Feinstein declared March 19 Gorman Day.

Many noted political figures and celebrities collected Gorman's work, including Elizabeth Taylor, Danny DeVito, Gregory Peck, Erma Bombeck, Barry Goldwater, Lee Marvin, Arnold Schwarzenegger, and Jackie Onassis. Andy Warhol silk-screened a portrait of Gorman that hung in his bathroom. Gorman was injured in a fall at his home. He died at age 74 on November 3, 2005, after treatment for a bacterial blood infection that resulted in several complications, including pneumonia. Upon his passing, New Mexico governor Bill Richardson, a friend of Gorman's, ordered flags in the state lowered in his honor.

The Navajo Nation's president, Joe Shirley Jr., said that Gorman was the "Picasso of the Southwest," an apparent reference to Gorman's notoriety, not his work itself, since the two artists' painting styles were very different. The *New York Times* did Shirley one better, calling Gorman the "Picasso of American Indian art" (Romancito and Clark, 2005). Shirley also called Gorman "a child of the Navajo. . . . He afforded us the opportunity to talk about ourselves to the world. When they talked about him, they talked about us" (Hardeen, 2005, 1).

During the late 1990s, the Federal Bureau of Investigation conducted an investigation into suspected pedophilia by Gorman during the previous 20 years, but no charges were filed. The FBI concluded that some of the evidence was credible, but a five-year statute of limitations had expired. Accusations that Gorman had been a pedophile resurfaced again after his death. Geoffrey

Francis Dunn, who worked as an author, historian, and filmmaker, as well as a lecturer at the University of California at Santa Cruz, reached back to 1967 to accuse Gorman of molesting him at the age of 12. An Albuquerque television station (KRQE-TV, Channel 13) broadcast Dunn's allegation on July 26, 2005, making the bit newsworthy because Gorman would have been 75 years of age on that date.

The station also obtained decade-old FBI reports alleging that Gorman was part of "a pedophile ring in Taos" that brought "runaways or uneducated" boys from Mexico, violating a federal law known as the White Slave Traffic Act (Sharpe, 2005). Gorman was known to have been gay, but people who knew him pointed out that sexual preference has no direct relationship to child molestation.

Virginia Dooley, who managed Gorman's career for 35 years, co-authored some of his books and was the personal representative of his estate, said that she didn't believe the allegations of pedophilia. Gorman was never formally charged with molesting a child.

See Also PART 2: CULTURAL FORMS: SPIRITUALITY: "Great Spirit": Reality and Fantasy

Further Reading

Baker, Kris. "RIP Artist RC Gorman." *Santa Fe New Mexican*, November 3, 2007. http://www.freenewmexican.com/news/34626.html. Accessed August 26, 2014.

Brody, J. J. *Indian Painters and White Patrons.* Albuquerque: University of New Mexico Press, 1971.

Gorman, R. C. *The Radiance of My People.* Houston: Santa Fe Arts Gallery, 1992.

Gorman, R. C., and Virginia Dooley. *Nudes and Food: R. C. Gorman Goes Gourmet.* Flagstaff, AZ: Northland Press, 1981.

Gorman, R. C., and Virginia Dooley. *R. C. Gorman's Nudes & Foods in Good Taste.* Santa Fe: Clear Light, 1994.

Hardeen, George. "Flags at Half-Staff for R.C. Gorman: President Calls Mr. Gorman the 'Picasso of the Southwest, Child of the Navajo Nation.'" Navajo-Hopi Observer. November 10, 2005. http://nhonews.com/print.asp?ArticleID=4364&SectionID=74&SubSectionID=1.

Monthan, Doris. *R. C. Gorman—A Retrospective.* Flagstaff, AZ: Northland Press, 1990.

"Obituary: R. C. Gorman; Renowned Navajo Artist's Works Coveted by Celebrity Collectors." *New York Times*, November 13, 2005.

Parks, Stephen. *R. C. Gorman, A Portrait.* Boston: Little, Brown, 1983.

Romancito, Rick, and Virginia L. Clark. "R. C. Gorman, 1931–2005: A Taos Original." *Santa Fe New Mexican*, November 3, 2005. http://www.freenewmexican.com/news/34600.html. Accessed August 26, 2014.

Sharpe, Tom. "Child-sex Accounts Emerge after Taos Artist's Death." *Santa Fe New Mexican*, August 5, 2006. http://www.freenewmexican.com/news/47435.html.

JEMISON, G. PETER (1945–)

G. Peter Jemison, an eighth-generation descendant of Mary Jemison, is a Heron Clan Seneca from Cattauraugus. Born in Silver Creek, New York, Jemison has directed the American Indian Community House Gallery in New York City. He has been the long-time manager of Ganondagan, a historic Seneca village site (designated as a state and federal historic site), 25 miles southeast of Rochester, New York. Jemison also has been active in national efforts to advocate the return of Native American remains and funerary objects from museums and other non-Indian archives. Jemison has also been an influential administrator, curator, editor, and writer. In 2004, he was elected board member at large of the American Association of Museums.

Jemison describes himself as a "faith-keeper," who organizes dance performers and banquets. "Members of your clan ask you to become a faith-keeper, and the only choice you have is to say you are ready, or not yet," says Jemison. "I was only ready when I was 50" (Kandell, 2006). Jemison's work, according to one observer,

> draws upon the concept of *orenda*, the traditional Haudenosaunee (Iroquois Confederacy) belief that every living thing and every part of creation contains a spiritual force. Presenting a challenge to reductive and exclusionary art historical structures, Jemison synthesizes the dual traditions of academic and traditional Native American arts. (*Eight Modern*, 2007)

Jemison (whose media as an artist include acrylics, pen and ink, charcoal, and colored pencils) began drawing as a boy. Encouraged by his parents and art teachers, he attended the State University of New York at Buffalo to study art (1962–1967). He also studied art at the University of Siena, Italy, during 1964.

In addition to being an artist, Jemison has served as chair of the Haudenosaunee Standing Committee on Burial Rules and Regulations. He is also well known in Haudenosaunee country as an organizer of shows for other artists. One example of many such shows that Jemison has organized was "Where We Stand: Contemporary Haudenosaunee Artists," which showed August 15–December 21, 1997, at the New York State Historical Association Fenimore House Museum. This show featured a number of Haudenosaunee artists active in a wide array of forms, from painting, to basketweaving, silversmithing, prints, and sculpture.

Jemison and fellow Senecas erected a full-scale replica of a longhouse and opened it to the public at Ganondagan in 1998 in order to give people an idea of how their ancestors lived. The longhouse, about 65 feet long, 20 feet wide, and 25 feet high, has been equipped with four roof smoke holes. As described by Jonathan Kandell in *Smithsonian* magazine,

Elm bark covers outer and inner walls and the roof. The floor is made of pounded earth. Dozens of raised platform beds line the walls. An assortment of gourd bowls, baskets woven from wood strips, corn-husk mats, fur blankets, snowshoes and lacrosse sticks are stored on ledges reached by notched wooden ladders. A bark-skin canoe hangs from the ceiling. (Kandell, 2006)

Jemison is also widely known as a curator of Native American arts. Some of Jemison's curatorial projects include "Pan-American Exposition Centennial: Images of the American Indian" at the Burchfield-Penney Art Center in Buffalo, New York, and "Stan Hill: The Spirit Released/A Circle Complete" at the Fenimore Art Museum, Cooperstown, New York. As a writer, with Anna M. Schein he co-edited *The Treaty of Canandaigua 1794: 200 Years of Treaty Relations between the Iroquois Confederacy and the United States* (2000).

Jemison's work has been collected by many museums worldwide, including the Heard Museum, Phoenix, Arizona; the Institute of American Indian Arts Museum, Santa Fe, New Mexico; the Denver Art Museum, Denver, Colorado; the British Museum, London, United Kingdom; and the Museum der Weltkultern, Frankfurt, Germany.

See Also PART 2: CULTURAL FORMS: ARTS: Cultural Tourism/Spotlight: Culture Bearers; **FAMILY, EDUCATION, AND COMMUNITY:** Wampum; **SPIRITUALITY:** Grandfathers (*Hadowi*): False Faces; Handsome Lake (*Gaiwiiyo*), Code of

Further Reading

Crowe, Kenneth C. "Museums Work to Restore Tribal Heritage." *Albany Times Union*, December 10, 1995, A-3.

Eight Modern. 2007. http://www.eightmodern.net/artists/bio/4250. Accessed August 26, 2014.

Jemison, Peter, and Anna M. Schein, eds. *The Treaty of Canandaigua 1794: 200 Years of Treaty Relations between the Iroquois Confederacy and the United States.* Santa Fe: Clear Light, 2000.

Kandell, Jonathan. "Steeped in History: New York's Breathtaking Finger Lakes District Has Inspired American Notables from Mark Twain to Harriet Tubman." *Smithsonian*, September 2006. http://www.smithsonianmag.com/travel/fingerlake.html?c=y&page=2. Accessed August 26, 2014.

LEDGER ART

Stemming from pictorial historical "winter counts" of Native peoples on the Great Plains (often inscribed on buffalo and other hides), "ledger art" continued a tradition of visual storytelling into the reservation era when buffalo became scarce, but paper (often ledger books used by immigrating European Americans) became available. Today many of these have been collected by museums, including the Smithsonian, the University of Montana's Maureen and Mike Mansfield Library, the Milwaukee Public Museum, and the Oklahoma Historical Society, among others. Private collectors also have acquired some of them. Contemporary artists sometimes now use the ledger as a background as they depict modern reservation life.

History and Origins

Plains peoples, who had no written language, preserved histories visually for many centuries before contact with European Americans, by recording their lives and experiences through pictographs, petroglyphs, and painted buffalo hides. As early as the 1830s, a few Native peoples on the Plains began drawing on ledger books brought by white traders, using pens, crayons, pencils, fountain pens, and occasionally watercolors that the Indians had acquired in trade or battle. They often drew over ledger entries entered by a book's previous owner. The earliest examples of this work have been lost, but from the early 1870s, some have been preserved in museum and private collections, often depicting events such as courtship and war.

In 1875, members of several Plains tribes who had been arrested and held at Fort Sill, Oklahoma, were sent to Fort Marion in St. Augustine, Florida. Members of the Kiowa, Arapaho, Cheyenne, and Comanche peoples (plus one man who was Caddo) were being supervised by Captain Richard Henry Pratt who, four years later, would start a nationwide network of Indian boarding schools at Carlisle, Pennsylvania.

As part of his work to "rehabilitate" (and assimilate) his prisoners, Pratt provided the 71 prisoners with watercolors, colored pencils, and paper to describe their experiences. Between 20 and 30 of the prisoners produced drawings. In 1878, 62 members of this group who had survived prison in an unfamiliar humid climate were released. Forty of them returned to Oklahoma, but 22 enrolled as students at Hampton Normal and Agricultural Institute in Virginia. Soon, the idea of ledger art was spreading among many Plains peoples, including the Blackfeet, Lakotas, Crows, and several others. The next year, 11 were sent to the Carlisle School, again under Pratt's supervision. Two years later, they also returned to Oklahoma.

A survey of the earliest ledger art said:

> The exiles' drawings differed greatly from their traditional imagery. While the subject matter included reminiscences of a number of former life

activities, hunting scenes, for example, replaced the earlier, traditional focus on warfare. Additionally, the prisoners recorded with remarkable clarity their lives at Fort Marion and the sights they saw. All this imagery was executed with much closer attention to detail of costume and scenery than previously demonstrated in American Indian art. (Weaver, n.d.)

After about 1880, ledger art was practiced by only a few people. Most of the former prisoners who had produced it became engaged in other modes of survival. Some became well known. Okuhhatuh (Sundance), known by the name "Making Medicine" during incarceration, took the Anglo-American name David Pendleton Okerhater, became a deacon in the Episcopal Church, and was designated a saint. Ohettoit and Zotom (both Kiowas) put their artistic talents to work in traditional forms, such as ornamenting tipis. Howling Wolf (a Cheyenne) and Tichkematse (aka Squint Eyes, tribal affiliation unknown) continued to work as ledger artists. A Kiowa, Haungooah (Silver Horn), and his brother, Ohettoit, also continued to produce ledger art as they also decorated tipis. Silver Horn's work helped shape a revival of ledger art during the 1920s by James Auchiah and Stephen Mopope at the University of Oklahoma, two of a group that came to be known as the "Kiowa Five."

Regional Variations

By the 1880s, a few artists were creating ledger drawings depicting warrior life, ceremonies, peace councils, and novel sights, such as a Native man riding a horse with an umbrella (to protect himself from the sun, not rain). These were sold to government agents, missionaries, soldiers, and traders. Some of these drawings were created to preserve memories of prereservation life. By the early 20th century, tourists and anthropologists were buying some of the ledger pieces.

Some ledger books were seized. For example, the Milwaukee Public Museum in 1897 purchased a book of 105 ledger drawings by Cetanluta (Red Hawk), an Oglala Lakota, from H. H. Hayssen of Chuncula, Alaska, that had been "captured" from Red Hawk near Wounded Knee, South Dakota, on January 8, 1891, within two weeks of the massacre there in which between 150 (the Army's estimate) and 350 (the Lakotas' tally) Native people were killed. Red Hawk's drawings show horse capture and warfare, such as "Chasing Crow on Horseback, Shoots Him in the Head." The Lakotas and the Crows were long-time enemies to the point that the U.S. Army hired Crow scouts to track the Lakotas.

Variations in style suggest that several artists contributed to this one ledger book. The book itself contains references to a large number of people in Lakota, English, or both:

Zuyaterila (Tough Soldier)

Tasunke Witko (His Crazy Horse)

Cetan Wa miniyomini (?) (Whirlwind Hawk)

Matonajiu (Standing Bear)

Unklekiraska (White Magpie)

Matoniyaluta (Red Living Bear)

Cetaniyotake (Sitting Hawk)

Mato Wanapeya (Scares the Bear)

Running Deer

Little Shield

Cetanluta (Red Hawk)

Wakinyano ranko (Quick Thunder)

Wiyaluaofra Zan (?) (Shows the Feather)

Kangi Wanbli (Eagle Crow)

Ki Sunsui (?) (No Braid)

Wahacankaska (White Shield)

Cetan Wankatuyo (High Hawk)

Pte Wakannajiu (Holy Standing Buffalo)

Wakinyan Witko (Crazy Thunder)

Itkaminyanke

Mato Huka

Kagisui yanke ("The Ledger," 2014)

Contemporary Forms

Until its modern-day revival, ledger art was nearly exclusively a male avocation. By the late 1960s, however, women such as Kiowa Virginia Stroud and Dorothy Dunn played a major role. One of the leaders in today's revival of ledger art is Dolores Purdy. In addition to creating ledger art, she studies its history and lectures on the subject. She also uses a variety of backgrounds, from old ledgers to musical scores.

"Ledger art has taken off but 10 years ago, when I started doing it, no one had heard of it," Purdy said. As a member of the Santa Fe Indian Market's Standards Committee, she was amazed at how much ledger art was submitted in 2013. "Now everyone has heard of it and a lot of people have jumped on the bandwagon. Unfortunately not all of them know exactly what the beginning, or what the history of ledger art, is all about" (Murg, 2013).

Purdy learned about ledger art as she researched her Caddo family, one of whom had been imprisoned at Fort Marion in 1875. "I started flipping through the book and saw some of the art that was coming out of Fort Marion and I couldn't believe how sophisticated their work really was," Purdy said. "They could take three colors: black, yellow, and red, and draw an entire huge team with 16 people and 17 horses. I'm a trained watercolorist but from that point on I just moved into ledgers because I was enthralled with them, and it's kind of cool being related to one of those guys" (Murg, 2013).

An online archive of ledger books and other information may be found at *Indian Ledger Art-Resources and Information,* http://www.amerindianarts.us /indian_ledger_art.shtml.

See Also PART 2: CULTURAL FORMS: FAMILY, EDUCATION, AND COMMUNITY: Education: Acculturalization and Boarding Schools; Pan-Indianism; LANGUAGE AND LITERATURE: Graphic Novels

Further Reading

Donnelley, Robert G., and Candace S. Greene. *Transforming Images: The Art of Silver Horn and His Successors.* Chicago: David and Alfred Smart Museum of Art, University of Chicago, 2000.

Greene, Candace S. *Silver Horn: Master Illustrator of the Kiowas.* Norman: University of Oklahoma Press, 2001.

Harris, Moira F., and Wo-Haw. *Between Two Cultures: Kiowa Art from Fort Marion.* St. Paul: Pogo Press, 1989.

"The Ledger Art Collection." The Milwaukee Public Museum. 2014. http://www.mpm .edu/research-collections/anthropology/online-collections-research/ledger-art-collection. Accessed January 18, 2014.

Lovett, John R., and Donald L. DeWitt. *Guide to Native American Ledger Drawings and Pictographs in United States Museums, Libraries, and Archives.* Westport, CT: Greenwood Press, 1998.

Murg, Wilhelm. "This Is Not Your Great-Great-Great-Grandfather's Ledger Art." *Indian Country Today Media Network,* October 25, 2013. http://indiancountrytoday medianetwork.com/2013/10/25/not-your-great-great-great-grandfathers-ledger-art -151920. Accessed August 26, 2014.

Pearce, Richard. *Women and Ledger Art: Four Contemporary Native American Artists.* Tucson: University of Arizona Press, 2013.

Petersen, Karen Daniels. *Plains Indian Art from Fort Marion*. Norman: University of Oklahoma Press, 1971.

Rushing, W. Jackson. "The Legacy of Ledger Art in Twentieth Century Native American Art." In Janet Catherine Berlo, ed. *Plains Indian Drawings: 1865–1935*. New York: Harry N. Abrams, 1996, 56–62.

Weaver, Bobby D. "Ledger Book Art." Oklahoma Historical Society. http://digital .library.okstate.edu/encyclopedia/entries/l/le003.html. Accessed January 19, 2014.

LUNA, JAMES (1950–)

With a daring sense of conception and cultural irony, performance artist James Luna has shaken up the world of Native American art. Having been called "one of the most dangerous Indians alive," Luna replies: "At times the message can be potent. One of my subjects is with ethnic identity—how people perceive us and how we perceive ourselves. Not everybody can talk about that, so I guess that makes me a dangerous character" (Fletcher, 2008).

Luna's work challenges stereotypes about American Indian life, art, and museums with a strong sense of storytelling and emotion. Much of Luna's work is bicultural (tricultural, if one includes his Latino heritage), and he is comfortable with it: "I'm a man of two worlds [and] I do it with ease," he has said.

Luna was born in 1950 in Orange, California. His mother was Luiseño and his father Mexican. Luna graduated in 1976 with a BA in art from the University of California–Irvine at a time when that school's art faculty and students were known for their daring approaches to conceptual and performance art. In 1983, Luna earned a master's degree in counseling at San Diego State University. He has long worked as a counselor at Palomar College, San Marcos.

He took the job as a counselor for financial security unavailable to most artists, and also to give him a connection to people outside the world of art, which he sometimes finds rather removed from reality. In the middle 1980s, Luna went into semi-seclusion. In 1986, however, David Avalos, curator at San Diego's Centro de la Raza, and Philip Brookman realized the potential of Luna's work, providing financial support and a studio.

Luna began his artistic life as a painter. With painting, however, he felt confined, unable to express emotions. Painting also limited his ability to express transition or motion. Luna has said that he "stumbled" into performance art while working with instructors Bas Jan Ader (from the Netherlands) and Jim Turrell at UC–Irvine. Luna quickly expanded his range of expression to include the design, installation, and performance of work that may include several media, including video, to challenge cultural and historical assumptions about Native Americans.

While painting usually involves an audience in a passive way, Luna enjoys performance art because the audience takes part in the act of expression with him. "I involve the audience," Luna said in an interview with *Smithsonian Magazine*. "People give you control of their imagination. I can have them outraged one moment and crying the next. That's the power the audience gives you. It's knowing that and knowing how to use it effectively" (Fletcher, 2008).

Luna resents being pigeonholed as an ethnic artist, "to be called upon only when his ethnicity is timely—as during the Christopher Columbus anniversary in 1992." He would rather be known as "James Luna, artist. Period. James Luna, artist who happens to be an Indian." To the avalanche of engagements offered in 1992, he replied, "Call me in '93" (Durland, 1998).

While Luna does not want to be stereotyped solely as an "Indian artist," he draws freely on Native American traditions and cultural practices as a major component of his artistic persona. He reserves the right, however, to be sharply critical of all assumptions, including those expressed in Native American cultures. "Authenticity," for example, to Luna, becomes a stereotype of a kind, a set of expectations beyond which Native people are not allowed to grow and change. Confronted with an occasional critic who accuses Luna of exploiting his own cultural background, he replies that all artists draw from their own experiences.

While Luna says that his work is not political, some members of his audience disagree. His strikingly original design and execution cannot help but involve political context, no matter how it is categorized. Some of Luna's work is autobiographical, as when he illustrates his own battle with alcoholism as part of a culture-wide problem. Some of the work is cathartic, perhaps reflecting his academic preparation as a counselor.

One of Luna's favorite targets is faux (e.g., "plastic") medicine men. In *Capitalists?* he combined a "high-technology" peace pipe mounted on the chassis of a desk telephone, a portrait of himself in beads and fringe, and a poem parodying a shaman who said he was from a long line of Cherokee holy men who completed a session in a commercial sweat lodge by singing a Lakota song, who "gave you a Seminole medicine pouch and a Kiowa name" (Dubin, 2002, 53).

Luna parodies stereotypes, as with his *End of the Frail*, a modern take on James Earle Fraser's iconic turn-of-the-20th-century *End of the Trail*, which displays a bowed, exhausted Indian on a weary horse, his spear pointed earthward. The original was displayed on a huge scale at the 1915 Panama-Pacific Exposition in San Francisco. In his tableau variation on *End of the Trail*, "Luna mimics the same lifeless pose, but the pony has been replaced by a weathered sawhorse, and the spear by a bottle of liquor. Nobility has been replaced by pathos. The exhaustion is no longer that of effort but that of despair" (Durland, 1998).

In one performance, Luna asks members of the audience to take photographs with him as a "real live Indian." Reactions of the audience become part of the art, Luna believes. He takes risks, depending on an unscripted audience to take part, aiming to "create a conversation" that will leave people changed in ways that a more passive exhibition wouldn't. Sometimes the conversation takes directions ("shock and dismay, sadness, empathy, association") that surprise even the artist. Once again, Luna's experience as a counselor comes into play as he appears once in Native regalia, then in typical non-Indian street clothes:

> There was an Indian in a breechcloth with everybody going "Oh wow, there's an Indian." Then I came out in my street clothes and they said "Oh, there's a guy." But when I came out in my regalia, I knew that it would get that response from the audience. Everybody went for it. There was a big ooh and aah when I stepped up on that pedestal with my war dance outfit. They forgot about all the rest and really lined up to have their picture taken. This is the memento that they really wanted. Even people that were art savvy fell for it. (Fletcher, 2008)

Luna's work often parodies the display of Native "artifacts" in museums. Luna is an iconoclast who will introduce you to yourself. Perhaps his best-known performance is *The Artifact Piece*, introduced in 1987 at the San Diego Museum of Man. It features a glass case in which *he* is the artifactual "Indian," confronting stereotypes. In this work, *he* is the object, "the other." Luna filled the display case with sand and "artifacts," some of his favorite music and books, legal papers, and labels describing scars acquired during his life. According to Paul Smith,

> Few works of contemporary Indian art have been so perfectly conceived and executed. Outrageous and brilliant, *The Artifact Piece* rumbled across Indian Country in the late 1980s like a quiet earthquake, making fine work by other Native artists suddenly look obsolete and timid. . . . Luna brought danger into the equation, and in the new atmosphere, anything seemed possible. (2009, 95)

As an artist, Luna reserves the right to be inconsistent. Occasionally, having said that his work is specific to North America, Luna does take his show on the road—far afield. In 2005, at the invitation of the National Museum of the American Indian, he took part in the Venice Biennale. In Belo Horizonte, Brazil, in 2005, Luna's work appeared at the Hemispheric Institute.

Luna continues, as he has since 1975, to live and work on the La Jolla Indian Reservation, a Luiseño community near Mount Palomar, north of San Diego. Luna's work has been portrayed on film, including a segment of *Race Is the Place*, a Public Broadcasting Service television magazine. He has taught on the faculty of Palomar College and San Diego State University, and lectured at Harvard University and other colleges and universities. Luna received an award at the American Indian Film Festival for best live short performance, as well as a Dance Theater Workshop of New York Bessie Award and an Eiteljorg Fellowship for Native American Fine Art. Luna also collaborated with filmmaker Isaac Artenstein on *The History of the Luiseño People*.

Luna was given an honorary doctorate by the Institute of American Indian Arts in 2012. Saying he was grateful, Luna wasn't sure he deserved it:

> I don't do this art thing to get wealthy. I don't do it for just me and I don't do it for awards. But every so often someone out there thinks we are deserving of what we do. And what we can do just blows my socks offs [*sic*] because it feels great to be acknowledged and have someone say you've done something important. ("Institute," 2012)

See Also PART 1: OVERVIEW: Nations, Tribes, and Other Native Groups: California's Plethora of Native Peoples; **PART 2: CULTURAL FORMS: Arts:** Cultural Appropriation: Questions and Issues

Further Reading

Dubin, Margaret, ed. *The Dirt Is Red Here: Art and Poetry from Native California.* Berkeley, CA: Heyday Books, 2002.

Durland, Steven. "Call Me in '93: An Interview with James Luna." Reading Room. Community Arts Network. In Linda Frye Burnham and Steven Durland, eds. *The Citizen Artist: 20 Years of Art in the Public Arena: An Anthology from High Performance Magazine 1978–1998.* New York: Critical Press, 1998. http://www.communityarts.net/readingroom/archivefiles/2002/09/call_me_in_93_a.php. Accessed August 26, 2014.

Fletcher, Kenneth R. "James Luna Is Known for Pushing Boundaries in His Installations, Where He Engages Audiences by Making Himself Part of a Tableau." *Smithsonian Magazine*, April 2008. http://www.smithsonianmag.com/arts-culture/atm-qa-james-luna.html. Accessed August 26, 2014.

"Institute of American Indian Arts Celebrates 50 Years and Bestows Two Honorary Doctorates." *Indian Country Today Media Network*, May 9, 2012. http://indiancountrytodaymedianetwork.com/2012/05/09/institute-of-american-indian-arts-celebrates-50-years-and-bestows-two-honorary-doctorates-112020. Accessed August 26, 2014.

Inventing "the Indian": The West as America; Reinterpreting Images of the Frontier, 1820–1920. Washington, DC: Smithsonian Institution, 1991.

"James Luna." Native Networks: National Museum of the American Indian. 2004. http://www.nativenetworks.si.edu/eng/rose/luna_j.htm. Accessed August 26, 2014.

Luna, James. *Encuentro: Invasion of the Americas and the Making of the Mestizo,* a catalog for a show of the same name presented at SPARC (Social and Public Art Resource Center), Los Angeles, 1991.

McHugh, Kathleen. "Profane Illuminations: History and Collaboration in James Luna and Isaac Artenstein's *The History of the Luiseño People.*" *Biography* 31, no. 3 (Summer, 2008): 429–460.

Nottage, James H., ed. *Diversity and Dialogue.* Seattle: University of Washington Press, 2008.

Smith, Paul Chaat. *Everything You Know About Indians Is Wrong.* Minneapolis: University of Minnesota Press, 2009.

"Urban (Almost) Rituals." Soundings Theatre, Te Papa, Wellington, Massey University College, New Zealand. May 14, 2009. http://www.onedaysculpture.org.nz/ODS_artist detail.php?idartist=12. Accessed August 26, 2014.

MOCCASINS

History and Origins

The word "moccasin" was adapted into English by the English founders of the Jamestown colony, from the Powhatan *mockasin*, meaning "shoe." Very quickly, wherever English was spoken, Native-stitched, tanned-hide footgear came to be called by that name. The word *Mekesen* first entered French at about the same time, although the phrase *souliers sauvages* (Indian shoes) was more common. By about 1650, French immigrants in Quebec were making their own moccasins.

Moccasins usually were decorated in specific patterns that varied between specific nations or tribes, so a person's origins could be determined by their design and ornamentation. Pieces of cloth, buttons, braids, quills, and dyes were used. Different cuts of moccasins also left specific tracks, so a scout who knew who was whom could determine "the T-shaped seam at the toe and heel of the northern Athapascan, the hard flat soles of the Plains Indian; the soft rounded soles of the Woodland Indian; or the seam along the side from the great toe to the heel of the Nez Perce" (Grant, 1989, 207).

Nearly as soon as they had a name for Indian footwear, non-Natives began wearing moccasins in lieu of more cumbersome European shoes and boots that were ill-adapted to frontier styles of life with long treks through forests. Priests, soldiers, fur traders, and farmers, as well as other immigrants of every type began adopting moccasins so widely that non-Indian manufacturing of them became established in the frontier town of Detroit in the middle of the 18th century. "The footwear's transition among non-Native wearers from cultural borrowing to homecraft to manufactured commodity reveals not only the considerable influences [but also] reveals the commercial sector's considerable skill in employing them," wrote Catherine Cangany in *William and Mary Quarterly* (2012, 266–267). As Detroit's population grew, so did the non-Indian moccasin market.

Advertisement for "Comfy Moccasin" by the Daniel Green Felt Shoe Company in New York, 1906. (Jay Paull/Getty Images)

Soon thereafter, moccasins became fashionable along the Eastern Seaboard and even in some parts of Europe, so the small-scale manufacturers in Detroit were eclipsed by larger shops closer to the center of sales. Before the American Revolution, Joseph Doddridge, an Anglican missionary, observed German immigrant farmers working their lands in moccasins and wrote that they were better than shoes.

Commercial manufacture could not duplicate the comfort and durability of hand-crafted "mocs" made by Native women with many generations of practice, so these were highly prized. The best moccasins were made of deer or elk skin, stretched on frames of sapling wood and made pliable over several days of tanning by women using cooking fires, soaking the skins in a solution of boiling deer brains, then oiling them. Since the tanning process made the skins porous as well as supple, the skins were coated in bear grease or fish oil as waterproofing.

Moccasins appealed not only to farmers but also to other people who did much of their work outdoors, such as soldiers, many of whom came to prefer them to regulation footwear, even against the orders of their superiors. In 1776, one soldier recommended "a kind of shoe from dressed leather, made without heels and straps and which, when new, does not look so very badly. In the winter we will have to try this shoe; for they tell us that our feet will freeze in our ordinary boots" (Cangany, 2012, 284). Hybrids came into use in both English and French colonies. One French adaptation had the shape of a boot.

Cangany described the manufacture of moccasins in Detroit as an exercise in transcultural adaptation:

> The tannery laborers, likely a mix of natives and non-Natives, cured Indian and white-supplied skins in European-style chemical tanning vats. They cut the skins with European scissors to fit native patterns, often supplementing the simple forms with European tongue pieces and soles. They then stitched the leather pieces with European needles and thread, and sent the hybrid moccasins to merchants' shops for retail to local consumers. In short, the process of fabrication depended on both Native knowledge and technique and European manufacturing methods and production structures for its success. (2012, 293)

Due to its central location vis-à-vis the waterways connected to the Great Lakes, Detroit moccasins spread quickly. By the 1780s, Detroit's moccasins had reached the East Coast. Newspapers advertised them in Massachusetts, and something of a fashion boomlet began. The footwear became a badge of "American" identity, as well as a tourist souvenir for the growing number of travelers drawn westward by the opening of the Erie Canal in 1825.

See Also PART 2: CULTURAL FORMS: ARTS: Clothing

Further Reading

Cangany, Catherine. "Fashioning Moccasins: Detroit, the Manufacturing Frontier, and the Empire of Consumption, 1701–1835." *William and Mary Quarterly* 3rd Ser. 69, no. 2 (April, 2012): 265–304.

Casse, Catherine. "The Iroquois Moccasin: Its Utilitarian and Symbolic Functions." *Dress* 10 (1984): 12–24.

Grant, Bruce. *Concise Encyclopedia of the American Indian.* New York: Wings Books, 1989.

NAVAJO WEAVING

History and Origins

While Anglo-American history often maintains that the Navajos learned weaving from Spanish immigrants (or from the Pueblos, who also are said to have learned from the Spanish), the weavers maintain that the entire process, from herding and shearing sheep to looming a rug or blanket, has its origins in antiquity. It is said that Spider Woman—half human, half spider—taught weaving to an outcast Kisani woman who taught not only her own people but the Diné (Navajos) as well. Whatever its origins, Navajo weaving has become a world-renowned art and expression of culture that has been sought by traders for more than 150 years. Hand-loomed Navajo rugs and textiles are among the best quality in the world.

Before they became collectors' items, Navajo textiles were used mainly by people on the reservation in their everyday lives, as saddle blankets, dresses, robes, cloaks, and shirts, as well as belts and sashes. By the year 1900, Navajo textiles were well known as commercial manufactures for export.

Navajo rugs and blankets are instantly recognizable for their distinctive geometric patterns. The patterns are decorative and serve no ceremonial role in Navajo culture. Before roughly 1850, most Navajo weaving utilized shades of brown, indigo (a trade dye), and white, but after that red, green, black, yellow, purple, and gray were added, colors that were imported via the railroads. Artists experimented with color combinations with the rise of the commercial market. New names for various colors, such as "Eyedazzler," came into use as well.

A Cultural History of Navajo Weaving

The origins of Navajo weaving are unclear. In addition to Navajos' own accounts that date to antiquity, some historians have traced them to Pueblo influences between 1300 and 1500 CE. Others believe that Navajos did not weave until the Spanish invasion after 1600 CE. Possibly, all of these factors played a role in shaping the Navajos' weaving culture. Navajos first used cotton acquired through trade, but after the Spanish invasion, wool became dominant. Pueblo-Navajo cultural communication continued after the arrival of the Spanish. After the Pueblo revolt (1680), many Pueblos sought refuge from Spanish repression with the Navajos.

By the year 1700, Spanish archival records describe the Navajos as excellent weavers. In 1804, a group of Navajos were killed at Massacre Cave in the Canyon de Chelly in present-day Arizona. They left behind a cache of fine textiles, but local Navajos did not enter the cave out of respect for the dead. About 100 years after the massacre, Sam Day, a trader, ignored the taboo and retrieved the textiles, then sold them to several museums. Some commercial sales of Navajo weaving had expanded during the 19th century, especially after the Santa Fe Trail opened in 1822.

The Navajo churro sheep that are the main source of wool for weavers were originally acquired from Spanish explorers late in the 17th century. The churro is adapted to the dry climate of Navajo country and produces a hand-spun long-staple wool, which was used until the 1860s, when the U.S. government seized Navajo livestock as part of a relocation at Bosque Redondo. In 1869, however, a peace treaty allowed the return of sheep and goats. Some Navajo rugs also were woven from three-ply, silky Saxony yarns. With the arrival of railroads, other yarns were imported from the eastern United States.

A major market opened during the late 1880s with the arrival of railroads. Wool production more than doubled in the area between 1890 and 1910, as textile production escalated more than 800 percent. (The difference was purchased yarn.) By 1894, Navajo textiles were being advertised in a catalog by C. N. Cotton. The manufacture of rugs and textiles by the early 20th century became a major part of the Navajos' cash economy.

Weaving is not a singular art; people who practice it sometimes herd their own sheep and shear them, picking out burrs and other contaminants, then soaking the wool in boiling water. The now-softened wool is then "carded"—straightened by pulling strands through spikes on planks of wood ("cards"). Only then is wool ready to be spun on a loom. Dyes are also prepared with care for colors, such as yellow, that are believed to promote harmony. Yellow also symbolizes female attributes and growth (the pollen of corn is yellow). Purple is usually avoided because mythology associates it with evil spirits.

Beauty as a Quest for Harmony

Spider Man is said to have created the first loom, which "contains all the important elements of creation. . . . The warp sticks were made of sun-rays (*sha bitlol*), the head stick of rock crystal (*tsa ghadindini*); the cord stick of sheet lightning (*atsolugghal*), the batten stick of sun halo (*oljekinaastle*), and the comb of white shell (*yolgat*)" (Brown, 2001, 77).

Beauty in a rug or blanket created on the loom is said to radiate out of the weaver in a quest for harmony (*hózhó*) that stems from antiquity, a vision that inspired First Man and First Woman to come into the world in search of it. The weaver expresses the desires of creation through the designs of the rug or blanket, calling upon the traditions of Spider Woman (who taught the art) and Spider Man (who made the first loom).

While families are still important conduits for Navajo weaving skills, today many weavers learn them in community colleges as well. In recent years, Navajo weavers' sales have fallen due to non-Indian imitations from outside the United States. A handwoven rug of moderate size averaged $800 in 2013.

See Also PART 2: CULTURAL FORMS: Arts: American Indian Arts and Crafts Fairs/Spotlight: Indian Arts and Crafts Act (1990)

Further Reading

Blomberg, Nancy J. *Navajo Textiles: The William Randolph Hearst Collection.* Tucson: University of Arizona Press, 1988.

Brown, Joseph Epes, with Emily Cousins. *Teaching Spirits: Understanding Native American Religious Traditions.* New York: Oxford University Press, 2001.

Haberland, Wolfgang. "Aesthetics in Native American Art." In Edwin L. Wade, ed. *The Arts of the North American Indian: Native Traditions in Evolution.* New York: Philbrook Art Center, 1986, 107–132.

Jacka, Lois Essary. *Beyond Tradition: Contemporary Indian Art and Its Evolution.* Flagstaff, AZ: Northland, 1991.

Maurer, Evan M. "Determining Quality in Native American Art." In Edwin L. Wade, ed. *The Arts of the North American Indian: Native Traditions in Evolution.* New York: Philbrook Art Center, 1986, 143–156.

M'Closkey, Cathy. "Towards an Understanding of Navajo Aesthetics." http://www.library.utoronto.ca/see/SEED/Vol4-1/M%27Closkey.htm. Accessed August 26, 2014.

Rodee, Marian E. *Old Navajo Rugs: Their Development from 1900 to 1940.* Albuquerque: University of New Mexico Press, 1983.

Salkeld, Stefani. *Southwest Weaving: A Continuum.* San Diego, CA: San Diego Museum of Man, 1996.

POTTERY

History and Origins

Remains of pottery, a fired ceramic made of clay, are often used to date many Native American cultures. Shards have traced the cultures that produced them as far back as 7,500 years in South America and 4,000 to 5,000 years in parts of the present-day United States. Similarities in pottery also have been used to trace trading networks, and as an indication that a culture adopted agriculture during a certain period of time. Pottery has many uses: to store and serve food, to carry human remains, as part of smoking pipes, musical instruments, toys, masks, ceremonial icons, and purely as decorative objects.

Pottery usually developed in tandem with agriculture to store water, aid in cooking, and to preserve seeds for subsequent seasons. The art of cooking developed along with pottery as various Native cultures became known for their distinct styles of decoration. Women, who often tended the fields (and stored what they produced) as men hunted, usually became the major creators of pottery. Many early pots were considered utilitarian objects; distinct artistic styles (and the idea of pottery as an expression of art for its own sake) came later.

Regional Variations

Native American pottery has been created in a dizzying array of styles, each distinct, including many works of exquisite beauty, ancient and modern. Pottery has been created by hundreds of well-known artists; the scholarly landscape is so complex that it has "schools," such as the San Ildefonso school of Maria Montoya Martinez (1887–July 20, 1980) (see Spotlight).

The art of pottery in all regions has some things in common. Clay must be gathered before pots can be formed and fired. Clay is then soaked in buckets to remove small twigs, pebbles, and other foreign material. The clays must be of proper consistency and are often gathered according to traditional cultural protocols. Many Native peoples have traditional areas to gather clay, and they recite prayers or make offerings to Mother Earth. Clays differ from region to region. In the Picuris and Taos pueblos, for example, clays flecked with mica provide sparkle to finished pots. Pueblos in the northern Rio Grande work ground volcanic sand into their clay. The Hopis also are careful to gather clay with the correct admixture of sand that experience tells them will make the best pots.

"Pueblo," from the Spanish, may refer to groups of houses, often assembled of adobe with support beams of lodgepole pine. The word also may refer to the people who live in the houses and their culture. Some Pueblo potters remove the impurities after the clay has been pulverized into powder, then run it through a sieve and mix it with water to make a malleable, paste-like substance that is then kneaded to remove air pockets that can cause explosions when fired. Clay may be rolled into long, thin "coils" that are formed into patterns to make a finished pot. With practice, a potter can use coiling to provide internal integrity (strength) to the finished pot. Native American potters fashioned their work by hand; potter's wheels were not used before sustained contact with Europeans.

Pigments were often mixed in a liquid suspension and applied to pots in several colors. Pots also can be designed by incision. Pots often are polished to shine with stones or other smooth, hard surfaces. In addition to burnishing with stones, Michael Simpson, author of *Making Native American Pottery*, has observed that one ancient Catawba potter used mastodon teeth. Mississippian Mound Builders created coiled pottery. One observer noted: "Their human and animal effigy pots are considered some of the finest North American Indian pottery of that period." As the Mound Builders created their first pots, the Anasazi in the U.S. Southwest fired "simpler black on white ceramics decorated with geometric patterns, and elaborated gray cooking pots" (*Coyote's Game*).

Precontact pottery usually was fired in pits or the open air. Kilns later were adopted from Europe. To fire pottery without kilns, some tribes along the U.S. southeast coast dug fire pits and lined them with materials that deflect heat, including sand, flat rocks, and ashes. The Cherokees fire pots in three- to four-foot-high mounds with bottom holes that aid air circulation, "cooking" the pots for several days, producing pottery that is black and very hard. Potters in many Pueblos build grates set off the ground, high enough to build a fire below with kindling or, if wood is scarce, animal dung. A flash of heat produced by any firing process hardens the pot and enhances its colors.

Clay pottery has been part of Pueblo culture for several thousand years, and distinctive styles (such as blackware pottery—see Spotlight biography of Maria Martinez) have evolved that can be identified with each pueblo. The backgrounds of pots were smoothed for designs and painted using materials made from finely ground metallic rocks and boiled plants with brushes shaped from the chewed ends of twigs or yucca fronds. Pots then hardened on an open bonfire that reached 1,300 degrees Fahrenheit. Those same methods are often used today.

Pueblo pottery follows Anasazi precedents, some of which have been unearthed by archaeologists, and are white or gray with geometric designs in black. Modern potters often combine traditional patterns with their own to create unique styles.

Each pueblo has its own styles. Taos and Picuris, pueblos in very northernmost New Mexico, for example, create undecorated pottery long used for storage and cooking. Classic Zuni pottery often uses images of deer, owls, frogs and dragonflies, rainbirds and feathers, as well as other animals, such as buffalo. Hopi orange clay is fired with colors that range from white to light red depending on the heat. Traditional Hopi pottery patterns, with typical decorations of splatters and lines made with plant- and mineral-based paints, come from the abandoned pueblo of Sikyatki. Various Hopi potters have evolved many styles on older patterns.

With the arrival of the railroad, trade in Pueblo pottery increased. Shortly after the turn of the century, potters were signing their works as they became collectors' items. Edgar Lee Hewett, acting on behalf of the Museum of New Mexico, the Heye Foundation in New York, and the Smithsonian Institution, sought the best work, bringing it to national and international attention. Nampeyo of Hano, Maria Martinez, and others became famous (see Spotlights).

Navajos created pottery mainly for household and ceremonial use until the advent of the railroads. Navajos' traditional arts have emphasized silverwork, weaving, jewelry painting, and basketry more often than pottery. At the same time, Anglo-American-imported kitchenware made of metal and plastic was replacing Navajo ware in everyday use. When they have taken up pottery, Navajo women often mix several types of clay. They do not recycle old pot shards into new clay, believing that old pots belong to their ancestors and should not be disturbed. The Navajos have a general taboo against touching anything owned by the deceased, including pottery.

Navajo pottery has its own style, "fabricated in the coil and pinch manner of old societies, [and the] bonfire. . . . Before the pot had cooled, hot melted pitch from piñon trees was poured or rubbed in a thin coating over the vessel, inside and out. This unusual technique distinguished the look and aroma of Navajo pottery" (Peterson, 1998). Navajo pottery is nearly waterproof, however, after it has been coated with piñon pine pitch, fired, and polished.

With the rise of the tourist and museum trade in pottery, Navajo work (traditionally unpainted in shades of brown and black) was often rejected by traders as "mud pots," lacking in design flourishes. A few Navajo artists (one example was Rose Williams) went against this trend, breaking into museum markets with two- to three-foot-tall cylindrical jars during the 1950s.

Many Navajo designs (such as those used in healers' sand paintings) are culturally circumscribed from commercial use and sale, which limits the creative range of potters. The *Yei bichai* (mythical Holy People) are used on pots by Lorraine Williams, who accommodates their sacred nature by leaving part of the design unfinished to allow the *Yei* spirit to escape.

Contemporary Forms

Pottery is a living art among Native peoples today. The creation and sale of many styles in many regions has been thriving. Traditions are preserved, but often combined with modern methods and artistic mastery. Dances, legends, and songs come alive in the potter's art and are communicated between generations. "The Indian philosophy is built into each pot," remarked Susan Peterson. "It determines the composition, the form, and the decoration. Today's continuation of the pottery tradition ensures that Indian aesthetics are still flourishing" (1998).

The roughly 20 pueblos in Arizona and New Mexico continue to be the epicenter of Native American pottery making, although distinctive styles of pottery exist in many areas. In regions where proper clay is not available, styles evolved with baskets or (on the north Pacific Coast) bentwood boxes of extraordinary beauty. Today's Pueblo potters' work is fluid, unconstrained by taboos, and sometimes even humorous. One may cross paths with a cowboy or Santa Claus on a pot that is otherwise traditional in form and function. Storyteller figurines that proved to be very popular were introduced in 1964 by Cochiti potter Helen Cordero, featuring grandfathers telling stories to children. Some pottery styles are introduced by accident. Horsehair pottery, for example, is said to have been invented by a Pueblo potter whose hair brushed against a hot pot being removed from a kiln, whereupon it stuck and singed. The same effect was later reproduced with a horse's tail. The idea has since spread to several other Native peoples.

The creation of pottery is often a family enterprise (and one that is passed down over many generations) in which women usually take the lead. While collectors often look for meanings in symbols on pottery, the artists sometimes discuss such things with reluctance. Symbols may be mainly embellishment or reflect sacred themes, as well as natural scenes (plants, animals, humans in their daily lives, the sun and moon).

A trading market has flourished along with the growth of trading posts and galleries throughout the U.S. Southwest. Among the Pueblo (and elsewhere to a lesser degree) some potters have opened their own galleries. The Santa Fe Indian Market on the third weekend of every August has become an important meeting ground for artists and collectors of pottery. Many lesser-known art fairs also offer similar sales and networking opportunities. Museums have expanded their collections as well.

See Also PART 1: OVERVIEW: NATIONS, TRIBES, AND OTHER NATIVE GROUPS: Pueblo Cultural Context; **PART 2: CULTURAL FORMS: ARTS:** American Indian Arts and Crafts Fairs/Spotlight: Indian Arts and Crafts Act (1990); Pottery/Spotlight Biography I: Martinez, Maria Montoya and Spotlight Biography II: Nampeyo; **FAMILY, EDUCATION, AND COMMUNITY:** Wedding Customs; **MEDIA, POPULAR CULTURE, SPORTS, AND GAMING:** Museums: National Museum of the American Indian (NMAI); **TRANSPORTATION AND HOUSING:** Pueblo Architecture

Further Reading

Cooper, Emmanuel. *Ten Thousand Years of Pottery*. Philadelphia: University of Pennsylvania Press, 2000.

Coyote's Game. 2014. http://www.coyotesgame.com/napotinfo.html. Accessed August 26, 2014.

Gibson, Jon L., and Phillip J. Carr, eds. *Signs of Power: The Rise of Cultural Complexity in the Southeast*. Tuscaloosa: The University of Alabama Press, 2004.

Peterson, Susan. "Pottery by Native American Women: The Legacy of Generations: The Avant-Garde. Women Artists of the American West." 1998. http://www.cla.purdue.edu/WAAW/peterson/petersonessay2.html. Accessed August 26, 2014.

Simpson. Michael. *Making Native American Pottery*. Happy Camp, CA: Naturegraph, 1991.

Trimble, Stephan. *Talking with the Clay: The Art of Pueblo Pottery*. Santa Fe: SAR Press, 2007.

Spotlight

MARTINEZ, MARIA MONTOYA (1887–1980)

From her home in the San Ildefonso Pueblo, 20 miles northwest of Santa Fe, Maria Montoya Martinez (who was born Maria Antonia Montoya) earned an international reputation for her pottery. Maria, her husband Julian, and other members of their family studied traditional styles of Pueblo pottery and worked them into modern forms. Maria and members of her family revived the older forms of Pueblo pottery and made them a high art. Blackware thus became more than a kitchen implement; it became museum-quality art.

Martinez received honorary degrees, several citations and medals from governments and institutions, and invitations to the White House from four presidents. The San Ildefonso people had been making pottery for 1,000 years by the time Martinez took up the work, but she elevated the art and shared her knowledge with other artists. She was, according to Michael Ettema, writing in *Western Art Collector* (2008), "one of the most famous craft artists in the world." Martinez was both a traditionalist and an innovator. "And most importantly," wrote Ettema, "through her high standards and generous sharing of techniques, Maria revived the art of pottery-making among her people, reconnecting them to their ancestral form of artistic expression and traditional Pueblo way of life."

As a child, Martinez learned traditional Pueblo pottery styles and skills from her aunt Nicolasa Montoya at a time when Spanish tinware and Anglo-American enamelware were said to have been making traditional Native pottery obsolete. By 1904, at age 17, newly engaged to Julian Pocano Martinez, Martinez already was notable enough to earn an invitation to the St. Louis World's Fair. The couple boarded a train to St. Louis hours after they had been married.

The blackware created by Martinez and her family evolved from remains of jet-black, polished pottery found in 1907 and 1908 during an excavation headed by Edgar Lee Hewett, professor of archaeology and director of Santa Fe's Laboratory of Anthropology (Peterson, 1977, 89). Julian worked on Hewett's excavation. Maria, visiting the excavation, became excited at its artistic implications. The blackware style could be traced to about 1600 but had been subsequently forgotten until it was revived by Martinez after she had observed the work of the matriarch Margaret Tafoya at Santa Clara Pueblo. Martinez worked on the technique until she developed the glossy black surface that became her family's trademark style. Afraid that she could not recreate the traditional style, Martinez at first hid her pots, but with practice that led to refinement of her techniques, they soon came into demand from collectors. During the next few years, refining their blackware work, Maria and Julian became recognized as among the best potters in the Southwest.

Julian assisted Maria, also enduring many trials and errors, as he specialized in decorating the pots that she had created. In 1918, he finished their first decorated black pot. Julian studied ancient Pueblo myths and made them part of the pottery designs. His most important contributions were his artistic and technical skills as well as his standout use of color.

By 1921, wrote Ettema (2008),

> the black-on-black process was widely recognized as the greatest innovation in Pueblo pottery in generations. Drawn irresistibly by its subtlety and elegance, non-Indian collectors flocked around Maria to buy every piece of black-on-black pottery she could make. The Museum of New Mexico collected their first of many examples as early as 1920, and Maria's work consistently took top prizes at the Santa Fe Indian Market, which started in 1922. By the early 1930s, Maria's annual income placed her family solidly in the financial middle class, and her work had become famous around the world.

Their success elevated the status of Pueblo pottery generally.

Creation of blackware pottery requires six distinct steps. According to Susan Peterson in *The Living Tradition of Maria Martinez*, these steps include (1) finding and gathering the clay; (2) forming a pot; (3) scraping and sanding the pot to make it smooth; (4) applying the iron-bearing slip and working it to a high, smooth sheen; (5) decorating the pot with another slip; and (6) firing the pot.

The Martinez family shared its techniques with other potters freely. "We want everybody to get something, so we tell others how to make the pottery," Maria said in 1934 (Ettema, 2008). Julian died in 1943, and Adam, her oldest son, and his wife, Santana, began to take his role as Maria's artistic partner. Later, around 1950, Maria's third son, Popovi Da, also became involved in decorating pots. By 1956, he was her major partner. The collaboration between Maria and Popovi produced some of the best pots of her long career. Maria died on July 20, 1980.

Further Reading

Bunzel, Ruth L. *The Pueblo Potter*. New York: Columbia University Press, 1972.

Ettema, Michael. "Maria Martinez, Legendary Potter of San Ildefonso Pueblo." *Western Art Collector,* September 2008. http://www.medicinemangallery.com/Maria-Martinez -article.lasso. Accessed August 26, 2014.

Frank, Larry, and Francis H. Harlow. *Historical Pottery of the Pueblo Indians 1600– 1880*. Boston: New York Graphic Society, 1974.

Hyde, Hazel. *Maria Making Pottery*. Albuquerque: Starline, 1973.

Peterson, Susan. *The Living Tradition of Maria Martinez*. New York: Kodansha International, 1977.

Spotlight

NAMPEYO (CA. 1859–1942)

Born in Hano, Arizona, about 1859, Nampeyo (Snake Girl; Tcu-mana, Nam-payu, Nampayo) was an internationally notable Hopi-Tewa potter. Her father was Qotsvena, of the Snake Clan, and her mother was Qotcakao, of the To-bacco Clan. As a young girl, she watched her grandmother make the large *ollas* (Spanish for water pots) and other vessels used in traditional Hopi vil-lage life. Her village, Hano, was adjacent to Walpi on First Mesa and was set up by Tewa people fleeing Spanish oppression in the Rio Grande val-ley after Pope's Rebellion. Although the Tewas intermarried with the Hopis, they retained much of their language and distinctive ceremonies into the 19th century.

Contemporary accounts describe Nampeyo as a stunning young woman. In 1879, she married her first husband, Kwivioya, who left her soon afterward because he believed that he could not keep other men away from her. In 1881, Nampeyo married a second and final time to Lesou from the neighboring village of Walpi.

About 1892, she began to revive the designs and forms present in ancient Hopi pottery because she thought that they were superior to contemporary styles. Initially, other Hopi artists scorned Nampeyo's work, but when they saw that her pottery sold at high prices, they began to copy her designs and techniques. When the archaeologist Jesse Walter Fewkes employed her hus-band in excavations at Sikyatki (an early Pueblo ruin) in 1895, old pottery shards unearthed there provided her with a treasure trove of ancient designs. Nampeyo also visited other archaeological sites at nearby Awatovi, Payupki, and Tsukuvi to expand her knowledge of ancient styles. Using bits of broken ancient pottery, she created her own motifs rooted in ancient Hopi forms. As Nampeyo's pottery improved, it took on a fluid, bold style that is still distinctive of her work.

By the end of the 19th century, Nampeyo had become a prominent Indian artist. In 1898 and 1910, she journeyed to Chicago to promote her work. In 1904 and 1907, she was employed by the Fred Harvey hotel company at its Grand Canyon lodge. Her partnership with Fred Harvey made Nampeyo a fig-ure of international renown. The Smithsonian Institution also began to collect her work.

Through Nampeyo's efforts, Hopi pottery was elevated to a commercially viable art form. When Nampeyo began her work, few Hopi women still pro-duced pots, but she single-handedly revived the craft and enhanced its aesthet-ics. By the 1930s, Nampeyo began to go blind and she could no longer create the remarkably precise, fine, and fluid decorations that became her hallmark. Her husband helped to create Nampeyo's pottery during her declining years, until he died in 1932. Her four daughters (Annie, Cecilia, Fannie, and Nellie) were also renowned potters in their own right. Nampeyo died at her home on July 20, 1942.

Further Reading

Bowman, John S., ed. *The Cambridge Dictionary of American Biography*. Cambridge: Cambridge University Press, 1995.

Champagne, Duane, ed. *The Native North American Almanac*. Detroit: Gale Research, 1994.

Garraty, John A., and Mark C. Carnes, eds. *American National Biography*. Vol. 16. New York: Oxford University Press, 1999.

Heller, Jules, and Nancy G. Heller. *North American Women Artists of the Twentieth Century—A Biographical Dictionary*. New York: Garland, 1995.

Jones, Deborah. *Women in World History*. Vol. 11. Waterford, CT: Yorkin, 1999.

Malinowski, Sharon. *Notable Native Americans*. Detroit: Gale Research, 1995.

ROCK ART

Rock art had several purposes, among them recording events in the histories of tribes and bands, displaying ceremonial icons, or providing directions to favored hunting areas. The literature on rock art is immense. An entire academic field has been devoted to its study, and a professional association (the American Rock Art Research Association [ARARA], http://www.arara.org) has collected considerable bibliographical resources.

History and Origins

The greatest concentration of Native American Indian rock art is located in the southwestern United States. Eastern Utah alone has more than 1,000 known rock art sites. New Mexico and Texas also contain a wealth of sites. Many other sites probably have not been identified. Sites have been found dated from about 10,000 BCE. In addition to cave walls, rock art may be found on rocks facing rivers or streams, as well as on cliff faces and ledges.

Scholars have classified Native American rock art in two categories: petroglyphs (incised, ground, pecked, scratched, or abraided) and pictographs (drawings or paintings using mineral pigments or drawings in one or more colors using dyes and mineral pigments). Many sites were executed using both methods. Many now display only petroglyph aspects because the paints and dyes have weathered. Context sometimes yields dating clues; for example, a horse indicates rock art created after 1540 CE, when the Spanish introduced them. Bows and arrows were used after about 500 CE.

Regional Variations

Native American Indian rock art can be found in many areas with exposed surfaces, but it is concentrated in the southwestern United States. ARARA's bibliography classification of studies shows how broadly rock art has diffused. It contains headings for North American surveys and general works on rock art, as well as more specialized studies on rock art in the Caribbean, Mesoamerica, the eastern United States, Central America, several parts of Mexico, California, Nevada, Utah, the Four Corners area, the Colorado Plateau, Arizona, New Mexico, Texas, the Plains, southern Plains and Midwest, and Canada's Pacific Coast.

Styles vary by location, reflecting different cultures. Individual pieces may be as small as an inch across or as large as 15 to 20 feet. Some Chumash also created portable painted rocks. Pigments that have withstood the elements for several centuries were made from pulverized rocks mixed with animal fat, most often red and black, but also orange, yellow, white, and brown, or in combination, depicting human figures (or their feet and hands), and several animals (such as buffalo, snakes, deer, birds, and mountain lions), framed by trees, sun symbols, and other natural motifs. Sometimes European American figures appear. Some symbols are spiritual or shamanistic.

Many rock art sites seem to have been completed within relatively short periods of time. Only a few evoke a longer-term evolution of a consistent style. One, according to a summary of Texas rock art, is

> at the junction of the Pecos River with the Rio Grande, and the Devils River with the Rio Grande in Val Verde County, the collection of rock art

Anasazi petroglyph, Mesa Verde National Park, Colorado. (Frank Bach/ Dreamstime)

known as the lower Pecos River style suggests an indigenous effort. The collection of paintings shows a beginning and development, a slow refining in style, and an eventual dying out—all in a geographically limited area that was seemingly isolated from outside artistic influences. Evidences of human habitation in the area date back perhaps 10,000 years. ("Indian Rock Art")

Elsewhere across Texas, except for a few sites influenced by older Puebloa cultures, rock art seems not to be consistent in style or evolution.

Chumash rock art in present-day Southern California (in the vicinity of present-day Santa Barbara, Ventura, and San Luis Obispo) was painted on cliffs and mountainsides, with new work completed as late as the 18th century. Some Chumash rock art was created by shamans on vision quests. Cliffs, caves, and bodies of water were believed to be portals to a sacred realm. Chumash artists created animals, humans, and celestial bodies, as well as images that may have spiritual meaning but appear ambiguous to the uninformed eye. Many present-day Chumash have been reluctant to talk about the symbols with archaeologists. One researcher, Alfred Kroeber, speculated in 1925:

> The cave paintings of [Southern California] . . . represent a particular art, or local style or cult. This can be connected, in all probability, with the technological art of the Chumash. [An] association with . . . religion is also to be considered, although nothing positive is known in the matter. Many of the pictures may have been made by shamans; and it is quite possible that medicine men were not connected with the making of any. (quoted in Grant, 1965, 80)

Contemporary Forms

Some rock art has been vandalized and weathered by nature, and other sites have been submerged under water due to construction of reservoirs, but a surprisingly large number of sites remain as tourist attractions. In the 1990s, rock art benefited from an emphasis on conservation and public education. Several state and national parks have aided in the preservation of rock art as well.

A typical tourist site is Grapevine Canyon in the Lake Mead National Recreation Area, which affords easy access to petroglyphs a quarter-mile from a parking area that were created when Yuman-speaking peoples chipped away the dark surface of cliffs to expose lighter rock, depicting figures of lizards and bighorn sheep. These designs range from 150 to more than 800 years of age. The area lies a few miles south of 5,639-foot Spirit Mountain, which the local Yuman peoples, resident in the area for almost 1,000 years, regard as their spiritual birthplace. Visitors are warned not to touch the petroglyphs because oils on human hands may corrode them.

Some of the plethora of rock sites in present-day Utah also are easily accessible, such as several in the Moab area. As is often the case, these sites are often tourist-oriented, along highways in recreational areas within short hikes to and from parking lots. In addition to the usual bighorn sheep, shields, scorpions, dogs, and birds, one well-known piece of rock art in this area depicts the birth of a baby.

Further Reading

The American Rock Art Research Association Home Page. http://www.arara.org. Accessed August 26, 2014.

"Books on Rock Art of North America by Area." *The American Rock Art Research Association*. http://www.arara.org/Books_by_Culture_Area_NAm.html. Accessed August 26, 2014.

Dewdney, S., and K. E. Kidd. *Indian Rock Paintings of the Great Lakes*. London: University of Ontario Press, 1967.

Grant, Campbell. *Rock Art of the American Indian*. New York: Crowell, 1967.

Grant, Campbell. *The Rock Paintings of the Chumash: A Study of the California Indian Culture*. Berkeley and Los Angeles: University of California Press, 1965.

"Indian Rock Art." *Texas State Historical Association*. http://www.tshaonline.org/handbook/online/articles/bqi03. Accessed March 10, 2014.

Penny, David W. *North American Indian Art*. London: Thames and Hudson, 2004.

Schoolcraft, Henry Rowe. *Travels Through the Northwestern Regions of the United States*. Albany: E. & E. Hosford, 1821. Reprinted 1966 by Microprint.

Wall, Deborah. "Native Indian Rock Art Adorns Canyon." *Las Vegas Review Journal*, February 27, 2014. http://www.reviewjournal.com/columns-blogs/deborah-wall/native-indian-rock-art-adorns-canyon. Accessed August 26, 2014.

SANDPAINTING

History and Origins

Native Americans, principally in the present-day U.S. Southwest, have used colored sands and other materials to create paintings over many centuries for sacred and commercial purposes. They are not alone. Wherever sand is available, people have used it for artistic expression, from Tibet to the Indian subcontinent, Singapore, Australia, Latin America (on some Christian holy days), and parts of Europe, as well as in Japan, where sandpainting has been traced to the 15th century. Sand art has been created in bottles in the United States for a century and a half.

Navajo sandpaintings (sometimes called dry paintings) are used in healing rituals or in seeking a bountiful harvest, or, with alterations, as museum-quality fine art or as a sale item for tourists. The figures on sandpaintings have been said to be symbolic representations of a story in Navajo mythology. They depict such objects as the sacred mountains where the gods live, legendary visions, dances, or chants performed in rituals ("Navajo Sandpaintings").

Creation and Uses

A Navajo *hatathli* (healer, or medicine man) creates a sandpainting (*ikaah*, "a summoning of the gods" in Navajo) on the floor of a hogan (home) before a healing ceremony. Such paintings also may be arranged on cloth or animal skin. The Navajo have several hundred traditional designs, each with its own meaning, all believed to have life and spiritual purpose. The paintings are usually composed of elements available in the local environment: sand of several colors, ochre, gypsum, charcoal, and sandstone, cornmeal, pollen, bark, and roots. The paintings utilize four sacred colors: blue, yellow, red, and black. Colors may

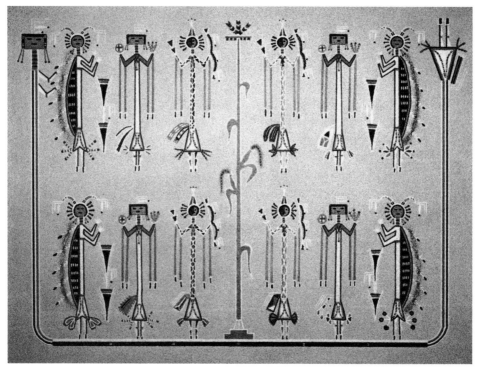

Navajo sandpainting with Yei figures and a corn plant. (Geoffrey Clements/Corbis)

be created as a painter would do it, by combining available materials (red and black combine to brown, red and white make pink, and so forth).

The *hatathli* chants while creating the painting to summon *yeibicheii*, the sacred presence, to the healing ceremony. The degree to which the pattern of the painting follows traditional patterns represents harmony that aids healing because the painting offers a door through which spirits pass. The subject of the healing ritual sits on the painting to absorb the spirits' medicine, which absorbs and removes illness. The healer also transfers the spiritual medicine by touching the sand figures, then the patient.

Having absorbed the illness, the painting is destroyed before sunset. A healing ceremony may require several chants, using a different painting each day, which is created and then destroyed by the healer. Immediately after each chant, the sand used in a painting is returned to the earth north of the hogan.

The chants are performed only by men; women who are menstruating are not allowed to attend these ceremonies, which are believed to injure unborn children. However, women who are past menstruating age may be called on to take part. Sandpaintings may be created only by healers with demonstrated credentials. Those who fake authority may be punished by the healers and the spirit forces. Outsiders usually are not allowed to attend the ceremonies, which are not tourist fare. Photography is nearly always forbidden. A healer may create a sandpainting to satiate outsiders' wishes, but its colorings and designs are not authentic. Creation of an authentic painting for non-sacred work is taboo. Paintings for commercial sale have been traced to about 1945. Unlike real sandpaintings, these are fixed in place.

Contemporary Forms

Sandpainting is widely practiced in Navajo country and elsewhere today. Eugene Baatsoslanii Joe, 63 years of age in 2013, a senior sandpainter who has practiced the art for more than a half century, co-authored a book on the subject, *Navajo Sandpainting Art*, published in 1978. He paints near Shiprock, New Mexico, on the Navajo reservation. "I sat here until I knew what I was supposed to do with my life," he told Alysa Landry of Indian Country Today Media Network in 2013. "I sat here until the insects were crawling over me and I was one with the earth." Joe apprenticed with his father, James C. Joe, who was himself continuing the traditions of Navajo sand art from ancient times.

James Joe was one of the first Navajo artists to use glue that fixed sand to boards, turning an impermanent healing art into a fine art suitable for museum display and commercial sale. Since Joe also was a *hatathli*, he helped to determine how commercially viable sand paintings must differ from those used for healing. James Joe produced contemporary sand art that did not include exact reproductions of the paintings used in healing ceremonies. One traditionally prescribed color may be switched with another, or the number of feathers on the head of a human figure may be changed.

While some elders protested that the senior Joe was debasing a sacred form of healing art, Ed Foutz, a trader, said that he and others jumped at the opportunity to market them. "There was some feeling that it shouldn't be done," Foutz said of the early paintings, which some elders viewed as disrespectful. "When [the artists] came in, they brought them in covered, or quietly. They were bought in a separate room—a safe—where other people didn't see them. There was feeling that things like that shouldn't be put on boards" (Landry, 2013). Once the use of fixed sandpaintings spread, the market was flooded.

"Back then, you bought sand paintings from one or two people, then all of a sudden there were thousands of them," Foutz said. "There were so many I used to joke that they would use up all the sand and the community would cave in." James Joe maintained the quality of his work and generally refused to sell them to tourists. "So many of the sand painters got a particular pattern or did different figures and just reproduced them in different sizes," Foutz said. "Eugene started down his own road. Instead of being just another sand painter, he had some talent and went on to perfect it. It got extremely—beautifully—artistic" (Landry, 2013). "Eugene was the one breaking the new ground when it came to sand painting," said Mark Bahti, of Tucson, Arizona, Eugene Joe's co-author. Many of the other artists who flooded the market were mimicking patterns with little understanding of what they represented. "They use designs they see in books instead of relying on the traditional background. Sand painting has become the fast food of Indian art. It is appeal without description" (Landry, 2013).

Further Reading

Caruna, W. *Aboriginal Art*. London: Thames and Hudson, 2003.

Joe, Eugene Baatsoslanii, Mark Bahti, and Oscar T. Branson. *Navajo Sandpainting Art*. Tucson: Treasure Chest, 1978.

Landry, Alysa. "Eugene Joe: Synonymous with Navajo Sand Art Painting." *Indian Country Today Media Network*, September 21, 2013. http://indiancountrytodaymedianetwork .com/2013/09/21/eugene-joe-synonymous-navajo-sand-art-painting-151361. Accessed August 26, 2014.

"Navajo Sandpaintings." *Navajo People*. http://navajopeople.org/navajo-sand-painting .htm. Accessed January 20, 2014.

Parezo, Nancy J. *Navajo Sandpainting: From Religious Act to Commercial Art*. Tucson: University of Arizona Press, 1983.

Villasenor, David. *Tapestries in Sand: The Spirit of Indian Sandpainting*. Healdsburg, CA: Naturegraph, 1966.

SILVERWORK

History and Origins

Working with silver, nearly unknown across North America before contact with Europeans, has become a means of artistic expression among Native Americans from coast to coast—Iroquois to Zuni pueblo. Silverwork has been adapted to items used in daily life, such as Navajo bowguards, bolo ties, belt buckles, and horse bridles. Silverwork often is ornamented with turquoise and sometimes other stones. Many Native American jewelers have earned international reputations, and their work has become the target of mimics, fakes, and forgeries worldwide, even though authentic Native American work is legally protected in the United States.

Some silverwork is used in daily life. The practical use of a *ketoh* (bowguard), for example, is to protect the wrist against the recoil snap of a bowstring. Such things were used in Europe as well ("bracelet," modified French for "brace," refers to a similar device). Before they were worked in silver and turquoise, *ketohs* were made of leather, about four inches wide, and laced to the wrist. Anthropologist John Adair, who described the rise of Navajo and Pueblo silverwork, wrote that "when the smiths became more proficient and as more tools were introduced, the designs became more elaborate" (Adair, 1944, 34). Navajo bowguards combine metal (often silver) with turquoise, other stones, and leather. Although they are highly ornamental, as an item of jewelry the bowguard has not been adapted for the tourist trade. The best-known bowguards are the *ketoh* of the Southwest, created by Navajo silversmiths beginning about 1895. Men wear bowguards, many of which are retained by families as heirlooms.

Regional Variations

Another distinctive form of silverwork in the Southwest is the concha, often arrayed in belts. The rounded shape of the concha actually originated among Plains peoples and spread to the Southwest. At first, conchas were plain, made in a domed shape. Later, they were ornamented with stamped designs and stones, most often turquoise. The earliest conchas were created with gaps in the middle through which belt loops passed; later, the belt was threaded through loops attached to their backs. Small conchas also have been used on broad-brimmed hats. The concha form, unlike bowguards, has been widely popularized by non-Indians.

Silverworking often runs in families. When a Navajo wants to learn how to make silver, Adair wrote, "He goes to a relative for instruction. Only if there are no silversmiths among his blood relatives, or among his relatives by marriage, will he turn to an outsider for instruction" (Adair, 1944, 87). Since most Navajo families contained at least one silversmith (Adair estimated that about 600 Navajos and 139 Zunis were working in metals as of 1940), working outside the family was rare.

The "squash blossom," composed of fluted beads, a necklace, and a crescent-shaped *naja* pendant, have become very popular among non-Navajos. The *naja* (meaning "crescent" in Navajo) and petals were adapted from a Spanish and Moorish "pomegranate" design late in the nineteenth century. The English term "squash blossom" was invented by traders, but the beads resemble them. These necklaces are worn by both men and women. The earliest ones were entirely silver, but designs utilizing coral and turquoise were fashioned after 1900. Some people associate the *naja* with fertility or protection against the "evil eye," but these beliefs are not shared among the Navajo. In fact, most of the patterns on Southwest jewelry have no symbolic meanings. They are solely design flourishes.

Some silver was worn in daily life, but the really heavy pieces, such as concha belts, came out on social occasions. "At that time, every Navajo will wear as much of his silver as he is able," Adair wrote (1944, 98). The use of the male pronoun was a convention of grammar of the time; Adair indicated that while both men and women wore copious amounts of silver, the women had an edge. "A Navajo obtains the same satisfaction in appearing at a . . . dance bedecked in silver and turquoise as he does when he gathers his sheep and goats together at the sheep dip where other Navajo have come with their flocks. This display of wealth is not so much a personal matter as a family matter" (Adair, 1944, 98).

The wearing of silver and turquoise was (and today remains) part of being properly dressed in public, an essential part of a Navajo's dress for both men and women. Adair said he had once asked Grey Moustache if he would stand for a photograph. "No, I won't let you do that," he said. "I do not have any of my turquoise and silver on. People who see it will say: 'Why, that Navajo doesn't have anything at all.'" Without his jewelry, Grey Moustache told Adair, he would feel like "a chicken with all his feathers plucked out." In 1881, a Lieutenant Bourke (who was quoted by Adair) described a "well-dressed" Navajo man:

> Frequently a dandy will enter the agency wearing large silver hoops in his ears, a necklace of silver balls the size of small cherries, a baldric [shoulder belt often used to carry a weapon] and belt as above described, silver buttons down the outside seam of his leggings from knee to ankle, and a corresponding amount of barbaric decoration upon his pony's bridle and saddle. (Adair, 1944, 49)

Within three generations (roughly one human lifetime) silver and turquoise had become a measure of wealth and an essential part of ceremonial costume as well as daily life. Navajo silversmiths told Adair that while Navajos wanted their silver shiny and new-looking, Anglo-American customers favored an old-pawn look, so the new pieces would be artificially oxidized.

Like the Navajo, the Zunis had carved turquoise for hundreds of years before they took up silverwork. Native peoples of the U.S. Southwest call turquoise the "sky stone" and credit it with spiritual significance, including healing properties. It is used in purification rituals and as a talisman against evil. Possession of jewelry ornamented with turquoise may be associated with wealth and prestige. Turquoise mined by hand was used for ornamentation before it was incorporated into silverwork. Depending on the amount of copper in a given stone, turquoise may be green, blue-green, or blue. A bluer stone indicates a higher proportion of copper; green is associated with iron. Combined also with aluminum, turquoise is usually found in the upper sections of copper deposits.

The Navajos are without question the largest producers of Native American silverwork. (They also are the largest Native group, after the Cherokees.) Silversmithing and other metalwork is not indigenous to Navajo country; about 1850, a few Navajos learned to work iron from immigrant Mexican blacksmiths. At about the same time, Navajos learned to work silver from Mexican *plateros* (silversmiths) in the upper Rio Grande valley. Silverwork had been imported from Spain, where the Moors used it (the Aztecs also worked in gold). To this day, metalsmiths in northern Africa work silver and turquoise in ways similar to Native American crafters in the U.S. Southwest. Navajo interest in metalsmithing also extended to copper. While they were being held at Fort Sumner by the U.S. Army between 1867 and 1868, some Navajo men created fake copper chits that were used to exchange for food rations.

Between the 1860s and 1890s, Atsidi Sani (which translates as Old Smith) became the first Navajo to become well known for his silverwork. Atsidi Chon was the first Navajo to set turquoise into a piece of silver jewelry about 1870 (he was active until the 1890s). Both men taught other Navajos. The trade then spread among the Pueblos. At first, Navajo and Pueblo silversmiths created jewelry only for Native people.

By 1910, a tourist trade had developed with the aid of traders and railroad vendors. Jewelry was sold on the Santa Fe line, both in stations and on trains in transit. By the 1950s, a class of jewelers who were notable to the outside world by name (such as Kenneth Begay) began to assemble and became innovative as their individual styles developed. A number of women, by early in the 20th century, worked their way into what had been a male-dominated line of work.

As early as 1700, the Haudenosaunee (Iroquois) Confederacy acquired silver objects in trade from immigrating Europeans. Silver also figured metaphorically in their diplomacy with the immigrants. Relations were said to be maintained through a "covenant chain." When relationships were good, the silver covenant chain was said to be in high polish. During bad times, it was tarnished.

Silver armbands, brooches, finger rings and earrings, and gorgets (worn across the chest) became popular among men and women, and Iroquois silversmithing became widespread shortly before the year 1800. It reached a peak at midcentury, then declined, to be revived during the 1930s. The revival continues today. Designs often mixed Native motifs with those of Europe, especially France and Great Britain.

Some of the most intricate silverwork is engraved and incised by Native artists from the Alaska Panhandle southward to coastal British Columbia and northwestern Washington State. The Haida, Kwakuitl, Tlingits, and Coast Salish, best known for their wood carvings (boxes, bowls, totem poles, canoes, and so on) applied the same artistry to the creation of jewelry, usually in silver. They also worked gold, bone, and copper, as well as ivory, which was fashioned into intricate scrimshaw. Artists were well established in the medium of silver by the 1880s, about the same time as the Navajos and Zunis.

The exquisite silverwork of the Northwest Coast peoples has its origins in trade with Europeans who brought brass, silver, and copper to the area. Coins were pounded down, shaped, and engraved to make various pieces of jewelry, many with Northwest Coast designs including bears, beavers, eagles, ravens, sharks, and whales.

The artistry that emerged in jewelry in part was a reaction to European American government bans on the potlatch and other ceremonies. Artistry that had been part of the gifting culture of the potlatch was commercialized for the tourist trade and received worldwide attention. The Canadian ban on the potlatch was not lifted until 1951.

Combating Fakery

By 1910, only a few years after the tourist trade developed in Navajo and Pueblo silver, a company in Denver hired non-Indian workers to mass produce their designs and undersell the market. Widespread fakery of Native American silver and turquoise jewelry from Asia has been rampant for decades. The fakes not only misrepresent authenticity but often use fake turquoise and silver as well. These pieces often are so bogus that anyone can spot them. More difficult to detect are pieces that utilize genuine silver and turquoise in imitation of "old pawn" styles or work by well-known artists. These can fool even veteran dealers and collectors.

Fakery negatively impacts the livelihoods of Native artists. As early as 1935, the Indian Arts and Crafts Board (an agency of the U.S. Department of the Interior) was established to combat forgeries, but its ability to police the market has been limited. The Indian Arts and Crafts Association, composed of members from private industry, was set up in 1974 with a similar purpose. By 1990, the authenticity of Native arts and crafts, including jewelry, also was protected by the Indian Arts and Crafts Act (P.L. 101-644 [104 Stat. 4662]).

See Also PART 1: OVERVIEW: Nations, Tribes, and Other Native Groups: Northwest Coast Culture Area; Pueblo Cultural Context; PART 2: CULTURAL FORMS: Arts: American Indian Arts and Crafts Fairs/Spotlight: Indian Arts and Crafts Act (1990)

Further Reading

Adair, John. *The Navajo and Pueblo Silversmiths.* Norman: University of Oklahoma Press, 1944.

Ashwell, Reg. *Coast Salish: Their Art, Culture, and Legends.* Saanichton, BC; Seattle: Hancock House, 1978.

Baxter, Paula, and Allison Bird-Romero. *Encyclopedia of Native American Jewelry.* Phoenix: Oryx Press, 2000.

Carter, William H. *North American Trade Silver: The Chain of Friendship.* London, Ontario: W. H. Carter, 1988.

Cirillo, Dexter. *Southwestern Indian Jewelry.* New York: Abbeville Press, 1992.

Dubin, Lois Sherr. *North American Indian Jewelry and Adornment: From Prehistory to the Present.* New York: Abrams, 1999.

Fredrickson, N. J., and S. Gibb. *The Covenant Chain: Indian Ceremonial and Trade Silver.* Ottawa: National Museums of Canada, 1980.

Jacka, Lois, and Jerry Jacka. *Navajo Jewelry: A Legacy of Silver and Stone.* Flagstaff, AZ: Northland Press, 1995.

Karasik, Carol. *The Turquoise Trail: Native American Jewelry and Culture in the Southwest.* New York: Abrams, 1993.

Pardue, Diana. *The Cutting Edge: Contemporary Southwestern Jewelry and Metalwork.* Phoenix, AZ: The Heard Museum, 1997.

Parker, Arthur Caswell. "The Origins of Iroquois Silversmithing." *American Anthropologist* 12 (July–September, 1910): 349–357.

Rosnek, Carl, and J. Stacey. *Skystone and Silver: The Collector's Book of Southwest Indian Jewelry.* Englewood, NJ: Prentice-Hall, 1976.

Smith, Scott S. "The Scandal of Fake Indian Crafts." *Cowboys and Indians*, September 1998. http://www.cowboysindians.com/articles/archives/0998/fakecrafts.html. Accessed August 26, 2014.

Woodward, Arthur. *Navajo Silver: A Brief History of Navajo Silversmithing.* Flagstaff, AZ: Northland Press, 1971.

TATTOOS

History and Origins

Tattooing has been widely used by Native American peoples since antiquity to establish individual and collective identity, as well as to denote societal rank and accomplishment, such as heroism in battle. Tattoos sometimes have been associated with the acquisition of supernatural powers, or as representing an infusion of power from a specific species of animal.

Before the advent of electric needles that apply ink under the top layer of skin, Native people (often a shaman or someone else practiced in this craft) used a sharp rock or the bone of a fish or turtle to carve a design into skin that was filled with dyes from plants and soot. The acquisition of a tattoo in this manner could be very painful, and a measure of endurance by itself. Tattooing also was performed with sharp flint and box elder wood or steel needles, after they became available through trade with immigrating whites. In desert areas of what is now the U.S. Southwest, several cactus thorns tied together acted as a brush.

Travelers and missionaries among the Caddos (in the southern Plains) reported during the spring of 1687 that many women wore skin clothing only over their lower bodies in warm weather, exposing their tattooed upper bodies, "thereof they make a particular show of their bosom, and those who have the most [tattoos] are reckoned the handsomest, though the pricking in that part be extremely painful to them" (Cox, 1905, 2:140–141). During the 19th century, in 1852, the Waco and Tawakoni (in what became western Oklahoma) women also were observed with tattoos on their faces and breasts. Josiah Gregg, traveling the old Santa Fe Trail, described Wichita women's tattoos as "a perfect calico of the whole underjaw, breast, and arms, and the mammae are fancifully ornamented with rings and rays" (Ewers, 1997, 130). These are a few of many similar descriptions.

Regional Variations

Tattoos often were used as identity markers, to keep records and denote accomplishments, and to indicate passage of stages in life. Among the Creeks, Seminoles, and Cherokees, a boy received a small tattoo at birth and another at maturity (when he had proved himself as a warrior). A Kiowa woman might be recognizable by a circle tattoo on her forehead. An Omaha girl might receive a four-pointed star on her breast and back if her father performed bravely in battle. An Osage carrier of the sacred pipe also received a tattoo to acknowledge that rank. Among the Chippewas, a tattoo was said to relieve pain, especially toothache.

Young Cherokee warriors might have the muscular parts of their arms embellished with designs of flowers and animals. Natchez men wore tattoos as war medals, illustrating their bodies from head to toe. Timuacas (in present-day Florida) painted by the English artist John White during the 16th century show elaborate tattoos on both men and women, both indicative of high status. The tattoos were applied with needles dipped in cinnabar or lampblack. Anyone who acquired tattoos without the proper status was forced to remove them—a very painful process.

Netsilik (Alaskan Inuit, or Eskimo) girls received a tattoo along the edge of the lower lip at maturity; at marriage, two more such lines were added. These tattoos were inscribed in a painful process: "Sinew threaded through an eyed needle was covered with soot and plant juice and laced beneath the skin. Alternately, the skin could be punctured and the wounds rubbed with the tattooing substance to produce a blue color" (Oswalt, 2002, 72). While facial tattoos were simple, larger and more elaborate ones were laced and punctured into the arms, hands, and thighs—a factor, many people believed, in admission to a favorable afterlife following death. "The souls of notable hunters, especially those who died violent deaths, and of women who had suffered the pain of having large and beautiful tattoos went to a place high in the sky in which life was good and they never aged," wrote Wendall Oswalt (2002, 92). The souls of lazy hunters and women without elaborate tattoos were said to huddle miserably under the surface of the earth, "with closed eyes and hanging heads with only butterflies as food" (Oswalt, 2002, 92).

Some Alaska Inuit (Eskimo) men kept a record of whales killed with indelible marks on their cheeks, arms, and chests. Young Yurok (in present-day Northern California coastal areas) girls were tattooed with three parallel bands from lower lip to chin to indicate that they were available for marriage. Upon marriage, and after having children, more bands were added.

Contemporary Forms

As Native American cultures have recovered their vibrancy, traditional tattoos have come back into vogue with both Native and non-Native people. However, Native people most often use tattoos as an expression of inclusion—identity with a group heritage—while non-Natives use them in an exclusive manner, as an indication of dissent from a mainstream culture in which several European-rooted religions regard "body art" negatively, as a defilement of the human body's divine design.

Among many Native peoples, the use of tattoos can express pride in heritage. Several women in Alaska and along the Pacific Coast have been described as acquiring facial tattoos as identity markers. A Mohawk tattoo artist has had a large design of a turtle tattooed on her lower back, which is emblematic of her clan. To her, it "represents my spiritual center. . . . It is a source of stability to me in my life . . . [that has] helped tie me to the past, and in weak moments in my life, [I] have been able to say: 'Well, how would a Mohawk woman behave in this situation?'" (Schwarz, 2006, 244).

Among non-Natives, American Indian–themed tattoos often have been associated with New Age spirituality. One informant, a tattoo artist (who is part Mohawk), told Maureen Trudelle Schwarz: "A lot of people are just drawn to the images; they're not really sure why. I get people . . . wanting medicine shields and dream catchers all the time who don't have any idea what they are. They just like them. . . . They identify very strongly with the Indian beliefs and traditions" (Schwarz, 2006, 234).

With the revival of tattooing and other forms of "body art" beginning during the late 20th century, many non-Native people have requested various forms of Native American designs. Like "plastic medicine men" and other forms of cultural appropriation, the use of traditional Native motifs (some of which have highly spiritual meanings or are earned for specific acts, like a soldier's medals and ribbons) is deeply resented by some American Indians as a form of cultural theft, as "playing Indian." Generic American Indian designs have even been marketed as temporary tattoos for children. Others use the images to express "independence, heritage, honor, independence" (Schwarz, 2006, 236).

A search of the Internet produced scores of websites flush with purported Native American designs along with advice not to use them unless the "tattooee" was certain of his or her Native identity. Once acquired, any tattoo can be removed only with considerable expense, time, and physical pain. Non-Native people carrying Native-design tattoos may be characterized as posers. Even a Native person who has a mistaken idea of his or her identity may run into problems. Cherokee men, for example, traditionally tattooed their faces, while among some Sioux peoples only women did so. A Native person with the wrong tattoo in the wrong place within a certain cultural context may look ridiculous.

Some scholars who coin phrases to describe sociological phenomena came to characterize the use of Native American tattoo designs by people who often do not know what they mean as a form of "imperialist nostalgia," defined as "people longing for what they themselves have destroyed" (Rosaldo, 1993, 87), which can hide the guilt over the destruction of people and cultures. Maureen Trudelle Schwarz noted, "Euro-Americans can be said to glorify American Indians as a means of mourning their own destruction of this continent's aboriginal inhabitants and subsequently the environment and its animal inhabitants" (2006, 232–233). They have also been described as "a mask of innocence to cover their involvement with a process of domination" (Rosaldo, 1993, 86).

Tattooing and other forms of body modification were widespread among indigenous peoples of what is now the U.S. Northeast until the 19th century, when colonization aided by missionaries inveighed against the practices. Native tattooing was revived late in the 20th century. By 2013, the revival had reached the point that the Iroquois Indian Museum opened its annual season with an exhibit, "Indian Ink: Iroquois and the Art of Tattoos," featuring tattoos' role in Iroquois history, identity, self-expression, cultural philosophy, and politics.

Opening the exhibit, Lars Krutak, an author and anthropologist, described worldwide indigenous body modification with an illustrated lecture on Native tattooing in the Philippines, Indonesia, and northeastern North America. Krutak has served as a consultant for *National Geographic* documentaries and acted as host for a Discovery Channel (USA) *Tattoo Hunter* program.

See Also PART 1: OVERVIEW: Nations, Tribes, and Other Native Groups: Northwest Coast Culture Area; **PART 2: CULTURAL FORMS: Arts:** Cultural Appropriation: Questions and Issues

Further Reading

Brandon, William. *The Last Americans.* New York: McGraw-Hill, 1974.

Caplan, Jane, ed. *Written on the Body: The Tattoo in European and American History.* Princeton, NJ: Princeton University Press, 2000.

Cox, Isaac Joslin, ed. *The Journeys of René Robert Cavelier Sieur a la Salle.* 2 vols. New York, 1905.

Ewers, John C. *Plains Indian History and Culture: Essays on Continuity and Change.* Norman: University of Oklahoma Press, 1997.

Gilbert, Steve. *The Tattoo History Source Book.* New York: Simon & Schuster/Juno Books, 2000.

Green, Rayna. "The Tribe Called Wannabe: Playing Indian in America and Europe." *Folklore* 99, no. 1 (1988): 30–55.

Krutak, Lars. *Spiritual Skin: Magical Tattoos and Scarification.* Aschaffenburg, Germany: Editions Reuss, 2012.

Kuwahara, Makiko. *Tattoo: An Anthropology.* London: Berg, 2005.

Maxwell, James A., ed. *America's Fascinating Indian Heritage.* Pleasantville, NY: Reader's Digest, 1978.

Oswalt, Wendell. *This Land Was Theirs: A Study of Native Americans.* 7th ed. New York: McGraw-Hill, 2002.

Rainier, Chris. *Ancient Marks: The Sacred Origins of Tattoos and Body Marking.* San Francisco: Mandala/Earth Aware Editions, 2006.

Rosaldo, Renato. *Culture and Truth: The Remaking of Social Analysis.* Boston: Beacon Press, 1993.

Schwarz, Maureen Trudelle. "Native American Tattoos: Identity and Spirituality in Contemporary America." *Visual Anthropology* 19 (2006): 223–254.

Sizemore, Donald. *How to Make Cherokee Clothing.* Summertown, TN: Book, 1997.

Uranga, Rachel. "Marks Across Time: For Some California Indians, Facial Tattoos Make a Bold Connection to a Fading [sic] Tradition." *Sacramento Bee*, August 31, 2001.

Van Dinter, Maarten Hesselt. *The World of Tattoo: An Illustrated History.* Amsterdam: KIT, 2005.

TOTEM POLES

History and Origins

Thirteen hundred miles of rugged, rain-washed forest from the panhandle of Alaska to northwest Washington State is home to several Native American nations who preserve memories of families and events on "totem poles." A sea-based culture of many tribes among islands, bays, and inlets, with steep mountains on one side and the open ocean on the other, the peoples of the Northwest Coast have been raising these heralds in increasing numbers since the 1960s. Many have been erected out of cultural context—in tourist destinations such as Seattle's waterfront, museums, and highway rest stops—but many others still rise in front of family houses.

Totem poles are carved from the trunks of the western red cedar. Locating a suitable tree takes some skill. It must be straight, without cracks or a surplus of knots, and positioned close to a watercourse for transport. Because of rugged terrain and sparse population, many Northwest Coast villages even today are not connected by roads. Once created, a totem pole is given a name. Other wooden works of art, from houses to canoes and feast bowls, also are named in a way that links them symbolically to their owners, to stories told by carvings, or to other circumstances of their histories. Poles can vary from a few feet in height to the world's tallest, 173 feet, at Alert Bay, British Columbia.

The name "totem pole" is a misnomer, since these unique artworks usually do not display totems, "a creature or object that a person holds in great respect or religious awe" (Stewart, 1990, 7). The name has been so widely used, however, that it has become denotative. Originally, the poles stood as family heralds

**A totem pole at the entrance of Tlingit Chief Sou-i-hat's home in Alaska.
(Library of Congress)**

outside sturdy pole-and-beam longhouses that opened on the water, greeting people arriving in canoes. The homes contained several related families in a culture based largely on rank and prestige. The poles described who lived in the houses and where they ranked in society. The poles are historical monuments that have great meaning for those who carved them. They communicate a people's lineage, origins, experiences with the supernatural, achievements and exploits, and successes. Totem poles record a people's cultural identity.

As an art form, totem poles predate contact with Europeans, but initially they were erected only by the Tsimshian people (who lived just south of the present-day Alaska Panhandle in coastal British Columbia) and the Haida Gwaii (on the islands the immigrants named after Queen Charlotte) and in the extreme southern Alaska Panhandle. After European contact, use of totem poles spread northward to the Tlingits in the Alaska Panhandle, as well as southward among the Nuxalks, Kwakwaka'wakw (formerly called Kwakiutl), and Nuu-chah-nulth, then further southward along the coast across Vancouver Island, coastal British Columbia, and parts of Washington State. Most poles that people see today were carved after the 1930s, except for a few that have been preserved in the controlled atmosphere of museums. In a natural setting, the humid atmosphere of the coast causes most totem poles to decay within a century.

Despite the assumptions of some Christian missionaries, totem poles are not religious shrines. People do not worship them. Nor are the poles considered sacred in a European religious sense.

The first Europeans to reach the Northwest Coast were awed by huge logs carved with designs set as house posts. Captain George Dixon, having visited the islands the English named after Queen Charlotte during the early 1790s, described "figures which might be taken for a species of hieroglyphics; fishes and other animals, heads of men and various whimsical designs . . . not deficient in a sort of elegance and perfection" (Stewart, 1990, 20). Another seaman, John Bartlett, described a tree trunk carved so that "the entrance was cut out of a large tree and the passage into the house was through his teeth" (Stewart, 1990, 20).

Regional Variations

At the same time, between the 1870s and 1920s, large museums all over the world became infatuated with Northwest Coast art, including totem poles. Museum agents were sent to the area to buy anything they could get at low prices, or even to steal art pieces from abandoned villages. Poles that were the centerpieces of illegal ceremonies in Canada were put on prominent display in large cities such as London, New York, Paris, and Berlin. The same Canadian government that had outlawed the potlatch in 1925 began to work with the Canadian National Railway to restore old totem poles. As the potlatch was relegalized, restoration efforts increased, spearheaded by the University of British Columbia Museum of Anthropology, which commissioned Mungo Martin to refurbish many old Kwakiutl poles. Museums and corporations across the United States and such places as Mexico City, England, Denmark, Germany, Argentina, China, Japan, and Australia sought poles.

First contact with Europeans brought a flush of prosperity to the Northwest Coast peoples, along with an increase in wealth that was reflected in demand for carvers to make larger and more ornate poles that displayed the Native nobility's status. The wealth came from the harvest of otter pelts, fashionable in Europe, which peaked about 1860. Soon thereafter fashions changed, harvests declined, and imported diseases ravaged the area. Cultures declined as villages were abandoned, and many splendid totem poles were destroyed and splintered for firewood. The potlatch was outlawed by the Canadian government in 1884 (a ban that lasted until 1951), and demand for objects used in it declined, although some were held out of official sight. Dance and ceremonial regalia, feast bowls and ladles, headdresses and masks all became scarce, along with totem poles. Carvers who had created all of these died without passing on their knowledge.

Totem poles serve many purposes, and designs vary based on the type of display being made. A "welcome pole," for example, erected by the Kwakiutl and Nuu-chah-nulth, usually erected on a village beach, may be recognized by its display of a large human figure with its arms held wide. "House posts," usually inside the homes of high-ranking leaders at the backs of houses (supporting roof beams), display carvings of family history in crests. Some houses use these poles at both ends. A "house frontal pole" stands outside a front entrance, with carvings similar to house posts including the histories, crests, and identity of the family within. A "house portal pole" is very similar in design and purpose, but encloses a door.

Other types include the "memorial pole," erected about a year after a chief's death in front of his house, which describes lifetime accomplishments. The pole may have been raised by the succeeding chief, who also used it to validate his position. A "mortuary pole," also for a person of high rank, is used to sheath remains in a cavity at the pole's upper end. A "shame pole" is erected by one chief to publicize something that may embarrass another person, such as an unpaid debt. If the matter in question is something that can be resolved, the pole is removed after restitution is made. "Commercial poles" are carved on commission by non-Natives, often private individuals, corporations, museums, or government agencies.

To steal a totem pole is believed to bring profound bad luck. While such a thing cannot be proved, Hollywood star John Barrymore provided an anecdotal example. Barrymore, who sailed his 120-foot yacht, *Infanta*, along the inland passage of the Alaska Panhandle about 1930, stole a memorial pole (probably used to inter human remains) on Prince of Wales Island, despite having been warned by "an American settler on Lemesurier Island . . . that removing such a tribal emblem from its appointed place meant bad luck" (Williams, 2015, 38). Between that time and his death in 1942, Barrymore, who had been wealthy, divorced four times and went bankrupt.

Totem poles include many natural (and some supernatural) images. Many are animals of the sea and land—whales and fishes, frogs, hawks, bears, beavers, wolves, and many others. The history on a totem pole should be "read" top to bottom. The English aphorism "low man on the totem pole" actually has status reversed, however. The "last" image, on the bottom of the pole, usually carries the most prestige.

The familiar figure at the top of many Haida poles wearing a very tall conical hat is the Watchman, who can appear on the pole singly, or in multiples of two or three. These figures are believed to have supernatural powers; they keep watch over a village, looking toward the sea for protection.

The Thunderbird is one of the most important supernatural creatures. A mythical creature, the Thunderbird is the most powerful of all spirits in Northwest Coast cosmology and may be taken as a crest only by the most high-ranking of leaders. The Thunderbird is said to be so large and powerful that it can swoop out over the ocean, seize a whale in its talons, then fly inland, into the steep mountains, to devour it, as thunder cracks from the beating of its wings and lightning streaks out of its eyes. Thunderbird also has a younger brother, Kolus (or Kulus, or Quous), covered in fine white down that the bird can remove to reveal a human image. Kolus has a more benign disposition than Thunderbird; it may use its great strength to lift roof beams into place for longhouses, for example.

Hokw-hokw, a very large cannibal bird, is notable on totem poles as the eagle-like bird with a long beak that can be used to crack open people's skulls to consume their brains. This bird also is used as a mask worn by a dancer that can open and shut loudly. Another mythical being, Sisiutl, is a sea serpent that can shape-shift in many ways. It can become a canoe that eats seals. Touching or looking at Sisiutl (even being looked at by it) can cause death—but conversely, it can bestow wealth. Rubbing its blood on a warrior will protect him from injury. Warriors don a headband bearing Sisiutl's image to protect them from harm. A similar image may be affixed over the entrance to a home.

Totem poles have been carved to mark historical events. A pole that stands outside Centennial Hall in Juneau, Alaska, carved by Nathan Jackson and Steve Brown, was erected in 1980 to record an atrocity nearly 100 years earlier (in 1883) by the U.S. Navy and depicts Uncle Sam with his top hat and red, white, and blue clothing.

The Wooshkeetan people of Angoon (in the Alaska Panhandle) had demanded 200 blankets to compensate them for the death of a kinsman who was killed in an accident on a whaling ship. The whaling company called for help from the U.S. Navy, which sent an armed ship, whose commander demanded that the Indians pay him 400 blankets for their hostile behavior. When they could collect only 82 blankets, the Navy bombed and burned the village, destroyed 40 canoes, and stole ceremonial furs and regalia. The United States never formally apologized or compensated the Wooshkeetans for the damage. As close as the Navy got to apologizing was a bland letter 100 years later stating that the "event" had been "unfortunate."

Another pole, erected in 1869 by Chief Ebbetts of Tongass Village, depicts William Seward, the U.S. official who purchased Alaska from Russia, as a boorish man sitting atop a box. Ebbetts had hosted an elaborate potlatch for Seward, who offended his hosts by failing to reciprocate.

Contemporary Forms

One prominent totem pole stands at the Seattle Center as a memorial to John T. Williams, a Native wood-carver shot to death by Seattle police officer Ian Birk in 2011 after he failed to drop a carving knife he was carrying. A later review revealed that the knife had been sheathed at the time. The police department's Firearms Review Board determined that the shooting was unjustified. By November, the Justice Department was investigating the SPD's civil rights record. Shortly after that, the King County prosecutor declined to bring charges against Birk. The shooting of Williams was found to have been unjustified by an internal police review, however, and Officer Birk resigned from the force.

On August 30, 2011, a year to the day after Williams was killed, hundreds of people gathered on the Seattle waterfront to dedicate a totem pole in his honor. "At 4:12 p.m. on Tuesday, the 30th of August," wrote Editor John Loftus in the *Muckleshoot Monthly*, "speechmaking, drumming, singing and dancing ceased as the hundreds who had gathered on the Seattle waterfront held hands in silence at the moment that four fateful shots had rung out precisely one year earlier" (Loftus, 2011, 1).

The 34-foot, 3,500-pound totem pole memorializing Williams later was hand-carried by about 85 people from Pier 57 on the Seattle waterfront to a designated site a few yards from the Space Needle at the Seattle Center, a mile and a half, mainly uphill on February 26, 2012, as several hundred people watched along the route, amidst singing and drumming. It was one day before what would have been Williams's 52nd birthday. The pole carried carvings of an eagle, a mother raven, and the figure of a wood-carver. Williams's friends and family had spent a year carving the memorial pole.

Late in the 20th century, competition developed regarding who could carve and hoist the tallest totem pole. In 1956, the *Victoria Times* sponsored a contest in which people could add their names to a scroll to be buried under a pole being carved by Kwakwaka'wakw master Mungo Martin. More than 10,000 people subscribed at 50 cents each, as Martin carved a 127-foot, 7-inch pole that was erected in Victoria, B.C.'s Beacon Park. Don Lelooska, a Cherokee, carved a 140-foot pole that was erected in Kalama, Washington, to draw tourists. In 1994, to commemorate the Commonwealth Games in Victoria, a pole was commissioned that ended up at 180 feet, 3 inches, carved by Bill and Alex Helin, Art Sterritt, Jessel Bolton, Richard Krenz, Nancy and Anthony Dawson, and Heber Reese. It was erected in Victoria's Inner Harbour, and city officials required a blinking light at its top to warn away landing seaplanes. The city later required that the pole, which was secured to the ground with wires, be shortened substantially.

Lummi Jewell (tse-Sealth; Praying Wolf) James (a lineal descendant of Chief Sea'th'l, after whom the city of Seattle was named) is also a master carver of healing poles, which have been presented around the world. For example, the Lummis presented two totem poles carved from red cedar trees to the Pentagon to support the families of the 184 people who died there September 11, 2001. "The totem pole isn't a sacred thing, it's the sacredness of love joining us together," said James, who wore a coned straw hat over his long, black, braided hair and a black vest with a shadowy gray wolf's head on the back as he presented the Liberty and Freedom totem poles on September 19, 2004 (Robins, 2007, 201).

See Also PART 1: OVERVIEW: Nations, Tribes, and Other Native Groups: Northwest Coast Culture Area; **PART 2: CULTURAL FORMS: Arts:** American Indian Arts and Crafts Fairs/Spotlight: Indian Arts and Crafts Act (1990); **Language and Literature:** Figures of Speech, Native American Origins; **Transportation and Housing:** Longhouses (Pacific Northwest)

Further Reading

Blankinship, Donna Gordon. "Justice Dept.: Seattle Police Used Excessive Force." Associated Press in *Seattle Times*, December 17, 2011. http://seattletimes.nwsource.com /html/nationworld/2017030040_apusseattlepolice.html. Accessed August 26, 2014.

Jonaitis, Aldona. *Discovering Totem Poles: A Traveler's Guide*. Seattle: University of Washington Press, 2012.

Loftus, John. "John T. Williams Memorial Totem Poles Blessed: A Family of Woodcarvers Honors Its Fallen Brother." *Muckleshoot Monthly*, September 2011, 1, 3.

Miletich, Steve, and Jennifer Sullivan. "Seattle Officer's Kicking of Suspect Prompts Call for Federal Civil-rights Review." *Seattle Times*, November 19, 2010, n.p.

Robins, Barbara K. "Healing Poles: Traditional Art for Modern Grief." *The International Journal of the Humanities* 5, no. 9 (2007): 201–208.

Stewart, Hilary. *Totem Poles*. Seattle: University of Washington Press, 1990.

Williams, Paige. "The Tallest Trophy: A Movie Star Made Off with an Alaskan Totem Pole. Would It Ever Return Home?" *The New Yorker*, April 20, 2015, 36–44.

FAMILY, EDUCATION, AND COMMUNITY

FAMILY, EDUCATION, AND COMMUNITY OVERVIEW

Family and community are the bedrock of most Native American cultures, as with many other peoples around the world. Every culture has its own distinct ways of welcoming newborns into the world, conducting weddings, and observing the end of a person's life. Each culture's family life has a historic economic base. On the Great Plains, buffalo (bison) culture is described here, with a Spotlight on buffalo hunt customs and protocols. Civic and military societies (with a Spotlight on coup and "counting coup") were closely tied to the buffalo culture. The historic context also includes the uses of wampum (generally in diplomacy, not as money).

Several aspects of Native American family and community life are distinctive and, at the same time, recent exemplars for European American societies, among them concepts regarding sexual orientation, gift-giving, and the importance of women's roles. These distinctive features have endured (but not without severe challenge) as large numbers of indigenous people have moved to urban areas.

In many Native American cultures, a person acquires influence not by accumulating possessions, as in many European societies, but by giving them away. People with the means to do so are generous, even in cultures (such as the Northwest Coast peoples) with hierarchies and a competitive nature. Note that the potlatches of the Northwest Coast peoples are expressions of rank and status. Gifts are an essential part of maintaining human relationships, and, done according to custom, the act of giving creates reciprocal obligations. A gift to a

195

Native American by a colonist "might pas[s] twenty hands before it sticks. . . . Wealth circulateth like the blood, all parts partake" William Penn observed (Black, 1976, 5). Trade is more than a commercial exchange; it involves reciprocal bonds maintained by giving.

Unlike most European societies, which were emphatically patriarchal until the 20th century, the vast majority of Native American cultures accord women a great deal of respect. With a few exceptions, societal and cultural models were (and today remain) matriarchal as well as matrilineal. While men often had leadership roles in diplomacy, trade, and other areas of endeavor that were visible to European immigrants, women influenced decision making. While some details differed, Haudenosaunee (Iroquois), Diné (Navajo), and Apache women (profiled in this section) were among many who exercised profound influence.

Traditional Native American gender roles can seem amazingly contemporary. Societies worldwide generally have become more accepting of gender fluidity as many Native peoples have long practiced it. In recent years, as laws prohibiting gay marriage have fallen, gay, lesbian, bisexual, and transgender (LGBT) relationships are described in at least 150 Native peoples' myths and stories. These roles have existed since the dawn of time, according to oral accounts. Heterosexuals usually are not threatened by variations of gender identity in their midst, but read into them special talents. Cross-gender work roles also generally are respected.

Education has been changing in Native American cultures as many peoples assume direction of their own schools. Economic self-determination—including the use and sale of resources (timber, oil, natural gas, and others) as well as proceeds from gaming, tourism, and other business activities—is making educational self-determination possible.

Native American education today is generally moving away from destruction of indigenous culture as official policy, which was the goal of an intensive program of cultural assimilation aimed at American Indians during the 19th and early 20th centuries in the United States and Canada. "Kill the Indian—Save the Man," an advertising slogan for boarding schools developed during the 1880s, has sometimes been called cultural genocide today. The policy sought to preserve living Indians scoured of their own cultural attributes (as an alternative to outright physical extermination), remade as Anglo-Americans. In 1900, barely two decades after the first one had opened, 307 boarding schools in the United States enrolled 21,568 young Native Americans. Today, Native education generally affirms Native cultural values, even at some of the remaining boarding schools. Revival of Native cultures is also prevalent elsewhere, as described in entries on pan-Indianism, reindigenization, and restorative justice.

Further Reading
Black, Nancy B., and Bette S. Weidman. *White on Red: Images of the American Indian.* Port Washington, NY: Kennikat Press, 1976.

BIRTHING CUSTOMS

History and Origins

As one might expect in cultures that are mainly matriarchal, several Native American origin stories begin with mythical births. Earth is often taken to be the "womb" from which the people emerge, midwifed by "Mother Earth." Navajo women gather with an expectant mother and sing the song of creation, the Changing Woman, a personification of the earth. To the Hopis, the creator is the Corn Mother. At birth, an ear of ceremonial corn is placed beside an infant. Corn pollen is a prominent element in a Hopi infant's welcome to the world:

> On the first day, the child was washed with water in which cedar had been brewed. Fine white cornmeal was then rubbed over his body and left all day. The next day, the child was washed and cedar ashes rubbed over him to remove the hair and baby skin. This was repeated for three more days. From the fifth day until the twentieth day, he was washed and rubbed with cornmeal for one day and covered with ashes for four days. Meanwhile, the child's mother drank a little of the cedar water each day. ("First People," n.d.)

On the twentieth day, at dawn, the Corn Mother that was laid beside the child at birth is passed over the infant four times, from navel to head. The child is named on the first pass, then wished a long and healthy life. A son is wished a productive life in work; a girl is wished to be a good wife and mother. After these wishes, aunts bestow clan names, after which all walk into the rising sun, praying silently, preceded by pinches of cornmeal. As the sun rises, the child, not having seen a sunrise before, is held before it. The child now belongs to both the family and to the Earth.

Regional Variations

Dutch immigrant Adrien Van der Donck described Mohawk and Mahican women's preparation for birth in present-day New York State during the 17th century. He wrote that women, when pregnant, would "depart alone to a secluded place near a brook, or stream of water . . . and prepare a shelter for themselves with mats and coverings, where, provided with provisions necessary for them, they await their delivery without the company or aid of any person. . . .

They rarely are sick from child-birth [and] suffer no inconveniences from the same" (Pearson, n.d.). This was not an eyewitness account. The writer, a European man, had no access to any Native American birthing practices. Despite the fact that such accounts are rather common, historians today doubt their accuracy. However, Inuit and Algonquins did maintain buildings dedicated to menses and birth, and Mi'kmaq and Bella Koola women gave birth in wooded areas, often near bodies of water.

Birthing customs varied among Native peoples, but as a whole they were more social than Van der Donck indicates. In fact, birthing usually involved many members of extended families who kept up the house while the mother was birthing, "while also pampering the mother with grooming, binding, special nourishing, washing, steaming, and massaging. . . . Many Native American cultures would swaddle the mother in a warm bed over heated stones, while others require steaming in special steam huts—women were respected, revered and pampered" (O'Donohue, n.d.). In the nine-day Navajo Blessingway, a pregnant woman is blessed and pampered with ceremonial grooming and cleansing, and provided nourishing food and gifts.

Navajo pregnant mothers are told not to look at dead animals in the belief that the child may take on their attributes. For example, it was believed that looking at a dead duck may provoke the birth of an infant with webbed feet. Women who were expecting children were advised not to expose themselves to death or any other traumatic experience, because this may cause bad luck. This is true even before a child is conceived. Navajo women who are expecting also are encouraged to walk, in the belief that this will keep the baby smaller than otherwise; walking also keeps a woman's hips wide and supple, aiding delivery. The baby's father is told not to tie animals in the belief that this will "tie up" the fetus, making delivery more difficult. Both mother and father are told to wash their hands frequently, at least daily.

Pregnant Native women often avoided strenuous activity and modified their diets to protect an unborn child. Pregnant Cherokees, for example, avoided eating raccoon or pheasant that they thought might make the baby ill (or even cause death). It was said that eating speckled trout might give the baby birthmarks; black walnuts could cause an oversized nose. Standing in doorways was said to delay delivery, and wearing a neckerchief might cause the umbilical cord to strangle the fetus. Healers were engaged to perform rituals that would ease delivery.

During the 19th century, James Mooney, an anthropologist, described a Cherokee ritual that was meant to accelerate delivery by frightening a child from the womb. A female relative of the mother would say: "Listen! You little man, get up now at once. There comes an old woman. The horrible [old thing] is coming, only a little way off. Listen! Quick! Get [off] your bed and let us run away!" The female relative then repeated the formula, substituting "little woman" and "your grandfather," in case the baby was a girl (Pearson, n.d.). Cherokee women also drank a beverage made of wild cherry bark to accelerate delivery by bringing on contractions. The journals of the Lewis and Clark expedition said that the Mandans (in present-day North Dakota and eastern Montana) used a few rungs of a rattlesnake's tail to accelerate delivery, broken into pieces and swallowed in water. Captain Meriwether Lewis reserved judgment on the idea but noted that he had watched a delivery take place within minutes of an expectant mother's use of it.

Native American women studied many herbal and natural means to aid labor, including wild yam partridgeberry, corn smut, red raspberry leaf, snakeweed, and American licorice. Broom buckwheat, black chokeberry, sumac, balsam, birth root, Hottentot fig, bayberry, and cotton root also were employed to aid in difficulties of childbirth, including extended labor and postpartum hemorrhage. Some Natives used songs, musical gourds, and chants to alleviate labor pains. According to Van der Donck, Mahican mothers-to-be drank a potion made mainly of root bark to ease labor pains.

Many pregnancies were attended by midwives and members of families. The Navajo called their midwives *Midewiwin*, meaning "the one who holds." To Inuit the midwife was "the cord mother." Men usually were not allowed to witness births. The Kickapoos, an exception, did allow men to assist in birthing. Women usually did not deliver babies from a prone position. They sat, stood, or kneeled, permitting gravity to aid delivery. Women also walked, strutted, crawled, danced, and swayed to aid delivery, reasoning that lying still on their backs (as has been common among Europeans) would inhibit the baby's movement along the birth canal.

Most commonly, a bed of leaves or other soft materials was prepared for the emerging infant. Statements of European Americans attest that infants often were plunged into cold water (usually rivers) routinely when very young. Such accounts are common from the Cherokees on the East Coast to the Coast Salish near Puget Sound. Lieutenant Henry Timberlake, a mid-18th-century British envoy to the Cherokees, said that cold-water immersion allowed "the children [to] acquire such strength, that no ricketty [*sic*] or deformed are found among them" (Pearson, n.d.). Women's quick recovery from childbirth surprised some European observers as well.

Contemporary Forms

Today many Native women give birth using a combination of modern and traditional practices. Traditional midwifery is often practiced within a hospital setting or at home. Today many Navajo women have returned to the Blessingway tradition. As such, mothers are advised to think of good things. Even discussing the cost of pregnancy or birth is deemed inappropriate "because motherhood was never looked at as a burden or inconvenience. . . . Pregnancy and motherhood [are] a blessing, and everything that made them a woman [is seen] as beautiful" (O'Donohue).

Some women have been replacing baby showers with the Blessingway tradition to prepare for the journey of motherhood physically, mentally, and emotionally. During the Blessingway, women surround the mother and rub her belly, providing foods that increase strength and stamina, giving talismans of strength, and singing the creation story of Changing Woman. Many practicing midwives today utilize Navajo (and other) indigenous birthing traditions. These often are combined with practices of modern medicine.

See Also PART 2: CULTURAL FORMS: FOOD: Agriculture/Spotlight: Corn and Culture

Further Reading

Deleary, Nicholas. "The Midewiwin, an Aboriginal Spiritual Institution. Symbols of Continuity: A Native Studies Culture-based Perspective." Carleton University (Ontario), MA thesis, 1990.

"First People: The Legends: Native American Legends: The Birth Ritual: A Hopi Legend." http://www.firstpeople.us/FP-Html-Legends/TheBirthRitual-Hopi.html. Accessed March 17, 2014.

Mooney, James. *Myths of the Cherokee.* New York: Johnson Reprint, 1970.

O'Donohue, Kayla. "Native American Birth Rituals: Postpartum." *Prezi.* http://prezi.com/09uo4lavbea8/native-american-birth-rituals/. Accessed March 18, 2014.

Pearson, Ellen Holmes. "How Did Native American Women Give Birth, or What Were Their Practices or Beliefs in Giving Birth?" *Teaching History.org.* http://teachinghistory.org/history-content/ask-a-historian/24097. Accessed March 17, 2014.

Perdue, Theda. *Cherokee Women: Gender and Culture Change, 1700–1835.* Lincoln: University of Nebraska Press, 1998.

Rountree, Helen. "Powhatan Indian Women: The People Capt. John Smith Barely Saw." *Ethnohistory* 45 (1998): 1–29.

Shoemaker, Nancy, ed. *Negotiators of Change: Historical Perspectives on Native American Women.* New York: Routledge, 1995.

Timberlake, Lt. Henry. *Memoirs of Lieutenant Henry Timberlake: The Story of a Soldier, Adventurer, and Emissary to the Cherokees, 1756–1765.* Edited by Duane H. King. Chapel Hill: University of North Carolina Press, 2007.

Van der Donck, Adrien. "A Description of the New Netherlands." 2nd ed. (Amsterdam, 1656). Translated by Jeremiah Johnson. *Collections of the New-York Historical Society,* 2nd ser. 1 (1841).

BUFFALO (BISON) CULTURE

History and Origins

On the high plains of North America, the buffalo was basic to Native American economic life and culture well into the 19th century. When European American settlement began to encroach on the area early in that century, an estimated 30 million buffalo lived in a large area from present-day Texas in the south to northern Alberta. East and west, buffalo ranged from present-day New York State to Alabama and Mississippi, to Idaho and eastern Oregon.

John Fire Lame Deer, a Brulé spiritual leader, recalled that, culturally, "The buffalo was part of us, his flesh and blood being absorbed by us until it became our own flesh and blood. Our clothing, our tipis, everything we needed for life came from the buffalo's body. It was hard to say where the animal ended and the man began" (Hedren, 2011, 92). Major Irving Richard Dodge was riding with the Third Cavalry in 1871 when he observed that "The whole country appeared one mass of buffalo." In 1876, another soldier said that "[A]s far as the eye could reach on both sides of our route . . . somber, superb buffalos were grazing in thousands! The earth was brown with them" (Hedren, 2011, 94).

Most Native peoples worked nature into their rituals and customs because their lives depended on the bounty of the land around them. Where a single animal comprised the basis of a Native economy (such as the salmon of the Pacific Northwest or the buffalo on the Plains), strict cultural sanctions came into play against killing such animals in numbers that would exceed their natural replacement rate. On the Plains, the military societies of the Cheyennes, Lakotas, and other peoples enforced rules against hunting buffalo out of season and against taking more animals than a people could use. Many Plains societies had special police who maintained discipline before and during communal buffalo hunts. An individual who began the hunt early could be severely punished.

Native peoples on the Plains used nearly every part of the buffalo in their everyday cultural economies. In addition to the meat that was eaten fresh or preserved as jerky, buffalo hides were tanned and used as tipi covers, moccasin tops, shirts, leggings, dresses, and other clothing, bedding, bags, and pouches. Rawhide was used for moccasin soles, shields, rattles, drums, saddles, bridles, and other horse tack, as well as snowshoes. Buffalo horns were fashioned into cups, spoons, and other eating utensils, toys, and rattles. The bones became knives, arrowheads, shovels, hoes, war clubs, and ceremonial objects, while buffalo hair was used in headdresses and ropes. Buffalo tails became fly brushes; the bladder could be fashioned into a watertight canteen. Buffalo chips were sometimes used as fuel when wood was unavailable.

Variation and Change

European immigration fundamentally altered many Native American cultures' relationship with the buffalo in two ways. First, the arrival and adaptation to horses imported from Europe changed semisedentary cultures that had mixed agriculture with occasional buffalo hunting into mainly nomadic peoples adapted to following buffalo herds and using them as their major source of sustenance. Second, the arrival of capitalist mercantilism drafted many Native Americans into industrial roles making buffalo robes for Europeans and European Americans—and thereby into the cash economy, with men hunting the animals and women dressing the robes. During the 1870s and the early 1880s, the Society for the Prevention of Cruelty to Animals (SPCA) made opposition to the buffalo hide trade one of its early campaigns.

The Native peoples were very sensitive to changes in their environments that preceded larger changes in their cultures wrought by the tide of immigrants. One such change was the arrival of European honeybees. By 1810, if not before, the bees, which had arrived in Virginia during the 1620s, had reached the Missouri River Valley. Naturalist John Bradbury wrote in 1810 that the honeybee had reached the Missouri River homeland of the U'ma'hos (Omahas), whom he called "Mahas": "Bees have spread over this continent to a degree, and with a celebrity so nearly corresponding with that of the Anglo-Americans that it has given rise to a belief, both among the Indians and the Whites, that bees are their precursors" (Bradbury, 1810, 58). Washington Irving noted swarms of honeybees and wrote in a travel book dated 1835 (*A Tour of the Prairie*), "The Indians consider them harbingers of the white man, as the buffalo is of the red man; and say that, in proportion as the bee advances, the Indian and the buffalo retire. The Indians also feared the honeybee as a sign that smallpox would soon devastate them."

The phrase "Indian summer" came into English as a signifier of cultural change during the 19th century. It refers to a period of mild weather, usually in early October, which followed the first frost (this cycle is often later today because of global warming). Native peoples were accustomed to moving between summer and winter camps. Following the incursion of European Americans, migrating Native peoples often found their way impeded by farms, livestock, railroads, and fences, so conflicts broke out. The nomadic lifestyle was supported by a trading culture with the whites that created a demand for skins not only of buffalo but also other animals, such as beaver, which also became fashionable on the East Coast and Europe during the 19th century.

Many Native peoples also knowingly adapted to a nomadic culture to avoid imported diseases, the most dangerous of which was smallpox. Sedentary peoples were much more likely to fall prey to contagions. Population estimates between 1780 and 1877 indicated that while sedentary peoples lost as many as 80 to 90 percent of their people (mainly to disease), nomads often lost 10 to 20 percent.

The nomadic way of life could be risky, with periods of abundance alternating with hunger. One captive of the Oglalas, Fanny Kelly, described a diet of bison leavened with locusts: "The Indians seemed refreshed by feasting on such small game" (Isenberg, 2000, 73). Andrew H. Long wrote in 1821 that the Plains Indians' "means of subsistence are precarious and uncertain . . . a state of constant alarm and apprehension" (Isenberg, 2000, 64). The chancy nature of life is also reflected in the folktales of the Lakotas and Cheyennes, which may cast the buffalo as "both a mythic source of social and environmental stability and a wily, elusive antagonist" (Isenberg, 2000, 75).

Andrew Isenberg speculated that the risky nature of life contributed to a communal culture that valued cooperation and relatively equitable distribution of food and other resources, although it did not eradicate class differences. Conflict sometimes broke out among various parts of the same group, especially among Sioux bands such as the Hunkpapas, who were known for being cantankerous. The customs of many civic societies among Plains peoples such as the Sioux and Cheyennes also stressed the virtues of charity for the poor. Scarcity also lay at the root of strong cultural taboos against waste.

Several eyewitness accounts indicated that the taboo against waste was frequently broken, especially during large summer hunts that might kill 200 to 300 bison in one afternoon, leaving a tribe with much more meat than anyone could process. A large hunt turned into a feast at which everyone ate as much as he or she could. Custom called for putting every part of an animal to good use, but in practice, the boom-and-bust cycle sometimes left the cleaning up to packs of wolves. Charles McKenzie observed that most of 250 carcasses were left to rot after a successful summer hunt, "on the field where they fell, excepting the Tongues which they dried for a general feast" ("Charles," 1985, 282).

The robe trade changed many Plains Native cultures quickly and fundamentally. The size of buffalo hunts exploded to as many as about 1,500 animals in one day. Any remaining taboos on waste vanished, as nothing often was taken from the dead buffalo except their hides and their tongues. The size of wolf packs following the hunting parties grew apace. "The White Wolves," wrote George Catlin, "followed the herds of buffaloes . . . glutting themselves on the carcasses of those that fall by the deadly shafts of their enemies" (Townsend, 1839, 21:170).

Men of prestige in northern Plains tribes had long taken more than one wife, but with the coming of the robe trade, two or three wives became five, six, and seven. Each woman represented a source of income when she dressed buffalo robes. The average age of weddings among the Blackfeet declined from the late teens to as young as 12 years of age. Anglo-American female captives sometimes were pressed into service as robe dressers.

Buffalo Slaughter

The number of bison (or buffalo) in North America, principally on the Great Plains, declined from between 25 and 30 million in 1800 to fewer than 1,000 by about 1900, after which their extinction was averted narrowly by carefully managed conservation efforts. The American Bison Society, a private group, cooperated with the tribes and government agencies to restore some of the herds. By 1995, a concerted effort to replenish buffalo herds had raised the population to an estimated 200,000.

The slaughter of the vast buffalo herds that had once roamed the plains and prairies began in the 1840s. During most years of the 1870s, a million buffalo a year were killed by non-Indian hunters on the northern Plains. The railroads ran special excursions along their newly opened tracks from which self-styled sportsmen shot buffalo from the comfort of their seats.

The near extermination of the buffalo was mainly a result of the European American incursion into the Plains, which seized their range for cattle that overgrazed buffalo habitats and spread diseases fatal to them, just as the Indians who had hunted them also were dying for the same reasons. Part of the population decline came about because of hunting for their skins, which became fashionable as coats among Europeans and their offspring in America. Part of the killing also was purposeful, without a trade stimulus, to deprive the Plains peoples of an animal vital to their cultures and economies. In this event, huge piles of buffalo carcasses were often left to rot, with only the tongues (a dietary delicacy) removed.

General Phil Sheridan of the U.S. Army viewed the slaughter of the buffalo as a weapon in the Army's arsenal against the last remaining independent Native Americans: "I would not seriously regret the total disappearance of the buffalo from our western prairies, in its effect upon the Indians, regarding it rather as a means of hastening their dependence upon products of the soil," Sheridan said (Morris, 1992, 343). At one point, Sheridan suggested that buffalo poachers be given medals with a dead buffalo engraved on one side and a discouraged-looking Indian on the other. Sheridan, never a man to mince words, remarked that buffalo hunters had done more to defeat the Indians than the entire regular Army.

Hunters utilize the new railroad to shoot buffalo on the Great Plains in the late 19th century. Tens of millions of buffalo were reduced to near extinction by the 1880s, depriving Native peoples of their main form of sustenance. (Library of Congress)

By the 1830s, steamboats were plying the Missouri and Mississippi rivers, hauling dressed buffalo robes to New Orleans *en masse*. In 1801, the annual exports could be counted on one's fingers; by 1825 to 1830, an average of 130,000 buffalo robes per year arrived from upriver at New Orleans. Among the Lakotas, Nakotas, Dakotas, Cheyennes, and other peoples, buffalo robes became the backbone of trade culture. All of this lasted a few decades, until the buffalo were nearly gone and robes went out of fashion. The many Plains peoples who had become suddenly prosperous suddenly descended into destitution. A Blackfoot band that called itself the Buffalo Followers called 1854 "The year we ate dogs" (Isenberg, 2000, 112).

The buffalo herds of the central plains were finished off during the 1860s with a technological boost from a new line of high-powered hunting rifles. The large buffalo herds that had roamed the southern Plains, sustaining thousands of Native people (who still lived as they preferred, with the buffalo at the root of their economies), were largely destroyed by the 1870s. Hunters of the dwindling herds were followed by skinners, who (depending on market conditions) might strip the hides, or just remove the slain buffaloes' tongues. No one ever counted the number of buffalo that fell.

The Speed of Extermination

The extermination of the buffalo on the Great Plains of North America oc- curred so quickly during the last half of the 19th century that an unknown number of Native Americans starved to death, unable to change cultures and economic systems in which the animal was the most basic food. Treaty com- missioners warned of the impending extermination beginning in the 1850s, but John C. Ewers wrote, "as long as there were buffalo to be hunted, their efforts to induce nomadic hunters to become sedentary farmers met with very little success. The Indians were too thoroughly committed by both experience and inclination . . . to a hunting-trading economy to abandon [it] as long as they had any choice in the matter" (Ewers, 1997, 58).

In many cases, the U.S. and Canadian governments also were unable to es- tablish alternative food sources quickly enough to prevent profound human suffering and death. Hunger provoked wars—one example being the Great Sioux Uprising, which began during 1862 in Minnesota when U.S. officials refused to release food stockpiles to starving Indians from warehouses. That uprising ended with the largest mass hanging in U.S. history (38 people) at Mankato, Minnesota. Locals wanted to hang more than 300, but President Abraham Lincoln pardoned most of them for lack of evidence.

By the 1870s, the West was being knit together by the railroads, and most of the Native peoples were confined to reservations. The bison hunt for the most part was being taken over by whites, who stepped up the slaughter. By this time, European Americans were killing more buffalo than Native Americans. Of 1.2 million buffalo skins shipped east on the railroads in 1872 and 1873, about 350,000 (28 percent) were supplied by Indians. The buffalo hides were being used for more than robes; they became the leather belts that ran indus- trial machinery. Buffalo bones by the ton were being ground into black pigment and fertilizer.

During one winter (1872–1873) hide dealers in Dodge City, Kansas, shipped out about 400,000 hides on the newly arrived Santa Fe Railroad. While the area around Dodge City had been thickly populated with bison in 1872, a year later, "where there were myriads of buffalo . . . there were myriads of carcasses. The air was foul with sickening stench, and the vast plain which only a short twelve months before had teemed with animal life was a dead, solitary, putrid desert" (Dodge, 1989, 150–151). By one estimate, the Santa Fe, Kansas Pacific, and Union Pacific Railroads shipped 1.4 million buffalo hides between 1872 and 1874. Many hides were ruined in processing and never were shipped, perhaps three to five to one. By the late 1870s, buffalo on the southern Plains had been nearly exterminated; a railroad spur opened to Miles City, Montana, and the process continued in that area. A *New York Times* reporter in Miles City wrote in 1880 that bison carcasses covered the prairies.

The Plains were swarming with unemployed railroad workers, would-be farmers whose homesteads would not sustain their families, and hopeful miners caught between gold rushes. Buffalo populations were reduced to levels that would no longer sustain the trade during the 1880s. There were an estimated 5,000 non-Indian hunters chasing them. By the early 1880s, the U.S. Army's version of total war against the Plains Indians had reached its goal: the buffalo were nearly extinct. Ten years earlier, some of the Plains Indians still had an ample supply of food; by the early 1880s, they were reduced, as General Sheridan had intended, to the condition of paupers, without food, shelter, clothing, or any of those necessities of life that came from the buffalo. The Great Plains buffalo culture was dying, but would revive.

Contemporary Buffalo

By 2012, buffalo in the United States numbered more than 500,000, many of them being raised as a lean alternative to beef. Ted Turner, who made a fortune in cable television and invested part of it in a large swath of the Nebraska Sand Hills, raised a large bison herd there. Upscale grocery stores sell bison steaks as a healthy alternative to beef. The National Bison Legacy Act, introduced in the U.S. Senate in 2012, would designate bison as the "National Mammal of the United States," a new designation. A white bison in Texas was slaughtered during 2011 in what may have been a racial hate crime.

Buffalo are still closely identified with Native American culture, so much so that when a rare white buffalo (one in 10 million) was born on a farm near Goshen, Connecticut, during June 2012, many American Indians traveled there for four days of festivities and a naming ceremony on July 28. A white bison is believed by many Oglala Lakotas to be a spiritual manifestation of the White Buffalo Calf Maiden, or *ptesan wi*, a prophet, who taught the Lakotas sacred rituals and provided their sacred pipe. The 30-pound calf was born on Peter Fay's farm in Litchfield County, Connecticut, an event that, according to an account in the *New York Times*, "made the Fay farm below Mohawk Mountain, for the moment at least, the unlikely epicenter of the bison universe" (Applebome, 2012).

People traveled to the Fay farm from across North America to see the white buffalo calf. "They're awesome animals, wild, not domesticated," Fay said. "You think of them in South Dakota, where it's a desert and hot in the summer and bitterly cold in the winter. They don't mind either one. And they don't get sick. They're not like a cow. They're very hardy. They can deal with anything" (Applebome, 2012). Fay said he carefully researched the bloodlines of the calf's mother and father, and he is confident the animal is all bison without any intermingling with cattle. But to be certain, he sent its DNA for testing. Keith Aune, senior conservation scientist with the Wildlife Conservation Society, said some white bison are albinos and have difficulty thriving in the wild because they lack the black skin that absorbs sunlight during harsh winters.

Marian White Mouse brought her family from Wanblee, South Dakota, on the Pine Ridge Oglala Lakota reservation, to see what they regarded as a major spiritual event. "They are very rare, and when a white bison is born there is a reason for each one to be here," White Mouse said. "It's such a blessing for someone to take care of a bison like Peter Fay will. I told him when it was born, 'You don't even know what you have on your hands here'" (Applebome, 2012).

See Also PART 1: OVERVIEW: POPULATION AND DEMOGRAPHICS: Disease, Depopulation, and Cultural Destruction; **NATIONS, TRIBES, AND OTHER NATIVE GROUPS:** Apache Culture; Cheyenne Cultural Context; Osage Economic Culture; Ponca Culture; **PART 2: CULTURAL FORMS: ARTS:** Clothing; Moccasins; **FAMILY, EDUCATION, AND COMMUNITY:** Spotlight: Buffalo Hunt Customs and Protocols; Civic and Military Societies

Further Reading

Applebome, Peter. "A Bison So Rare It's Sacred." *New York Times*, July 12, 2012. http://www.nytimes.com/2012/07/13/nyregion/sacred-white-bison-is-born-in-rural-connecticut.html. Accessed October 29, 2014.

Bradbury, John. *Travels in the Interior of America in the Years 1809, 1810, and 1811.* London: Sheerwood, Neely, and Jones, 1810. In Reuben Golf Thwaites, ed. *Early Western Travels: 1748–1846.* Vol. 5. Cleveland: Clark, 1904.

Branch, Douglas E. *The Hunting of the Buffalo.* Lincoln: University of Nebraska Press, 1973.

"Charles McKenzie's Narratives." In W. Raymond Wood and Thomas D. Thiessen, eds. *Early Fur Trade on the Northern Plains: Canadian Traders Among the Hidatsa and Indians, 1738–1818.* Norman: University of Oklahoma Press, 1985.

Dodge, Richard I. *The Plains of North America and Their Inhabitants.* Newark: University of Delaware Press, 1989.

Ewers, John C. *Plains Indian History and Culture: Essays in Continuity and Change.* Norman: University of Oklahoma Press, 1997.

Garretson, Martin S. *The American Bison: The Story of Its Extermination as a Wild Species and Its Restoration under Federal Protection.* New York: New York Zoological Society, 1938.

Hedren, Paul L. *After Custer: Loss and Transformation in Sioux Country.* Norman: University of Oklahoma Press, 2011.

Hodgson, Bryan. "Buffalo: Back Home on the Range." *National Geographic* 186, no. 5 (November 1994): 64–89.

Hornaday, William T. "The Extermination of the American Bison with a Sketch of Its Discovery and Life History." *Annual Report of the Smithsonian Institution.* 1887. Vol. 2. Washington, DC: Government Printing Office, 1889, 367–548.

Irving, Washington. *A Tour on the Prairie.* Edited by John Francis McDermott. Norman: University of Oklahoma Press, 1956 (1835).

Isenberg, Andrew C. *The Destruction of the Bison: An Environmental History, 1750–1920.* Cambridge: Cambridge University Press, 2000.

Johnson, Lowell, ed. *The First Voices.* Lincoln: University of Nebraska Press, 1984.

Klein, Alan M. "The Political Economy of the Buffalo Hide Trade: Race and Class on the Plains." In John H. Moore, ed. *Political Economy of North American Indians.* Norman: University of Oklahoma Press, 1993.

"Montana's Indian Puzzle." *New York Times*, April 4, 1880, 2.

Morris, Roy, Jr. *Sheridan: The Life and Wars of General Phil Sheridan.* New York: Crown Publishers, 1992.

National Bison Legacy Act website. *votebison.org.* Accessed October 29, 2014.

Townsend, John K. *Narratives of a Journey Across the Rocky Mountains to the Columbia River.* Boston: Perkins and Marvin, 1839.

Spotlight

BUFFALO HUNT CUSTOMS AND PROTOCOLS

Before they acquired horses, Native bands sometimes hunted buffalo by herding them over "jumps," cliffs that were nearly invisible to the stampeding animals until they were crowded over the edge by animals behind them, after which they would be killed with arrows. Following such a stampede, the hunters and their wives worked quickly to preserve the meat, often by drying it in the sun to make jerky. In the heat of summer, when buffalo were usually hunted, undressed meat could spoil within a day.

Before they acquired horses from the immigrating Europeans, the traveling range of Plains Native peoples was limited. Many of them lived east of the areas that they later utilized as buffalo hunting ranges. The Lakotas, Nakotas, and Dakotas (called Sioux by the immigrants), for example, lived mainly in present-day Minnesota, where they pursued a mixed agriculture, raising corn and other crops, hunting buffalo when they came within a range that could be reached on foot.

A pedestrian buffalo hunt could be undertaken without a bluff. It required careful organization and planning by the people of several villages, and it tended to encourage a culture of clans organized in a hierarchical manner. A leader was chosen and given absolute obedience during the hunt. Individual hunting that might incite an unplanned stampede was strictly forbidden and punished. "The leader organized all members of the village(s) to form a large circle around the herd," wrote Andrew Isenberg (2000). "On cue, the hunters slowly closed the circle, careful not to alarm the animals. Once they had closed the circle they fired the prairie grass, enclosing the herd, and proceeded to shoot the trapped animals with arrows" (p. 38).

Native acquisition of the horse had an immense impact both on the hunting of buffalo and on the economic behavior and social structure of Native societies. A large number of Native societies transformed themselves into roving buffalo hunting bands. Elite societies of young men skilled at buffalo hunting emerged, forming the basis of the Plains warrior societies, who pursued the animals. A male buffalo can weigh a ton and can charge at 30 miles an hour.

When the men of a village realized that a buffalo herd was within a few hours' journey, they met to decide whether to organize a hunt. Unless other affairs intervened, the ready presence of sustenance was enough to get people moving. A crier was sent through the village or camp, announcing plans for the hunt, urging all able-bodied men to assemble with their horses, arrows at the ready, knives sharpened. Women also sometimes accompanied men on the hunt to dress meat and hides, or just to ride along. Sarah Olden wrote (1999), "The whole band . . . in feathers and war paint, bearing knives, clubs, bows, and arrows then mounted their lively, knowing, little horses and rushed out of camp to the beating of drums and the singing of songs for the buffalo chase" (p. 113).

The group usually appointed two leaders to enforce discipline. Guns were forbidden on buffalo hunts, and anyone using one could be beaten on the spot. Back in camp, an offender's tipi might be destroyed as well. The sound of gunfire could cause a stampede and wreck a hunt. Reaching the herd's range, the hunting party stopped to plan a strategy. The hunt was a team effort, and anyone who showed off by running ahead of the group was whipped and forced back into line—again, too much agitation could startle the animals and ruin the hunt.

At the leaders' signal, the hunters advanced on the buffalo, which at first usually stood their ground, as if dazed. After a prearranged sharp shout, the buffalo took off, with the mounted Indians following, isolating as many animals as needed and killing them. Occasionally, a bull might reverse field and charge into the hunting party. Some men died this way. After the hunt women dressed the meat and hides, which were loaded onto extra horses brought along for that purpose. Some of the meat was cooked and eaten as part of a celebratory feast before everyone returned home. Some of the dried meat and carcasses might be wrapped in hides and buried in the cool earth for future use.

The tanning of hides was hard work:

> First the thick fat was scraped from the inside with a horn, and a mush or paste made of the brain, liver, and gall was rubbed over it again and again. The hide was turned toward the sun for a day or two and then soaked for some time in an infusion of sage brush. It was dried thoroughly and rubbed all over with a large stone . . . [to] make it soft and pliable. (Olden, 1999, 121)

During the 1860s and 1870s, the number of non-Indians in Arapaho country exploded, and buffalo herds declined markedly, largely at the hands of white sharpshooters who destroyed much of the Arapahos' traditional culture and economy, as it had been modified by the fur trade.

Further Reading

Isenberg, Andrew C. *The Destruction of the Bison: An Environmental History, 1750–1920*. Cambridge: Cambridge University Press, 2000.

Long, Stephen H. "A General Description of the Country Traversed by the Exploring Expedition." In Reuben Golf Thwaites, ed. *Early Western Travels: 1748–1846*. Vol. 5. Cleveland: Clark, 1904.

Olden, Sarah. "Part II: The People of Tipi Sapa." In Vine Deloria, Jr. *Singing for a Spirit: A Portrait of the Oglala Sioux*. Santa Fe: Clear Light, 1999.

Walker, James R. *Lakota Society*. Edited by Raymond J. DeMallie. Lincoln: University of Nebraska Press, 1982.

CIVIC AND MILITARY SOCIETIES

History and Origins

Native American nations across the Great Plains of North America maintained a variety of civic and military societies such as the Omahas' *Hethu'shka* society, described by Alice C. Fletcher and Francis LaFlesche in 1911, that maintained rules that tended to enforce peace and harmony within the tribe. The society also reinforced cultural continuity in an oral culture, which Fletcher and LaFlesche called "an heroic spirit among the people . . . [to] keep alive the memory of historic and valorous acts" (Fletcher and LaFlesche, 1972 (1911), 2:459, 462). The Apache societies also maintained continuity with the past.

Civic societies often played a role in staging pow wows and other ceremonies. This was true of the Kiowa and Apache rabbit societies, which staged their dances in conjunction with warrior societies. Like the Lakota societies, the Apaches' civic societies were charged with aiding the poor. This practice helped to distribute wealth. Members of the Pawnee Crazy Dog Society maintained a custom of removing their moccasins during ceremonial dances to "put them on a needy bystander" (Murie, 1914, 580).

Regional Variations

The Ponca *He-thus-ka* society supported people who were mourning the loss of loved ones by collecting gifts, caring for the indigent, and entertaining visiting tribes. Lakota culture included several civic societies that supported the moral fiber of communities. The Society of Braves (*Cante Tinza Okodakiciye*) and the Society of Owls' Feathers (*Mawatani Okodakiciye*) each were led by seven senior officers, a doorkeeper, and a crier. Both inducted new members, who were male (except for women who aided in singing), and charged them with maintaining societal standards, which included generosity (defined as giving horses to the elderly, poor, and orphans). Morals offenses (such as going off with a woman who was married to another man) could result in expulsion for a Brave.

The main difference between the two societies was the age and experience of members. Braves, who were relatively young, were charged with protecting the people when needed through acts of valor. Owls' Feathers members, who were generally older, acted as senior advisors. Owls' Feathers members were instructed to never mistreat their wives; if a member's wife eloped with another man, he was restrained from pursuing her. However, the transgressing wife's character was considered forfeit, and she was unwelcome in the village until she returned to her husband on her own. At that point, the Owls' Feathers member was bound to treat her kindly. Like Braves, Owls' Feathers members were instructed to share with the elderly, poor, and orphans.

The Plains peoples' warrior societies made preparation for and conduct of war a way of life. By 10 years of age, a boy's life could resemble a little boot camp, in which they "were made to take long runs, go without food and water for long periods of time, roll in snow, dive into icy water, and learn to stay awake for hours on end. . . . Use of the lance, the bow and arrow, and skill in horsemanship were also learned at an early age" (Dugan, 1985, 48).

Members of the Grass, Wolf, Warrior, and Crow societies, most of whom shared experience in battle, were elected much like those of the other groups, with an emphasis on courage in battle. An annual meeting was held to share accounts of these feats. Like the other societies, the Grass Society elected seven principal men, a doorkeeper, and a crier. The killing of at least one man was a qualification for office. Acts of self-denial were much esteemed.

Grass Society members lined their moccasins with grass to keep them warm and carried grass in their pockets so they could start fires quickly. They cut their hair on the sides of their heads but grew and braided the middle, adding a second braid to the first. To this string of braids they added ornaments, including feathers representing the number of men killed in battle. "Sometimes the feathers were so numerous," wrote Sarah Olden (1999), "that they were stuck in the braid . . . and often extended through the whole length of it to the ground" (p. 159). A Grass Society member used his body as a canvas to record feats of valor in battle—stealing a horse from an enemy or saving a compatriot. Eagle feathers colored red denoted an injury in battle (resembling a Purple Heart in the U.S. Army). A severe wound would be marked by red paint around the mouth.

Other military societies included the Society of Foxes, who pulled out their hair on the sides of their heads by its roots, except for tufts on either side. Hair on the middle of the head was grown long and braided, then ornamented. As a civic society, the Foxes worked in much the same manner as the Braves and Owls' Feathers—to be brave and to share what they had with an eye toward others' welfare. Among the Sioux *Akicitas*, or police societies, the Foxes were dedicated to preparing to die for the protection of their people, as embodied by their song:

> *I am a Fox*
> *I am supposed to die*
> *If there is anything difficult,*
> *If there is anything dangerous,*
> *that is mine to do.* (Hassrick, 1964, 21)

A sense of personal rigor and self-control as well as a toughening of the body were also part of youth life among the Coast Salish. Thus, young children might be toughened by bathing in cold water, to the point of a winter dunk in a river through a break in thin ice. Except when ill, adults continued such immersions throughout life, just as canoe families in our time sometimes take morning baths in the cold waters of Puget Sound.

Further Reading

Dugan, Kathleen Margaret. *The Vision Quest of the Plains Indians: Its Spiritual Significance.* Lewiston, ID: Edwin Mellen Press, 1985.

Ellis, Clyde. *A Dancing People: Powwow Culture on the Southern Plains.* Lawrence: University Press of Kansas, 2003.

Elmendorf, William W. *The Structure of Twana* [Skokomish] *Culture.* Pullman: Washington State University Press, 1960.

Fletcher, Alice C., and Francis LaFlesche. *The Omaha Tribe.* 2 vols. Lincoln: University of Nebraska Press, 1972 (1911).

Hassrick, Royal B. *The Sioux: Life and Customs of a Warrior Society.* Norman: University of Oklahoma Press, 1964.

Murie, James R. "Pawnee Indian Societies." *Anthropological Papers of the American Museum of Natural History* XI, Part VII (1914): 543–644.

Olden, Sarah. "Part II: The People of Tipi Sapa." In Vine Deloria, Jr. *Singing for a Spirit: A Portrait of the Oglala Sioux.* Santa Fe: Clear Light, 1999, 159.

Skinner, Alanson. "Ponca Society and Dances." *Anthropological Papers of the American Museum of Natural History* XI, Part IX (1915): 779, 801.

Spotlight

COUP, COUNTING COUP

Many Plains warriors acquired prestige in battle by "counting coup"—that is, touching an enemy without injuring or killing him. To do so (and escape without retaliation) required a great deal of physical skill. Battle under such conditions took on aspects of an athletic contest rather than a fight to the death, as in much of European warfare, especially after adoption of horses, but before guns made warfare bloodier.

Coup (French for "a blow") counted for higher value if a warrior took greater risk. The degree of risk had more value than the outcome of a battle or raid. Counting coup on an armed foe was more valuable than killing him, and more praiseworthy at council gatherings to which the warrior who had scored the coup would recount his act of valor. Wounding an enemy from a distance without first having touched him scored no coup. The greatest coup included capture of a foe's weapons, horses, and ceremonial paraphernalia. Having been touched by an enemy incurred considerable dishonor. At council, coups were recalled in detail with the aid of witnesses, and a feather from a male golden eagle could be awarded that a warrior would wear on his scalp lock or war bonnet with other awards he had earned.

Even after guns came into use, coup could be awarded for striking an enemy with a gun, or with a bow, a lance, or a coup stick. Additional coup was awarded for killing an enemy after striking him. A coup stick was bent at one end and festooned with various things, such as shreds of otter fur. Coup sticks were valued in families as inheritance.

Other actions, such as stealing a horse from an enemy, also credited coup. One also could score coup by entering an enemy village stealthily and touching a tipi or lodge. The warrior had then "captured" an enemy lodging and earned the right to use its decorative designs on his own. To enter a village, count coup on an enemy lodging, then kill him and steal his horse was a coup trifecta of sorts. However, the original touching of an enemy was generally considered a higher honor than killing him. Killing without counting coup first was not honorable. Some peoples, such as the Assiniboine, Crows, and Arapahos, allowed as many as four warriors to earn coup by touching an enemy before killing him.

Warriors observed coup by wearing certain feathers, much as modern military personnel earn medals. Blackfoot warriors earned white weasel skins; Crows attached wolf tails to the heels of their moccasins.

Further Reading

Maxwell, James A., ed. *America's Fascinating Indian Heritage*. Pleasantville, NY: Reader's Digest, 1978.

CLIMATE CHANGE AND NATIVE PEOPLES

Climate change induced by human consumption of fossil fuels impacts everyone on Earth and has become the signature environmental issue of our time. Native peoples of North America, with their close connection to the Earth and subsistence styles of life, are among the first to be significantly affected by a rapidly changing climate. This is most evident in the Arctic, which is the swiftest warming area on Earth, where an Inuit world built on ice is melting away. Alaskan Native communities also face climate-induced change, including relocation of entire coastal villages. Elsewhere in North America, Native water resources and food sources already have been damaged by a warming climate.

"We need to be worried about climate change because it's clearly already affecting our region in ways that impact many areas—we're seeing landscapes burning, dying because of heat and dryness," lead author Jonathan Overpeck, of the Southwest Climate Science Center, told Indian Country Today Media Network. "We're seeing reservoirs that were full just ten years ago now only half full on the Colorado. These are visible harbingers of what might come. What we need to do as a society is talk about it and figure out how to deal with these challenges" (Allen, 2012).

Iqaluit, capital of Nunavut, Canada, on Baffin Island, has endured record warmth as the proportion of greenhouse gases rises in the lower atmosphere. (AP Photo/ Beth Duff-Brown)

American Indians Feel the Effects of Climate Change Most Intensely

A National Wildlife Federation report, *Facing the Storm: Indian Tribes, Climate-Induced Weather Extremes and the Future for Indian Country*, suggests that American Indians suffer more intensely than other ethnic groups from climate change. The report said, "The high dependence of tribes upon their lands and natural resources to sustain their economic, cultural and spiritual practices, the relatively poor state of their infrastructure and the great need for financial and technical resources to recover from such events all contribute to the disproportionate impact on tribes" ("American Indians," 2011). Not only does Native American spirituality emphasize relationships with nature, but Alaska Natives and American Indians depend more on natural resources, as well as rivers and oceans. Tribes suffer from a lack of resources and feel the negative impacts even more from extreme weather.

"Climate change is reshaping the daily lives of many Native peoples," according to reporting on the Indian Country Today Media Network, "especially that of coastal communities. They have witnessed the destruction of their freshwater streams, lakes, watersheds, coral reefs, and the devastating decline of fish and wildlife" ("First Stewards," 2012). At a First Stewards Symposium convened during July 2012 in Washington, D.C., coastal tribes and nations of Washington State (Makah, Quileute, Hoh, and Quinault Indians) drafted a resolution sent to the U.S. Congress and President Obama that "requests formal recognition of the coastal indigenous people and their expertise in understanding and adapting to changes in their natural systems" ("First Stewards," 2012). "We are girding our loincloth and sharpening our spears to undertake this project and are asking President Obama, the U.S. Congress and others to engage in sincere and earnest consultation with us, so our cultures, our peoples and our world can survive and thrive," said Kitty Simonds, vice chair of the First Stewards board of directors. Lawrence Snow, land resources manager for Utah's Shivwits Band of Paiutes, explains:

> Our 30,000-acre reservation is pretty dry because of drought. Wildfires in the last decade have burned half our acreage and changed the landscape. We've got less trees, and bark beetles are trying to kill off the ones we do have. Once the fires happened and took out the ground cover, major storms brought big flooding. Seasons have changed; winter hangs around now until May. It's weird the way the weather is changing. (Allen, 2012)

Consulting with Native Peoples

Greenpeace activists during 1997 gathered information about global warming from Yup'ik and Inupiat Inuit. They embarked on the organization's 150-foot ship, *Arctic Sunrise*, on a route north to Barrow along Alaska's Arctic coast. The activists reported that Savoonga whalers brought home no whales in 1997 due to a quick and early breakup of ice that forced them to come home earlier than usual. Inuit said that for several years they have been routinely catching fish heretofore not considered native to the Arctic, including chum and pink and silver salmon. Like observers the width of the Arctic, Inuit interviewed by Greenpeace said they had observed birds that are new to higher latitudes, such as various types of swallows, finches, and robins.

A Canadian government report, *Responding to Global Climate Change in Canada's Arctic*, released late in 1997, did its best to put a positive spin on how global warming in the Arctic affects Native peoples. Reading closely, however, one realizes that most of the benefits accrue to industrial society's incursion into the Arctic. The report noted that reduced ice cover would aid offshore oil and gas production and extend the shipping season. In the western Arctic, said the same report, opportunities for agriculture would arise.

Most of global warming's debits are accruing to the Inuit, the animals of the region, and their traditional relationship. The report expects that precipitation will increase as much as 25 percent during the century with the advent of rapidly rising temperatures. When the precipitation falls as snow and ice, caribou and other grazing animals will have a harder time finding food during lean winter months. The study anticipates that heavier snow cover will lead to smaller, thinner animals, which will be forced to go further afield for food in winter. The same animals will be plagued by increasing numbers of insects during warmer summers. Environmental stresses during the next century could, in a worst-case scenario, lead to complete reproductive failure of the caribou.

The United States Geological Survey (USGS) also has been consulting with Arctic peoples. "Many climate change studies are conducted on a large scale, and there is a great deal of uncertainty regarding how climate change will impact specific regions," said USGS social scientist Nicole Herman-Mercer (Observations, 2011). The USGS, for example, describes thinning ice on the Andreafsky and Yukon rivers and notes that Arctic peoples use frozen rivers as transportation routes using snowmobiles or dogsleds. Early melting and late freezing disrupts hunting patterns and trade.

Warming's Pervasive Effects

The cascading effects of climate change on North American Native peoples became the sole focus of an entire issue of the scientific journal *Climatic Change*, published in October 2013. Special attention was paid to the congruence between Native elders' observations and meteorological records, finding widespread agreement. Native subsistence was a major focus of this scientific forum, from observations that moose seem less healthy, to effects of diminishing sea ice on walrus, effects on salmon runs, and damage from increased storm intensity and rising seas. Some shore-dwelling tribes along the Washington coast (Quileute and Hoh, for example) have moved, or are considering leaving seafront homelands inundated by rising storm surges.

Many Native residents of the Arctic have asserted that the climate in which they live has become stormier as weather has warmed. Late in 2009, two scientists in the School of Earth Sciences at the University of Melbourne, Victoria, Australia, provided statistics that support those assertions. Ian Simmonds and Kevin Keay studied the month of September because sea ice has been markedly reduced from 1979 through 2008, and found that cyclonic storms had become stronger, although the number of storms had not changed significantly. "The findings reinforce suggestions that the decline in the extent and thickness of Arctic ice has started to render it particularly vulnerable to future anomalous cyclonic activity and atmospheric forcing," they wrote in *Geophysical Research Letters*.

The beaver population has risen as the weather warms, and they run the risk of contracting "beaver fever" or giardia, an intestinal infection. "In general, people could drink from [the creeks and rivers] freely. Now they have beavers defecating into the river," said Michael Brubaker, director of the health consortium's Center for Climate and Health ("Climate Change," 2011).

Rising temperatures enhance the probability of disease in many fish on which Native peoples depend. For example, Chinook salmon are now infected with a new parasite. Salmon, a cold-water fish, are very sensitive to warming water, which debilitates them and often makes them ill. In the summer of 2003, salmon were forced to pause their upstream migration at the Bonneville Dam on the Columbia River for several weeks until temperatures cooled. Warmer water is causing mussels to disappear in some Pacific Northwest waters. Rising ocean acidity also is imperiling shellfish. Along some parts of the Pacific Coast shellfish have stopped reproducing because sea water contains so much carbon dioxide that it has become acidic.

Crow elders' observations describing rising temperatures and diminishing snowpack in southeastern Montana were compared to weather observations and fleshed out with effects on people. For example, with both drought and extreme rainfall events increasing, floods and wildfires (at different times) have become more damaging. With stream flow generally declining (except in occasional floods), distribution of fish on which Native people depend has become more precarious. Areas previously covered in snow and frozen from November to March are now bare grass.

In Crow country, berries often bud out earlier and then become vulnerable to sudden freezes in spring, killing the blossoms. Longer autumns mean that buffalo berries dry out before the first frost, making them worthless. Because of warmer winters, trees may emerge from dormancy and then die in sudden subsequent freezes. Increasingly hot late springs and summers have made fasting for a Sun Dance in late May or June risky for people's health. The average temperature in Hardin, Montana, has risen from 45.6°F in the 1950s to 50.1°F after 2000. Snow used to melt slowly, ensuring summer water supplies. Now, shorter winters and hotter summers threaten water supplies in the hot season. Persistent drought in the southern tier of states is forcing Navajos to travel longer distances for potable water and forcing the early sale of livestock. Premature snowmelt on the Pine Ridge provoked by temperature spikes to as high as 70°F during what used to be prethaw times has caused early flooding, as stranded residents had to have emergency drinking water delivered to them. Meanwhile, tribes in coastal Louisiana are losing land to rising sea levels, subsiding land, and erosion.

See Also PART 2: CULTURAL FORMS: FAMILY, EDUCATION, AND COMMUNITY: Spotlight: Climate Change and Alaska Natives; FOOD: Food Sovereignty; Wild Rice

Further Reading

Allen, Lee. "Southwest Tribes Struggle with Climate Change Fallout." *Indian Country Today Media Network*, June 14, 2012. http://indiancountrytodaymedianetwork.com/article/southwest-tribes-struggle-with-climate-change-fallout-118386more-beavers-defecating-and-disease.

"American Indians Feel the Effects of Climate Change at Higher Rate Than Other Groups." *Indian Country Today Media Network*, August 9, 2011. http://indiancountrytodaymedianetwork.com/article/american-indians-feel-the-effects-of-climate-change-at-higher-rate-than-other-groups-46365.

"Climate Change Puts Health of Arctic Villagers on Thin Ice." *Indian Country Today Media Network*, March 07, 2011. http://indiancountrytodaymedianetwork.com/article/climate-change-puts-health-of-arctic-villagers-on-thin-ice-21391.

Cozzetto, K., K. Chief, K. Dittmer, M. Brubaker, R. Gough, K. Souza, F. Ettawageshik, S. Wotkyns, S. Opitz-Stapleton, S. Duren, and P. Chavan. "Climate Change Impacts on the Water Resources of American Indians and Alaska Natives in the U.S." *Climatic Change* 120 (2013): 569–584.

Doyle, John T., Margaret Hiza Redsteer, and Margaret J. Eggers. "Exploring Effects of Climate Change on Northern Plains American Indian Health." *Climatic Change* 120 (2013): 643–655.

"First Stewards Resolution Asks U.S. Congress to Formally Recognize Ecological Knowledge of Coastal Indigenous People." *Indian Country Today Media Network*, September 30, 2012. http://indiancountrytodaymedianetwork.com/article/first-stewards-resolution-asks-u.s.-congress-to-formally-recognize-ecological-knowledge-of-coastal-indigenous-people-136802.

George, Jane. "Sierra Club Focuses on Arctic Global Warming." *Nunatsiaq News*, January 31, 2000. http://www.nunatsiaq.com/archives/nunavut000131/nvt20121_04.html.

Lynn, Kathy, John Daigle, Jennie Hoffman, Frank Lake, Natalie Michelle, Darren Ranco, Carson Viles, Garrit Voggesser, and Paul Williams. "The Impacts of Climate Change on Tribal Traditional Foods." *Climatic Change* 120 (2013): 545–556.

"Observations of Climate Change from Indigenous Alaskans. USGS: Science for a Changing World." September 13, 2011. http://www.usgs.gov/newsroom/article_pf.asp?ID=2931.

Simmonds, Ian, and Kevin Keay. "Extraordinary September Arctic Sea Ice Reductions and Their Relationships with Storm Behavior over 1979–2008." *Geophysical Research Letters* 36 (October 14, 2009). L19715, doi:10.1029/2009GL039810.

Wilkin, Dwane. "Global Warming Poses Big Threats to Canada's Arctic." *Nunatsiaq News*, November 21, 1997. http://www.nunatsiaq.com/archives/back-issues/71121.html#6.

Spotlight

CLIMATE CHANGE AND ALASKA NATIVES

Climate change is swiftly transforming the lives of Alaskan Native peoples. This is most evident in the Arctic, which is the swiftest warming area on Earth, where an Inuit world built on ice is melting away. Alaskan Native communities also face climate-induced change, including relocation of entire coastal villages. Gunter Weller, director of the Center for Global Change and Arctic System Research at the University of Alaska in Fairbanks, said mean temperatures in the state have increased by 5°F in the summer and 10°F in the winter over the last 30 years. Moreover, the Arctic ice field has shrunk by 40 to 50 percent over the last few decades and has lost 10 percent of its thickness, studies show. "These are pretty large signals, and they've had an effect on the entire physical environment," Weller said (Murphy, 2001, A-1).

Alaskan Natives (such as Yup'iks in St. Mary's and Pitka's Point) have told the scientists that weather has become more unstable in ways that affect their lives. For example, less melting snow means that thawing rivers carry less of the driftwood that Native peoples use for cooking and heat. In Point Hope, Alaska, 330 miles south of Point Barrow, a 4,500-year-old Alaskan Native village of 900 people, thawing has caused problems with food storage. Juliet Eilperin (2012) wrote in the *Washington Post*:

> Fermented whale's tail doesn't taste the same when the ice cellars flood. . . . Whaling crews in this Arctic coast village store six feet of tail—skin, blubber and bone—underground from spring until fall. The tail freezes slowly while fermenting and taking on the flavor of the earth. Paying homage to their connection to the frozen sea, villagers eat the delicacy to celebrate

the moment when the Arctic's ice touches shore. But climate change, with its more intense storms, melting permafrost and soil erosion, is causing the ice cellars to disintegrate. Many have washed out to sea in recent decades. The remaining ones regularly flood in the spring, which can spoil the meat and blubber, and release scents that attract polar bears.

Stored in an electric freezer, the fermented whale's tail loses its distinctive taste. "So much of our culture is being washed away in the ocean," said Point Hope mayor Steve Oomittuk. "We live this cycle of life, which we know because it's been passed from generation to generation. We see that cycle breaking" (Eilperin, 2012). Melting ice deprives hunters of firm footing and obliterates paths that used to be reliable. Instead of poking their heads through holes in the ice, seals remain submerged in water, evading hunters.

A Winter without Walrus

Hunting, including walrus, is still key to survival for Native peoples across the Arctic. Imported food is not only culturally unappealing but also so expensive that few Native people can afford it. Wild swings in weather and ice conditions has devastated harvests of walrus, the main subsistence staple in some Alaskan Native villages. In recent years, ice, the primary habitat for walrus, has been too scarce—except, as in the winter of 2012–2013, when weather was so cold and ice so thick that hunters could not get out often enough to provide for their families.

Food imported by air to the one small grocery store in Gambell, Alaska (in extreme northwest Alaska within sight of Siberia's Chukchi Peninsula) is no alternative. A single chicken costs $25. Families that once put 20 to 25 walrus into their meat lockers each spring, meant to last until the next winter, have been storing only a handful in recent years because of retreating ice. "If this continues, we will seriously starve," said Jennifer Campbell, 38 years of age in 2013, mother of five, whose family caught only two walrus in the autumn of 2013, down from about 20 previously (Carlton, 2013, A-4). The Yup'ik Eskimos harvest the walrus from passing ice floes in May and June using small boats. In 2013, however, the hunt lasted only a week. "The ice was so bad we couldn't get out," said Brian Aningayou, a hunter who took only four walrus, who feeds an extended family of 40 people (Carlton, 2013, A-4). He has been shooting birds, which provide little meat compared to a walrus that can be the size and weight of a small car.

With ice receding hundreds of miles offshore of Alaska and Russia during the late summer of 2007, walrus gathered by the thousands onshore in Alaska and Siberia. Joel Garlich-Miller, a walrus expert with the U.S. Fish and Wildlife Service, said that walrus began to gather onshore late in July, a month earlier than usual. A month later, their numbers had reached record levels from Barrow to Cape Lisburne, about 300 miles southwest, on the Chukchi Sea.

Walrus usually feed on clams, snails, and other bottom-dwelling creatures below the ice. In recent years, the ice has receded too far from shore to allow the usual feeding pattern. A walrus can dive 600 feet, but water under ice shelves in late summer is now several thousands of feet deep. The walrus have been forced to swim much farther to find food, using energy that could cause increased calf mortality. More calves are being orphaned. Russian research observers also reported many more walrus than usual on shore, tens of thousands in some areas along the Siberian coast, which would have stayed on the sea ice in earlier times.

Walrus are prone to stampedes once they are gathered in large groups. Thousands of Pacific walrus above the Arctic Circle were killed on the Russian side of the Bering Strait where more than 40,000 had hauled out on land at Point Schmidt, as ice retreated farther north. A polar bear, a human hunter, or noise from an airplane flying close and low can send thousands of panicked walrus rushing to the water.

"It was a pretty sobering year, tough on walruses," said Joel Garlach-Miller, a walrus expert for the U.S. Fish and Wildlife Service. Several thousand walrus died late in the summer of 2007 from internal injuries suffered in stampedes. The youngest and the weakest animals, many of them calves born the previous spring, were crushed. Biologist Anatoly Kochnev of Russia's Pacific Institute of Fisheries and Oceanography estimated 3,000 to 4,000 walrus out of a population of perhaps 200,000 died, or two or three times the usual number on shoreline haulouts (Joling, December 14, 2007).

The reports support expectations of the walrus' fate once the ice retreated, notes wildlife biologist Tony Fischbach of the U.S. Geological Survey. "We were surprised that this was happening so soon, and we were surprised at the magnitude of the report," he said (Joling, December 14, 2007). Walrus lacking summer sea ice that they use to dive for clams and snails may strip coastal areas of food, and then they starve in large numbers.

Villages Fall to Encroaching Seas

Several coastal Alaskan Native villages have been declared disaster areas following a series of severe storms. By 2013, more than 30 Alaskan Native villages were experiencing or facing relocation due to climate change, including Shishmaref and Newtok. "Alaska is seeing all these things the rest of the country hasn't seen yet," said Dr. Jerome Montague, Native Affairs and Natural Resources Advisor for the Alaskan Command Joint Task Force (Jessepe, 2012). A new sea wall costing $3 million was built to quell erosion during 2006 in the village of Kivalina on Alaska's seaward side.

In Kivalina, erosion and flooding has poured sediment into the community water system, requiring filtration to prevent ingestion of unsanitary water. About 400 people in Kivalina could take only sponge baths and had limited access to laundry for the winter. "As hand-washing and bathing decreased, respiratory and skin diseases increased," health aides said ("Climate Change," 2011). In Point Hope, algae blooms clouded a lake used for drinking water. Kivalina hangs precariously on a slender, eroding peninsula that the U.S. Army Corps of Engineers projects the sea will wipe off the map by 2025.

And, in addition:

> The threat of food poisoning increases with rising temperatures. Meat stored in ice cellars carved from melting permafrost can become contaminated with pathogens that cause sickness. "We used to have frozen

whale meat and maktuk all winter and summertime, too," said Joe Towksjhea, a Point Hope resident, in the consortium's report. "It is not frozen anymore." ("Climate Change," 2011)

The Indian Country Today Media Network reported: "The Yup'ik village of Kotlik, Alaska, along with Unalakleet and other predominantly Native communities, were ravaged beginning November 9 [2013] by a series of four storms [that] battered hundreds of miles of Alaska's west coast with near hurricane-force winds, a sea surge as high as nine feet, freezing rain, and snow. . . . The storm surge wrecked food supplies" ("Yup'ik," 2013). For a time, the entire town was flooded with seawater and chunks of ice. Rising seas and coastal erosion directly threaten Tuktoyaktuk, a Dene and Inuit community located at the edge of the Arctic Ocean. Ice that once protected the coast has receded out to sea. Extensive erosion washed away the school and has forced the village to relocate many other structures.

These Native villages have been washing into the sea during increasingly stormy weather for several years. Six hundred people in the Inuit village of Shishmaref on the Chukchi Sea, about 60 miles north of Nome, have been watching their village erode into the sea. The permafrost that had reinforced its coast is thawing. "We stand on the island's edge and see the remains of houses fallen into the sea," wrote Anton Antonowicz of the London *Daily Mirror*. "They are the homes of poor people. Half-torn rooms with few luxuries. A few photographs, some abandoned cooking pots. Some battered suitcases" (Antonowicz, 2000, 8). Percy Nayokpuk, a village elder, runs the local store, which now perches dangerously close to the edge of the advancing sea. "When I was a teenager, the beach stretched at least 50 yards further out," said Percy. "As each year passes, the sea's approach seems faster" (Antonowicz, 2000, 8). Five houses have washed into the sea; the U.S. Army has moved or jacked up others. The villagers have been told they will soon have to move.

Shishmaref hunters are being forced to search up to 200 miles from town for walrus because of retreating ice. They also now use boats to hunt seals that they used to track over ice. "This year the ice was thinner, and most of the year at least part of the ice was open. We don't normally see open water in December," said Edwin Weyiouanna, an artist who has lived most of his life on the Chukchi Sea (Murphy, 2001, A-1). In earlier years, the sea was more likely to be frozen during much of the stormy winter season. With warming, the erosive, wind-whipped ocean corrodes Shishmaref's waterfront. The town's residents have come to fear the full moon with its unusually high tides.

Point Hope, on a spit of land that juts into the Chukchi Sea, has been losing its battle against the sea. Almost $2 million was spent to shore up its runway, the only connection with the outside, except for an evacuation road restored by the Army Corps of Engineers for $433,000.

Increasing coastal erosion isn't limited to Shishmaref; it is now general on the shores of the Bering Sea, as increasing storm surges crush ice packs that retreat several weeks earlier than 30 years ago. Sea ice extent in the Arctic has decreased Arctic-wide by 0.35 percent per year since 1979. During the summer of 1998, record reduction of sea ice coverage was observed in the Beaufort and Chukchi seas. In Tuktoyaktuk, a town near the mouth of the Mackenzie River, several buildings have been lost to erosion by the sea. In addition to a reduction in Bering Sea ice cover, more precipitation is falling in many areas of Alaska. During the fall of 1998, sea ice formed in northern Alaska more than a month later than usual, postponing the annual seal and walrus hunt. Average temperatures at the mouth of the Mackenzie River were 9°F above long-term averages during 1998. Several decades ago, miners in the area deposited toxic wastes in ponds that were expected to remain frozen (and the toxic materials sealed by the permafrost). With warmer temperatures, some of these toxic dumps may thaw and leak.

See Also PART 2: CULTURAL FORMS: FAMILY, EDUCATION, AND COMMUNITY: Climate Change and Native Peoples

Further Reading

"Anglo American Withdraws from Pebble Mine." *Environment News Service*, September 20, 2013. http://ens-newswire.com/2013/09/20/anglo-american-withdraws-from-alaskas-pebble-mine/

Antonowicz, Anton. "Baking Alaska: As World Leaders Bicker, Global Warming Is Killing a Way of Life." *London Mirror*, November 28, 2000, 8–9.

"Bristol Bay Tribes' Fight to Fend off Pebble Mine Highlighted in National Geographic." *Indian Country Today Media Network*, November 19, 2012. http://indiancountrytodaymedianetwork.com/bristol-bay-tribes-fight-to-fend-off-pebble-mine-highlighted-in-national-geographic.

Carlton, Jim. "A Winter without Walrus: Harvesting of Food Staple for Remote Eskimo Villages Plummets; Disaster Declared." *The Wall Street Journal*, October 4, 2013, A-4.

Chythlook-Sifsof, Callan J. "Native Alaska, Under Threat." *New York Times*, June 28, 2013. http://www.nytimes.com/2013/06/28/opinion/native-culture-under-threat.html.

"Climate Change Puts Health of Arctic Villagers on Thin Ice." *Indian Country Today Media Network*, March 07, 2011. http://indiancountrytodaymedianetwork.com/article/climate-change-puts-health-of-arctic-villagers-on-thin-ice-21391.

Eilperin, Juliet. "Alaskan Arctic Villages Hit Hard by Climate Change." *Washington Post,* August 5, 2012. http://www.washingtonpost.com/national/health-science/alaskan-arctic-villages-hit-hard-by-climate-change/2012/08/05/e9dbd4a6-d5b0-11e1-a9e3-c5249ea531ca_print.html.

Jessepe, Lorraine. "Alaskan Native Communities Facing Climate-Induced Relocation." *Indian Country Today Media Network*, June 21, 2012. http://indiancountrytodaymedianetwork.com/article/alaskan-native-communities-facing-climate-induced-relocation-119615.

Joling, Dan. "Walruses Abandon Ice for Alaska Shore." *Washington Post,* October 4, 2007. http://www.washingtonpost.com/wp-dyn/content/article/2007/10/04/AR2007100402299_pf.html.

Joling, Dan. "Thousands of Pacific Walruses Die; Global Warming Blamed." Associated Press, December 14, 2007 (in LEXIS).

Murphy, Kim. "Front-Row Exposure to Global Warming; Climate: Engineers Say Alaskan Village Could Be Lost as Sea Encroaches." *Los Angeles Times*, July 8, 2001, A-1.

"Yup'ik Villages Ravaged by Fierce Alaska Storms." *Indian Country Today Media Network*, November 20, 2013. http://indiancountrytodaymedianetwork.com/2013/11/20/yupik-villages-ravaged-fierce-alaska-storms-152341.

EDUCATION: ACCULTURALIZATION AND BOARDING SCHOOLS

"Acculturalization" (the destruction of indigenous culture as official policy) was the goal of an intensive program of cultural assimilation aimed at American Indians during the 19th and early 20th centuries in the United States and Canada. "Kill the Indian—Save the Man," an advertising slogan for boarding schools developed during the 1880s, has sometimes been called cultural genocide today. The policy sought to preserve living Indians scoured of their own cultural attributes (as an alternative to outright physical extermination), remade as Anglo-Americans. In 1900, barely two decades after the first one had opened, 307 boarding schools in the United States enrolled 21,568 young Native Americans.

History and Origins

Boarding schools were part of a broader system to remake Native Americans' cultural landscape. The "Rules for the Court of Indian Offenses" on the Pine Ridge Reservation in 1908 included a ban on "the sun dance and all other similar dances and so-called religious ceremonies." An Indian convicted of dancing could, on the first offense, be deprived of rations for up to 10 days. A second offense called for deprivation of rations for 15 to 30 days, or by up to 30 days in the agency prison.

In 1875, Congress moved to make Indians on reservations subject to federally supervised policing. Family, religious, and economic affairs of Indians were strictly regulated by the Bureau of Indian Affairs in 1882, and Congress set up mechanisms to enforce an individualized property-holding ethic among Indians in the General Allotment Act of 1887.

From the points of view of many Native Americans, cultural assimilation was the essence of political oppression on a very personal level. Winnebago Reuben Snake recalled:

> The steamrolling effort of the "civilized society" upon the Indian people has wreaked a havoc which extends far beyond that of loss of material possessions. The American Indian and Alaskan Native are caught in a world

American Indian students participate in a mathematics class at the Carlisle Indian School in Carlisle, Pennsylvania, circa 1903. (Library of Congress)

wherein they are trying to find out who they are, and where they are. . . . The land that was once their "mother," giving them food and clothing, was taken. Their spiritual strengths were decried as pagan and familial ties broken. Their own form of education, i.e. that of legends, how to live, how to respect themselves and others, were torn asunder by the White society's reading, writing, and arithmetic. No culture could, or can be, expected to be thrust into a world different from its own and adapt without problems of culture shock. (French, 2003, 62)

Josiah Black Eagle Pinkham, an ethnographer with the Nez Perce Cultural Resource Department, said: "Things like . . . boarding schools were meant to completely remove all of that wisdom that we had amassed over generations. The idea was to make us like the new people" (Chapman, 2001, 106). The schools' engines of assimilation led many of their Native students, such as Luther Standing Bear, George Eastman, and Gertrude Simmons Bonnin (Zitkala-Ša), among others, to criticize their methods (and those of Anglo-American society generally). "This is a story," writes Ruth Spack (2002), "of language and how people used it to further their own political and cultural agendas" (p. 7). As with all communicative acts, influence flowed both ways, not only in the single direction that the monolinguists had planned.

Regional Variations

Much of U.S. policy toward American Indians, expressed through boarding schools, was based on assumptions that a greater social good required that Indians become absorbed into "mainstream" society. A number of policies, from the establishment of schools and churches to the allotment of Indian land, have been implemented with the same ulterior motive of cultural assimilation.

Nevertheless, as early as 1819, the U.S. Congress passed an act to establish a "civilization fund" for Indians, notably the construction of schools by benevolent societies. The act urged that the schools be used to introduce among the Indians "habits and arts of civilization," including agriculture, reading, writing, and math. The act asserted that its provisions would be "for the purpose of providing against the further decline and final extinction of the Indian tribes." Congress allotted $10,000 a year for the fund.

One position in the late-19th-century Anglo-American debate over the future of Native Americans and their cultures held that Indians could only be divorced from the land by extermination, the rawest form of genocide, a point of view that was advocated by such prominent Anglo-Americans as L. Frank Baum, who later authored the *Oz* books, and Horace Greeley, the newspaper editor and abolition advocate.

While extermination and assimilation were the two major poles of popular debate, a wide variety of opinions were expressed on the "Indian problem" by non-Indians. In contrast to the hunt-them-down mentality of Baum, a minority of whites expressed beliefs that Indian societies would model some aspects of America's future. Opinions of this kind were expressed by the poet Walt Whitman, as well as feminist pioneers Matilda Joslyn Gage and Elizabeth Cady Stanton.

The predominant axis of opinion in this debate was sketched by the *New York Times* in an editorial published April 15, 1875. The editorial demarcated two main attitudes toward Native Americans and their cultures in non-Indian America, "the Manifest Destiny policy," which "hardly is willing, in any division of the spoils of this continent, to give the red man the buzzard. . . . It looks to no future for him but extermination" (Hayes, 1997, 69). The extermination advocates, said the *Times*,

> Remorselessly appropriate his hunting grounds, wantonly kill the game upon which he subsists, civilizes him enough to appreciate whiskey, and then gets him drunk and swindles him out of every valuable he possesses. . . . It then declares him a savage, [and] declares him incapable of civilization. (Hayes, 1997, 69–70)

"The other policy," wrote the *Times* editorialist, "is that of humanity." The *Times* favored this policy, which, it said, provided Indians with rights as original inhabitants of the continent. The humanitarians were said to believe that "the Indian's savagery . . . is not incurable" (Hayes, 1997, 70). The *Times* noted that government policy seemed to have been an amalgamation of these two poles of belief, molded by the pressures of special interests, whether they were Indian-baiting frontier squatters, the Army's high brass, various religious orders, or various other "friends of the Indian."

According to historian Francis Paul Prucha, schooling and private ownership of land were advanced late in the 19th century to break up the common history, purpose, and destiny of tribes. In 1872, the commissioner of Indian affairs was quoted as saying that the reservation must become "a legalized reformatory," where Native Americans would adopt non-Indian ways peaceably, and if not, forcibly.

Some supporters of assimilation put the case for it in more ethnocentric terms, such as the office of the Commissioner of Indian Affairs, in 1901:

> Indian dances and so-called Indian feasts should be prohibited. In many cases these dances and feasts are simply subterfuges to cover degrading acts and disguise immoral purposes. You [Indian agents] are directed to use your best efforts in the suppression of these evils. (Johansen, 1998, 23)

General William Henry Pratt became known as a major advocate of Indian cultural assimilation through education. In 1879, Pratt founded the Carlisle Indian Industrial School, the prototype for a nationwide network of such institutions. Pratt believed (contrary to a minority of extermination advocates) that "the Indian" could be salvaged from the ruins of conquest only if Indians assimilated into majority society as individual land-owning farmers and urban workers. Pratt's sense of mission was shared by a number of Bureau of Indian Affairs superintendents whose memoirs found sizable audiences. All advocated remaking Native Americans (especially children) in the white man's image through instruction in farming (on allotted land), education, and organized religion. Both sides in this debate were preparing dwindling numbers of Indians for eventual extinguishment of their now-fragmented cultures and land bases.

To recruit students for his new school, Pratt visited the Sioux of the High Plains. One hundred and sixty-nine students traveled eastward in 1879 to form Carlisle's first class. Included was Luther Standing Bear, who later became a well-known author. Standing Bear recalled his days at Carlisle in *My Indian Boyhood*. Luther Standing Bear's Sioux name was Plenty Kill when he entered the first class at Carlisle School in 1879 at the age of 11. While Standing Bear and his father thought the school was doing him some good, other parents were not so sure. Spotted Tail, for example, withdrew his three children from Carlisle after a visit.

Carlisle's curriculum included both academic and industrial education; the goal was to teach Native American young people to read, write, and speak English, and to acquire trades that would afford them employment. The goal was lofty, but in practice many Native young people returned to reservations where the only full-time employment was monopolized by Indian Bureau patronage employees. Young men trained in blacksmithing, wagon making, carpentry, tailoring, farming, and other trades rarely found employment at home on the reservations. Young women were taught Anglo-American domestic skills.

The Carlisle School was run on an Army model. Students were strictly regimented and forced to divest themselves of all vestiges of Indian identity. They wore uniforms, their hair was cut, and they were forbidden to speak their own languages. Missionaries were brought in to teach them Christianity. Runaways were punished severely; many students died of disease or other causes. This system produced a notable amount of alienation among some Native American young people, such as Plenty Horses, a young Sioux. It also produced some notable success stories, such as those of Jim Thorpe and Luther Standing Bear. The boarding school experience was traumatic for Indian children who suffered from racism and culture shocks, with many dying of disease, suicide, and heartbreak.

By 1903, Pratt's last year as Carlisle's superintendent, the school enrolled more than 1,200 pupils at a time. During Pratt's 24 years as head of the school, it educated 4,903 Indian boys and girls. During the 1880s, congressional appropriations for Indian schools rose from $150,000 to more than $1 million a year. Because of political conflicts, and despite a record that seemed exemplary by the Army's standards, Pratt was forced to retire as Carlisle's superintendent in 1904. He died at an Army hospital in San Francisco on April 23, 1924, at 84 years of age.

By the turn of the century, Carlisle was the prototype for 25 Indian industrial schools in 13 states. Within a decade after Pratt died, however, even the government was losing faith in forced assimilation. The boarding schools began to close after enactment of reform legislation under Franklin Delano Roosevelt and John Collier in the 1930s. By that time, inklings of Indian self-determination were surfacing in the making of policies in which Native Americans had at least some voice in plotting their own futures.

"Talking Back" to the System

As surely as the boarding schools' inventors understood that language is the vessel of culture, none of them gave much thought to the ways in which Native Americans would use English to critique the schools into which many of them had been unwillingly enrolled. Boarding school students were unwilling to surrender as victims. Amelia Katanski's *Learning to Write "Indian"* (2005) describes how Native American students in boarding schools often forged new identities, taking a degree of authorial control even as they were victimized by an intense campaign to deny them indigenous language, culture, and identity. Zitkala-Ša, who was both a student in and a teacher at boarding schools, wrote critically enough in the *Atlantic Monthly* during 1900 and *Harper's* in 1901 to acutely embarrass Pratt, who attacked her writings in retaliation. She took up English, said Katanski, to "wage a linguistic rebellion against the boarding-school ideology" (Katanski, 2005, 122). Ruth Spack, writing in *America's Second Tongue: American Indian Education and the Ownership of English, 1860–1900* (2002), added: "It is a story of linguistic ownership, and the meaning of ownership keeps shifting, depending on whether one is perceived to own English or to be owned by it. . . . Language can be used to justify to resist oppression" (Spack, 2002, 7).

Many boarding school students exercised a sense of ownership of the words they spoke and wrote, making of English a device by which culture, identity, and sovereignty could be preserved in a bilingual world. The boarding schools' emphasis on monolingualism was not universally accepted as it was being implemented. Spack quotes from a series written by Zitkala-Ša in the *Atlantic Monthly* during 1900 that favored a bilingual approach much more congruent with prevailing educational attitudes a century later. Several Native Americans advocated bilingualism as an alternative. One example was Sarah Winnemucca, who served as a translator for General Oliver O. Howard (who played a major role in the founding of Howard University). Winnemucca designed an entire bilingual curriculum for Native American boarding school students during the 1880s and won some congressional support. Many Native parents also opposed monolingualism. The "Americanists," however, refused to utilize her program in the boarding schools. Spack does an excellent job of delineating the political context that spurred the defeat of such initiatives.

The schools' military-industrial model and Anglo-American ethnocentricity affected students in very different ways. The discipline that Pratt built into his system inculcated star athletes such as James Thorpe and literary talents, including Standing Bear, Eastman, and Zitkala-Ša. It also filled graveyards with young suicides. Spack's book brilliantly describes the former; it is less successful at describing the pain of young men and women who coped less successfully with the forceful stripping away of their languages and cultures. They were the silent ones, leaving few historical records from which to quote. Of roughly 20,000 Native students enrolled in boarding schools, according to Spack's account, only 40 left behind extensive autobiographical accounts of their educations. Some of the students who left only brief records summed up how they felt by comparing their experiences to those of prisoners of war facing firing squads. Others, described by Zitkala-Ša, felt like "little animals driven by a herder" (Spack, 2002, 116).

Contemporary Native American Education

Many Native elders became dubious about education because of their experiences in boarding schools. They recalled being told that their cultures, languages, and families were not valued, as they lived for years in an atmosphere that repressed the cultural attributes that had helped their ancestors survive for thousands of years. Negative experiences in boarding schools were a major reason for the emphasis on Native-controlled education that helped propel self-determination efforts beginning in the 1960s.

Today, answering acculturalization, many Native peoples maintain their own school systems. Planning distribution of casino profits, for example, the Muckleshoots' first priority has been education on their reservation near Seattle. At first schools were started in temporary quarters, but by 2010 students were housed in a new complex of Muckleshoot-run schools that equaled or surpassed anything that public schools offered, with one important difference: curricula were designed to reinforce Native identity and keep students in school. The Muckleshoots also started a scholarship and financial aid program to provide funds to Indian students attending any four-year college or university in the United States.

The Muckleshoot schools were designed as an alternative to public schools and government boarding schools, part of a widespread movement since the early 1970s among Native peoples across North America that included teaching American Indian culture to improve overall academic achievement. This was a reaction to a facet of colonialism that dictates what children would learn and in what cultural framework, as in the boarding school system. When traditional forms of education were destroyed, so were Native societies' methods of raising new leaders. The new systems restore these traditions in a modern context.

The parents of the generation who built today's Native-controlled schools had been forced to wear military uniforms, march in ranks, and suffer punishment for speaking their Native languages. At the same time, many children were taken from parents and placed in non-Indian foster homes during the 1950s and 1960s, away from their reservations and extended families and culture. The Indian Child Welfare Act (ICWA, 25 USC 1901) was adopted in 1978 to deal with these problems.

See Also PART 1: OVERVIEW: POPULATION AND DEMOGRAPHICS: Cultural Genocide; **PART 2: CULTURAL FORMS: FAMILY, EDUCATION, AND COMMUNITY:** Spotlight: Boarding School Profiles: Chemawa Indian School and St. George's Indian School; Spotlight: Education Revival: A Muckleshoot Case Study; **LANGUAGE AND LITERATURE:** Bonnin, Gertrude (Zitkala-Ša)/Spotlight: Cradleboard Teaching Project; Language Reclamation: Eastern Tribes; Language Recovery in Indigenous North America

Further Reading

Barsh, Russel Lawrence, and James Y. Henderson. *The Road: Indian Tribes and Political Liberty*. Berkeley: University of California Press, 1980.

Calloway, Colin, ed. *Our Hearts Fell to the Ground: Plains Indian Views of How the West Was Lost*. Boston: Bedford Books/St. Martin's Press, 1996.

Chapman, Serle. *We, the People: Of Earth and Elders, Volume II*. Missoula, MT: Mountain Press, 2001.

French, Laurence Armand. *Native American Justice*. Chicago: Burnham, 2003.

Hayes, Robert G. *A Race at Bay:* New York Times *Editorials on the "Indian Problem."* Carbondale: Southern Illinois University Press, 1997.

Johansen, Bruce E., ed. *The Encyclopedia of Native American Legal Tradition*. Westport, CT: Greenwood Press, 1998.

Katanski, Amelia V. *Learning to Write "Indian": The Boarding School Experience and American Indian Literature*. Norman: University of Oklahoma Press, 2005.

O'Brien, Sharon. *American Indian Tribal Governments*. Norman: University of Oklahoma Press, 1989.

Pommersheim, Frank. *Braid of Feathers: American Indian Law and Contemporary Tribal Life*. Berkeley: University of California Press, 1995.

Porter, Joy. *Land and Spirit in Native America*. Santa Barbara, CA: Praeger/ABC-CLIO, 2012.

Pratt, Richard Henry. *Battlefield to Classroom: Four Decades with the American Indian, 1867–1904*. Edited by Robert M. Utley. Lincoln: University of Nebraska Press, [1964] 1987.

Spack, Ruth. *America's Second Tongue: American Indian Education and the Ownership of English, 1860–1900*. Lincoln: University of Nebraska Press, 2002.

Stannard, David. *American Holocaust: The Conquest of the New World*. New York: Oxford University Press, 1993.

Spotlight

BOARDING SCHOOL PROFILES: CHEMAWA INDIAN SCHOOL AND ST. GEORGE'S INDIAN SCHOOL

Chemawa Indian School

The Chemawa Indian Training School opened on February 25, 1880, the second "Indian industrial school" in the United States in what became a nationwide system (the first, in Carlisle, Pennsylvania, Colonel Pratt's flagship, had opened a year earlier). Chemawa was built at nearly the same time as Carlisle, under the supervision of a Colonel Wilkinson.

During its history, Chemawa has been known by several names: Harrison Institute, Salem Indian Industrial and Training School, and United States Indian Training and Normal School. The school was first located on four acres in Forest Grove, built by a team of Puyallup boys under the direction of General O. O. Howard with a $5,000 federal grant in 1880. The first class, 18 students (14 boys and 4 girls) all came from Washington State, 17 Puyallups and one Nisqually. By the early 1880s, with increasing appropriations from Congress, the school was looking for a larger site that could accommodate farming. A 171-acre site was chosen in 1885 five miles north of Salem, Oregon. The first wooden buildings were demolished after a few years and brick structures replaced them. Farming, including animal husbandry, poultry raising, and dairy, became the mainstay of the school.

Male and female students were taught geography, history, English, and arithmetic. The boys were also were taught agriculture, blacksmithing, wagonmaking, electrical engineering, plumbing, shoe and boot manufacturing, tinsmithing, gardening, tailoring, and carpentry. Girls were taught cooking, sewing, painting, nursing, vocal and instrumental music, and laundering. The boys grew most of the food that the students consumed, and the girls cooked it.

The school maintained 345 acres of farmland by 1905, half of which had been donated by the city of Salem. Pupils at the school and alumni pooled their savings from picking hops to buy 84 acres. The farm also maintained orchards that produced plums, apples, strawberries, blackberries, raspberries, pears, and cherries "in profusion" (*Chemawa*, 1905, 9). Four literary societies met in the evenings, with public debates governed by parliamentary procedure. On Sundays, attendance at church and Sunday school was mandatory. The football and baseball teams were competitive with many non-Indian schools in southern Oregon. In 1905, the school assembled a large display to celebrate the 100th anniversary of the Lewis and Clark expedition.

Also in 1905, the school celebrated its silver (25th) anniversary with a special edition of its weekly newsletter, *The Chemawa American* (Vol. 7, No. 56, March 3, 1905). This edition included several advertisements from local businesses—grocers, furniture stores, men's clothiers, booksellers, jewelers, bakers, beekeepers, photo studios, and the Northern Pacific Railroad, which maintained a station near the school on its Portland to San Francisco line. "Chemawa's beautiful grounds and rose-covered gardens have given the school the name of being the most beautiful in the Indian Service," the newsletter said. "Flowers bloom nearly the whole year round, and the grass is always green, studded with tall firs . . . due to the warm, mild climate of Oregon" (*Chemawa*, 1905, 5). In 1905, a hospital was under construction at Chemawa.

Chemawa reported 690 students in 1913 from a wide geographical area, including 175 Alaskan Native children. By 1922, 70 buildings had spread over 40 acres as the school's land base grew to more than 400 acres. In 1926, the school enrolled more than 1,000 students. In 1927, the school became a fully accredited high school and dropped its elementary grades. During the early 1930s, however, Chemawa nearly closed due to federal funding cuts, but pressure from local political figures and newspapers kept it open. Chemawa remained open after boarding schools in Washington State closed. After the Carlisle school closed, Chemawa became the oldest Indian boarding school in the United States with a record of continuous operation.

Children sometimes ran away from Chemawa, walking and hitchhiking home. Sometimes parents hid their six-year-old children to avoid having them taken away. Lawney Reyes (brother of Seattle activist Bernie Whitebear), who attended Chemawa, wrote that by the 1950s the school had relaxed prohibitions on the practice of Native cultures:

> I did not experience any harsh restraint against Indian culture or tradition at Chemawa. Generations of Indians before me had already felt the full force of that practice. I learned that in earlier years, speaking the Indian language had been forbidden. White authority had dealt harshly with Indian dancing, singing, and drumming. Students were not allowed to braid their hair or wear any ornaments with Indian design motifs. During my time, efforts to teach the white way were still in force, but attempts to abolish or restrain Indian culture were past. The practice of Indian culture, however, was not encouraged or discussed. (Reyes, 2002, 117)

During the late 1970s, Chemawa built a new campus; most of the original brick buildings were removed. Four buildings that were not destroyed were listed in the National Register of Historic Places in 1992. Today, Chemawa numbers its graduates in the thousands.

St. George's Indian School

St. George's Indian School was the first educational institution in or near the small town of Milton, near Tacoma, Washington, which was first called Mill Town after its main industry. As the town's residents sought to incorporate, they discovered that the U.S. Post Office would not award a fourth-class office to a town with more than one word in its name. The name thus became "Milton." St. George's Indian School was endowed in 1878 by Katharine Drexel, an heiress from Philadelphia who also founded the Catholic religious order that constructed it. The school was built mainly to educate Indian children in reading, writing, and agriculture. St. George's was designed to be as self-sufficient as possible. The boys farmed and the girls, even the youngest, processed food and cooked it. The school enrolled European American immigrants' children as well as Indians until shortly after 1900 because Milton, in its earliest years, had no schools of its own. They studied side by side through the first eight grades. The whites then went to Stadium High School in Tacoma, and the Native students went to Cushman School until it was closed in 1920. (A hospital by the same name operated on the Puyallup reservation from 1929 to the late 1950s.)

The most prominent headmaster of the school in its early days was Father Hylebos, an immigrant from Belgium, born in 1848, one of the first Catholic missionaries at St. George's. Hylebos was ordained as a priest in 1870 and began his trek to Puget Sound as a divine calling. In addition to St. George's, he started hospitals and homes for orphans and destitute women. When people in Tacoma tried to expel Chinese immigrants, Hylebos defended them with a plea for interethnic peace. A local creek named after Hylebos was known as such a rich source of salmon that local people said they could hear them roiling the water during spawning season.

An electric commuter railway, the Interurban, connected Milton with Tacoma and Seattle. It supplied a cheap ride (15 cents, transfers free). Young people were not always told to avoid the train's dangerous charged third rail. A young Native boy, a student at St. George's, was long remembered after he dragged a wet salmon over the third rail on the line, not realizing the current would kill him.

Further Reading

Adams, Vera S. "Early History of Milton, Washington." Milton: unpublished, 1948. Manuscript in City of Milton archives. www.cityofmilton.net/file_viewer.php?id=2095. Accessed August 27, 2014.

Chemawa American, Anniversary Number. 7:56 (March 3, 1905). Copy in Muckleshoot Preservation Program Archive.

Marino, Cesare. "History of Western Washington Since 1846." In Wayne Suttles, ed. *Handbook of North American Indians: Northwest Coast*. Vol. 7. In William C. Sturtevant, general ed. *Handbook of North American Indians*. Washington, DC: Smithsonian Institution, 1990, 169, 179.

Olive, Shirley. "Milton, Washington: The Early Days." Historic Tacoma, Instructor: Chris Cherbas, July 1982. Manuscript in City of Milton archives. www.cityofmilton.net /file_viewer.php?id=1668. Accessed July 27, 2014.

Reyes, Lawney. *White Grizzly Bear's Legacy: Learning to Be Indian*. Seattle: University of Washington Press, 2002.

Spotlight

EDUCATION REVIVAL: A MUCKLESHOOT CASE STUDY

Planning the distribution of casino profits, the Muckleshoots' first priority has been education. At first schools were started in temporary quarters, but by 2010 students were housed in a new complex of Muckleshoot-run schools that equaled or surpassed anything that public schools offered, with one important difference: curricula were designed to reinforce Native identity and keep students in school. The Muckleshoots also started a scholarship and financial aid program to provide funds to Indian students attending any four-year college or university in the United States.

The Muckleshoot schools have expanded steadily from the opening of the first tribal school (kindergarten through fourth grade) in 1984–1985, to the tribal college built in 1995–1996. Schools were expanded to kindergarten through 12th grade in 2009. Early childhood education was added in 2010, completing seamless pathways so students can always see the next classroom on a 37-acre campus that offers prekindergarten through community college education, according to Joseph Martin, assistant tribal manager of operations for education.

"When we had bingo, we could help out a little. But now . . . it's covered. And if we had a cutback, that [education] would be the last one," said John Daniels Jr., speaking as Tribal Council chairman in 2002. Casino money also buys supplies and new clothes for children "so they can go to school with their heads up," Daniels said (Mapes, November 3, 2002). When budget cuts hit the Auburn public schools, the Muckleshoots stepped in with aid. In addition, the Muckleshoot Indian Tribe cooperates with the Auburn School District to support Native students in public schools with several hundred thousand dollars per year for added staff and Indian education programs.

Pride in Head Start

Muckleshoot self-determination in education began in a small way with the youngest of pupils. The Head Start program, directed by Muckleshoot Virginia Brown, a 1957 Auburn High School graduate, became a point of pride and self-determination on a reservation of about 300 people where, by the late 1960s, community organization was becoming widespread.

Interest in a Muckleshoot preschool had begun five years before the Head Start program was funded with help from the Saltwater Unitarian Universalist Church in Des Moines, Washington, a suburb south of Seattle. A number of women from several churches were taking part with Muckleshoot women in a quilting circle at which they discussed the fact that Muckleshoot children were lacking preschool skills. These discussions grew into a preschool on the reservation with cooperation from the tribal government, the Saltwater Unitarian Church, the Family Life Group of the Seattle Public Schools, the American Friends Service

Committee (Quakers), and Erna Gunther, a well-known anthropology professor at the University of Washington. Several churchwomen (Marian Fairbanks, Doreen Johnson, Carolyn McMichael, and Lee Landrud) served as teachers at the school and enrolled their own children there. After three years of volunteer efforts, the school received financial support from the Auburn School District. Many of the Muckleshoots' educational leaders stemmed from the Head Start program, with certification and training through that program that served as a basis for development of the entire Native-run system of today.

The Muckleshoot Preschool, which enrolled about 30 children a year, met in an old Government Services Administration building owned by the Auburn School District. It had started in 1958 with donations from local churches and volunteer teachers; in 1965, Muckleshoot received one of the first two federal Head Start grants for Native Americans (the Navajos, the largest Native nation in the United States, was the other funded program). This has been a point of pride at Muckleshoot for decades, regarded as the takeoff point for education defined and controlled by the tribe. The $24,000 annual Head Start grant always seemed to be in jeopardy, however, because of politics in Washington, D.C. For several weeks in 1967, the funds were delayed, and mothers and teachers, according to a report in the *Tacoma News-Tribune*, "ran the program on their own time" (Jeffords, 1968).

Parents helped to make the 25 percent nonfederal match by volunteering, fundraising, and obtaining donations. Parents held raffles, bake sales, cakewalks, rummage sales, and Indian taco sales. Some parents even raffled off blankets, rugs, beadwork, vests, lamps, horses, cars, bikes, radios, and television sets. Muckleshoot Head Start enrolls children who are Muckleshoot, from other Native tribes, black, Latino, European American, and Asian. The staff also is ethnically mixed.

The Head Start program had a unique requirement: mothers were asked to accompany their children to school at least once a week. The mothers worked as teachers' aides, kept the students "at ease," and "picked up an interest in what the children [were] accomplishing," according to the newspaper report (Jeffords, 1968). Robert J. Terrell, principal of Chinook Elementary School, where most of the children went to school after Head Start, told the Tacoma *News-Tribune*, "Prior to the Head Start program, the Muckleshoot children usually were a little behind in their learning, but never in intelligence. Now the situation really is improving and the Indian children are catching up much quicker."

Building a School System

The value placed on education was reflected by the lead story in the *Muckleshoot Monthly* of June 15, 2002, an edition filled with photographs of graduates from Head Start to college that featured events honoring graduates from the Muckleshoot tribal community. Graduation from Head Start, as from college, is celebrated with a cap, gown, and diploma. The special section has become a regular annual feature of the newspaper, celebrating a week when graduation from all manner of schools is the main business of the reservation.

Four years after adding high school grades in 1997, the Muckleshoots' school system (with 125 students in kindergarten through 12th grade at the time) welcomed its first two graduates in June 2001. The students, brother and sister Matt and Ginger Allen, were hailed as "a shining example for generations to come," by school administrator Amy McFarland (Pemberton-Butler, 2001). The Allens, both Tulalips who grew up at Muckleshoot, were the first of their family's grandchildren to complete high school. Each Muckleshoot student who graduates from high school, on or off the reservation, receives a Pendleton blanket and a two-week trip to Hawaii from the Muckleshoot government.

By 2010, what had come to be known as "Graduation Season" produced the Muckleshoot school system's largest high school commencement ceremony, with 19 graduating seniors, compared with a total of 32 in the nine years since the first high school seniors had graduated in 2001. In addition, the school awarded 10 GEDs in 2010. In 2011 the Muckleshoot schools graduated 19 high school seniors for the second year in a row. Muckleshoots also earned eight master's degrees in cooperation with Antioch University—Charles Gordon (environment and community), Mitzi Judge (management), Leo V. LaClair and Todd LeClair (strategic communication), Ada McDaniel (environment and community), and Noreen Milne, Dena Starr, and Linda Starr (all in management).

A total of 224 Muckleshoots graduated at various stages of their educational careers in 2011: Head Start, 40; kindergarten, 34; fifth grade, 18; eighth grade, 18; high school, 19; other local high schools, 13; college degrees, 21; postsecondary certificates, 37; GEDs, 24—a 20 percent increase in a year. By 2011, the Muckleshoots had access to education for early childhood through high school all on one campus. By 2013, 241 graduated.

During late spring of 2011, the Muckleshoot schools reached a milestone: full recognition by the Northwest Accreditation Commission (NAC). The school system had operated under provisional accreditation for several years as it built a new facility and increased enrollment. Formal accreditation meant that Muckleshoot Tribal Schools (MTS) had accomplished their task of providing students with standard and rigorous teaching and learning. Joseph Martin said:

> Accreditation certifies that the school has undergone a process of intense self-examination that has been validated by an outside team of educational experts. In addition, NAC accreditation will ensure that academic credits earned at MTS will be fully transferable to all other accredited high schools and will be accepted by colleges and universities. (Martin, 2011)

Nearly forgotten songs have been revived, said Virginia Cross, Muckleshoot Indian Tribal Council chair. "I think if we don't retain it, it will be gone forever" (Pemberton-Butler, 2001). With the songs come memories, and reconstruction of history. One teacher who has helped with recapture of culture has been David Horsley, formerly a Federal Way educator, a non-Indian who gained his knowledge through research. Early curricula that included emphasis on culture, such as traditional arts and Whulshootseed, the Muckleshoots' language, reduce drop-out rates. Roberto Enríquez, a teacher in the Muckleshoot schools, said: "We're about our culture, our language, we're about promoting pride in one's cultural identity," he said. "When people have a healthy identity of themselves and where they came from, I think they're going to be more positive" (Pemberton-Butler, 2001).

Casino Profits Become Scholarships

By 2002, the Muckleshoots were converting $1 million a year worth of casino profits and other business income into college scholarships for 132 students. Behind every one was a personal story. Lynda Mapes of the *Seattle Times* described Denise Dillon, the first member of her family to enter college, who became the first Muckleshoot to earn advanced degrees from large institutions of higher learning on the East Coast of the United States. Behind her was a determined mother, Cathleen Schultz, whose education had ended in the eighth grade, who decided that college was not a question of "if" for her daughter, but "when."

The odds were long. In Washington State, during the late 1990s when Denise began her college career, about 4 percent of Native Americans earned graduate or professional degrees. Attending Western Washington University in Bellingham, Washington, on a full-ride Muckleshoot scholarship, she earned a bachelor's degree. Then she completed a master's in health sciences at Duke University and, in 2002, a physician assistant's surgical residency program through the Yale School of Medicine.

By 2007, more than 700 students held Muckleshoot scholarships. In 2008, 564 students were on scholarships. The program was producing long-term results as well. The annual graduation dinner in 2008 recognized five students who had earned master's degrees in the previous years, as well as several others who had completed college programs.

See Also PART 1: OVERVIEW: POPULATION AND DEMOGRAPHICS: Cultural Genocide; **PART 2: CULTURAL FORMS: FAMILY, EDUCATION, AND COMMUNITY:** Education: Acculturalization and Boarding Schools/Spotlight: Boarding School Profiles: Chemawa Indian School and St. George's Indian School; Spotlight: Reindigenization; **LANGUAGE AND LITERATURE:** Language Recovery in Indigenous North America

Further Reading
Jeffords, Edd. "Muckleshoot Preschool Prepares Tots for Burgeoning Education." *Tacoma News-Tribune*, May 12, 1968.

Mapes, Lynda. "Washington Tribes Invest Casino Proceeds by Sending Members to College." *Seattle Times*, November 3, 2002. http://community.seattletimes.nwsource.com/archive/?date=20021103&slug=yale03m. Accessed October 29, 2014.

Martin, Joseph J. "Graduations 2011: MIT Enjoys Another Excellent Graduation Season." *Muckleshoot Monthly*, August, 2011, P-1.

"Muckleshoot Celebrates Educational Achievement." *Muckleshoot Monthly*, June 15, 2002, 1.

Noel, Patricia, and Virginia Cross. *Muckleshoot Indian History*. Auburn, WA: Auburn Public School District No. 408, 1980.

Pemberton-Butler, Lisa. "Huge Day for Muckleshoot School: Its First Two Grads." *Seattle Times*, June 19, 2001. http://community.seattletimes.nwsource.com/archive/?date =20010619&slug=muckleshoot19m. Accessed October 29, 2014.

"Tribal School Receives Accreditation." *Muckleshoot Monthly*, June, 2011, 1.

FUNERARY CUSTOMS

History and Origins

With more than 600 Native American nations, tribes, and bands within the present-day United States, traditions regarding death (often phrased as "passing over") vary greatly. Many traditions are thousands of years old. Generalizations can be perilous, but some general patterns stand out.

Many Native Americans evoke a common belief that the deceased's soul does not die. A common thread in many Native funerary rituals is a belief that a deceased person should be comfortable after having passed over. Death is often characterized not as an end to life but as passage into another world. In many traditional cosmologies, passage of the soul to this new life can be aided by provision of a horse or (depending on location) a canoe. An opening might be provided at the burial place so that the deceased's spirit can escape. The deceased thus influences spiritual forces that play a role in the everyday reality of the living.

Items that a person may need in the next world often are placed at a site of interment: various favorite foods, familiar weapons, tools, pots, jewelry, gifts, and others. In the past, in some cultures, the deceased's wife, slaves, or horses might have been sent on the journey as well. A medicine man (shaman) often leads rituals, as ancestors are summoned in spirit. The symbol of the circle is often used as an icon of life without end. Death is regarded as a natural outcome of life, a belief that is common among the Navajo in the words of one observer, "reflect[ing] the ancient traditions that death itself is not something to be feared, [and] that the deceased would return to visit the living" (Redmond, n.d.).

Another common element is the customs that often prescribe purification as the deceased is being prepared for the journey. A body might initially be cremated or exposed to the elements, then interred after a period of time. Native peoples on the Plains as well as some in the Pacific Northwest commonly built above-ground burial sites with scaffolds, trees, and canoes. Some California tribes practiced cremation. Some in the central and south Atlantic areas embalmed and mummified the deceased, until epidemics of smallpox forced them to use mass graves.

The ancient Hopewell mound-building societies in the Mississippi Valley used elaborate tombs. Chambered and crematory mounds were used in the

Indian Mound Park, St. Paul, Minnesota, c. 1898. (Library of Congress)

Mississippi River drainage. Remains of these mounds are visible today. Earthenware jars or urns were used in some parts of the present-day U.S. Southeast and Southwest.

Regional Variations

Some Native peoples believe that mention of a person's name after death impedes the soul's journey to its final resting place. Chief Sea'th'l, after whom Seattle (which is Anglicized) was named, is said to have objected to the naming on these grounds. Sea'th'l, who was Duwamish and Suquamish, objected strenuously enough to have his personal canoe paddled 60 miles from the site of the new city to Olympia, the territorial capital, where he asked Governor Isaac Stevens to revoke the naming of the city. The immigrant whites ignored him and considered the naming an honor. The Choctaws, in eastern North America, also avoided mentioning the name of the deceased in the belief that it agitates the spirit.

The Shoshone-Bannock often erect a tipi with a campfire burning near the entrance to house a body. Visitors pay their respects, and women relatives feed them. The deceased may be dressed in full regalia, moccasins, and jewelry for his or her journey.

In Navajo belief, the deceased go to an underworld; burial includes rituals to keep the dead from reemerging. There is a taboo against looking at the body or handling the deceased person's possessions. The body may be touched only by people with the need to do so. A shaman and family members remain with the person until death is certain, at which time only one or two close relatives who agree to be exposed to evil spirits remain. If a Navajo dies suddenly, from illness, suicide, or violence, it was believed that a *chindi*, a ghost, might provoke trouble for his or her family.

Under traditional protocols, when the death of a Navajo is near, he or she will be removed from home. If death occurs in the home before the dying person is removed, the lodging must be destroyed. After death, two men prepare the body for burial. They wear no clothes, only moccasins, having covered their bodies in ashes (to protect against evil spirits). The body is carefully washed and dressed; caution is required because a body that is not prepared properly may return to its home site as an evil spirit. Two other men prepare a grave, and funeral rites are held as quickly as possible, often the next day, with only the four men who prepared the body present at the burial site. Other family members do not attend under traditional protocols. If a coffin is used in a Navajo burial, it may not be completely closed, so the spirit may escape.

One observer described a Navajo burial as follows:

> The deceased person's belongings are loaded onto a horse and brought to the grave site, led by one of the four mourners. Two others carry the body on their shoulders to the area. The fourth man warns those he meets en route that they may want to stay away from the area. Once the body is interred, great care is taken to ensure that no footprints are left behind. The tools used to dig the grave are destroyed. (Redmond)

Because the Navajos regard death as part of a natural cycle, expression of grief is usually avoided. This is not to say that Navajos do not grieve, but restraint is a sign of respect to the deceased, whose necessary journey may be impeded by expression of grief by the living.

The Apaches, like the Navajos, buried the dead as quickly as possible and burned the homes of the deceased. The family of the deceased moved to a new home to escape ghosts. Many Native peoples cut their hair while mourning, most notably widows. Some wore ashes on their faces. In contrast to the Navajos, members of some California tribes wailed during long funeral ceremonies and marked anniversaries one and two years after a death with similar rituals. The Hopis allowed a day of grief on the day of death and a year later.

Precontact Choctaws left the deceased to decompose naturally. Two or three years later, some of the bones were used in an honoring feast. The Hopis prepared the deceased for a journey with a body wash of yucca suds before it was dressed in traditional clothes.

New Mexico's Pueblos have combined traditional practices with those imported during the Spanish conquest almost 500 years ago. Many of their precontact practices were abandoned or modified following the arrival of European American immigrants, especially missionaries. According to one account, the Pueblo peoples first experienced contact with Hispanics in the 16th century when their lands were colonized. Burials took place within the church grounds and graveyards of the Roman Catholic missions according to Christian doctrine for those who had converted. Native Americans also continued their traditional practices, in secret when necessary.

A report from the National Park Service described a combination of Native and European burial practices in Alaska:

> Throughout the period of the fur trade in the North Pacific, beginning in the late 18th century, Russian Orthodox missions were established among the native populations settled along the coastline and mainland interior of Russian-occupied Alaska. At Eklutna, a village at the head of Cook Inlet, north of Anchorage, an Athabascan cemetery adjacent to the 19th century Church of St. Nicholas . . . illustrates continuity of a burial custom widely recorded in historic times, that of constructing gable-roofed wooden shelters over graves to house the spirit of the dead. In the cemetery at Eklutna, the spirit houses are arranged in regular rows, have brightly-painted exteriors fronted by Greek crosses, and are surmounted by comb-like ridge crests. In this particular example, variation in the size of the shelters is an indication of social status, while clan affiliations are identified by color and by the styling of the crest. ("Native American Burial," 2014)

Contemporary Forms

Traditional funerary rituals may be combined with modern (Western) funerals. The Shakers of the Pacific Northwest, a religion that combines Native traditions with Christian precedents, conduct church services but also remove all images of the deceased from view for a year and put away their possessions. At the end of the year, pictures come out and possessions are given away.

The importance of funeral traditions is evident today in the Native American Graves Protection and Repatriation Act (NAGPRA), a U.S. law that took effect November 16, 1990. The law requires federal agencies, as well as institutions that receive federal money, to return "cultural items," including human remains, funerary objects, sacred objects, and objects of cultural patrimony, to Native tribes and lineal descendants.

The NAGPRA statute also penalizes traffic in Native American human remains with a prison term of up to one year or a fine of up to $100,000 for a first offense. The law is meant to reunite human remains and cultural artifacts with their owners and to prevent pillage of gravesites, both important issues among many Native peoples today. Looting of human remains of the 500-year-old Slack Farm burial mound in Kentucky during 1987 was a major provocation for NAGPRA. Native peoples have sought to remove human remains from museums and government agencies and return them to the earth for proper burials. During the 19th and 20th centuries many burial mounds were destroyed. Today, others have been threatened by golf courses, housing developments, and office parks. Indian activists have been called upon to defend their burial sites even with NAGPRA in force.

See Also PART 1: OVERVIEW: Population and Demographics: Disease, Depopulation, and Cultural Destruction; Nations, Tribes, and Other Native Groups: Pueblo Cultural Context; **PART 2: CULTURAL FORMS**: Family, Education, and Community: Native American Graves Protection and Repatriation Act (NAGPRA) (1990)

Further Reading

Fine-Dare, Kathleen S. *Grave Injustice: The American Indian Repatriation Movement and NAGPRA*. Lincoln: University of Nebraska Press, 2002.

Garbarino, Merwyn S. *Native American Heritage*. Boston: Little, Brown, 1976.

Jones, P. *Respect for the Ancestors: American Indian Cultural Affiliation in the American West*. Boulder, CO: Bauu Press, 2005.

McKeown, C. T. *In the Smaller Scope of Conscience: The Struggle for National Repatriation Legislation, 1986–1990*. Tucson: University of Arizona Press, 2012.

"Native American Burial Customs." *National Register Bulletin*. U.S. Department of the Interior, National Park Service. 2014. http://www.cr.nps.gov/nr/publications/bulletins/nrb41/nrb41_5.htm.

Native American Graves Protection and Repatriation Act (NAGPRA). Pub. L. 101-601, 25 U.S.C. 3001 et seq., 104 Stat. 3048.

Redmond, Jodee. "Navajo Burial Customs." *Love to Know*. http://dying.lovetoknow.com/Navajo_Burial_Customs. Accessed March 19, 2014.

Theobald, Donna. "Native American Death Rituals." *Love to Know*. http://dying.lovetoknow.com/native-american-death-rituals. Accessed March 19, 2014.

GIFT-GIVING

History and Origins

In many Native American cultures, a person acquired influence in a cultural context not by accumulating possessions, as in many European cultures, but by giving them away. The ability to distribute gifts indicated wealth and status.

Gifts were an essential part of maintaining human relationships, and, done according to custom, created reciprocal obligations. A gift given to a Native American by a colonist "might pas[s] twenty hands before it sticks. . . . Wealth circulateth like the blood, all parts partake" William Penn observed (Black and Weidman, 1976, 5).

The "giveaway," a ceremony in which the host honors guests with presents, is practiced among many Native peoples across the North American continent. In recent times, the giveaway has become a part of pan-Indian cultural observances in many areas. Giveaways have functioned in the reservation period to fill the gaps in uncertain local economies and to compensate for erratic and arbitrary government social services. This network facilitates exchange and redistribution, and is important because it provides needy Native American families with goods and services necessary to sustain life. At a Native American giveaway, the guest of honor often does not receive gifts, as in most European American gift-giving. Instead, the guests of honor observe while their sponsors give away food, money, blankets, dishes, and other goods.

Regional Variations

Gift-giving became an important part of trade in North America between different Native American groups, as well as between Native peoples and European immigrants who adopted their customs to trade in America. Trade and diplomacy in the mid-18th century was tied into gift-giving protocol. Some traders also built alcoholic beverages into the gift-giving routine, with devastating results.

Traditional Native American leaders often were expected to give away most of what they acquired for the benefit of their people. A Cheyenne leader also was expected to be generous with his material possessions. Ethnologist John H. Moore describes how such leveling behavior is still practiced:

> They are constantly called upon for help in the form of money, food, a ride, or a long-distance phone call (although most chiefs don't have phones because they can't pay their phone bills). . . . Because of the heavy obligations imposed on council chiefs . . . they frequently are reluctant to accept the invitation to join the council. (Moore, 1996, 163)

English traders and diplomats were quick to realize that giving gifts could pay dividends. Historical accounts relate that gift-giving was so entrenched among Iroquois leaders that British diplomats established private gift-giving ceremonies at which leaders benefited personally. Trader John Long told a story about William Johnson, British superintendent of relations with the Iroquois.

Johnson was well known among the Iroquois. Having married into the Mohawks, Johnson often fought alongside them, other Iroquois, and their allies against the French. Johnson also joined in Mohawk councils. One night a Mohawk admired Johnson's finely laced English coat and said he had had a dream in which Johnson gave the coat to him. Understanding the gift-giving protocol, Johnson realized that he was being called upon to give up the coat. He did so, after which the Mohawks agreed that Johnson needed land on which to build a house. They then gave him 66,000 acres.

If a Tlingit man wants someone to give him something, according to ethnologist Kalervo Oberg,

> He gives that person a preliminary gift and makes his wish known. He will not ask the man outright, but will admire the object he desires. . . . The social norm demands that a man accept a gift and also that he will return one. . . . The value of objects is very well known, so that if one wishes an object of quality he is forced to give the maker a gift of the proper value in return. The craftsman can always retaliate upon a stingy giver by making a poor article. (Oberg, 1973, 94)

The Laguna Pueblo of New Mexico has a giveaway called a "grab," in which, once a year, water and bread, toys, and other gifts are thrown from the rooftop of a home to people below, a ceremony during which a community gives thanks and prays for renewal in the year to come. It is also a feast-day celebration that honors the pueblo's patron saints. Native filmmaker Billy Luther created a documentary on the "grab," which was shown at the 2011 Sundance Film Festival, the first time in the "grab's" 300-year history that cameras were allowed to record it.

Giveaways marked certain kinds of social occasions among the Coast Salish, not just for wealth display or distribution. Namings, weddings, funerals, healings, and so forth still continue today. A century ago, however, the tourist trap "Golden Potlatch" summoned European Americans to Seattle for ersatz "Indian" parades downtown. As Seattle was playing up the Golden Potlatch for tourists, in 1906 the Bureau of Indian Affairs was forbidding Indians' own potlatches as pagan rituals. The real potlatches were held in secret.

Barbara Lane wrote:

> Distribution was effected through complex exchange systems involving voluntary gift-giving to kin and friends, reciprocal gifting to specified . . . kin which sometimes became competitive, intercommunity feasting, potlatching, and outright sale and trade beyond the local community and sometimes over great distances. (Lane, 1973, 10)

In the potlatch ceremony as practiced along the north Pacific Coast, people gathered by invitation of the host to distribute wealth among invited guests. Social and economic standing was acquired and enhanced in a contest of giving. Such a ceremony would not have been possible in an impoverished society. This ceremony was practiced by Native peoples from northern Puget Sound to the panhandle of Alaska. Once banned by the governments of European American immigrants, the potlatch has been revived.

The anthropologist T. T. Waterman (1973) described the potlatch about 1920, including the nuances of distributing wealth, acquiring social standing, and intertribal competition, "a combination of feasting, entertainment, disbursement of property, and religious ceremonies" (p. 75). The potlatch might be tied into other events, such as "purchase" of a wife, payment for a homicide, or a funeral. Property at Puget Sound potlatches was distributed "with the definite expectation of getting back an equivalent" (p. 77). All participants had to understand the social status acquired by giving and its reciprocal nature. Waterman indicated that Indians east of the Cascades did not practice the customs of potlatch, "so to invite them to such a performance was sheer waste" (p. 78).

The potlatch also included tests of strength between groups, or a tug of war using a long hemlock pole. In this contest, wrote Waterman, "apparently anything short of outright murder was considered legitimate. It was customary to trip an opponent, or to stick him gently in the calf of the leg with a knife-point. Sometimes a man was collared and dragged bodily over the pole. This was spoken of as a 'capture'" (Waterman, 1973, 79).

The fulcrum of Haudenosaunee (Iroquois) economics was its egalitarian distribution system, which was founded on spiritual precepts. The Haudenosaunee believe that Mother Earth and her bounty were created for the benefit of all, not the hoarding of a few. The bounty law that Europeans called "Indian hospitality" had a much wider application than feeding a few European stragglers, however. Bounty law reflected the spiritual precept that Mother Earth existed independently of human effort and was not, therefore, the property of this or that person. Neither labor nor proprietorship conferred entitlement to her produce. Instead, *all* human beings were *equally* the guests of Mother Earth, who did (and still does) all the providing.

Consequently, everyone had an equal right to all goods and services necessary to life, especially food. Anyone entering any lodge at any time was instantly fed, by order of the clan mother of the longhouse. The ill, the poor, and the mentally infirm had immediate claim on anything they might need out of the common stock. Travelers, in view of their exertions, were entitled to a double portion of food. If food was scarce, guests were fed first; hosts would go hungry rather than hold back from their stores, however meager. Since sharing was the rule, greediness (especially in the form of gluttony) was frowned upon; children were warned that the *Sago/dăkwŭs,* a hungry bogey, would "'get' [eat] them if they gorged" (Parker, 1968, 64).

During the course of the year, all goods and amenities were carefully maintained, transported, and distributed by the women. Most importantly, women controlled the food supply, whether agricultural or game. (Although men kept, divided evenly, and ate whatever they might need during the actual hunt, the fruits of the hunt were "kept" by the women.) As Nancy Bonvillain (1989, 15) summed up the situation, "Women controlled the distribution of the products of their own labor and, significantly, the products of men's labor as well."

The mystique of the frail female is European; Haudenosaunee women were proud of their physical strength. Carrying carcasses home from the hunt was their *right,* part of women's general custody of all material goods, as was toting large harvest baskets. Women also had sole control of cooking, which included the processing of all food: drying meat and fruits, pounding corn, seasoning foods, and so on.

Running the household was another firm prerogative of women, who "owned" the longhouses of their clans and everything contained therein. This included men's implements of war, which were only shared out as the Clan Mothers' Council deemed proper. Women also managed the fuel supply. In March and April, they collected, cut, and stored firewood, another task performed collectively and organized by clan. (Men had already severed limbs from the living tree in large chunks, making them "dead," that is, carcasses under the rightful control of women.)

Day-to-day living did not consume all the goods available. Large surpluses existed, not only of food but also of every other item imaginable. The Haudenosaunee were rich people. Unlike the Europeans, however, whose socioeconomic structures led to extremes of possession and dispossession, the Haudenosaunee evenly distributed Mother Earth's surplus gifts among all her children. Denys Delâge (1985) aptly described the institutional mechanism that developed to manage equitable distribution as *"le règle du don,"* that is, "the order (or rule) of the gift" (p. 64). Instead of the marketplaces, proprietary concerns, capital accumulations, commodity bartering, mercantilism, and commerce of Europe, the clan-based networks of Iroquoia redistributed all goods, of whatever origin, among all members of the community through organized gift-giving, or "gifting." As Delâge observed, *"le don constitue la clé de l'universe social"* ("gifting constitutes the key to the social universe") of the Iroquoian nations in a continuing *"obligation de donner, obligation de recevoir, obligation de rendre"* ("obligation to give, obligation to receive, [and] obligation to give back [again]" (p. 64).

Men's travel networks of trails and waterways facilitated large-scale, international gifting circles, bringing many foreign goods into Iroquoia: wampum from the Atlantic coastal nations, conch shell ornaments from the Gulf of Mexico, tobacco from the Petuns of Canada, copper from west of Lake Superior, jasper from Pennsylvania, and quartz from the high northern tip of Labrador. Although Western scholars now call these exchanges "trading," they were really gift-giving rituals intended to solidify foreign alliances. Friendly parties met, gave gifts, and departed. The gifts cemented goodwill and set up continued friendly relations.

Contemporary Forms

Gift-giving continues to be important in Native societies. The animating spiritual analogy behind gifting is the generosity of Mother Earth, who gives to the living, receiving back thanks and gifts from them, only to give anew. Native American economics is, therefore, a spiritual cycle of reciprocities based on connections forged over time. Clans had the same duty as Mother Earth to give freely of all they have, acquiring something of her spiritual stature in the process. Sara Stites (1905) correctly noted that "the only object in amassing a surplus [of any sort of goods] was to give it away and so to gain prestige" (p. 75).

Time is a prime factor in distribution, as parity was achieved over time, not all at once. Thus, gifting occurred at a series of periodic and occasional festivals that were held throughout the year and commenced largely for that purpose. Periodic festivals included the Dream Feast; occasional feasts included condolence councils (for the dead). Gifting circles bound together the clans, towns, and nations of Native America.

Because of its ability to cement friendly relations, gifting is also a means of establishing peaceful alliances with foreign nations. Gifting was deliberately expanded to include as many clans, nations, and strangers as possible. The failure to respond to a gift constitutes an affront. On the other hand, the giving of a gift is the prelude to establishing cordial relations with strangers.

Bruce E. Johansen and Barbara Alice Mann

See Also PART 1: OVERVIEW: General Historical Considerations: Treaty Diplomacy, Cultural Context; **PART 2: CULTURAL FORMS: Family, Education, and Community:** Restorative Justice/Spotlight: Reciprocity; Trade, Cultural Attributes

Further Reading

Black, Nancy B., and Bette S. Weidman. *White on Red: Images of the American Indian.* Port Washington, NY: Kennikat Press, 1976.

Bonvillain, Nancy. "Gender Relations in Native North America." *American Indian Culture and Research Journal* 13, no. 2 (1989): 1–28.

Delâge, Denys. *Le Pays renversé: Amérindiens et Européens en Amérique du Nord-est, 1600–1664*. Montréal: Boréal Express, 1985.

Lane, Barbara. "Political and Economic Aspects of Indian-White Culture Contact in Western Washington in the Mid-Nineteenth Century." May 10, 1973. Typescript in Muckleshoot Indian Tribe Preservation Program Archives.

Moore, John H. *The Cheyenne*. Cambridge, MA: Blackwell, 1996.

Moore, John H. "How Giveaways and Pow-wows Redistribute the Means of Subsistence." In John H. Moore, ed. *The Political Economy of North American Indians*. Norman: University of Oklahoma Press, 1993.

Oberg, Kalervo. *The Social Economy of the Tlinget Indians*. Seattle: University of Washington Press, 1973.

Parker, Arthur C. "The Iroquois Uses of Maize and Other Food Plants." In William N. Fenton, ed. *Parker on the Iroquois*. Syracuse, NY: Syracuse University Press, 1968 (1913), 5–119.

Stites, Sara Henry. *Economics of the Iroquois*. Dissertation Monograph. Series, vol. 1, no. 3. Bryn Mawr: Bryn Mawr College Monographs, 1905.

Waterman, T. T. *Notes on the Ethnology of the Indians of Puget Sound*. Indian Notes and Monographs. Misc. Series No. 59. New York: Museum of the American Indian/Heye Foundation, 1973.

NATIVE AMERICAN GRAVES PROTECTION AND REPATRIATION ACT (NAGPRA) (1990)

The Native American Graves Protection and Repatriation Act of 1990 has been lauded as major human rights legislation. It has also been criticized as removing items from museum shelves, or hindering science. Looking back on almost 25 years of the development and administration of the law, the promises of restoration of cultural property rights to Native Americans is coming to fruition, while museum shelves are not and will not be emptied of Native American cultural items. Forward-thinking scientists have come to realize the importance to science of information obtained in consultation with tribes and Native Hawaiian organizations (NHOs) that outweighs any loss of control of Native American human remains and some cultural items.

History and Origins

Since 1906, the United States has taken management authority over the cultural and scientific resources under its jurisdiction. The 1906 Antiquities Act

(16 U.S.C. §§431–433) and later the Archaeological Resources Protection Act (ARPA, 16 U.S.C. §§470aa–mm, 1979) established permitting authority for scientific data recovery on federal and Indian lands. The items removed from the ground, mostly Native American human remains and burial items, were to remain under government control and became stored in perpetuity largely in government and university repositories. Attempts by tribes to reclaim the remains of their ancestors and tribal property were unsuccessful (Echo-Hawk, 1986). When the Onondaga Nation went to court in 1899 to retrieve the wampum belts held by the New York State Museum, they found that courts did not acknowledge the nation as having enforceable property rights (*Onondaga Nation v. Thacher*, 61 N.Y.S. 1027 [N.Y. App. Div. 1899]).

At the end of the 20th century the American public and the U.S. government began to recognize the culture of American Indians as meriting respect and protection on a formalized basis. In 1986, the board of the New York State Museum voted to return the wampum belts to the Onondagas. Congress passed the American Indian Religious Freedom Act (AIFRA, 42 U.S.C. §1996, 1994), and the president issued the Sacred Sites Executive Order (E.O. No. 13,007, 61 Fed. Reg. 26771, May 24, 1996) supporting the rights of Native Americans to practice traditional ceremonies. The National Historic Preservation Act (NHPA, 16 U.S.C. §§470a et. seq., 1992) was amended to recognize traditional cultural places meriting listing on the National Register of Historic Places and established Tribal Historic Preservation Officers who could replace state authority on tribal lands. Specific legislation to address the cultural property rights of Native Americans was the Native American Graves Protection and Repatriation Act (NAGPRA, 25 U.S.C. §§3001–3013, 1990).

After compromises reached on the language and scope of the law by the archaeological, museum, and tribal communities, the NAGPRA legislation received unanimous support in Congress. NAGPRA is a law with four attributes: property law, Indian law, human rights law, and administrative process.

Property Law   NAGPRA enfranchises tribes and Native Americans in the common law of property and Fifth Amendment property rights. The law recognizes that although human remains are not property and cannot be owned under the common law, descendants have the obligation and right to direct the disposition of their ancestors (Bowman, 1989). Funerary objects, sacred objects, and objects of cultural patrimony removed from tribes and Native American individuals without their permission, which are held in the control of federal agencies and museums that receive federal funds, must be returned to claimants under NAGPRA. If the museum has a lawful chain of ownership and transfer for the item, it may assert the right of possession. Under NAGPRA no taking shall occur.

NAGPRA Provisions and Applications

Protected items in NAGPRA are the human remains of Native Americans and Native Hawaiians and cultural items. Cultural items include funerary objects, those items placed with or intended for burials; sacred objects, those ceremonial items needed by traditional Native American religious leaders for the practice of traditional religion by present-day adherents; and cultural patrimony, the inalienable items owned by the group that have ongoing historical, traditional, or cultural importance and were considered as such at the time the object was separated from the group.

The parties with standing to receive NAGPRA-protected items held in the collections of federal agencies or museums are lineal descendants of named individuals with their associated funerary items, and federally recognized tribes or Native Hawaiian organizations. When there are newly exhumed burials and NAGPRA-protected items located on federal or Indian land, the priority of claimants is established as follows: lineal descendants; then tribal landowners on their tribal land regardless of cultural relationship; culturally affiliated federally recognized tribes and Native Hawaiian organizations on federal land; then federally recognized tribes or Native Hawaiian organizations that are the aboriginal occupants of the area regardless of cultural affiliation, unless another group with standing has a stronger claim of relationship.

Indian Law   NAGPRA acknowledges the unique relationship between the federal government and tribes and Native Hawaiian organizations (25 U.S.C. §3010). As such, the law requires consultation with federally recognized tribes and with Native Hawaiian organizations on a government-to-government basis at each stage of the process. That NAGPRA is contained within Title 25 of the United States Code, the Indian law section, brings to the interpretation of the law those general tenets of Indian law. One such Indian law provision applicable in the NAGPRA process is the absence of a time-bar for claims brought to establish title of Indians to human remains of their descendants and to cultural property. (See *County of Oneida v. Oneida Indian Nation*, 470 U.S. 226 [1985]).

Human Rights Law   NAGPRA does not provide Native Americans with any greater rights than would otherwise be afforded to those seeking to make claims recognized under the common law and to seek relief from a "taking" under the Fifth Amendment of the Constitution. As such, NAGPRA may be seen as "equal protection" law. Enfranchising Native Americans with property rights due but not historically respected is the essence of human rights law.

Administrative Process   The NAGPRA process establishes separate means to approach "repatriation" of Native American and Native Hawaiian human remains and cultural items separated from the land and held in museum and federal agency collections from the immediate determination of "ownership" upon the discovery of human remains and cultural items excavated on federal or Indian lands after the date of the law, November 16, 1990. NAGPRA is a congressionally mandated management plan that requires federal agencies and museums that receive federal funds to proactively ascertain the provenance of Native American items in their collections, consult with tribes, move forward with repatriations, and do so on an ongoing basis.

Use of NAGPRA Today

Federal agencies and institutions that receive federal funds and have possession of or control over Native American cultural items—the definition of a museum—must catalog their Native American and Native Hawaiian collections and produce a NAGPRA summary, sent to all possibly interested tribes and NHOs. The federal agency or museum need not know if the items generally described in a summary are NAGPRA-protected items. If a tribe or NHO wishes to consult on an item and make a claim, the obligation of the federal agency or museum is to entertain consultation and respond to the claim. The claimant will identify the item as a funerary object, sacred object, or object of cultural patrimony, or a combination of categories.

As to human remains and associated funerary objects, federal agencies and museums must consult with tribes, take the information they possess and that gained in consultation, and produce an itemized list of human remains and their funerary objects. This list, the NAGPRA inventory, is a decision document. Either a decision is made that the human remains are Native American—with the number of individuals represented, and the cultural affiliation of each individual—or inability to determine cultural affiliation is established. Cultural affiliation is a shared group identity that is fact based and is cultural, not political, and thus not limited to present-day tribes. Present-day tribes are identified in a NAGPRA inventory as those able to receive the human remains of a tribe, people, or culture (25 USC § 3001[9]). If there is no cultural connection to present-day tribes, then the individual is culturally unidentifiable, and the federal agency or museum makes a decision on the tribes with a tribal or aboriginal land connection. Tribes or NHOs will request to receive the individuals, acting on the decisions in the NAGPRA inventories.

NAGPRA requires publication of notices in the Federal Register, prior to transfer of control to tribes or NHOs, to provide an opportunity for objection prior to finalizing repatriation. Notices of Inventory Completion are the published decisions of the museum or federal agency, which act to enfranchise the tribes and NHOs in the notice to receive the human remains and their associated funerary objects. Notices of Intent to Repatriate are the responses of federal agencies and museums to claims of tribes and NHOs, which enable transfer of control to the claimant. In either notice, if there are no competing requests or claims, on the 31st day repatriation—that is, transfer of control—can occur. Timing of transfer of possession is subject to consultation in each case.

NAGPRA does not require that science be undertaken to make a cultural affiliation determination. It does not prohibit science undertaken in consultation with the interested parties. It does allow a museum or federal agency with NAGPRA-protected items in the collection to receive permission from the Secretary of the Interior to retain items until the end of a study that is of major benefit to the United States. Such a request has never been made.

Disputes over repatriation factual issues may be referred to the Review Committee for an advisory opinion. This is not a predicate to court action but provides a means to have the facts examined by an expert neutral panel. Also, a museum may resist the claim of a tribe if the museum can carry the burden of proving that they have the right of possession—that is, under the common law of property, they hold title that began with permission of the initial owner to acquire the item.

NAGPRA requires consultation with tribes and NHOs prior to the removal of human remains or cultural objects from federal or tribal land including Hawaiian Homes Commission land. When there is an agreement in place prior to the discovery of a NAGPRA-protected item, the event is called an "intentional excavation." The disposition of newly discovered items follows the agreement. When no agreement is in place the event is called an "inadvertent discovery" and all work must cease for 30 days while consultation occurs to reach an agreement on disposition. Thus, advance planning is better than stopping a project to do remedial decision making. Native American human remains and associated funerary objects that are not claimed remain in federal control pending future regulations on disposition.

NAGPRA makes it a crime to traffic in Native American human remains and cultural items (18 U.S.C. §1170). As to human remains, it is illegal to sell, purchase, use for profit, or transport for sale or profit the human remains of a Native American, taken from any location, of any age, unless the actor has the right of possession. Under the common law this would mean only the descendant with authority to put the remains into the marketplace may lawfully do so. If the same activity is undertaken with Native American cultural items in violation of the act, it is also a crime. Violation of NAGPRA can be committed by either removing the item from federal or Indian lands, including the lands of a Native Hawaiian organization, or by trafficking in items from museum or federal agency collections that are subject to the repatriation provisions. For instance, a museum that holds back a NAGPRA-protected item from the NAGPRA process so that it may be offered for sale at an auction has committed an act of trafficking. The first offense is a misdemeanor and the second offense is a felony.

NAGPRA seeks to rectify historic practices of disregard for Native American cultural property rights by adherence to the constitutional guarantees of equal protection and of rights to property, as well as to the common law treatment of human remains and personal, group, and sacred property. However, a sea change in ethics has not occurred without raising issues.

Culturally Unidentifiable Native American Human Remains   There are 130,000 Native American individuals listed in NAGPRA inventories as culturally unidentifiable individuals (CUI), in contrast to the 34,000 individuals recognized as culturally affiliated in published notices. Over 80 percent of the human remains on the CUI database were exhumed by archaeologists. A second look needs to be taken of the CUI inventories by each originator, applying the reasonable basis standard for cultural affiliation determinations after consultation with tribes.

Identification and Repatriation of Funerary Objects   Tribes are beginning to ask, "Why do so many of our repatriated ancestors have no funerary objects?" It can be expected that tribes will desire to see the excavation records to assist them to locate funerary objects, establish cultural affiliation, and request their repatriation.

Consultation: With Whom, By Whom   Consultation with tribes by museums and federal agencies is central to the NAGPRA process, whether the circumstances arise from collections or new discoveries on the land. A document is not a NAGPRA inventory unless it is the product of consultation.

Resolving Interests of Native American Groups   Not all Native Americans are in federally recognized "tribes." NAGPRA seeks to make cultural, rather than political, connections between exhumed or collected human remains and present-day tribes. However, "tribes" have standing to make claims under NAGPRA that politically unrecognized "groups" do not. As a matter of legal status, not fact, such human remains and items are culturally unidentifiable.

Designing State Law to Fit with NAGPRA   NAGPRA jurisdiction covers collections in the possession or control of federal agencies and museums that receive federal funds, which include state and local museums. When Native American human remains and cultural items are retrieved from state, local government, or private land or burials and come under state possession or control, the collections side of NAGPRA applies to those collections. States can develop protocols for an efficient state/federal process. Undisturbed burial places are subject to state and local law, not NAGPRA.

Tribal Compliance and Tribal Code   Tribes that have collections of Native American human remains and cultural items, or have new discoveries on their lands, are also required to comply with NAGPRA. NAGPRA defers to tribal sovereignty, so the challenge that now exists for tribes is to develop tribal cultural codes to deal with resolution of items.

Other Causes of Action   That NAGPRA exists is not cause for other remedies to disappear. NAGPRA expressly acknowledges that other remedies are available but does not require a choice of action. NAGPRA does not require excavation or prohibit land development. In those actions, other laws will apply.

   When viewed against the option of litigation, NAGPRA is an orderly, efficient means to resolve cultural property rights of Native Americans and Native Hawaiians.

Sherry Hutt

See Also PART 2: CULTURAL FORMS: FAMILY, EDUCATION, AND COMMUNITY: Wampum; SPIRITUALITY: Grandfathers (*Hadowi*): False Faces; Mound Cultures of the Ohio Valley

Further Reading

Bowman, Margaret B. "The Reburial of Native American Skeletal Remains: Approaches to Resolution of a Conflict." *Harvard Environmental Letter* 13 (1989): 167.

Echo-Hawk, Walter. "Museum Rights vs. Indian Rights: Guidelines for Assessing Competing Legal Interests in Native American Resources." *New York University Review of Legal and Social Change* 14 (1986): 437.

McKeown, C. Timothy, and Sherry Hutt. "In the Smaller Scope of Conscience: The Native American Graves Protection and Repatriation Act Twelve Years After." *UCLA Journal of Environmental Law and Policy* 21 (2002–2003): 153–212.

National NAGPRA Program Website. www.nps.gov/nagpra. Accessed October 31, 2014.

PAN-INDIANISM

"Pan-Indianism"—the amalgamation of many disparate Native American peoples into one group for common political effort—was born in paradox. Historically, many Native American groups operated largely as small groups in isolation. Their names in their own languages often meant "people," or "human beings," defining an inside and an outside. Rivalries were common.

Even before they were confronted by an invasion of outsiders from Europe, however, Native peoples were forming alliances and confederacies via intermarriage and trade. This was true to some degree across the continent. Confederacies were used for trade, cultural interchange, and political power-sharing the length of what is today the U.S. East Coast, as well as in the Plains and in the Pacific Northwest, where Coast Salish peoples traveled east of the Cascades to intermarry with the Yakamas and others. The Plains Indian peoples developed sign language to facilitate communication among peoples who needed to cross the barrier of language. The horse also increased range and, therefore, intercultural contacts.

The Haudenosaunee (Iroquois) Six Nations were the best-known confederacy to the immigrating Europeans, some of whose leaders (most notably Benjamin Franklin) used their model as an example for the British colonists' own federal structure. The Iroquois' culture, which supports a confederacy that is almost 1,000 years old, was pervaded by an early example of "pan-Indianism," as the white roots of their symbolic Tree of Peace (a Great White Pine) were said to reach outward, inviting other peoples to renounce violence and gather under the shade of the tree. On an individual level, the Haudenosaunee adopted people from other nations, even Europeans, which brought diverse cultural practices into their confederacy.

Panoramic view of a group of Iroquois (or Haudenosaunee) people on April 8, 1914. (Library of Congress)

The coming of Europeans also provoked Native peoples to find common cause. For the first time, the immigrants often defined Native peoples as a single ethnic group rather than along lines of separate tribal and national identities. The Europeans also forced Native peoples to endure assimilative pressures to coerce an abandonment of "Indian" cultural attributes. "Indians" in boarding schools mixed, mingled, and shared their forbidden languages and other cultural attributes.

Later, during the 1950s, the Bureau of Indian Affairs' relocation program increased the movement of American Indians to cities, where many different peoples mixed and formed a political and cultural basis for an activist movement that began to reclaim land, language, and cultures under the aegis of groups of continental scope. The modern movement toward pan-Indianism actually began early in the 20th century in the Society of American Indians (among other groups), and spread in the 1940s with the National Congress of American Indians.

The activist groups that formed during the 1960s did not spring from a vacuum, therefore, but from a long tradition of pan-Indian combinations. The American Indian Movement was mainly born in cities (the first being Minneapolis), among peoples, most of them young, who returned to reservations in search of cultural roots. The National Congress of American Indians was composed mainly of young people with reservation roots. Ad hoc groups developed to advance specific political goals, such as the United Indians (at Alcatraz) and the United Indians of All Tribes (at the occupation of Fort Lawton in Seattle). Their names were evocative of common goals hewn by a wide variety of peoples from across the continent. Paradoxically, the younger people used pan-Indianism to organize in opposition to the older groups, whom they criticized as doing too little to combat problems related to poverty, racial discrimination, and other problems shared by many Native peoples.

Pan-Indian spirituality provided another avenue, with the Ghost Dance serving as an example. The Native American Church (the peyote way) also grew out of pan-Indian cultural sharing. Pow wows also provide communication between many cultures. Cross-cultural communication is full of paradoxes. One result of American Indian pan-tribalism in the 20th century, for example, has been the use of English as a common language among people whose ancestors used many different Native languages. The pan-Indian movement thus spread knowledge of issues concerning many Native peoples as their languages declined. Later, pan-Indian groups came to advocate federal funding and other efforts to restore the many diverse cultures, the basis of which was revitalization of languages.

Another paradox of pan-Indianism was its emphasis on generic Plains Indian cultural attributes, such as pow wow formats generated by Buffalo Bill's

Wild West Show, along with a proliferation of feathered headdresses and tipis into areas where other cultural attributes were more traditional or had been lost. The "Pan-Plains" style of modern pan-Indianism thus sometimes came into competition with other Native peoples' traditions and created some resentment and factionalism. "In some tribes, these [Pan-Plains] traits exist side-by-side with older aboriginal forms. In other tribes where aboriginal traits have disappeared, these symbols of 'Indianness' are the distinctive traits of the community," anthropologist Robert K. Thomas wrote in 1965 (p. 78).

See Also PART 2: CULTURAL FORMS: ARTS: American Indian Arts and Crafts Fairs; **FAMILY, EDUCATION, AND COMMUNITY:** Spotlight: Reindigenization; Urban American Indians; **FOOD:** Food Sovereignty; Food Sovereignty: Local and Regional Examples; **LANGUAGE AND LITERATURE:** Language Reclamation: Eastern Tribes; Language Recovery in Indigenous North America; **MEDIA, POPULAR CULTURE, SPORTS, AND GAMING:** Indian Country Today Media Network; **MUSIC AND DANCE:** Native American Music Awards & Association (NAMAA); Pow Wows

Further Reading

Howard, James. "The Pan-Indian Culture of Oklahoma." *The Scientific Monthly* 18, no. 5 (November 1955): 215–220.

Thomas, Robert K. "Pan-Indianism." *Midcontinent American Studies Journal* 6, no. 2 (Fall, 1965): 75–83.

Spotlight

REINDIGENIZATION

Reindigenization, which is the conscious recovery of Native cultural attributes on a personal and collective level, has flourished in the late 20th and early 21st centuries after several centuries of colonization that sought to eradicate Native American languages, economic infrastructure, and other attributes of a sustainable culture. Reindigenization practiced at a tribal or national level is related to legal self-determination (most notably the protection of treaties and land bases in the United States) and nation building, as well as the use of economic resources to improve Native reservations.

"For many of us," wrote Melissa K. Nelson in *The Original Instructions* (2008, 24), "re-indigenization means we have to decolonize our minds, hearts, bodies, and spirits and revitalize healthy cultural traditions. We also have to create new traditions . . . to thrive in this complex world." Quoting John Mohawk, Nelson continued: "We're in recovery from more than five centuries of what only can be described as cultural madness" (p. 14). An Ojibwe scholar calls this state of mind "Post-Apocalyptic Stress Disorder" (Gross, 2003, n.p.).

Recapture of traditional diet is an important part of reindigenization on a personal level. At a time when Native foods have been widely adapted in mainstream culture (salmon and corn are two examples), reservation fare had often come to be characterized by what some Indians joked were the four food groups: Spam, commodity cheese, frybread, and Pepsi. Cooperative projects such as Renewing America's Food Traditions (RAFT) have been started to reindigenize diet.

Jeanette Armstrong makes a case that indigenous cultural knowledge has something to offer Western economics as well as science. Indeed, in a time when the pollution of capitalist enterprise overwhelms Earth's capacity to cleanse and cope, "reindigenization" is essential to framing a sustainable future. She quotes John Mohawk: "I think that when we talk about re-indigenization, we need a much larger, bigger umbrella to understand. It's not necessarily about the Indigenous Peoples of a specific place; it's about re-indigenizing the peoples of the planet" (Armstrong, 2011, 115).

To this Daryl Posey has added: "To reverse the devastating cycle which industrialized society has imposed on the planet, we have to re-learn ecological knowledge and earnestly deal with the question: Can sustainable practices harmonize with trade and increased consumption?" (Armstrong, 2011, 115). Posey calls upon indigenous environmental knowledge as a guide, "the re-indigenization of the world" (p. 115). Jerry Mander, in *Paradigm Wars*, also calls upon indigenous ecological models to guide non-Native activists who "remain hesitant to mention that such prevailing paradigms as economic growth, corporatism, capitalism, and the ideologies of the global market are all, by varying degrees, the root causes of the grave environmental and social crises of our time" (Mander and Tauli-Corpuz, 2006, 197).

"Indigenous knowledge does not fit comfortably into the Eurocentric concepts of 'culture'" because, as Battiste and Henderson comment, "most Indigenous scholars choose to view life from two different but complementary perspectives: First, as a manifestation of human knowledge. Heritage and consciousness, and second as a mode of ecological order" (2004, 35).

See Also PART 1: OVERVIEW: GENERAL HISTORICAL CONSIDERATIONS: Consensus in Governance as a Cultural Value; **PART 2: CULTURAL FORMS:** FAMILY, EDUCATION, AND COMMUNITY: Pan-Indianism; Urban American Indians; FOOD: Food Sovereignty; Food Sovereignty: Local and Regional Examples; LANGUAGE AND LITERATURE: Language Reclamation: Eastern Tribes; Language Recovery in Indigenous North America; MUSIC AND DANCE: Native American Music Awards & Association (NAMAA)

Further Reading

Armstrong, Jeannette C. "Indigenity: Situating the Tribal and the Local in the Global." In Kerstin Knopf, ed. *North America in the 21st Century: Tribal, Local, and Global*. Trier, Germany: Wissenschaftlicher Verlag Trier, 2011, 111–129.

Battiste, Marie, and James (Sa'kke'j) Youngblood Henderson. *Protecting Indigenous Knowledge and Heritage: A Global Challenge*. Saskatoon, SK: Purich, 2004.

Gross, Lawrence. "Cultural Sovereignty and Native American Hermeneutics in the Interpretation of the Sacred Stories of the Anishinaabe." *Wicazso Sa Review* 18, no. 2 (Fall, 2003): 127–134.

Mander, Jerry, Victoria Tauli-Corpuz, and International Forum on Globalization, eds. *Paradigm Wars: Indigenous Peoples' Resistance to Globalization.* San Francisco: Sierra Club Books, 2006.

Nelson, Melissa K. *Original Instructions: Indigenous Teachings for a Sustainable Future.* Rochester, VT: Bear, 2008.

RESTORATIVE JUSTICE

History and Origins

Native societies worked vigilantly to create and maintain harmony and balance, and they used a variety of means to return to harmony when relations between people or groups were out of balance. When dealing with acts that Western society today considers crimes and torts (civil injuries), the emphasis was on restoring harmony between the parties. This might involve punishment or compensation for harm as part of the harmonizing process. As far as possible, when someone had committed an offense, the emphasis was on reintegrating the wrongdoer back into society as a good citizen. Only in extreme cases, where reintegration seemed unattainable and the offender was considered sufficiently dangerous, was a perpetrator exiled or killed.

Numerous indigenous nations, including the Navajo Nation, whose peacemaking process is the best known, continue to settle disputes through participatory processes involving all the concerned parties, in line with the inclusive participatory decision making of virtually all traditional indigenous societies. This is based upon respect for all people, indeed all beings, and upon the view that each person has a unique perspective to contribute to the whole, so that everyone impacted by a decision is entitled to a voice in it, and that to the extent possible, everyone's concerns are to be included in the decision.

By contrast, in the United States and numerous Western societies the emphasis in the criminal justice process has been first in retribution, applying appropriate punishment, and most often only secondarily, if at all, providing restitution to victims and rehabilitation for offenders. This has usually left victims of crimes, and sometimes their communities, unrestored from the harms of crimes. There often also have been high recidivism rates among those convicted of crimes, who are frequently greatly limited in their ability to obtain desirable employment. As with the history of organizations in the West, which, since the late 19th century, step by step introduced modifications in a defective hierarchical organization model, before beginning to replace it with an effective participatory system of organization consistent with traditional indigenous ways of functioning, there have long been some modifications occasionally introduced into the corrections model in North America to deal with shortcomings in the corrections model, such as providing psychological services to convicts and halfway houses to provide employment and ease convicts' reintegration to society. More recently, an alternative approach, restorative justice, has been applied in the United States beginning in the 1970s, in different forms and to different extents, which derives directly from American Indian experience.

Restorative justice, when fully applied, is an attempt to restore solid relationships among all those who have suffered loss from a criminal act: the victim, other members (individuals and/or groups) of the community, and, if possible, the offender. For the victim, involvement in the process is very often quite empowering and healing. Victims have an opportunity to know what is being done about the harm done to them, and they may be able to discover why the harmful act was committed, while being heard through telling their stories. As with participatory decision making, simply having a voice in many instances is extremely important to the speaker. Often, the victim is able to receive restitution from the perpetrator, either concretely or symbolically. Where concrete restitution is not possible, the restorative justice process can be augmented by victims' compensation from the government or community, as exemplified by the California Victim Compensation Program (CalVCP: http://www.vcgcb .ca.gov/victims/) that helps pay bills and expenses resulting from certain violent crimes. Victims of crime who have been injured or have been threatened with injury in many instances are eligible for assistance. It may also be possible for the victim to receive an apology from the perpetrator.

For communities, restorative justice provides an opportunity to be involved in matters that concern them, which is not possible in standard Western judicial proceedings, where the full responsibility is with the government (at whatever level). Crime affects communities, making them stakeholders, as secondary victims, when it occurs in their midst. Having a role in a criminal proceeding allows the community and its members to participate in forums to address issues of crime and to support victims in their midst, while building a sense of mutual accountability and strengthening the bonds of community. It encourages community members to take on their obligations for the welfare of their members, encompassing victims and offenders in the course of fostering conditions that promote healthy communities, much the way citizen participation in community policing can be empowering in building healthy communities and reducing crime.

Restorative justice has been found to be extremely important for a high proportion of offenders as well. While it is not always proper for offenders to be directly involved with victims in a restorative justice process, they can still be involved indirectly when that is the better course of action. The participation of offenders, in whatever form, is important as it encourages offenders who admit their guilt to face up to what they have done and to see the impact of their behavior. Depending on the circumstances, this also often provides an opportunity for offenders to move toward making things right, at least with an apology (which usually is not accepted unless it appears genuine, with understanding of the harm inflicted, which offenders' participation confronts them with) and in many instances with restitution. In cases of less serious offenses involving property damage or minor injuries, this may involve the perpetrator repairing the damage or earning the money to pay for the repair or compensation. All of these aspects of offender participation tend to enhance rehabilitation, and recidivism rates are generally lower for offenders who have gone through a restorative justice process than an adversarial criminal justice process. This is partly the case because one aspect of restorative justice is to consider and take steps to assist the offender in attaining rehabilitation, and where appropriate, reintegration with the community. This may involve such actions as the offender participating in substance-abuse programs; undertaking counseling or psychological treatment; undertaking anger management, nonviolence training, or other appropriate education; and supervised probation or halfway house living (either alone or following incarceration, where that is appropriate).

Regional Variations

In situations where the offender is also a victim (though the offense is not an appropriate response to victimhood, which the restorative process needs to effectively lead the offender to understand), steps also need to be taken to correct that injustice, as the ultimate aim of restorative justice is to return all the parties, and at times the community, to balanced, harmonious relations. To do this requires examining each case holistically to understand the full set of relations involved and to work to bring them into harmony so far as possible. This is more complex than the normal workings of Western criminal justice systems that focus narrowly on the offender's act in isolation, though mitigating (or aggravating) circumstances may be taken into account in sentencing. A key to working well with offenders—as with everyone else—is to speak and act with respect; criticism should be directed toward inappropriate and harmful behavior and work to correct wrong thinking (while honoring a person's views and experience, so far as practicable in a mutually respectful dialogue) and to try to assist people in moving to be more fully who they really are.

Thus, the underlying principles of restorative justice work in the following ways. Crimes and equivalent harms are a violation of people and of interpersonal relationships. Since we are all related and interconnected, the violation creates an obligation for all parties, including the offender, to put things right—to restore proper relationships—so far as possible (and where relationships were previously imperfect, to improve them, a situation that may be illuminated by a harm).

Contemporary Forms

Restorative justice processes may take any number of a wide variety of forms and be applied for different purposes. In 20th-century North America, much of their use has been as alternative sentencing programs, following a standard judicial process to determine guilt. This has had some special applications in the development of drug courts that can focus on rehabilitation in alternative sentencing; in family courts in dealing with domestic sex crimes; and in juvenile courts and restorative programs, where young people are widely considered generally more open to social and psychological reeducation. In addition, restorative justice is sometimes also used more broadly as the process for handling crimes, as remains the case in some indigenous nations, as exemplified by Navajo peacemaking courts. Moreover, following the indigenous model, restorative justice can be utilized in dealing with all harms and injuries, civil as well criminal, and is so used outside the legal system in some institutions, including workplaces and schools.

One example is the application of the Native Hawaiian problem-solving process, *ho'oponopono*, a form of restorative justice, by a variety of social services, beginning in Hawaii in the 1970s. Although varying slightly in form, *ho'oponopono* follows the same basic principles of the indigenous and restorative processes previously discussed. It is "a method for restoring harmony that was traditionally used within the extended family. According to Pukui, it literally means "setting to right . . . to restore and maintain good relationships among family, and family and the supernatural powers" (Shook, 2002, 10). While first used to solve a case involving traditional Hawaiians, the practice quickly spread in Hawaii to include non-Hawaiian clients and practitioners in a variety of social service activities involving resolving conflicts and restoring relationships. *Ho'oponopono* was applied, for example, to resolve family and business disputes, and it was applied as an alternative mental health strategy to solve clients' psychological and psychiatric problems. Since the 1980s, *ho'oponopono* has been applied internationally, with many variations, as a method of conflict resolution. (A version of *ho'oponopono* has become internationally popular as a meditation method for individuals to attain inner harmony; see http://www.ancienthuna.com/ho oponopono.htm, and http://www.bing.com/search?q=ho'oponopono&form=AP MCS1, accessed December 28, 2013.)

Thus, restorative justice practices are related to the whole expanding field of conflict resolution and conflict transformation, which encompasses a large number of participatory processes for solving interpersonal and intergroup (or institutional) problems, as well as a number of inclusive participatory strategic planning methods. Good examples of large- and small-scale participatory processes for transforming conflict into collaboration and for preventing open conflict through inclusive dialogue are the work of the National Coalition for Dialogue and Deliberation (http://ncdd.org/), the Network for Peace Through Dialogue (http://ncdd.org/), and Search for Common Ground (www.sfcg .org), while an excellent example of a participatory strategic planning process employed to restore community harmony and empower effective community actions is the Indigenous Leadership Interactive System (ILIS) used by the Comanche Nation of Oklahoma to discuss issues and build consensus in the nation on proposals for the tribal government. The rise and expansion of these participatory processes, particularly since World War II, is an indication of the increasing relevance of traditional indigenous principles, values, and ways of being for the wider world of the 21st century.

In the fully participatory society (which all traditional Native societies are), applying indigenous values, restorative justice would be the general approach used to find justice in both the criminal and civil law, and it would be used informally, in various forms, as appropriate, in many institutions and organizations for dealing with inappropriate behavior. It is important to note that restorative justice uses punishment and compensation, when and as appropriate, as criminal and civil courts in the West have been doing for centuries. The difference is that restorative justice is broader, focusing on people and the full set of relations involved in each case or situation.

Stephen M. Sachs

See Also PART 2: CULTURAL FORMS: FAMILY, EDUCATION, AND COMMUNITY: Pan-Indianism/Spotlight: Reindigenization; Spotlight: Harmony Ethic, Cherokee; Spotlight: Reciprocity

Further Reading

Brown, Lee P. *Community Policing: A Practical Guide for Police Officials.* Washington, DC: National Institute of Justice, 1989.

California Victim Compensation Program (CalVCP). 2013. http://www.vcgcb.ca.gov /victims/. Accessed October 29, 2014.

Farole, Donald J., Jr., Nora Puffett, Michael Rempel, and Francine Byrne. "Applying the Problem-Solving Model Outside of Problem-Solving Courts." *Judicature* 89, no. 1 (July–August 2005): 40–42.

Goldstein, Herman. "Toward Community Oriented Policing: Potential, Basic Requirements and Threshold Questions." *Crime and Delinquency* 33 (1988): 6–30.

Greene, Jack R., and Stephen D. Mastrofski, eds. *Crime and Delinquency.* New York: Praeger, 1988.

Hanley Duncan, Susan, and Ida Dickie. "Family Group Conferencing: A Pilot Project within the Juvenile Court System in Louisville, Kentucky." *The Prevention Researcher* 20, no. 1 (2013): 11–14, http://www.nxtbook.com/nxtbooks/integratedresearchsrvcs/ pr_201302/#/16.

Hantzopoulos, Maria. "The Fairness Committee: Restorative Justice in a Small Urban Public High School." *The Prevention Researcher* 20, no. 1 (2013): 7–10. http://www .nxtbook.com/nxtbooks/integratedresearchsrvcs/pr_201302/#/12.

Harris, LaDonna, ed., and Stephen M. Sachs and Barbara Morris, gen. eds. *Recreating the Circle: The Renewal of American Indian Self-Determination.* Albuquerque: University of New Mexico Press, 2011.

Johnston, Kirsty. "Alternative Road for Victims of Sex Crime." *Fairfax* (New Zealand) *News,* December 22, 2013. http://www.stuff.co.nz/national/9544771/Alternative-road -for-victims-of-sex-crime.

McCaslin, Wanda D., ed. *Justice as Healing: Indigenous Ways, Writings on Community Peacemaking and Restorative Justice from the Native Law Centre.* St. Paul: Living Justice Press, 2005.

Melton, Ada Pecos. "Indigenous Justice Systems and Tribal Society." In Wanda D. Mc-Caslin, ed. *Justice as Healing: Indigenous Ways, Writings on Community Peacemaking and Restorative Justice from the Native Law Centre.* St. Paul: Living Justice Press, 2005.

Moore, Mark Harrison. "Problem-Solving and Community Policing." In M. Tonry and N. Morris, eds. *Modern Policing.* Chicago: University of Chicago Press, 1992, 99–158.

Nielsen, Marianne O., and Robert A. Silverman. *Native Americans, Crime and Justice.* Boulder: CO: Westview Press, 1996.

Pavelka, Sandra. "Practices and Policies for Implementing Restorative Justice within Schools." *The Prevention Researcher* 20, no. 1 (2013): 15–17.

Pranis, Kay, Barry Stuart, and Mark Wedge. *Peace Making Circles: From Crime to Community.* St. Paul: Living Justice Press, 2003.

Ross, Rupert. *Returning to the Teachings: Exploring Aboriginal Justice.* Toronto: Penguin Canada, 1996.

Sachs, Stephen M. "Expanding the Circle: Developing an American Indian Political Theory for Living Well in the Twenty-First Century." *Proceedings of the 2014 Western Social Science Association Meeting American Indian Studies Section. Indigenous Policy* 25, no. 2 (Fall 2014).

Sachs, Stephen M. "Los Angeles and Somalia: Community Service Policing and Community Empowerment." *Nonviolent Change* VIII, nos. 2–3 (Winter–Spring, 1994). Reprinted in *COPRED Peace Chronicle* 19, no. 2 (December 1994).

Shook, Victoria. *Ho'oponopono: Contemporary Uses of a Hawaiian Problem Solving Process.* Honolulu: University of Hawaii Press, 2002.

Trojanowicz, Robert, and Bonnie Bucqueroux. *Community Policing: A Contemporary Perspective.* Cincinnati, 1990.

Weisheit, Ralph A., L. Edward Wells, and David N. Falcone. "Community Policing in Small Towns and Rural America." *Crime & Delinquency* 40, no. 4 (October 1994): 549–567.

Wilson, James Q., and George L. Kelling. "Making Neighborhoods Safe." *Atlantic Monthly* 263, no. 2 (February 1989).

Zehr, Howard. *The Little Book of Restorative Justice.* Intercourse, PA: Good Books, 2002.

Zion, James, and Elsie B. Zion. "'Hazho's Sokee'—Stay Together Nicely: Domestic Violence under Navajo Common Law." In Marianne O. Nielsen and Robert A. Silverman, eds. *Native Americans, Crime and Justice.* Boulder: CO: Westview Press, 1995, 96–102.

Spotlight

HARMONY ETHIC, CHEROKEE

The Cherokees occasionally went to war with other Native American nations, but within their settlements, the highest value was placed on what was sometimes called a "Harmony Ethic." This code of behavior placed a great deal of emphasis on eliminating interpersonal conflict, especially face-to-face anger; it may be compared in some ways to the Iroquois code of behavior developed in the Great Law of Peace. The Harmony Ethic governed the way in which Cherokees treated each other and how they defined their relationship with nature.

In Cherokee society, a person was conditioned by social norms to avoid giving offense to others. A good person was supposed to avoid expressing anger or causing others to become angry; a leader earned respect by listening carefully and not expressing his views until he had heard all sides in a conflict. A third person often was brought in to resolve conflicts between two individuals in this manner. If a conflict was not reconciled, the two parties often went about their business, studiously avoiding each other. Robert K. Thomas cites examples of such behavior into the mid-20th century; Cherokee children in off-reservation schools sometimes asked a third party (usually another child) to ask the teacher if they could use the bathroom, for example. Some Cherokees took companions with them to apply for jobs, or when they had to appear in court.

In the face of conflict, the Harmony Ethic directed both parties to withdraw. If a conflict could be resolved through generosity, a good Cherokee was expected to give of himself and his belongings to retain a semblance of social well-being. This value was especially evident with respect to sharing food. The

Cherokee language contains a special word that indicates stinginess with food, as compared to stinginess with other possessions.

A person who engaged in behavior contrary to the Harmony Ethic would at first become the target of gossip and ostracism. If verbal methods of social control failed, and if a pattern of antisocial behavior became entrenched, the people who were offended by it might hire a conjurer, whose rituals were said to prepare the way for the offending person to become seriously ill, with death the eventual result in the most extreme cases. Even when preparing to kill such a person, however, a third party was always engaged. Face-to-face conflict was avoided at all costs.

Further Reading

Cooter, Robert, and Robert K. Thomas. *The People and the Strangers: Narratives and a Theory of American Indian Life.* Unpublished, 1995. Available at: http://works.bepress .com/robert_thomas/1.

Spotlight

RECIPROCITY

The idea of reciprocity—if one receives or takes away, one must also give back—is shared by many Native American cultures. It is also an expression of an emphasis of thinking in cycles as opposed to a Eurocentric emphasis on linear expression. All things are said to be related; the Lakota phrase *Mitakuye Oyasin* ("all my relatives") is a way of expressing a familial relationship with all of nature. "This relatedness not only ties together seemingly disparate beings but also identifies humans with all of creation," wrote Joseph Epes Brown (2001, 87). Many Native myths contain stories of shape-shifting humans changing into animals and vice versa.

Native American economic relationships often were carried on according to principles of reciprocity involving mutual gift-giving. Trade among Native peoples often was conducted as an exchange of gifts. Notions of reciprocity permeated the daily lives of many Native American peoples. Among the Tlingits, for example, the two major clans (Wolf and Raven) built houses for each other, a process that was accompanied by feasting and gift-giving. Among the Wyandots (Hurons), relations of friendship and material reciprocity were extended beyond the Wyandot Confederacy in the form of trading arrangements. Foreign trade was not merely an economic activity; it was embedded in a network of social relations that were, fundamentally, extensions of the kin relationships within the Wyandot Confederacy. Like the Iroquois, the Wyandots sometimes formally adopted traders with whom they had frequent and mutually beneficial relations. Traders so adopted often lodged with their friends while visiting; sometimes traders, who were male, took Native American wives.

The bonds of reciprocity extended to the relationships of humans and animals—many Native peoples thanked a source of food for its sustenance before removing its life force—"or, more generally, between humans and all form and forces of nature" (Brown, 1982, 125). Joy Porter (2012) points to a wider belief shared by many indigenous communities that a basic reciprocity exists between the human world and the spirit world. This relationship supersedes the profit motive. For example, anyone who attempts to sell "false face" Iroquois ceremonial masks (many traditional people call them "grandfathers") may be warned about "the dangers of handling 'dangerous material'" (Porter, 2012, 73). Some things are not for sale.

Further Reading

Brown, Joseph Epes. *The Spiritual Legacy of the American Indian*. New York: Crossroad, 1982.

Brown, Joseph Epes, with Emily Cousins. *Teaching Spirits: Understanding Native American Religious Traditions*. New York: Oxford University Press, 2001.

Porter, Joy. *Land and Spirit in Native America*. Santa Barbara, CA: Praeger/ABC-CLIO, 2012.

Trigger, Bruce G. *Children of the Aataentsic: A History of the Huron People*. Montreal: McGill-Queen's University Press, 1976.

SEXUAL ORIENTATION

History and Origins

Gay, lesbian, bisexual, and transgender (LGBT) relationships are part of at least 150 Native peoples' myths and stories. Jim Elledge compiled an anthology that contains such stories from, among many others, the Arapahos, Assiniboine, Chemehuevis, Comanches, Coos, Crows, Dakotas, Fox, Hopis, Kamias, Menominees, Mohaves, Navajos, Ojibwe, Passamaquoddy, Pawnees, Sioux (Lakotas), Tewas, Western Monos, Yokuts, and Zunis. These roles have existed "since the dawn of time," according to Elledge, and "were often at least of equal standing with other members of their tribe, if not more powerful than those in whose midst they existed" (Elledge, 2002, xv). Heterosexuals usually were not threatened by variations of gender in their midst, "but saw the two-spirits as individuals with special talents which they offered the tribe for its continued existence, its prosperity, and its safety" (Elledge, 2002, xviii). Cross-gender work roles also generally were respected.

According to Barbara Mann, an important factor in many Native ways of thinking is that *all* human beings have two spirits, and not—as modern urban legend has it—only gays and lesbians. That legend was deliberately invented and spread in the 1980s, but it is a New Age concept, not a traditional idea.

We-Wa, a Zuni two-spirit, weaving, c. 1890. (National Archives)

Traditionally, one inherits a Breath spirit from one's father and a Blood spirit from one's mother, as reflected in one's dual membership in a nation (Breath) and a clan (Blood).

Being gay or lesbian is not a spirit quality but the border-crossing quality of the Third Gender, which traditional thought recognizes alongside the male and female genders. Three is an important number to cultures that use binary math. Especially in the Eastern Woodlands, three is the number that means "Pay attention." It signals that important information is at hand, so that belonging to the Third Gender is an automatic "Listen up" (Mann, 2012).

This point of view was echoed in recent times by Erna Pahe, a Navajo community activist:

> We're the one group of people that can really understand both cultures. . . .
> You go out there into the straight world and it's really amazing, the stereo-
> types. Men can do this and women can't do that. Or women can do this
> and men can't do that. In our culture, in our little gay world, anybody can
> do anything. (Roscoe, 1998, 65)

A Crow tribal elder said in 1982: "We don't waste people the way white society does. Every person has their gift" (Roscoe, 1998, 4). One of those talents
in many cases seems to have been matchmaking.

A minority of scholars dissent from these ideas. Chicano gender historian
Ramón Gutiérrez criticized what he called a "queer-friendly" approach by Will
Roscoe and others as "an unsubstantiated 'gay liberationist' white projection of
idealizing and projecting queer freedom onto Native American pasts" (Estrada,
2011, 171).

According to Elledge (2002), "Typically, the two-spirit individual was a gay,
lesbian, bisexual or transgendered person—in the western definition of gender
variance—who often, but not always, adopted the clothing, habits, and/or social roles of the opposite sex" (p. xiv). Many assumed such roles in youth, aided
by dreams or visions. In many cases, an individual's peers performed a ritual to
recognize the change. Such roles had a valuable place in many Native societies and were not morally condemned as a matter of religion as in European
American cultures.

While some gay, lesbian, bisexual, and transgender people formed intimate
relationships with others of similar orientation, more often "two spirits" formed
relationships with heterosexual partners: "Their partnerships were overwhelm-
ingly with individuals who were comfortable with the roles assigned them by
virtue of their gender. Thus, a male two-spirit formed a sexual relationship . . .
with an individual who was, in terms of his social status, a 'heterosexual man';
likewise, a female two-spirit would form a relationship with a 'heterosexual
woman'" (Elledge, 2002, xiv). Long-term, male two-spirits often were considered "wives" and "husbands" of their respective partners. "For many Native
Americans," noted Elledge, "sexuality seems to have been more fluid than the
polarized notion of heterosexuality at one extreme and homosexuality at the
opposite extreme allows" (p. xv). In recent years, Western gender science has
come to agree with the point of view that a person may have both attributes in
varying proportions.

Regional Variations

Will Roscoe (1998), a prominent scholar of sexual orientation in Native American cultures, noted that some people had criticized the use of the term "berdache,"
finding it a Western imposition (actually, its linguistic roots were Persian). He
had his doubts that "two spirit" was any less Western. He tended to use both
terms, or to use "third gender" for male homosexuals and "fourth gender" for
lesbian females. Roscoe documented male same-sex relationships in at least 155
Native American groups and female relationships in a third as many (p. 7).

During the colonization of North America, the fluidity of gender and cultural roles among Native Americans confounded Europeans whose cultures confined behavior according to gender roles with a rigidity unknown today. Many Native men not only blurred gender barriers, but crossed them, back and forth, many times during their lives. Some preferred the company of other men but also married women and fathered children. The same men also may have performed tasks usually identified with women, such as farming and dressing hides, until they shed their female roles and led other men in war. Some men (and a smaller number of women) were bisexual, and others abstained from sex altogether.

The Lakotas called men who affected women's roles *winkte*. Such people were not ostracized but generally respected as *wakan*, having powers that other men did not. Although *winktes* did not go to war, they sometimes were said to be able to foretell the future, so warriors consulted with them about upcoming battles. Luther Standing Bear wrote: "Everyone accepted the *winktes* with kindness and allowed them to choose their own work, be it either men's or women's, and one of the bravest men I ever knew was a *winkte*. They were scarce, however, and in my life I have not known more than half a dozen" (Standing Bear, 1933, 93).

Early in 1801, the trader Alexander Henry encountered a young Anishinaabe (Ojibwe) man whose dress and mannerisms were feminine but who was known as a superlative warrior whose feats of bravery were legendary—he had once, in fact, routed an entire Sioux war party with a bow and a single quiver of arrows. "This person," wrote Henry, "is a curious compound between a man and a woman. He is a man in every respect both as to members [sexual organs] and courage but still he seems to appear womanish, and dresses as such" (Carpenter, 2011, 148). Henry reported that some of the young man's compatriots (including his own father) disapproved of his gender bending, but others admired it.

The Illinois singled out young boys who played with women's toys ("the spade, the spindle, and the axe") and dressed them as girls, including tattoos on their cheeks and breasts. "They omit nothing that can make them like the women," an observer wrote (Carpenter, 2011, 151). The Hidatsas believed that effeminate men had been blessed by a female deity. They were believed to be favored as religious leaders. An Omaha man was described as having been commanded by the moon to shift gender roles—he was an outstanding husband and father but feminine in his dress and cultural behavior.

Hernán Cortés, Spanish conquistador of the Aztecs, regarded every man in his new subject kingdom as a sodomite: "We have learnt and been informed for sure that they are all sodomites and use that abominate sin," he wrote. His fellow conquistador Bernal Diaz del Castillo thought that "all the rest were sodomites, especially those who live on the coasts and in warm lands; so much so that young men paraded around dressed in women's clothes to work in the diabolical and abominable role" (Slater, 2011, 47). He assumed that cross-dressing guaranteed homosexuality.

Cabeza de Vaca wrote of the Karankawas of present-day Texas in 1540: "I saw a most brutish and beastly custom . . . a man who was married to another and these be certain effeminate and impotent men, who go clothed and attired like women, and perform the office of a woman" (Roscoe, 1998, 4). About the same time, in 1513, the Spanish explorer Vasco Nuñez de Balboa encountered 40 male homosexuals dressed as women in present-day Panama. He had them killed by hunting dogs, an act that was praised by a Spanish historian a century later as "a fine action of an honorable and Catholic Spaniard" (Roscoe, 1998, 4).

Edwin T. Denig arrived in Crow country during 1833 as a trader with the American Fur Company. For 23 years, he remarked at what he thought was the alien nature of Native cultures. One aspect that often perplexed Denig was how the Crows regarded diversity of gender. He found that some of the Crows' most highly regarded people were men who dressed as women and did women's work. Conversely, some women led men into battle. Denig noted that such behavior in European Americans could lead to a person's jailing, persecution, and even execution as their sexual orientation was condemned as unnatural. One prominent Crow, who was known as Woman Chief, had four wives, led men into battle, and was highly esteemed by her peers. Originally a Gros Ventre, she was captured at the age of 10 by the Crows. She was described by Denig as taller and stronger than most women and "desired to acquire manly accomplishments" (Roscoe, 1998, 78).

The German prince Maximilian, who traveled on the northern Plains between 1832 and 1834, wrote: "They have many berdaches, or hermaphrodites, among them" (Roscoe, 1998, 25). Navajo families welcomed children who displayed berdache tendencies and gave them special care and encouragement. Anthropologist Willard Hill wrote, "As they grew older and assumed the character of *nadle*, this solicitude and respect increased, not only on the part of their families but from the community as a whole" (Roscoe, 1998, 43).

Laguna Pueblo author Leslie Silko noted, "Pueblo men in sacred kiva spaces can become possessed by female spirits, momentarily and appropriately embodying mixed gender energy" (Estrada, 2011, 169). Christianity, Western law, and cultural biases often inhibit expression of "these fluid gender realities" in public, but this mode of expression survives in oral history. Paula Gunn Allen, Silko's cousin (and also a Laguna Pueblo author), makes strong statements on lesbian and gay roles: "It is my contention that gayness, whether female or male, traditionally functions positively within tribal groups." Furthermore, she asserted that "same-sex relationships may have been the norm for primary pair-bonding before opposite-sex bondings would occur." She also notes that such expressions have been repressed by Christianity (Estrada, 2011, 169–170).

Contemporary Forms

American society generally has become more accepting of gender fluidity as many Native peoples practiced it, as illustrated in an account by Ruth Padawer in the *New York Times Sunday Magazine*:

> Many parents and clinicians now reject corrective therapy, making this the first generation to allow boys to openly play and dress (to varying degrees) in ways previously restricted to girls—to exist in what one psychologist called "that middle space" between traditional boyhood and traditional girlhood. These parents have drawn courage from a burgeoning Internet community of like-minded folk whose sons identify as boys but wear tiaras and tote unicorn backpacks. Even transgender people preserve the traditional binary gender division: born in one and belonging in the other. But the parents of boys in that middle space argue that gender is a spectrum rather than two opposing categories, neither of which any real man or woman precisely fits. . . . What is clear is that in the last few years, challenges to the conventional model have become increasingly common in the United States and Europe, in medical publications and among professionals and parents themselves. "The climate has changed," said Edgardo Menvielle, head of one of the world's few programs for gender-nonconforming youth, at Children's National Medical Center in Washington [D.C.]. (Padawer, 2012)

As support for same-sex marriage increased rapidly around the world early in the 21st century, members of many American Indian tribes found themselves caught up in the same debate. A few tribal councils had approved same-sex unions by 2013, but the vast majority had remained silent, pending a landmark ruling by the U.S. Supreme Court on the federal Defense of Marriage Act (DOMA) (the Court struck down DOMA in June 2013). Some Native governments (such as the Suquamish in Washington State) had approved same-sex marriages in the 11 states (by May 2013) that had approved them. In the meantime, the Navajos were standing by a ban on same-gender marriage between close blood relatives that their council had passed in 2005.

Strong feelings and debates exist in Indian country, points out Elizabeth Ann Kronk, director of the University of Kansas School of Law's Tribal Law and Governance Center, who also is a member of the Chippewa Sault Ste.

Marie Tribe of Michigan. "What you see in Indian country is this struggle between the historical accepting of the two-spirit individuals versus the relatively new but yet very strong Christian influences" (Hotakainen, 2013).

See Also PART 2: CULTURAL FORMS: ARTS: Cultural Appropriation: Questions and Issues

Further Reading

Carpenter, Roger M. "Womanish Men and Manlike Women." In Sandra Slater and Fay A. Yarbrough, eds. *Gender and Sexuality in Indigenous North America: 1400–1800.* Columbia: University of South Carolina Press, 2011, 146–164.

Devereux, George. "Institutionalized Homosexuality of the Mohave Indians." *Human Biology* 9 (1937): 498–527.

Elledge, Jim. *Gay, Lesbian, Bisexual and Transgender Myths: From the Arapaho to the Zuñi.* New York: Peter Lang, 2002.

Estrada, Gabriel S. "Two-Spirit Histories in Southwestern and Mesoamerican Literatures." In Sandra Slater and Fay A. Yarbrough, eds. *Gender and Sexuality in Indigenous North America: 1400–1800.* Columbia: University of South Carolina Press, 2011, 165–184.

Fletcher, Alice C., and Francis La Flesche. *The Omaha Tribe.* Smithsonian Institution: Bureau of American Ethnology *Annual Report 27* (1905–1906): 132–133.

Hill, W. W. "Note on the Pima Berdache." *American Anthropologist* new series, 40 (1938): 339.

Hotakainen, Rob. "Among Indian Tribes, a Division over Gay Marriage." *Washington Post*, May 13, 2013. http://www.washingtonpost.com/politics/among-indian-tribes-a -division-over-gay-marriage/2013/05/12/4c77bf3e-bb3a-11e2-9b091638acc3942e_print .html. Accessed October 29, 2014.

Mann, Barbara Alice. Personal communication, April 13, 2012.

Olden, Sarah. "The People of Tipi Sapa." In Vine Deloria Jr. *Singing for a Spirit: A Portrait of the Dakota Sioux.* Santa Fe, NM: Clear Light, 1999.

Padawer, Ruth. "What's So Bad About a Boy Who Wants to Wear a Dress?" *New York Times Sunday Magazine*, August 12, 2012. http://www.nytimes.com/2012/08/12/magazine /whats-so-bad-about-a-boy-who-wants-to-wear-a-dress.html. Accessed October 29, 2014.

Roscoe, Will. "Bibliography of Berdache and Alternative Gender Roles Among North American Indians." *Journal of Homosexuality* 14, no. 3 (1987): 81–171.

Roscoe, Will. *Changing Ones: The Third and Fourth Genders in Native North America.* New York: St. Martin's Press, 1998.

Slater, Sandra. "'Nought but Women': Construction of Masculinities and Modes of Emasculation in the New World." In Sandra Slater and Fay A. Yarbrough, eds. *Gender and Sexuality in Indigenous North America: 1400–1800.* Columbia: University of South Carolina Press, 2011, 30–53.

Slater, Sandra, and Fay A. Yarbrough. *Gender and Sexuality in Indigenous North America: 1400–1800.* Columbia: University of South Carolina Press, 2011.

Spier, Leslie. "Transvestites." In *Klamath Ethnology*. Berkeley: University of California Press, 1930, 51–53.

Standing Bear, Luther. *Land of the Spotted Eagle*. Lincoln: University of Nebraska Press, 1933.

TRADE, CULTURAL ATTRIBUTES

History and Origins

Before European colonization, Native American peoples carried on active trading relationships across North America. Unusual items, such as turquoise from New Mexico, found their way to the East Coast via trade routes that covered the continent and often paralleled the routes of modern interstate highways. Copper from Lake Superior and pipestone from Minnesota were carried thousands of miles from their sources. Aztec artifacts have been found along the U.S. Gulf of Mexico coast. Trade shaped cultures across the continent.

Regional Variations

According to Bruce G. Trigger and William R. Swagerty, trade was very active across much of North America even in prehistorical times:

> Eastern North America was . . . crisscrossed by exchange networks, many of which were of considerable antiquity. Trade across ecological boundaries sometimes involved staples, such as the surplus corn that the Hurons traded with the Nipissings, and possibly with other Northern Algonquian peoples, in return for pelts and dried fish. Most trade, however, was in luxury items, including marine shells, copper, and fancy furs. Exotic cherts continued to be passed from one band to another throughout the boreal forests. (Trigger, 1996, 329)

Some Native peoples, such as the Ottawas, had a reputation for being far-ranging traders. After contact, the Pawnees acquired a reputation as horse traders on the Plains. Rock carvings above watercourses in the American West that looked haphazard to European American eyes sometimes contained information for travelers, as intelligible to Native American travelers as road signs on a modern interstate highway. Where some European Americans saw a trackless wilderness, Native Americans saw a vital network of trade.

Trade patterns in North America seem to have been well formed as early as 2,300 years ago; the Adena and Hopewell cultures of the present-day U.S.

Midwest traded for Lake Superior copper, Gulf of Mexico shells, and North Dakota flint. They used obsidian that originated in Wyoming's Yellowstone region, quartz from Arkansas, and silver from Canada.

As the European trade frontiers expanded, Native Americans in different regions specialized in certain kinds of trade. Many in what would later be called the U.S. Southwest specialized in the horse trade. Those to their northeast specialized in guns and furs. At times, Native American peoples who shared neighboring territories evolved symbiotic trade relationships over time. The Crows, for example, routinely produced a surplus of meat and other buffalo products that often were traded to the Hidatsas for their surplus of agricultural products. Different segments of the same tribe or nation also sometimes evolved symbiotic trade relationships.

Certain bands of Cheyennes specialized in various modes of economic production. For example, southern bands specialized in horse raiding, while central bands specialized in the making of buffalo robes. The northern bands usually had a surplus of trade goods, such as knives and kettles, from trade along the upper Missouri River. Whenever people from two different Cheyenne bands were married, ceremonies included substantial gift-giving, which performed an economic function of redistributing goods for mutual benefit.

While trade among Native peoples served the same material purposes as similar forms of exchange among non-Indians, trade was viewed by most Native Americans as something more than an economic exchange. Trade also cemented political alliances. In some Plains Native cultures (the Hidatsas, for example) non-Indian traders were adopted ceremonially. Other links were created by traders' marriages to Native women. In trading relationships, bargaining often was not carried on directly in trade between Native American peoples, who considered an argument over price as a breach of friendship. The consideration of a profit motive also was considered uncouth in public. Trade was generally meant to be a mutually advantageous exchange of gifts.

The beaver trade was brief but intense as the pelts of the animals entered and then vanished from fashion among whites. Nearly every Native people from the Great Lakes to the northeastern Great Plains experienced a cultural shock of intense, quickly passing prosperity. David Thompson recalled in his memoirs that

> "for several years all of these Indians were rich. The Women and Children, as well as the Men, were covered with silver brooches, Ear Rings, Wampum, Beads, and other trinkets. Their mantles were of scarlet cloth, and all was finery and dress. . . . The Canoes of the Furr [sic] Traders were loaded with packs of beaver." A Cree man was quoted by Thompson as

anticipating a time when the beaver would be gone and "we [shall] soon be poor." (Isenberg, 2000, 52)

Many Native peoples associated trade with the formation of a kinship bond; trade very quickly became much more than the simple commercial transactions used in European societies. Among the Cheyennes, trade was accompanied by the "making of relatives." Influence accrued to the person with the largest network of "relatives" or "relations." Marriage was regarded as only one way of many that such a network could be built. When non-Indian traders arrived here—as in many other Native societies where relations were construed similarly—some were incorporated this way.

European traders quickly learned Native American customs of trade and adapted them to their purposes. Because Indian trading customs valued reciprocity, Europeans found that generosity on their part would often be returned. The commercial traffic in furs often was carried on according to Native trading customs, just as early diplomacy in America often took place according to Native American protocol.

From a Native point of view, much of the trade of the Plains was perceived to be reciprocal gift-giving in association with the calumet, or peace pipe. The calumet had been used for hundreds of years in rituals that enabled peoples who were otherwise hostile to meet and trade in peace. Lewis and Clark's journal explains the ritual: "The party delivering generally Confess their Errors and request a peace[;] the party receiving exult in their Suckcesses [*sic*] and receive the Sacred Stem" (Wishart, 1994, 32). Bows and arrows, skins, food, guns, and other "gifts" might then be exchanged.

Trade traffic in the early years after contact often was characterized by an influx of manufactured goods, such as metal kettles, linen shirts, blankets, spinning wheels, Italian glass beads, shoes, drills, and many other items. The fact that the Industrial Revolution began first in England provided that country with the most extensive inventory of trade goods and had a major influence on swinging the balance of power toward England, away from France and Spain, by the mid-18th century. The two most important European trade items during the first years of contact were probably guns and horses, the advance guard of the cash economy. To purchase guns, ammunition, horses, and riding tack (among the many other trade items that came with time), Native American peoples needed a commodity in exchange, usually the skins of fur-bearing animals.

Because of trade, by the time of the American Revolution, many Mohawks had living standards comparable to those of nearby European Americans. Some of the Mohawks' Oneida neighbors, according to historian Colin Calloway, "lived in frame houses with chimneys and painted windows, ate with spoons from pewter plates, drank from teacups and punch bowls, combed their hair with ivory combs, used silk handkerchiefs, and wore white breeches" (Calloway, 1997, 46). The Cherokees, in a material sense, were living much like their non-Indian neighbors before they were expelled from their homelands on the Trail of Tears in the late 1830s, partially due to the trade.

Native American peoples adopted European trade goods because they made life easier, but many, such as the Onondaga sachem Canassatego, expressed misgivings in the 18th century about becoming dependent on outsiders' manufacturers. Some of the imports, such as firearms, increased the level of violence in Native societies. As Indians adopted European manufactured goods, their own inventory of cultural and economic skills declined as well.

North Pacific Coast peoples used a network of trails to traverse lands on the eastern side of Puget Sound, the Cascade Mountains, and along rivers and saltwater bays. Many of today's highways and other roads follow old trade routes. Intertribal trade was commonplace during the 19th century, before widespread non-Indian immigration. Coast Salish peoples conducted commerce within a wide geographic area. Native trading parties traveled east and west over the Cascade Mountains for trade and barter. Indigenous peoples of various nations often traded seafood. Following contact with European Americans, trade continued, as salmon, other fish, oysters, and clams were sold to allow purchase of new technology, including metal items (such as cooking pots) and tools that aided in carving canoes.

Trails laced the dense forests of western Washington, developed for trade and other communication. In some areas, the ground was worn by years of foot traffic. Trails led to saltwater areas for harvesting clams, to berry fields and fishing streams. One trail led from Puget Sound to the Cowlitz River. Another traversed the Cascade Mountains to the Yakima Valley. The trails helped maintain social relationships. Linkages between and within groups were facilitated by a number of cultural practices. Marriages cemented relationships along the coast. Similarly, marriages also created bonds between people from both sides of the Cascade Mountains. Many people from the east side of the Cascades escaped its harsh climate by wintering on the west side of the mountains. All of this maintained alliances, as well as trading and family relationships.

Shell money of several types was used by the Coast Salish to facilitate trade. These items were subject to scarcity value. East of the Cascades, for example, discs of white clam shells about a centimeter in diameter (*tc !au'wai*) became more valuable. Discs were smoothed with rough stones and a hole was drilled in each bead so they could be used in strings. "Solax" was made from tubular beads traded from the north, usually "strung in pairs with a round bead between"

(Haeberlin and Gunther, 1930, 29). Larger clam shells from the north had greater value because they were scarce. Some of the shells were worn in strings as adornment, or as ear ornaments by chiefs. Haeberlin and Gunther published a scale of purchasing power: so many Solax, for example, were generally worth one basket. A larger number might buy a small canoe. Tribes from the north who held slaves also converted their value into the various forms of shell money.

See Also PART 1: OVERVIEW: GENERAL HISTORICAL CONSIDERATIONS: Treaty Diplomacy, Cultural Context; **PART 2: CULTURAL FORMS:** FAMILY, EDUCATION, AND COMMUNITY: Restorative Justice/Spotlight: Reciprocity; MUSIC AND DANCE: Pow Wows

Further Reading

Albers, Patricia. "Synthesis, Merger, and War: Contrasting Forms of Intertribal Relationship Among Historic Plains Indians." In John H. Moore, ed. *The Political Economy of North American Indians*. Norman: University of Oklahoma Press, 1993, 99–128.

Anderson, Terry L., and Fred S. McChesney. "Raid or Trade: An Economic Model of Indian-White Relations." *Journal of Law and Economics* 37 (April 1994): 39–74.

Calloway, Colin. *New Worlds for All: Indians, Europeans, and the Remaking of Early America*. Baltimore: Johns Hopkins University Press, 1997.

Fixico, Donald L. "As Long as the Grass Grows: The Cultural Conflicts and Political Strategies of United States–Indian Treaties." In Winston A. Van Horne and Thomas V. Tonnesen, eds. *Ethnicity and War*. Madison: University of Wisconsin Press, 1984.

Haeberlin, H., and Erna Gunther. *The Indians of Puget Sound*. University of Washington Publications in Anthropology 4 (1930): 1–84. Seattle: University of Washington Press.

Isenberg, Andrew C. *The Destruction of the Bison: An Environmental History, 1750–1920*. Cambridge: Cambridge University Press, 2000.

Moore, John H. *The Cheyennes*. Oxford: Blackwell, 1997.

Trigger, Bruce G. "Entertaining Strangers: North America in the Sixteenth Century." In Bruce G. Trigger and Wilcomb E. Washburn, eds. *The Cambridge History of the Native Peoples of the Americas*. Cambridge: Cambridge University Press, 1996, 325–398.

Wishart, David J. *An Unspeakable Sadness: The Dispossession of the Nebraska Indians*. Lincoln: University of Nebraska Press, 1994.

URBAN AMERICAN INDIANS

History and Origins

Native American urbanization began late in the 19th and early in the 20th centuries with several U.S. government programs meant to (as President Teddy Roosevelt phrased it at the time) "pulverize the tribal mass" by making reservation life (and cultural bases) unappealing and economically unsustainable.

Boarding schools were established beginning in 1879 at Carlisle, Pennsylvania, to strip young American Indians of their languages and cultures, as well as to teach them attitudes and skills suitable for the urban workforce. Land was allotted, and the reservation infrastructure was dismantled.

After a brief respite under Franklin D. Roosevelt during the 1930s when some reservation land base was restored, a new wave of policies during the 1950s—relocation and termination—aimed to break up reservations, often sending Native peoples to urban areas. This process began to reverse in the 1960s with Indian self-determination meant to restore the land base with an accompanying cultural and economic revival. Much of the activism sprung from urban populations, however, who were rediscovering their reservation heritage. Revival of cultural context has been part of this revival. Today, urban and reservation peoples often support each other, with cultural activity aided by many urban Indian centers.

Regional Variations

"Termination," which abolished reservation land bases and scattered their inhabitants (as well as relocation programs urging Indians to move from reservations to urban areas) were expressions of the same assumptions that produced removal policies during the 1830s and 1840s: break down Indian societies, annex their land, and absorb the people, shorn of their languages and cultures, into the European American "melting pot." By the 1950s, most Americans lived and worked in cities. Advocates of termination and relocation saw themselves generally as modernists and realists, promoting the eradication of Native land, identity, and lifeways for the Indians' own good, to ease their transition into a modern industrial economy.

Under termination, land and resources were purchased from tribes and the proceeds distributed to individual members, who sometimes found themselves temporarily enriched in cash but suddenly deprived of land and community. Through various legal devices, much of the purchased land was then transferred into the private sector, often through lease for a specific purpose (such as logging or mineral exploration) or outright sale.

Between 1954 and 1966, Congress passed legislation terminating federal recognition and services to 109 Native American nations and bands. Some of them disappeared as organized communities as their members dispersed, many of them to cities, through the Bureau of Indian Affairs (BIA) "relocation" program. Congress sometimes held up land claims payments until the Native tribe or nation in question also agreed to termination proceedings. In 1963, for example, the Claims Commission awarded the Kalispels $3 million, an award that was held by Congress (under legislation passed at the behest of Idaho senator Frank Church) until they agreed to termination.

The Klamaths, holding title to a million acres of prime timber in Oregon, agreed to terminate after BIA agents promised them per capita payments of $50,000. Only afterward did the Klamaths learn painfully that "going private" can be expensive. They found themselves paying rent, utilities, health care costs, and taxes they had never faced before. Following their termination in 1953, the Klamaths lost more than 880,000 acres of ponderosa pine, 90,000 acres of which was quickly sold to Crown Zellerbach, a timber company. Most of the rest of their land was incorporated into two national forests. Both have since been heavily logged. Payments for the land to individual Klamaths were soon spent. Landless, the Klamaths scattered, often to urban areas, and became prey to alcoholism, poverty, suicide, increased incarceration rates, increasing infant mortality, and declining life spans. Within a few years, according to the Native American Rights Fund, 52 percent of the Klamaths were dying before age 40. This was a far cry from their economic status before 1953, when Klamaths had earned 93 percent of the national median income.

The Menominees of Wisconsin shared ownership of property valued at $34 million when their termination bill was enacted in 1953. By 1961, the federal government was out of Menominee Country, and each member of the former tribe had become the owner of 100 shares of stock and a negotiable bond valued at $3,000, issued in the name of Menominee Enterprises, Inc. (MEI), a private enterprise that held the former tribe's land and businesses. Governmentally, the Menominee Nation had become Menominee County, the smallest (in terms of population) and poorest (in terms of cash income) in Wisconsin.

As a county, Menominee had to raise taxes to pay for its share of services, including welfare, health services, and utilities. The only taxable property owner in the county was MEI, which was forced to raise the funds to pay its tax bill by restructuring so that stockholders had to buy their homes and the property on which they had been built. Most of the Menominees had little savings except for their $3,000 bonds, which were then sold to MEI to make the required residential purchases. Many Menominees faced private-sector health costs, property taxes, and other expenses with no more money than they had possessed before termination. Unemployment rose to levels that most of the United States had known only during the Depression of the 1930s. By 1965, health indicators in Menominee County indicated that tuberculosis afflicted nearly 35 percent of the population, and infant mortality was three times the national average. Termination, like allotment, had been an abject failure at anything other than reallocating Indian land to non-Indians.

Many of termination's opponents were Native American traditionalists, who believed that distinct cultures and land bases should be maintained. During the renaissance of Native activism in the 1960s, they were joined in this effort by the young, urbanized children of an earlier generation that had made its own long marches, one by one or family by family, from their homelands to the cities at the behest of the BIA. Between 1953 and 1972, more than 100,000 Native Americans moved to urban areas; by 1980, about half of the Native Americans in the United States lived in cities. Young Native Americans raised in urban areas in the 1960s began to reverse relocation's effects. Sometimes college-educated, and other times veterans of the Vietnam War and terms in state and federal prisons, many young urban Indians by the 1970s were returning to the reservations.

The San Francisco Bay Area was a major relocation site for the Bureau of Indian Affairs during the 1960s, so when Indian political activism began, the area became a major center. Native peoples organized through self-help organizations that provided social contacts and services that the BIA had ignored. The Bay Area had about 30 "social clubs" serving Native families who had immigrated to the area by the time the call went out to occupy "the island" (Alcatraz). A new generation of young Native people was growing up in the cities, going to college, and sharing experiences that led to a sense of betterment, according to Troy R. Johnson, who has written incisively about the subject:

> The Alcatraz occupation came out of the Bay Area colleges and universities and other California college campuses where young, educated Indian students joined with other minority groups during the 1969 Third World Liberation Front strike and began demanding that colleges offer courses relevant to Indian students. Indian history written and taught by non-Indian instructors was no longer acceptable to these young students, awakened as they were to the possibility of social protest to bring attention to the shameful treatment of Indian people. (Johnson, 1996)

Contemporary Urbanization

Roughly two-thirds of American Indians lived in urban areas in the United States as of 2012, according to the U.S. Census, compared to 45 percent in 1970. The top five cities' Native populations were New York City, 111,749; Los Angeles, 54,236; Phoenix, 43,7824; Oklahoma City, 36,572; and Anchorage, Alaska, 36,062.

Native American cultures have been revived through American Indian urban centers, such as the Daybreak Star in Seattle. Shortly after the occupation of Alcatraz Island in San Francisco Bay, similar circumstances provoked an occupation of the former World War II–era U.S. Army base in Seattle called Fort Lawton in Seattle's Magnolia neighborhood, which had been used as a troop transshipment point during World War II. The Army had declared the property surplus in 1964 as operations moved to Fort Lewis, near Tacoma. Fort Lawton, about 1,100 acres of woods, beaches, and fields about three miles northwest of downtown Seattle, was prime urban real estate.

Community activist Bernie Whitebear led an alliance that occupied Fort Lawton, as the media sensed the irony of Indians "attacking" an Army fort during the spring of 1970. A half-mile-long caravan of cars lined up to blockade the base's northern and southern entrances. Indians and their allies climbed fences, hauled in tipi poles, and prepared camps. The military police evicted them, after which they returned again. Activists stormed fences and gates several times, as troops beat them back. The occupiers of Fort Lawton included Native people from parts of Canada and the U.S. Great Plains, as well as California (some were veterans of the Alcatraz occupation). Thus the group's name: United Indians of All Tribes.

The battle for Fort Lawton lasted long after the physical confrontation ended. It took several years of bureaucratic wrestling before a compromise was reached: the city of Seattle received most of the old fort for a park, as the United Indians of All Tribes received land on which to build the Daybreak Star Center, construction of which began in 1975. It opened two years later. The occupation of Alcatraz never had a community center as one of its goals, but Seattle's event did.

Daybreak Star's groundbreaking was September 27, 1975, with a wide array of funding: the U.S. Economic Development Administration, City of Seattle, U.S. Department of Commerce, donations from the Makah, Colville, and Quinault tribes, the Campaign for Human Development of the Catholic Church, and the Weyerhaeuser Corporation. The center developed urban Indian programs related to housing, education, counseling, cultural awareness, and health. By 2010, the Daybreak Star Center was providing services for people regardless of ethnicity, including child care and Head Start. The center's main constituency, however, is more than 85,000 Native people who have immigrated to western Washington from across the United States, 20 percent of whom live in poverty. Daybreak Star maintained a presence for decades under the aegis of United Indians of All Tribes, led by Whitebear as its director, a position he held for almost 30 years until his death in 2000 after a three-year battle with colon cancer.

See Also PART 2: CULTURAL FORMS: FAMILY, EDUCATION, AND COMMUNITY: Pan-Indianism

Further Reading

Fixico, Donald. *The Urban Indian Experience in America.* Albuquerque: University of New Mexico Press, 2000.

Johnson, Troy R. *The Occupation of Alcatraz Island: Indian Self-Determination and the Rise of Indian Activism.* Urbana: University of Illinois Press, 1996.

LaGrand, James. *Indian Metropolis. Native Americans in Chicago, 1945–75.* Champaign: University of Illinois Press, 2002.

Parham, Vera. "Something Worth Going Up That Hill For." *Columbia Magazine* 21, no. 3 (Fall 2007): 24–32. http://columbia.washingtonhistory.org/magazine /articles/2007/0307/0307-a3.aspx. Accessed October 29, 2014.

Reyes, Lawney L. *Bernie Whitebear: An Urban Indian's Quest for Justice.* Tucson: University of Arizona Press, 2006.

Smith, Sherry L. *Hippies, Indians, & the Fight for Red Power.* New York: Oxford University Press, 2012.

Weibel-Orlando, Joan. *Indian Country L.A.: Maintaining Ethnic Community in Complex Society.* Urbana: University of Illinois Press, 1991.

WAMPUM

History and Origins

Wampum (from the Algonquian word *wampumpeag*) are strings or patterns of quahog and periwinkle seashells, cut and formed into beads and strings, that have been used by many American Indians in the Northeast to preserve accounts of history, to conduct diplomacy, and to complete some commercial transactions. Although the use of wampum as "money" has been emphasized by some historians, its other uses were probably more important in history.

Nearly every important treaty negotiated in the 18th century was sealed with the presentation of wampum belts. The shells that comprised the belts were harvested and traded to inland Native American nations on the coast. Before seashells were used to make wampum, it existed in other forms, including the quills of porcupine and eagles, as well as pieces of wood painted black and white. The shells were used until mass-produced trade beads from Europe replaced them.

Although wampum was used principally in diplomacy, the settlement of disputes, and the recitation of history, it also was used sometimes as currency. The Dutch first began to use wampum as "money" to facilitate trade, because European coinage was in short supply in the colonies. For a time, wampum was accepted as payment of tuition at Harvard University. By 1660, however, with the import of silver coinage from Europe, wampum lost much of its monetary

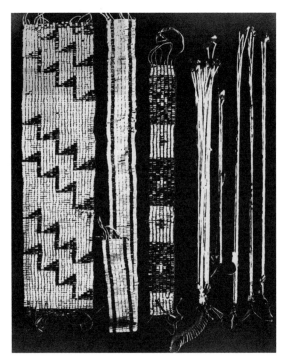

Haudenosaunee (Iroquois) wampum belts styled as jewelry, late 19th and early 20th centuries. (National Archives)

function in the colonies. At about the same time, the importation of European drills made wampum easier to manufacture and eroded its status value among New England Indians by dramatically increasing supplies.

Regional Variations

To negotiate with Native Americans whose nations bordered the English and French colonies in eastern North America, as well as to do business, European Americans learned that they had to know wampum diplomacy; most treaty councils and trading sessions opened with long speeches of welcome (and sometimes of condolence), in which wampum was exchanged according to a protocol. The importance of a message often was demonstrated by the size of the wampum belt handed over the council fire at its conclusion. Acceptance of the wampum by the receiving party often carried the same message as the signing of a treaty or contract. One also could demonstrate rejection of proposed terms by casting a wampum belt or string aside dramatically.

Peace among the formerly antagonistic Iroquois nations was procured and maintained through the Haudenosaunee's Great Law of Peace (*Kaianerekowa*), which was passed from generation to generation by use of wampum, using symbols (written communication) that outlined a complex system of checks and balances between nations and genders. During a complete oral recitation of the Great Law, which can take several days, wampum belts acted to prompt the memory of a speaker.

Wampum also was used by the Iroquois as a payment of damages in cases of murder. Under the Iroquois Great Law, as introduced by Hiawatha at the time that the League of Peace was founded, the blood feud (a major source of bloodshed before the Great Law) was forbidden and replaced by a condolence ceremony. Hiawatha and Deganawidah (the Peacemaker) replaced a political system based on blood revenge with one based on peacemaking. Part of their system was the use of wampum to "console or wipe away the tears of Hiawatha, whose heart was heavy because of the loss of his daughters" (Tehanetorens, 1983, 3). This was the first use of wampum for consolation.

Strings of wampum also were used by members of the Haudenosaunee Grand Council as credentials or a certificate of authority. Likewise, every chief of the confederacy possessed a string of wampum that established his or her authority to speak on official matters. Treaties not accompanied by wampum had no meaning. Belts were exchanged at treaty councils as signs of good will.

Wampum was used to express powerful cultural and political symbols within the Iroquois Confederacy. The Circle Wampum, with 50 strings of white wampum arrayed around a center, symbolized the 50 chiefs of the confederacy's Grand Council, 49 living men and one seat set aside for the Peacemaker. White wampum signifies purity, peace, unity, and friendship; purple signifies sorrow, death, and mourning. One of the strings is longer than the others, a signature of Hononwiyendeh, an Onondaga who keeps the records of the council. Another belt, with a pine tree at the center and two squares joined at each end (the League Belt), symbolizes the structure of the confederacy—Senecas and Mohawks ("Elder Brothers") at the ends, Cayugas and Oneidas ("Younger Brothers") between, and the Onondagas, keepers of the central fire, represented by the Great White pine tree in the center. The Six Nations Peace Belt reminds leaders to mentor their people in the ways of peace. Other belts served as invitations for other nations to become allies of the confederacy. The Wing or Dust Fan belt represented the branches of the Great White Pine under which all peoples were invited to take shelter.

Wampum strings could also be used as discipline for chiefs who violated the rules of the Council. Black wampum was shown to an erring chief as a warning, and if he persisted in violations (often violence, including murder), he could be removed, his credentials of office stripped away by the women who had nominated him and by war chiefs. In the worst cases, often murder, a war chief holding in his hand a bunch of black wampum strings shall say to the erring chiefs: "You have not heeded the warning of the general council of women, [nor] the warning of the men. There is only one course to adopt." At that point, the war chiefs drop strings of black wampum, and the men shall spring to their feet and club the erring chiefs to death. (Tehanetorens, 1983, 25)

The Ransom Belt was used by the chiefs in council to confirm the adoption of an individual, a family, or several families from outside the league, just as "friendship belts" were used to forge alliances with several dozen Native nations and tribes across eastern North America. Prisoners of war sometimes became Iroquois family members, adopted to replace members lost in war. The adoptions also absolved the grief of these families.

Under the Iroquois Great Law of Peace, the blood feud was outlawed and replaced by a Condolence ceremony that assessed penalties in wampum. Under the Great Law of Peace, when a person committed murder the grieving family could forego the option of exacting clan revenge (the taking of the life of the murderer or a member of the murderer's clan). Instead, the bereaved family could accept 20 strings of wampum from the slayer's family, 10 for the dead person and 10 for the life of the murderer himself. If a woman was killed, the price was 30 wampum strings. A woman's life was judged to be more valuable than a man's because women bear life.

Condolence wampum strings also played a role in public observances when leaders passed to the other world. "When a Head Chief or lesser chief of the Confederacy dies, a runner is sent to each nation carrying proper wampum strings. He walks from one end of the reservation to the other, and every once in a while he will give a certain call ('Kwee!') . . . three times, one call after another" (Tehanetorens, 1983, 5). The messenger's walk ends at the Council House, where the news is conveyed and wampum distributed. The wampum was offered with a condolence ceremony meant to "wipe the tears from off your eyes so that you may see clearly" (Tehanetorens, 1983, 34).

Over a wide span of years, many of the Iroquois' large historical wampum belts were removed to museums. In recent years, some of them have been returned to Iroquois possession. Today, given the scarcity of their constituent shells, only wampum strings are used in ceremonies.

The Cherokees used wampum in a ceremony meant to provide for the poor. During a special war dance, each warrior was called on to recount the taking of his first scalp. During the ceremony, anyone with something to spare, according to Henry Timberlake, "a string of wampum, piece of [silver] plate, wire, paint, lead" heaped the goods on a blanket or animal skin that had been placed on the ground (Corkran, 1962, 91). Afterward, the collection was divided among the poor of the community, with a share reserved for the musicians who had provided entertainment during the ceremony.

In 1612, John Smith of Virginia visited the Susquehannocks in the northern regions of the Chesapeake Bay. There, he encountered the use of wampum, and he found hints of the existence of the Iroquois Confederacy. During the course of their meeting, the Susquehannocks implored Smith to defend them against the "Atquanahucke, Massawomecke and other people [that] inhabit the river of Cannida." The Susquehannocks draped "a chaine of white beads (waighing at least 6 or 7 pound) about" Smith's neck while reciting an "oration of love" (Johansen, 1997, 1353).

Contemporary Forms

Belts are still used to remind treaty parties of their equity in diplomacy. The Two Row Wampum reminds European immigrants' descendants that they are not superior. A Record Belt reminded all parties that in the early days Native people and their cultures helped the People with White Faces survive in their new home. Another belt documents the coming of French immigrants who tortured and killed Indians, as a historical record. Individuals who made common cause with Iroquois could be adopted. Belts were provided for that purpose. Some belts are brought out to offer hospitality to visitors. Clan unity is symbolized by other belts. The role of women in political culture is observed with the Nominating Belt, used when new male chiefs are installed on the council. Wampum culture is very much alive, as today's Haudenodsaunee have sought return of their belts from New York State museums.

See Also PART 1: OVERVIEW: GENERAL HISTORICAL CONSIDERATIONS: Treaty Diplomacy, Cultural Context; **PART 2: CULTURAL FORMS: ARTS:** Jemison, G. Peter; **FAMILY, EDUCATION, AND COMMUNITY:** Native American Graves Protection and Repatriation Act (NAGPRA) (1990); **MEDIA, POPULAR CULTURE, SPORTS, AND GAMING:** George-Kanentiio, Douglas Mitchell

Further Reading
Barreiro, Jose. "Return of the Wampum." *Northeast Indian Quarterly* 7, no. 1 (Spring 1990): 8–20.

Corkran, David H. *The Cherokee Frontier: Conflict and Survival, 1740–1762.* Norman: University of Oklahoma Press, 1962.

Fenton, William N. "The New York State Wampum Collection: The Case for the Integrity of Cultural Treasures." *Proceedings of the American Philosophical Society* 115, no. 6 (December 1971): 437–461.

Grinde, Donald A., Jr., and Bruce E. Johansen. *Exemplar of Liberty: Native America and the Evolution of Democracy*. Los Angeles: UCLA American Indian Studies Center, 1991.

Hill, Richard. "Oral Memory of the Haudenosaunee: Views of the Two-Row Wampum." *Northeast Indian Quarterly* 7, no. 1 (Spring 1990): 21–30.

Jacobs, Wilbur. "Wampum: The Protocol of Indian Diplomacy." *William and Mary Quarterly* 3rd Ser. 6 (October 1949): 596–604.

Jemison, G. Peter. "Sovereignty and Treaty Rights We Remember." *St. Thomas Law Review* 7 (1995): 631–643.

Johansen, Bruce E. "Wampum." In D. L. Birchfield, ed. *The Encyclopedia of North American Indians*. New York: Marshall Cavendish, 1997, 10:1, 352–1, 353.

Mann, Barbara A. "The Fire at Onondaga: Wampum as Proto-writing." *Akwesasne Notes*, new series, 1, no. 1 (Spring 1995): 40–48.

Tehanetorens, Ray Fadden. *Wampum Belts*. Onchiota, NY: Six Nations Indian Museum; Irocrafts, 1983.

Waters, Frank. *The Book of the Hopi*. New York: Penguin Books, 1963.

Williams, Robert A., Jr. "Linking Arms Together: Multicultural Constitutionalism in a North American Indigenous Vision of Law and Peace." *California Law Review* 82 (1994): 981–1052.

WEDDING CUSTOMS

History and Origins

As with birthing and funerary customs, Native American ways of uniting individuals in matrimony vary widely. Jack Forbes, a Powhatan-Delaware scholar, notes that every tribe has its own traditions, "but more importantly, every mature individual was guided by his or her own dreams, visions, and personal spiritual calling" (Forbes, 2004). Although customs varied, according to Forbes, Native American marriage customs often were more fluid than European Christian traditions. Plural marriages (usually several women with an often older male), the young marrying the old, and remarriages after the death of a spouse were all common. Same-gender unions also were widely respected in pre-Columbian times, which caused considerable consternation among missionaries.

Regional Variations

In pre-Columbian times, many Native American unions (Lakota and Cherokee, for example) were arranged by parents, with a bride price, often clothes, food, and (after they were adopted from the Spanish) several horses, depending on the affluence of the negotiating families. Youthful romance usually had little to do with it, but it could have an influence. Accounts exist of young men emerging outside a favored companion's family tipi, playing his flute and making his affections obvious. Even the strongest cultural traditions did not always eclipse the influence of youthful hormones. Among some Northern California traditions, including those of the Klamaths, the Modocs, and the Yuroks, a marriage might be characterized as "full" or "half," depending on how much the man or his family could pay, among other factors.

In family negotiations over a Lakota, Nakota, or Dakota marriage, political alliances were a factor, as well as social relations, and acquisition (in the case of a man) of a hunter who would help to support an extended family. Fathers did most of the negotiating, but mothers had a very important advisory role. Marriage often occurred shortly after a girl had reached puberty, but older women remarried if spouses had died. Boys were expected to have proved their worthiness through horse raids and battle. People could remarry after divorce, but it was not encouraged. Many divorced people remained single for the rest of their lives. Some who remarried were ostracized.

Lakota, Nakota, and Dakota marriages included considerable feasting, as well as a dance for women and children in which four or five drummers beat a drum,

> while others . . . dished out soup and meat to the persons composing the circle. These, as soon as they had partaken of food, joined the dancers within the circle and danced until they were weary and then fell back to the circle and in a sitting posture rested and ate again. This dance continued during the entire day. As late afternoon approached, the betrothed couple, accompanied by a number of their friends, visited their new abode and made an inspection of the premises and visited until the master of ceremonies appeared on the scene and announced that the hour of proclaiming their marriage had arrived. ("Sioux Courtship," n.d.)

Some Lakota, Dakota, and Nakota men married more than once and had more than one wife, mainly because the gender ratio was skewed in favor of women due to deaths in hunting accidents and battles. Men might marry their sisters. According to one observer, family ties helped to minimize jealousy among wives. A man could have as many wives as he could support. This also meant that a woman living in a multiwife household might have less work to do.

Among the Cherokees, mothers were most influential in arranging marriages, and a girl was allowed to reject it. Cherokees usually married in their mid-teens, although a few were arranged before the age of 10. Marriage ages varied widely among other Native peoples. Choctaws usually waited until their

20s, and while Blackfoot women often married in their teens, Blackfoot men often waited until age 35 or older.

> In Cherokee tradition, when a couple was considering marriage, a young Cherokee man would bring a deer hindquarter or a sack of corn to her lodge and leave it. If the girl didn't want to marry him, she just left the food untouched and the man would have to retrieve it and choose another mate. If she wanted to marry him, she would cook the deer meat or pound the corn into flour and make him bread. This courtship ritual took place only after the matriarchal women of both clans had agreed to the match. ("Cherokee Courtship," n.d.)

Venison symbolized his intention to keep meat in the household and her corn symbolized her willingness to be a good Cherokee housewife.

Any matrimonial union also was subject to approval by a village's senior shaman, who interviewed both parties and tested for impediments to the relationship, including the possibility of supernatural intervention. Elder men then hosted a dinner for the young man, and the elder women did the same for the young woman. The wedding ceremony could be simple or elaborate, suited to the preferences of the participants. Ceremonial gifts often were presented in baskets. The two newlyweds folded their blankets together, representing union, and she gave him corn or wheat bread, symbolic of nurture and support.

For the wedding ceremony, a sacred spot was blessed for seven consecutive days before the event. On the wedding day, "The bride and groom approach the sacred fire, and are blessed by the priest and/or priestess. All participants of the wedding, including guests are also blessed. Songs are sung in Cherokee, and those conducting the ceremony bless the couple. Both the bride and groom are covered in blue blankets" ("Old Cherokee," n.d.). After this, according to one source, "Close relatives of the couple would then step forward and cover them both in a single white blanket. This blanket represents their joining together, their new life of happiness, fulfillment and the peace they will share together with their spirits joined. The town's main chief would come forward and announce to the guests that 'the blankets are joined,' and the wedding [ceremony] would be over" ("Cherokee Courtship," n.d.). Feasting and dancing followed, often including a Stomp Dance.

Cherokee unions were often temporary, and separation was common and acceptable. The Cherokee word for "husband" meant "The man I am living with for now" ("Cherokee Courtship," n.d.). Divorce often was announced by a woman when she placed the man's possessions outside the door of the matrilineal home (Navajo women did this as well).

Hopi courtship traditions were described this way:

> The Hopi Native girl, after undergoing important rites of adolescence (usually between the age of 16 and 20) was ready to receive suitors. In former days it was customary to give an informal picnic on the day following an important ritual. If a girl had decided on a youth as a future mate, she would extend to him an invitation to accompany her and would present him with a loaf of *qomi*, a bread made of sweet cornmeal in lieu of *somiviki* (maiden's cake). Since this invitation was tantamount to being engaged, boys would only accept the invitation from girls they were willing to marry. A Hopi young man would propose to a maiden by preparing a bundle of fine clothing and white buckskin moccasins. He would leave the bundle at her doorstep and if she accepted it, she accepted him as her future husband. ("Hopi Traditions," n.d.)

Among the Hopi, no marriages were sanctioned by society inside of nuclear families. Usually, no one who had annulled a marriage could enter another such relationship. Young men and women usually agreed to marry on their own, and once they had done so, the boy went to the girl's house after supper to make a proposal to the girl's parents. If they approved, he returned home to his own parents with the news. The girl then ground corn and baked bread for the prospective husband. If his mother accepted the bread, a wedding was planned. More exchanges followed, all symbolic of a new home's creation and a bond forged between families. Many Native families continue to be matrilineal, so a man often moves in with his wife's family.

Contemporary Forms

Many Native weddings today fuse traditional rites with European religious traditions—so well mixed, in fact, that it can be tough to separate the two. Today, wedding ceremonies, for example, may include a "Sioux Wedding Prayer," "Apache Wedding Prayer," or a "Cherokee Wedding Prayer" in a European-style ceremony. This prayer first appeared in the 1950 western movie *Broken Arrow* and has no connection to any specific American Indian culture or tradition. Widely available on the Internet (and used in New Age weddings as well), it goes:

> *Now you will feel no rain,*
> *For each of you will be shelter to the other.*
> *Now you will feel no cold,*
> *For each of you will be warmth to the other.*
> *Now there is no more loneliness,*
> *For each of you will be companion to the other.*

Now you are two bodies,
But there is only one life before you.
Go now to your dwelling place
To enter into the days of your togetherness
And may your days be good and long upon the earth.

Among the Navajos and Pueblos, decorated baskets are presented to the couple being married that contain corn, which serves as a symbol of nourishment, as well as a fertility symbol. Today, the Navajos and Paiutes use willow wedding baskets holding cornmeal. Baskets and pottery are widely used today as wedding gifts, often a vessel with two spouts, out of which both of the people who are being married can drink at the same time. Baskets often are filled with housewarming gifts. Water is taken to symbolize purification, so modern brides and grooms continue to wash their hands at wedding ceremonies to rid themselves of evil, as well as past associations.

Wedding vases were first used in the Southwest, but have become pan-Indian symbols of union in matrimony in a context of reverence for nature and the Earth. Drinking from a vase is much like exchanging wedding bands. The vase is usually retained as a reminder of the wedding day. Since they are made of fired clay, the vases (like any other pottery) can hold water or other liquids for only a short period without doing damage. After a wedding ceremony they should be emptied and dried.

See Also PART 1: OVERVIEW: NATIONS, TRIBES, AND OTHER NATIVE GROUPS: Cherokee Political and Legal Culture; **PART 2: CULTURAL FORMS: ARTS:** Cultural Appropriation: Questions and Issues

Further Reading

"Cherokee Courtship and Wedding Customs." *Native Arts.com.* http://www.aaanativearts.com/mailbag-archive/1476-cherokee-and-sioux-courtship-and-wedding-customs.html. Accessed March 21, 2014.

Forbes, Jack D. "What Is Marriage? A Native American View." *News from Indian Country*, May 3, 2004. http://yeoldeconsciousnessshoppe.com/art161.html. Accessed October 29, 2014.

Gourse, Leslie. *Native American Courtship and Marriage Traditions.* New York: Hippocrene Books, 2000.

"Hopi Traditions." *The Indian Sun. www.indiansun.com.* Accessed March 23, 2014.

"Old Cherokee Wedding Traditions." *Cherokee Tribe of Oklahoma.* http://www.cherokee.org. Accessed March 24, 2014.

"Sioux Courtship and Wedding Customs." *Native Arts.com.* http://www.aaanativearts.com/mailbag-archive/1476-cherokee-and-sioux-courtship-and-wedding-customs.html. Accessed March 21, 2014.

WOMEN IN NATIVE AMERICAN CULTURES

Unlike most European societies, which were emphatically patriarchal until the 20th century, the vast majority of Native American cultures accorded women a great deal of respect. With a few exceptions, societal and cultural models were (and today remain) matriarchal as well as matrilineal. While men often had leadership roles in diplomacy, trade, and other areas of endeavor that were visible to European immigrants, women influenced decision making. While some details differed, Haudenosaunee (Iroquois), Diné (Navajo), and Apache women exercised profound influence. Iroquois women, whose example has been especially influential, are described in Barbara Alice Mann's accompanying Spotlight entry.

History and Origins

Native American origin stories often are cast in female terms from the date of creation. Earth is characterized as "mother." In Navajo myth, the first human was Changing Woman (also known as White Shell Woman), whose twin sons prepared the Earth for human residency by ridding it of monsters and other dangers. The role of an originating mother and twin sons is also an important part of many other Native origin stories, including that of the Haudenosaunee (Iroquois), as Mann describes in more detail. In the Navajo creation story, Changing Woman finds herself alone on the Earth and is impregnated by the rays of the sun, then by rain. The twins are born of lightning (of the sun) and water (of the rain). Changing Woman never dies; in old age she walks eastward, sees herself coming, then meets and merges with her younger persona.

Regional Variations

Navajo girls reenact the creation story at their coming-of-age ceremony, *kinaalda* ("baking her cake"). The Apache "sunrise ceremony" shares several of the same attributes (Mails, 1993, 98–104). The power of Changing Woman is said to enter the girl at maturity. These rituals are considered private matters and, beyond the general outline, are not usually discussed in public. Discussion or description is believed to diminish the power of the ceremonies. Published descriptions of these ceremonies are widely available, however (see "Further Reading"), as are descriptions of traditional women's roles.

As teenagers, Navajo and Apache girls often took the initiative in courtship. As adults, a woman who was dissatisfied with a marriage could simply place her husband's saddle outside the door as a signal that his time with her had ended. After divorce, children stayed with their mothers.

When women's rights advocates first began organized activity in the United States during the 19th century, leaders such as Elizabeth Cady Stanton, Susan B. Anthony, and Matilda Joslyn Gage paid heed to Native American examples. Among Native peoples, generally a person became part of his or her mother's clan at birth, which influenced choices of marriage partners. Women usually owned family homes, and men, when they married, moved into them, a fact that impressed early feminists in a society where women were often not allowed to own property and had little political influence. Women often owned prized, valuable animals, such as horses and sheep.

The early suffragists were developing their work at the same time as Lewis Henry Morgan, the pioneer anthropologist whose work describing Iroquois society provided the groundwork for the field in the United States. According to Sally Roesch Wagner (1988), Stanton specifically referred to Morgan's work in her address (titled "The Matriarchate or Mother-Age") to the National Council of Women in 1891. Stanton referred to the influence of Iroquois women in national councils, and to the fact that their society was descended through the female line and also that American Indians professed "a higher degree of justice for women than American men in the 19th century, professing to believe, as they do, in our republican principles of government" (Stanton, 1891, 2).

Wagner asserts that "nineteenth-century radical feminist theoreticians, such as Elizabeth Cady Stanton and Matilda Joslyn Gage, looked to the Iroquois for their vision of a transformed world" (1988, 32–33). She also uses the work of male students of the Iroquois who wrote at roughly the same time as Stanton, Gage, and other early feminists, to illustrate just how appealing the Iroquois example must have been to women locked in a culture that considered them their husbands' property. She quotes Henry Schoolcraft, writing in 1846, two years before the Seneca Falls conference:

> Marriage . . . appears to be a verbal contract between the parties, which does not affect the rights of property. Goods, personal effects, or valuables of any kind personal or real, which were the wife's before, remain so after marriage. . . . Marriage is therefore a personal agreement, requiring neither civil nor ecclesiastical sanction, but not a union of the rights of property. Descent being counted by the female may be either an original cause or effect of this unique law. (Wagner, 1988, 32–33)

Stanton (1891) quoted the memoirs of the Reverend Asher Wright:

> Usually the females ruled the house. The stores were in common, but woe to the luckless husband or lover who was too shiftless to do his share of

the providing. No matter how many children, or whatever goods he might have in the house, he might at any time be ordered to pick up his blanket and budge; and after such an order it would not be healthful for him to attempt to disobey. The house would be too hot for him, and unless saved by the intercession of some aunt or grandmother he must retreat to his own clan, or go and start a new matrimonial alliance with some other. (p. 4)

Contemporary Native American Women

As Western societies have evolved to resemble Native American models in some ways, and as Native American cultures have been reviving in the late 20th and early 21st centuries, new attention has been paid to the role of women. Gender equity has become a global issue even as most societies remain patriarchal. At the same time, however, Native American women on reservations and in urban areas have been afflicted with domestic violence that was not part of traditional cultures, often provoked by abuse of alcohol and other drugs. Native American women have organized in groups such as Women of All Red Nations (WARN), which formed within the American Indian Movement to resist sexism.

Many Navajo families ceased performing the *kinaalda* coming-of-age ceremonies during the 1950s and 1960s, as Western religions (most notably Mormonism) gained influence. Many young Navajos and Apaches spent their teenage years in boarding schools during these years, where practice of Native rituals was forbidden. Later, many of them regretted having missed an important milestone in their personal development. In recent years some families have revived it, using written descriptions such as Frisbie (1993), Leighton and Kluckhohn (1947), Begay (1983), and Roessel (1981).

Many Native American women face acute contemporary challenges that are described in relatively recent cultural anthropology, such as *Weaving Women's Lives* (Lamphere et al., 2007), which follows three Navajo women's lives in real time as they face the toll of alcohol and drugs on families, pressures as single parents, and requirements of off-reservation careers. Other women struggle to maintain traditional knowledge in a changing world, such as knowledge of herbs and plants' healing properties. Several women have taken up the work of *hatathli* (medicine man or healer), traditionally a male role. As with all cultures, Native American ways of life continue to evolve.

See Also PART 1: OVERVIEW: GENERAL HISTORICAL CONSIDERATIONS: Consensus in Governance as a Cultural Value; **PART 2: CULTURAL FORMS: ARTS:** Spotlight:

Culture Bearers; **FAMILY, EDUCATION, AND COMMUNITY:** Birthing Customs; **SPIRITUAL-ITY:** Spirituality: Haudenosaunee (Iroquois)

Further Reading

Anthony, Susan B., Elizabeth Cady Stanton, and Matilda Joslyn Gage, eds. *History of Woman Suffrage.* Salem, NH: Ayer, 1985.

Begay, Shirley M. *Kinaalda: A Navajo Puberty Ceremony.* Rough Rock, AZ: Navajo Curriculum Center, Rough Rock Demonstration School, 1983.

Boyer, Ruth McDonald, and Narcissus Duffy Gayton. *Apache Mothers and Daughters: Four Generations of a Family.* Norman: University of Oklahoma Press, 1992.

Carr, Lucien. "On the Social and Political Position of Woman among the Huron-Iroquois Tribes." *Peabody Museum of American Archaeology and Ethnology, Reports 16 & 17,* 3, nos. 3–4 (1884): 207–232.

Deyhle, Donna. *Reflections in Place: Connected Lives of Navajo Women.* Tucson: University of Arizona Press, 2009.

Frisbie, Charlotte Johnson. *Kinaalda': A Study of the Navajo Girl's Puberty Ceremony.* Salt Lake City: University of Utah Press, 1993 (1967).

Lamphere, Louise, with Eva Price, Carole Cadman, and Valerie Darwin. *Weaving Women's Lives: Three Generations in a Navajo Family.* Albuquerque: University of New Mexico Press, 2007.

Leighton, Dorothea, and Clyde Kluckhohn. *Children of the People.* Cambridge, MA: Harvard University Press, 1947.

Mails, Thomas E. *The People Called Apache.* New York: BDD Illustrated Books, 1993.

McCloskey, Joanne. *Living Through Generations: Continuity and Change in Navajo Women's Lives.* Tucson: University of Arizona Press, 2007.

Mihesuah, Devon Abbot. *Indigenous American Women: Decolonization, Empowerment, Activism.* Lincoln: University of Nebraska Press, 2003.

Perrone, Bobette, H. Stockel, and Victoria Krueger. *Medicine Women, Curanderas, and Women Doctors.* Norman: University of Oklahoma Press, 1989.

Reichard, Gladys A. *Dezba: Women of the Desert.* New York: J. J. Augustin, 1939.

Roessel, Montty. *Kinaalda: A Navajo Girl Grows Up.* Minneapolis: Lerner, 1993.

Roessel, Ruth. *Women in Navajo Society.* Rough Rock, AZ: Navajo Resource Center, Rough Rock Demonstration School, 1981.

Stanton, Elizabeth Cady. "The Matriarchate or Mother-Age." Address before the National Council of Women, February 1891. *The National Bulletin* 1, no. 5 (February 1891).

Wagner, Sally Roesch. "The Iroquois Confederacy: A Native American Model for Non-sexist Men." *Changing Men* (Spring–Summer 1988): 32–33.

Wagner, Sally Roesch. *Matilda Joslyn Gage: She Who Holds the Sky.* Aberdeen, SD: Sky Carrier Press, 1999.

Spotlight

WOMEN IN HAUDENOSAUNEE (IROQUOIS) CULTURE

The Haudenosaunee, or People of the Iroquois League, are matriarchal, as are the cultures of the Eastern Woodlands generally. Thus, women played, and still play, a central role in the economic, social, political, and spiritual life of the people. The term for a woman acting in her official capacity is *gantowisas*, indicating a woman of the lineage sisterhood.

History and Origins

The primacy of Iroquoian women is bolstered and explained by creation tradition, under which the Iroquois count their descent as a people from two women: the First Woman, variously called Aetensic, Sky Woman, and Grandmother, and her daughter, called The Lynx or Hanging Flowers. Since Turtle Island (North America) was specifically created for Sky Woman by the animals and seeded with plant life by Sky Woman and The Lynx, the land mass is seen as properly "belonging" to the women. This assumption is reflected in the women's provisions, or the "Clans and Consanguinity" sections of the Great Law or Constitution of the Iroquois, which clearly stipulates that women "shall own the land and the soil" (Parker, 1916, 42).

Creation tradition also recounts that Sky Woman's fall to earth was interrupted by the Great Birds, Heron and Loon, who called down to Turtle, asking what to do about the Woman Falling from the Sky. Turtle—who is really female, as Mother Earth, but whom anthropologists gender-bent to "Grandfather"— called a council, at which it was decided to make solid ground for the strange woman. Once the animals had collaborated in that feat, Sky Woman was eased down onto the new land, upon which she immediately planted the seeds she had brought with her from Sky World: Corn, Beans, and Squash, known as "The Three Sisters." As she walked forth, more land rushed out ahead of her. While on Planet Earth, Sky Woman gave birth to her daughter, The Lynx, who also became instrumental in its foliage, not the least by creating potatoes.

As a consequence of this history, Iroquoian women have strong economic power, which begins with the sole ownership of the land. This accords the women complete control of agriculture, which was conducted on a large scale over thousands of acres of land, boggling the first Europeans who saw the bounty of their fields. Over the millennia, the skill of these female farmers developed not only such advances as fertilizers and soil conservation techniques, but also the co-planting of corn, beans, and squash. Traditionally, the economic power of women did not solely reside in their agricultural duties, but also in their disposition of the fruits of the hunt, which was deposited with the clan mother of the hunters immediately upon return.

Since the European invasion, the amount of land on which women can plant has been massively reduced. Nevertheless, it is still very common to find even Iroquoian women in the cities planting their Three Sisters. Grandmothers look forward to the day that they can take their little, fat-faced granddaughters outside to show them how to raise the mounds. Some will start with mini-mounds, just the right size for little girls to dirty their hands in, as the child learns how many seeds to plant, how deeply and how far apart; how to put Little Sister Bean around the stem of Big Sister Corn; and how to space out Sister Squash, who—unless one is careful—will overwhelm the space available. Similarly, it is not unusual to see men teaching little boys to turn over deer meat and fresh fish to their mothers.

"The Progenitors of the Nation"

Socially, the Constitution states that, because the women are "the progenitors of the Nation," descent is counted through "the female line" (Parker, 1916, 42). There is more attendant on this edict than sheer descent. The women traditionally controlled marriage and fertility, with men bowing to their dictates within the family. Traditionally, among other things, this meant that young girls were not forced into monogamous marriages from which there was no recourse, as in Western culture. Instead, it was expected that young women, from puberty into young adulthood, would experiment with multiple sexual partners, a fact that staggered and horrified the early European explorers and missionaries. A girl might go through 12 or 15 lovers before she settled on a particular mate. She did not have to name the father of her child, if she did not wish to do so, and she was under no compulsion to carry a pregnancy to term, should she decide against it. There were herbal methods of abortion, which were freely used by the women. Although the Third Epoch *Gaiwiiyo*, or *Code of Handsome Lake*, presumed to outlaw abortion, to this day, Iroquoian women listen to themselves and their mothers on the matter, just as they listen to themselves and their mothers on the issue of marriage and divorce.

When a girl decided to marry, it was in consultation with her clan mothers, who would then propose to the clan mothers of the boy in question. He was expected to say "yes." Once the young couple was married, the girl's mothers watched him closely and, should he fail in his duties of hunting, harmony, respectfulness, and protection, they could and would orchestrate a divorce.

Politically, Iroquoian women have a long history of governmental control. In a portion of the Great Law tradition that is still too little told, it was the Jikonsaseh, or head clan mother, who provided the grounding for the Peacemaker. It was she who welcomed him to Iroquoia, a very crucial act, for no one who is not properly welcomed to a polity may speak in it. Clan mothers are, therefore, very careful about whom they welcome. It was also the Jikonsaseh who spread the word of corn cropping throughout Iroquoia and who fed the people during their long struggle—some say it was 100 years—to implant the league. It was she alone who had the power to call for and put the horns of office on the first male officials. It was also she alone who held the medicine song that finally allowed the Peacemaker and Ayonwantha [Hiawatha] successfully to approach and subdue the Adodaroh, or Tadadaho, the fearsome head priest of the old order, who had been killing the children of peace. It was due to the Jikonsaseh that the Constitution finally given included the strong matriarchal sections that allowed the league to climb to greatness.

In replication of the binary complements of the Iroquoian cosmos, government was twinned. Contrapuntal to the Men's Grand Council sat, and still sit, the Clan Mothers' Councils, with the grandmothers firmly in control of titles of office and the right to nominate all officials—male as well as female. Again, the invading Europeans did the culture great damage by working, from the first, to disempower the clan mothers, scorning Iroquoian men for being proud to have been "made women," that is, judges and peace counselors. At the same time, wherever they could impose themselves, missionaries beat and abused women into the silence customary to European women, while the U.S. government forced them out of their fields to make them sit by spinning wheels. When that effort succeeded but poorly, the U.S. government imposed the Constitution of 1848, which deprived women of all but the power to sell land. In 1868, a new and even more woman-unfriendly Constitution was imposed. However, the women continued, if on the sly, to operate in the old way, so that they did not lose their habits of direction, which are reemerging so forcefully today.

Today: Powers of the *Gantowisas*

Important powers of the *gantowisas* include the ability to appoint public officials and to impeach errant officials, as well as to adopt or grant citizenship to newcomers. The women alone retain the power to "nominate" people to office, which effectively means to put them into an office. This happens because the mothers of any particular lineage own the titles to office in the keeping of that lineage. These include clan motherhoods and corn-plant chieftainships as well as the men's chieftainships on the Men's Grand Council. The only restriction on this power is that mothers may not nominate their own sons, unless literally no one else is left available (a circumstance that European invasion and genocide managed to bring about). If a lineage goes extinct, then the titles it holds go into abeyance. The Men's Council may bring that lineage back into the league—as was done with the Jikonsaseh's Wolf Clan lineage when the Attiwendaronk were brought into the league in 1649.

The women, and women alone, are able to impeach officials. This is not a power taken lightly, and it was only exercised when an official, male or female, had gone seriously astray. Lying was, and still is, seen as a very bad thing—much worse than murder. Murder kills only one person at a time, whereas lying kills everything, all at once, so that lying is an impeachable offense. In colonial times, the cultural disruption visited by conversion to Christianity became another impeachable offense, so that even a chairman of the Men's Grand Council was impeached in 1874 for converting. Catholics might feel that they have honored the Iroquois by canonizing the Mohawk convert Kateri Tekakwitha, but her conversion was considered treasonous and traditionals are not at all thrilled by her sainthood.

Granting citizenship is another power solely in the hands of women. Called "adoption," it means replacing a lost group member with an incumbent who originated in another group. This was a very commonplace happenstance in colonial times, with roots going long back to the founding of the league in 1142, when all nations were invited to come sit beneath the Tree of Peace and become members of the league. Eventually, six full nations and another 60 partial nations did this. Spreading the peace means accepting, not ostracizing, others. Adoption of newcomers was seen as an extension of childbirth and almost a form of farming, activities that no one but the women control. Thus, these new tubers, growing new citizens, were grafted onto the people by the women.

Although missionaries and Western governments did all in their power to destroy female political power, the women refused to accept the sovereignty of any outsiders, quietly continuing to wield power. Today, as Westerners finally figure out that women must be citizens equal to men in all facets of life, Iroquoian women are again strongly asserting their traditional legal rights in the league.

Spiritually, Iroquoian women have always represented half of the spiritual life of the people. They embody Blood (Earth) medicine, which is fully half of the cosmic order. To Europeans, "blood" signals danger or murder—the patriarchal interface with blood—but for the Iroquois, the Blood half signals successful childbirth and the continuation of the people. The healthful use of Blood medicine belongs entirely to women, for the only way men can make Blood medicine is by killing something. Women, however, naturally use Blood medicine to create life.

Barbara Alice Mann

Further Reading

Converse, Harriet Maxwell. *Myths and Legends of the New York State Iroquois.* Edited by Arthur C. Parker. New York State Museum Bulletin 125, Education Department Bulletin, no. 437. Albany: University of the State of New York, 1908.

Hale, Horatio, ed. *The Iroquois Book of Rites.* Toronto: University Press, 1978 (1883).

Hewitt, J. N. B. "Iroquoian Cosmology, Second Part." In *Forty-third Annual Report of the Bureau of American Ethnology to the Secretary of the Smithsonian Institution, 1925–1926.* Washington, DC: Government Printing Office, 1928, 453–819.

Jemison, Pete. "Mother of Nations: The Peace Queen, a Neglected Tradition." *Akwe:kon* 5 (1988): 68–70.

Johnson, Elias. *Legends, Traditions and Laws of the Iroquois, or Six Nations.* Reprint ed. New York: AMS Press, 1978 (1881).

Mann, Barbara Alice. *Iroquoian Women: The Gantowisas.* New York: Lang, 2006.

Mann, Barbara Alice. "The Lynx in Time: Haudenosaunee Women's Traditions and History." *American Indian Quarterly* 21, no. 3 (Summer 1997): 423–49.

Mann, Barbara, and Jerry L. Fields. "A Sign in the Sky: Dating the League of the Haudenosaunee." *American Indian Culture and Research Journal* 21, no. 2 (1997): 105–163.

"The Mohawk Creation Story." *Akwesasne Notes* 21, no. 5 (Spring 1989): 32–29.

Parker, Arthur C. *The Constitution of the Five Nations, or the Iroquois Book of the Great Law*. New York State Museum Bulletin No. 184. Albany: The University of the State of New York, 1916.

Rothenberg, Diane. "The Mothers of the Nation: Seneca Resistance to Quaker Intervention." In M. Etienne and E. Leacock, eds. *Women and Colonization*. New York: Praeger, 1980, 63–87.

Shimony, Annemarie Anrod. *Conservatism among the Iroquois at the Six Nations Reserve*. Syracuse, NY: Syracuse University Press, 1994.

FOOD

While popular imagination sometimes stereotypes them solely as nomadic hunters, many, if not most, of North America's Native American peoples practiced agriculture, the domestication of plants and animals for human consumption. In fact, a large proportion of foods consumed by peoples worldwide today originated with Native Americans. Some are very well known, such as corn, potatoes, many kinds of melons, turkey, peanuts, and chocolate. The origins of others have largely been lost to popular history. Consider "Indian" (East Indian) curry. The spices that comprise it actually began as a chili in what is now Brazil. They were transported to India by Portuguese sailors, then mixed with Asian spices to produce the mixture we know today.

The domesticated fowl that would come to be called "turkey" in English was first eaten by Native Americans in the Valley of Mexico, including the Aztecs, who introduced it to invading Spaniards. By the time the Pilgrims reached Plymouth Rock, Massachusetts, in 1620, turkeys had been bred in Spain and exported to England for almost a century. The passengers on the *Mayflower* had some turkeys on board their ship. The American bird was not new to them.

Corn, the major food source for several agricultural peoples across the continent, enjoyed a special spiritual significance among many Native peoples. Often corn and beans (which grow well together because the beans, a legume, fix nitrogen in their roots) were said to maintain a spiritual union. Some peoples, such as the U'ma'has (Omahas) of the eastern Great Plains, "sang up" their corn through special rituals.

Native Americans today sometimes wax nostalgic about frybread and commodity cheese, two staples of Indian humor. According to an old reservation joke: "You could be Indian if you think that the four basic food groups are Spam, commodity cheese, frybread, and Pepsi." In actual historical fact, however, frybread is what creative minds and hungry stomachs came up with after the buffalo had been slaughtered, guns and horses had been seized, and all the residents of reservations had to eat (and eat with) was a fire, a skillet, lard, and white flour, often of questionable quality. Frybread also was the Native introduction to a diet of "commods"—government-provided surplus food—and all the health problems associated with it, beginning with diabetes, which is still epidemic in Indian Country.

Today, many Native Americans are reclaiming their traditional diets, as well as reconstructing age-old agricultural systems (including recovery of heirloom seeds). Often, the "food empowerment movement" or "food sovereignty" is taking place collectively in a conscious effort to bring the era of commodity cheese to a close. Along the way, Native peoples also are finding that maintaining sustainable traditional agriculture also requires fending off environmental challenges, from proposed mines to a galaxy of contaminants in country food and fish.

Food sources varied widely across the continent. While buffalo was a staple on the Plains (as described in the section on "Family, Education, and Community"), salmon were the dominant food source for Pacific Northwest first peoples, and a very regular one, with an annual migration cycle. Five types of salmon are caught, in order of their runs: spring (*yo'batc*), humpback (*ha'do'*), silver (*skwa'xits*), dog (*L!xwai'*), and steelhead (*skwa'wiu'l*). Salmon was highly prized, dried, and traded hundreds of miles inland in what is now Idaho and eastern Washington.

Wild rice, the only grain indigenous to North America, has been harvested for thousands of years by Native peoples from the shores of shallow glacial lakes in areas bordering on the Great Lakes eastward to Maine. Many of the wild rice beds have been lost to recreational development and dredging, so areas still harvested by Native peoples today center in Minnesota. Wild rice is facing a number of environmental threats. One is rising levels of sulfates, mercury, and phosphates in the water, all caused at least in part by rising mining activity. Another threat is climate change.

AGRICULTURE

History and Origins

While popular imagination sometimes stereotypes them solely as nomadic hunters, many, if not most, of North America's Native American peoples practiced agriculture, the domestication of plants and animals for human consumption. At least half of the Earth's staple vegetable foods, the most important being corn and potatoes, were first cultivated by American Indians, who often drew their sustenance from hunting, gathering, *and* agriculture. By 800 CE, agriculture was an established way of life for many Native peoples in North America. At first sight, many immigrating Europeans did not recognize Native American agriculture because it did not resemble their own. Indians did not domesticate draft animals and only rarely plowed their fields. Sometimes crops were grown in small clearings amid forests.

Corn is intertwined with the origin stories of many Native American peoples. The Pueblos say that corn was brought to them by Blue Corn Woman and White Corn Maiden, who emerged to the surface of the earth from a great underground kiva, a sacred place. Corn was first domesticated in the highlands of Mexico about 7,000 years ago from a wild grass called *teosinte*. The first corn cobs were the size of a human thumbnail. As the use of maize ("Indian corn") spread north and south from Mexico, Native peoples domesticated hundreds of varieties and bred them selectively so that the edible kernels grew in size and numbers.

Agriculture among Native American peoples enabled higher population densities. According to William Cronon, Indians in Maine, who did not use

A Navajo hogan in a cornfield near Holbrook, Arizona, c. 1889. (National Archives)

widespread agriculture, sustained an average density of about 40 people per 100 square miles, while Native Americans in southern New England, who raised crops (corn being their major staple), averaged 287 people (seven times as many) on the same amount of land.

Native American agriculture often seemed disorderly to European eyes accustomed to large monocultural fields of one crop. Native fields showed evidence of thought and practice, however. Samuel de Champlain described how Indians planted corn on small hills mixed with beans of several types. "When they grow up, they interlace with the corn, which reaches to the height of five to six feet; and they keep the ground free from weeds," Champlain wrote (Cronon, 1983, 43). John Winthrop, describing Indian fields in Massachusetts within a generation of the Pilgrims' arrival, said that their agriculture "load[ed] the ground with as much as it will beare" (Cronon, 1983, 44). Indian farming methods (usually the responsibility of women, except when growing tobacco) not only kept weeds at a minimum but also preserved soil moisture.

Native American cornfields seem unkempt to non-Indian eyes because they also contain medicinal plants that monocultural farmers would remove as "weeds." Commercial herbicides also kill plants that traditional Native American agriculturalists deem valuable for their healing properties. Notions of sustenance and sacredness are intertwined in Native agricultural traditions. "When the Hopi say that all life is sacred, they mean it," writes Salmón (2012, 56). Pueblo katsinas (kachinas) have magical and healing powers, but in a climate often notable for its scarce precipitation, they also bring rain, which the culture sees as both magical and healing.

The production of food is woven into Native American spiritual life. Among the Haudenosaunee (Iroquois) and many other Native peoples, for example, festivals emphasize the role of the "three sisters" (corn, squash, and beans). Archaeologists tell us that the food complex of corn, beans, and squash was transferred northward from Mexico as a set of rituals before it was an agricultural system. By practicing the rituals, Native Americans in the corn-growing areas of North America became farmers. Corn requires a 160-day frost-free growing season; the northern limit of corn cultivation also often marks the limit of intensive Native agriculture.

Many Native peoples offer their thanks to the plants as well as the animals that they consume, out of a belief that the essence of life that animates human beings also is present in the entire web of animate and inanimate life and objects. Long before a science of "sustained yield" forestry evolved, Native American peoples along the Northwest Coast harvested trees in ways that would assure their continued growth, as part of a belief that trees are sentient beings. Some Native Americans charted farming cycles through complicated relationships with the sun and moon. In addition to domesticating dozens of food plants, they also harvested the wild bounty of the forests for hundreds of herbs and other plants used to restore and maintain health.

Corn, the major food source for several agricultural peoples across the continent, enjoyed a special spiritual significance. Often corn and beans (which grow well together because the beans, a legume, fix nitrogen in their roots) were said to maintain a spiritual union. Some peoples, such as the Omahas of the eastern Great Plains, "sang up" their corn through special rituals.

In addition to "singing up the corn," the Pueblos cleaned their storage bins before the harvest, so the corn would be happy when they brought it in. The Pawnees grew 10 varieties of corn, including one (called "holy" or "wonderful" corn) that was used only for religious purposes and never eaten. The Mandans had a corn priest who officiated at rites during the growing season. Each stage of the corn's growth was associated with particular songs and rituals, and spiritual attention was said to be as important to the corn as proper water, sun, and fertilizer. Among the Zuni, a newborn child was given an ear of corn at birth and endowed with a "corn name." An ear of maize was put in the place of death as the "heart of the deceased," and later used as seed corn to begin the cycle of life anew. To Navajos, corn was as sacred as human life.

At birth, each infant is given the seed from an ear of corn as a fetish to carry for life, as a reminder that the Corn Mothers brought life to the Pueblos. The corn fetish has a practical side as well: should a harvest completely fail due to drought or for other reasons, the fetishes may become the seed corn for the next crop.

Some Native peoples used fire to raze fields for farming and to drive game while hunting. These were not fires left to blaze out of control, however; Navajos who used range fires customarily detailed half of their hunting party to contain and control the fire, and to keep it on the surface, where the flames would clear old brush so that new plant life could generate, instead of destroying the forest canopy. When Europeans first laid eyes on North America, it was much more densely forested than today. The park-like appearance of many eastern forests was a result of Native American peoples' efforts to manage plant and animal life.

When colonists arrived in eastern North America, many of the Native peoples they met farmed corn in large tracts. Native Americans taught the Puritans which seeds would grow in their territory. Most of the seeds that the Puritans had brought from England did not sprout when planted in the area that the colonists called "New England."

Farming—and eating what is grown—involves a set of decisions that invoke culture and politics. Enrique Salmón, in *Eating the Landscape: American Indian Stories of Food, Identity, and Resilience* (2012), writes, "Through our choices to eat locally or to eat food that has traveled 2,000 miles to reach our grocer's shelves, we support a process. The latter process consumes precious fossil fuels; wastes clean drinking water in order to raise animal products; knocks down fragile rain forests and desert landscapes; and increases nutrition-related diseases primarily among poor, low-income, and uneducated populations" (p. 8).

Regional Variations

Oneida Corn Culture   Like other members of the Haudenosaunee (Iroquois) Confederacy, the Oneidas adopted corn as a staple crop at roughly the year 1000 CE, a change that was followed, within a few generations, by the formation of the Iroquois Confederacy. By the time European Americans encountered the Oneidas and other Iroquois, this confederacy was a trading and diplomatic power among the Native American peoples of eastern North America. The Oneidas enjoyed a commanding position astride the only relatively flat passage between the Hudson River and the Great Lakes; in the 19th century, this country would be traversed by the Erie Canal, a major economic lifeline before the spread of railroads a few decades later. "Oneida" is probably an anglicization of this people's own name for themselves, *Ona yote ka o no,* meaning Granite People or People of the Rock.

The first European to visit Oneida country who left a historical record was a Dutch surgeon, Harmen Meyndersten van den Bogaert, who traveled westward from Fort Orange (Albany) in 1634 and 1635. The Oneidas sheltered the Dutchman during the deepening winter and fed him venison, salmon, bear meat, cornbread baked with beans, baked squash, and beaver meat.

The fact that the Oneidas could bring such a feast out of winter storage spoke volumes about the abundance of their economy. Van den Bogaert described storehouses of beans and maize; he estimated that one of these contained 300 bushels of corn stored for the winter. According to his accounts, the Oneidas traded salmon to the Mohawks, perhaps for bear meat. Traveling Mohawk traders passed through Oneida settlements while van den Bogaert lived there. To reciprocate for the Oneidas' hospitality, he gave them salt, tobacco, knives, needles, axes, cloth, ham, and beer, as he discovered that he was not the first to introduce them to European trade goods. The French had arrived earlier, leaving some of the Oneidas with French clothing and razors.

During the early 1660s, continuing into the 1690s, Oneida and other Iroquois populations were sharply reduced by a series of epidemics, principally smallpox. By the late 1660s, according to French observers, two-thirds of the Oneidas were adopted Wyandot (Huron) and Algonquin captives. Alcohol was already taking a toll on the Oneidas as well. At about the same time, the religion frontier reached Oneida as the Jesuits arrived. By 1690, the new English government at Albany was issuing permission for purchase of Indian land in Iroquois country. Oneida population and economic bases continued a protracted decline.

The Oneidas, unlike a majority of other Iroquois, supported the patriots during the American Revolution. The Oneidas' corn surplus, an asset in peacetime trade, was put to use in 1777 feeding General George Washington's hungry troops during their desperate winter at Valley Forge. Because of the Oneidas' acumen as farmers of corn, General Washington got to know the Oneida chief Skenandoah (sometimes anglicized as "Shenandoah"), who lived to the age of 110, an anomaly at a time when the average lifespan was between 35 and 40. An Oneida, Polly Cook, served as Washington's cook for much of the war. Washington was said to have preferred Indian corn to European wheat, and to have made a patriotic point of it.

Mayan Agriculture   While the Mayas are known for their temples in such places as Tikal, Copan, and Palenque, most Mayas, the commoners who supported the small elite that maintained the temples, spent most of their time cultivating food, principally corn. Most of the Mayan ceremonial centers were surrounded by very large earthworks, which were used for agriculture. These artificial ramparts were not discovered by modern archaeologists until they started using satellite images of the land, since today the earthworks often are submerged in jungle and thus very difficult to see from ground level. The earthworks included complex irrigation channels and raised fields, often hewn from reclaimed swampland. The Mayas dredged nutrient-rich soil from the bottoms of the irrigation ditches to fertilize fields that they raised above the flood-level of the rainy season. The fields were so rich that they produced several crops a year to feed the people of the urban ceremonial centers.

The discovery of complex agricultural earthworks among the Mayas caused scholars to question earlier assumptions that the Mayas had practiced slash-and-burn agriculture that was said to have deforested the land, exhausted and eroded the topsoil, and played a role in the collapse of the "classic" age of the Mayas. Today, the collapse of the Mayas is usually ascribed not to deforestation caused by agriculture, but to ecological damage and social disorganization caused by escalating warfare between city-states. Not all of the Mayas' earthworks were constructed to aid agriculture. Some ramparts were defensive, and as war became more common and deadly, the Mayas' complex agricultural system suffered immensely.

Pueblo Agricultural Roots   About the same time that the Mayan civilization collapsed, the ancestors of today's Pueblos were building a corn-based culture in the Chaco Canyon area of present-day New Mexico. The Pueblos of the Rio Grande are cultural and economic inheritors of the Mogollon, Anasazi, and Hohokam communities to the west and southwest of the upper Rio Grande Valley. Cultivation of corn was introduced into the area about 3000 BCE. About 2000 BCE, beans and squash were added. Cotton later became a fourth staple crop.

Also about 2,000 years ago, irrigation was introduced to supplement dry farming in the area. The Pueblos used brief, heavy precipitation to advantage by constructing some of their irrigation works at the bases of steep cliffs that collected runoff. The residents of this area constructed roads that often ran for hundreds of miles to provide a way to share food surpluses—if one pueblo had a bad harvest, others would make it up. The cultivation of corn in Chaco Canyon supported a civilization that constructed the largest multifamily dwellings in North America. Such a high degree of agricultural organization supported a culture that dominated the turquoise trade in the area. Turquoise was important as a liquid asset, a medium of trade. Pueblo centers such as Pueblo Bonito became centers of trade, manufacturing, and ceremony.

The vital role of water and irrigation in Pueblo agriculture is illustrated by the fact that the great classic Pueblo civilizations were destroyed by a drought so severe that not even ingenious water management could cope with it. In the 13th century CE, most Pueblo settlements outside of the Rio Grande valley had been abandoned after 50 years of nearly rainless drought, which destroyed their agricultural base.

Following the Spanish colonization of New Mexico, access to water became a crucial cause for conflict. Land without water is worthless in the arid Southwest. Paradoxically, the Pueblos in 1680 used the waters of the Rio Grande to defeat the Spanish; they staged their revolt while the river was flooding to keep Spanish reinforcements out.

Irrigation of farmland is *the* key factor in Pueblo agricultural land use. In order to plan, construct, and maintain elaborate land systems, cooperation between several villages was crucial. Irrigation systems need routine maintenance, which rendered clans inefficient, so nonkinship associations were created to cope with such work. This organizational framework had other community functions, and it revolved primarily around the spiritual life of the Pueblos. The basic rationale for the nonkinship associations was irrigation, however.

Contemporary Agriculture

Eating culturally appropriate foods recalls memories and evokes history. Family recipes recall not only the preparation of food but also cultural context. Salmón (2012) wrote, "Eating is not only a political act, but also a cultural act that reaffirms one's identity and worldview. . . . Culture is performed by humans every minute of every day. . . . We have to eat in order to survive; therefore food becomes a medium through which a complex of collective memories . . . remain alive and intact" (pp. 8–9). The transfer of knowledge about plants' healing powers also keeps culture alive, as when Salmón recalls that his grandmother taught him that a tea made of wild spearmint "makes your insides smile."

While Western (European) history usually focuses on eminent human beings (heroes)—people who influence the course of events—indigenous cultural history often emphasizes a people's relationship with their homeland, "trees, plants, animals, and children" (Salmón, 2012, 14). People share the landscape rather than conquer it. Successful cultures maintain a relationship with the land base that sustains them. Enrique Salmón points out that cultural (including linguistic) diversity is related to biological diversity. Native cultures often see plants as relatives. Ceremonies invoke the abundance of the land: "Cultural histories speak the language of the land" (Salmón, 2012, 30).

Native Americans first cultivated many of the foods that are taken for granted as everyday nourishment today. The main ingredients of Crackerjacks (peanuts and popcorn), for example, are both indigenous to the Americas, as are all edible beans except horse beans and soybeans, all squashes (including pumpkins), Jerusalem artichokes, the "Irish" potato, the sweet potato, sunflowers, peppers, pineapples, watermelons, cassava, bananas, strawberries, raspberries, gooseberries, and pecans.

Native American agriculture has influenced eating habits around the world so completely that many people forget their culinary origins. Before the voyages of Columbus, the Italian food of today (with its tomato-based sauces) was unknown. The Irish cooked their food without potatoes. Europeans satisfied their sweet tooth without chocolate. Corn was unknown outside the Americas. These crops were produced by experimentation of many Native American cultures over thousands of years. Knowledge of plant life was passed along from generation to generation with other social knowledge, usually by the elder women of a Native tribe or nation.

See Also PART 2: CULTURAL FORMS: FOOD: Spotlight: Corn and Culture; Food and Culture: North Pacific Coast; Foods and Medicines from Native American Cultures/ Spotlight: Examples of Foods Native to the Americas; Spotlight: Native American Vegetal Remedies Used Today; Food Sovereignty; Food Sovereignty: Local and Regional Examples; Wild Rice; **SPIRITUALITY:** Thanksgiving

Further Reading

Ballantine, Betty, and Ian Ballantine. *The Native Americans: An Illustrated History.* Atlanta: Turner, 1994.

Brandon, William. *American Heritage Book of Indians*. New York: Dell, 1961.

Cronon, William. *Changes in the Land: Indians, Colonists, and the Ecology of New England*. New York: Hill and Wang, 1983.

Deloria, Vine, Jr. *God Is Red*. Golden, CO: North American Press, 1992.

Dozier, Edward P. *The Pueblo Indians of North America*. New York: Holt, Rinehart & Winston, 1970.

Grinde, Donald A., Jr., and Bruce E. Johansen. *Ecocide of Native America*. Santa Fe: Clear Light, 1995.

Hughes, J. Donald. *American Indian Ecology*. El Paso: Texas Western Press, 1983.

Iverson, Peter. "Taking Care of the Earth and Sky." In Alvin Josephy, ed. *America in 1492: The World of the Indian Peoples Before the Arrival of Columbus*. New York: Alfred A. Knopf, 1992, 87–98.

Richards, Cara E. *The Oneida People*. Phoenix: Indian Tribal Series, 1974.

Salmón, Enrique. *Eating the Landscape: American Indian Stories of Food, Identity, and Resilience*. Tucson: University of Arizona Press, 2012.

Sando, Joe S. *The Pueblo Indians*. San Francisco: Indian Historian Press, 1976.

Spotlight

CORN AND CULTURE

Corn's biological name is *Zea mays*, from which the name maize is derived. The first distant relative of today's foot-long ears of corn were probably grown in central Mexico, in caves near Teotihuacán, about 7,000 years ago. Early corn was small, perhaps three to four inches long, with two rows of mismatched kernels. Utilization of corn spread to South America as well as to the Anasazi country in present-day Arizona and New Mexico, first as a wild grain, then as an agricultural product, gradually gaining length and kernels along the way. Corn was firmly established as a staple in the Southwest by about 1,500 years ago. By 1,000 years ago, corn had spread over all parts of North and South America having the requisite warmth and growing season, and it had become a staple crop of many Native peoples across the hemisphere.

Corn was introduced in eastern North America about 200 CE, and it became the dominant food source across much of the region (from southern Ontario to northern Florida) by about 800 CE. During this time, Native American farmers took part in selective breeding of several strains of corn to increase production, as well as hardiness in the face of freezes and drought. By 900 CE, a major advance in breeding, commonly called "flint" or "eastern eight row," secured corn's dominance of food production throughout the east because it was even hardier than earlier strains. The spread of corn as a staple crop did not reach its greatest extent until a hundred years before Columbus's first voyage.

Corn also enhanced the role of agriculture in many Native American economies. The Iroquois' oral history, for example, holds that corn had a key role in
establishing agriculture as a major economic enterprise. The increasing role
of agriculture had far-reaching cultural as well as economic effects among the
Iroquois, including support of matrilineal social structures and establishment of
a confederation based on the Great Law of Peace.

Following their unification under Deganawidah's Great Law, the Haudenosaunee (Iroquois) became an economic and political confederation of five
previously separate nations, the Mohawks, Cayugas, Oneidas, Onondagas,
and Senecas. A sixth nation, the Tuscaroras, was brought into the confederacy
in the early 18th century. With the arrival of Europeans, the Iroquois came
to occupy a pivotal position between the warring English and French. They
were pivotal geographically, occupying the only relatively level land pass between the Atlantic Ocean and the Great Lakes, a matter of great economic
importance at a time when the most expeditious form of transportation was by
water. Later, the Erie Canal would be carved through Iroquois Country, providing the first large-scale economic link between the Eastern Seaboard and the
Great Lakes.

The Haudenosaunee Confederacy adopted corn as a staple crop as its constituent nations developed large-scale architecture shortly after 1000 CE. The
Haudenosaunee ability to produce a surplus of corn played a role in the political influence of the confederacy, which reached, through a chain of alliances,
from their homelands in present-day upstate New York across much of New
England and the Middle Atlantic regions.

The Iroquois' adoption of corn-based agriculture, along with cultivation
of beans and squash (called "the three sisters") played an important role
in their adoption of a matrilineal social structure and a consensus-based
political system. Before roughly the year 1000 CE, the Iroquois had been
less prone to alliance and more frequently disposed to murder for revenge.
An older confederacy to the north, probably the Wyandots (Hurons), are said
to have sent an emissary, Deganawidah, to persuade the Haudenosaunee to
make peace with each other and outlaw the blood feud, which was threaten-
ing social stability. Deganawidah and Hiawatha, the Mohawk co-founder of
the Haudenosaunee Confederacy, spent most of their adult lives persuading
the feuding Haudenosaunee to accept their vision of peace. According to cal-
culations by Barbara Mann and Jerry Fields, the confederacy was finally accepted in 1142 CE, within living memory, perhaps, of its adoption of corn as a
staple crop.

Corn, the major food source for several agricultural peoples across the
continent, also often enjoyed a special spiritual significance. Corn and beans
(which grow well together because the beans, a legume, fix nitrogen in their
roots) often were said to maintain a spiritual union. Some peoples, such as the
Omahas of the eastern Great Plains, "sang up" their corn through special
rituals. In addition to "singing up the corn," the Pueblos cleaned their storage bins before the harvest, "so the corn will be happy when we bring it in"
(Brandon, 1961, 116). The Pawnees grew 10 varieties of corn, including one

(called "holy" or "wonderful" corn) that was used only for religious purposes and never eaten. The Mandans had a corn priest who officiated at rites during the growing season. Each stage of the corn's growth was associated with particular songs and rituals, and spiritual attention was said to be as important to the corn as proper water, sun, and fertilizer. Among the Zunis, a newborn child was given an ear of corn at birth and endowed with a "corn name." An ear of maize was put in the place of death as the "heart of the deceased," and later used as seed corn to begin the cycle of life anew. To Navajos, corn was as sacred as human life.

Further Reading

Brandon, William. *American Heritage Book of Indians*. New York: Dell, 1961.

Iverson, Peter. "Taking Care of the Earth and Sky." In Alvin Josephy, ed. *America in 1492: The World of the Indian Peoples Before the Arrival of Columbus*. New York: Alfred A. Knopf, 1992, p. 98.

Mann, Barbara, and Jerry L. Fields. "A Sign in the Sky: Dating the League of the Haudenosaunee." *American Indian Culture and Research Journal* 21, no. 2 (1997): 105–163.

FISHING CULTURE, PACIFIC NORTHWEST

History and Origins

In the Coast Salish peoples' telling, there existed far out in the ocean five villages to which salmon traveled when they departed local streams. The first spring salmon is believed to be a scout for its village. If it is not treated with respect, no others may return. Thus, the Ceremony of the First Salmon has been practiced since antiquity and continues today. Each year the first salmon to return from the saltwater sea to the freshwater streams of its origin—a spring Chinook—is ceremonially captured as an honored guest. Its flesh is cooked, then meticulously removed from its bones and ceremoniously shared by all members of the community. Later, the skeleton of the salmon is carried back to the river at the head of a torch-bearing, singing, dancing, and chanting procession. It is placed in the water facing upstream in hopes that it will tell its brother and sister salmon of the fine hospitality it received from the Muckleshoot people, so the fish will return.

While the first peoples of the Pacific Northwest also hunted land animals, the salmon were their dominant food source, and a very regular one, with an annual migration cycle. Five types of salmon are caught, in order of their runs: spring (*yo'batc*), humpback (*ha'do'*), silver (*skwa'xits*), dog (*L!xwai'*), and steelhead (*skwa'wiu'l*). Spring salmon were most highly prized. Smelt, herring, flounder, cod, halibut, trout, rock cod, and skate, seal, sea lion, sea otter, porpoise, and whale also were caught in large numbers during ancestral times. As today, shellfish were important to the diet—mussels, clams, oysters, barnacles, and crabs. When the tide is out, local people long have said, the table is set. In ancestral times, if barnacles were harvested often enough, they became large and juicy, and often were preferable to oysters. However, barnacles had to be taken from areas with swiftly running tides. Those harvested in stagnant water could be toxic. Salmon swam in huge numbers from their headwater spawning areas, downriver and through an intricate array of saltwater inlets to the open ocean. After a period at sea, sometimes several years, the red-fleshed fish reversed direction and returned through the Strait of Juan de Fuca, Puget Sound, and other bodies of water to the exact spots on the same rivers and streams where they had been born, to breed. These destinations once were free of pollution, roadways, and hydroelectric dams. Since those early days, Native fishing peoples have harvested salmon with nets and spears, preserving them by smoking and drying. Like other Native peoples in the area, indigenous peoples have long traded salmon in dried form several hundred miles inland. Fish oil, kept in waterproof bags, was used as a flavoring much as olive oil is used in cooking today.

Coast Salish peoples fished for other species in addition to salmon, such as halibut and cod. They devised a unique way to catch cod: "They made a shuttlecock device which was lowered to the bottom on weights, and then freed by means of a trip. The cod, fascinated by the whirling motion of the device, followed its rise to the surface and were speared by the waiting fishermen" (Ashwell, 1978, 43).

Villages were constructed to maximize food gathering, often built adjacent to rivers where their residents launched fishing expeditions when salmon started swimming upstream. Salmon harvesting techniques (sun drying, wind drying, and smoking) were well developed, and preservation technologies allowed their use year-round domestically as well as for wide-ranging inland trade, which involved not only food but also many necessities and luxuries of life not available locally. Peoples west of the Cascades traded salmon, dried clams, camas, and other goods for sheep's wool, porcupine quills, embroidery, grass that could be used to make thread, and other things. Sometimes, dried salmon from the Yakima Valley was sold westward across the Cascades to people who preferred its taste to their own from Puget Sound.

Regional Variations

Pacific Coast peoples became adept at fishing in a variety of settings because their livelihood depended on it. In Coast Salish country, water contamination was not permitted when a salmon run was imminent—no food scraps or other rubbish was allowed in a host river; canoes were not bailed out; and women in menstrual seclusion were not allowed to swim in the watercourse.

While spears were designed for fishing in river rapids where nets were useless, fish traps were designed to catch salmon early in their run upriver. Fishing devices built and improved for thousands of years; fishing people used dip nets, set nets, and fish traps. Smaller nets were constructed for dipping out fish from traps. Bigger nets were used for dipping fish directly out of the water. One fish trap was called a *yidahd*, a grill-like structure that was placed atop narrow streams. Fishing people would scare the trout downstream toward the trap, where the grill would "leave them floundering" (Ballard, 1951, 155). Anthropologist Arthur C. Ballard said he had never seen such a trap himself, but a Native person known to Ballard as Abb said one was used near the mouth of Neuwaukum Creek. He also said that white people had destroyed such traps.

The weir was called *tsilósid* and was used mainly from midsummer into autumn for harvesting large fish, such as king salmon, silver salmon, and dog salmon. Weirs were constructed to block the passage of fish in shallow areas of rivers, or to guide them into traps. The latticework was put up during fishing season and then taken down. Fishing nets and traps allowed the capture of smaller fish than could be taken with spears. The fishing season began in the spring and continued through the fall, until people had enough to last the winter. If runs were sparse, they continued to fish into winter.

The weirs were so effective at harvesting fish that social pressure was brought to bear on families living downstream along the Green River to allow enough fish to escape so that their upstream neighbors could share the bounty. Ballard indicated that those who did not cooperate risked damage to their weirs inflicted by felled trees.

Other traps also were used, such as the "funnel snare," which was laid into riverbeds awaiting migrating steelhead. Ballard described one such snare that was about seven feet in length, "with a circular opening about eighteen inches in diameter at the entrance . . . converging to a point at the lower end," woven of willow stems. Planks were placed at either side of the funnel to guide fish into it. A "grill" was used to catch steelhead and trout. The grill was about eight feet long and wide, placed in a channel buttressed by dirt and gravel that led fish into a platform, where "they floundered about helplessly" (Ballard, 1957, 43).

Fishing was conducted primarily (but not solely) by men, while women usually smoked, dried, and stored the catch. Once caught, fish were cooked quickly, usually on ironwood sticks set alongside or over an alderwood fire. Seawater or seaweed, with its salt content, served as a flavoring. Fish also were cleaned and then dried for several days, hung on racks in small smokehouses, where a continuous fire fed with sweet-smelling woods gave the cured fish a distinctive flavor that is still prized today. Shellfish also would be smoked, dried, and stored for trading. The cured fish also were preserved for several months, through winter when fresh fish were unavailable. Fish, as the basis of the Coast Salish economy and ceremonial life, were used for trade as well as food. The smoking of fish made them portable and useful in trade.

Each Native nation, tribe, or band generally used certain defined fishing and hunting grounds. In reality, however, day-to-day relations were complex. Although fishing and hunting grounds usually were respected by others, at river weir sites no visitor was left without a share of fish. Marine fishing areas were freely shared among multiple groups. The marine fishery included an extensive shellfish harvest on the shores of Puget Sound, as well as trolling in saltwater for salmon and the harvest of other species, such as porpoise. Hunting areas away from winter villages also often were shared. Marriages between people from different tribes led to sharing of resources. Saltwater fisheries and upland root and hunting grounds were shared, with exceptions at the river weir fisheries where intensive labor established priority of use.

The ancestors of the fishing peoples also preserved the runs by keeping only the smaller fish so that the larger ones could spawn upstream. This sort of rough genetic selection contributed to an increase over time in the size and weight of salmon, some of which reached roughly 100 pounds. Even after contact, a 30-pound fish was not unusual. On one occasion, the elderly Louis Starr, who was born at Muckleshoot on September 6, 1898, recalled having hooked a salmon that was so big it "literally pulled him out of his dugout canoe" (Tollefson, 1993, 13). Once non-Indians in fishing boats began to snatch the biggest fish at sea before they returned to spawning streams, this system no longer worked.

With fish so large and skills honed by years of practice, spear fishing was more efficient than it might seem to later generations accustomed to devices, such as nets, weirs, and fish wheels, that caught fish *en masse*. A traditional fishing spear usually was 14 to 16 feet long with removable barbed harpoon points so that "a harpooned fish could be played and pulled ashore or into a canoe. . . . Once a fish was speared it was seldom lost" (Tollefson, 1993, 14). The harpoon's head was fastened to the shaft with a cord made of sweetgrass, obtained in trade from peoples east of the Cascades, and it was said to be more durable than rope.

Many foods that the Salish used were dried for storage and convenient transport. Salmon was roasted on tongs over an open fire. Clams were cooked in underground pits lined with hot rocks, their juices providing steam, then smoked on racks. Deer and bear meat, obtained in communal hunts, usually in the fall, also were smoked for the winter after cooking in earthen ovens lined with hot rocks. Huckleberries and camas roots were laid in the sun to dry.

Fishing Today: A Landmark Federal Fishing Decision

To defend their fishing rights, Puget Sound Native peoples called upon non-Indian allies, most notably the multiethnic collation forming in Seattle around such issues as the Indian occupation of Fort Lawton and the birth of El Centro de la Raza. Seattle was unusual for its alliances across racial lines; at the same time that defense of fishing rights reached fever pitch, Latino, Asian, black, and white allies were asserting economic rights and identity in the urban area. They aided each other. The interethnic alliance put bodies on the line, with the sit-in being the most familiar tactic. In the case of the fishing rights battles, non-Indians lined the shore as Native people took to their boats with nets, forming a human chain between those who were fishing and the state game and fishing agents who were determined to prevent activity that the Indians (later supported by federal law) insisted was legal under the treaties.

The ground-level fishing wars peaked September 9, 1970, during a fish-in on the Puyallup River near the Tacoma, as a multiethnic camp of about 100 fishing rights supporters standing vigil for an array of treaty Indians on the river was torn apart by about 300 police in riot gear who arrested about 60 people. Four shots were fired at the police, who then dispersed the crowd with a volley of their own fire and a haze of tear gas. This confrontation contributed to the filing of *United States v. Washington*, which produced the Boldt ruling in 1974.

The Boldt ruling provoked a revolution in federal law regarding Native American fishing rights. Upheld by higher courts, Judge Boldt's ruling affirmed the treaty and the fishing peoples' decades-long assertions of their rights, fundamentally and explicitly. Documented with the research of Barbara Lane, an anthropologist, Boldt used an 1828 edition of *Webster's American Dictionary* for his contemporary definition of "in common with" as entitling Native people to as much as half the salmon catch running through their *traditional* waters, *before* the treaties had been signed.

See Also PART 1: OVERVIEW: NATIONS, TRIBES, AND OTHER NATIVE GROUPS: Northwest Coast Culture Area; **PART 2: CULTURAL FORMS: FOOD:** Agriculture; Food and Culture: North Pacific Coast; Food Sovereignty; Food Sovereignty: Local and Regional Examples; **TRANSPORTATION AND HOUSING:** Longhouses (Pacific Northwest)

Further Reading
Ashwell, Reg. *Coast Salish: Their Art, Culture, and Legends.* Saanichton, BC, and Seattle: Hancock House, 1978.

Ballard, Arthur C. "The Salmon Weir on Green River in Western Washington." *Davidson Journal of Anthropology* 3, no. 1 (Summer 1957): 37–53. Copy in archives of Muckleshoot Indian Tribe Preservation Program.

Ballard, Arthur C. Testimony, Indian Claims Commission of the United States. *The Muckeshoot Tribe of Indians on Relation of Napolean Ross, Chairman of the General Council, Claimant, vs. The United States of America, Defendant,* vol. 1, Seattle, November 26–28, 1951. 2 vols.

Elmendorf, William W. *The Structure of Twana* [Skokomish] *Culture.* Pullman: Washington State University Press, 1960.

Haeberlin, H., and Erna Gunther. *The Indians of Puget Sound.* University of Washington Publications in Anthropology 4 (1930): 1–84. Seattle: University of Washington Press.

Lane, Barbara. "Political and Economic Aspects of Indian-White Culture Contact in Western Washington in the Mid-Nineteenth Century." May 10, 1973. Typescript in Muckleshoot Indian Tribe Preservation Program Archives.

"Overview: The Muckleshoot Indian Tribe." http://www.muckleshoot.nsn.us/about us/overview.aspx. Accessed October 30, 2014.

Tollefson, Kenneth D. "Remembering the Old Ways: Louis Starr's Reflections on Traditional Indian Subsistence Living." *Columbia Magazine* (Fall 1993): 13–16.

FOOD AND CULTURE: NORTH PACIFIC COAST

History and Origins

For several thousand years preceding immigration to western Washington by European Americans, indigenous peoples lived there in a density higher than nearly anywhere else in Native North America north of Mexico. This population density was centered on the watercourses of the region and was dependent on the skillful harvesting and use of available food resources, several species of salmon being the most important. The dense forests, with a few exceptions, were usually light on game animals. The bear, cougar, lynx, raccoons, squirrels, and mice that populated the forests were of little use as food, although Native people did harvest deer and elk on the prairies, which were the first areas taken by immigrant European Americans who wanted to farm without clearing thick forests and underbrush.

The land and especially the rivers and sea were abundant, but that didn't mean life was easy. People could not obtain everything they needed in a stroll around their villages. Native peoples had to work to maintain their lives. "This was not a 'lotus land,' in which the native fishermen in a few hours' time could obtain a year's supply of food for his family," wrote anthropologist Barbara Lane (1973, 11). Muckleshoot ancestral Salish culture is based on more than technologies of woodworking and fishing; it includes technologies of construction, basketry, weaving, hunting, gathering, exploration, trade economy, gaming and horse racing, art and design, popular and elite sports, as well as highly developed oral traditions, including songs and histories, teaching stories, religious practices, and healing arts.

The coastal region west of the Cascades has a mild, marine climate, with rare episodes of extreme heat or cold. While the Cascades and the Olympic Peninsula (including its western and southern slopes) receive heavy rain and snowfall in the late fall, winter, and early spring, the plateau on which the Muckleshoots' ancestors live is partially sheltered by the Olympics, limiting rainfall to about 40 inches a year.

Regional Variations

Although some anthropologists assumed that ancestors of Northwest Coast Native American peoples reached cultural complexity mainly without agriculture, a rarity in world history, this idea was simplified. They did not forgo agriculture entirely. Its forms were not easily recognized by Europeans, however. Some plants were cultivated, including root crops. Basket materials also were cultivated, and periodic burning was practiced to improve habitat. The fires created park-like landscapes of prairies that were attractive to European American immigrants. Areas were burned to enhance berries and animal forage.

Nature provided raw materials for clothing, shelter, and tools upon which a highly developed culture based on the technologies of woodworking and fishing thrived. Traditional life was (and remains) rich in artistry with roots in both ceremony and everyday life, including fine basketry and artistic woodcarvings, while developing a social structure with a nobility, a middle class, and a few slaves. The class system was complex but not as strictly structured as societies farther north. Hierarchies of expertise and knowledge also existed.

In *Notes on the Ethnology of the Indians of Puget Sound*, Thomas Talbot Waterman provides detailed descriptions of Puget Sound Native peoples' lifeways and technologies, from weaving of baskets (which he found to be of very high quality), to blankets, which could be woven of dog and goat wool, as well as that of sheep. Woodworkers also fashioned spoons, dishes, roasting skewers, mauls, adzes, spears, cradle boards, and canoe paddles, among many other things.

Waterman was especially fascinated by types of south Puget Sound berry pickers that were found nowhere else and showed "a considerable measure of ingenuity" (Waterman, 1973, 53). An elderberry picker was fashioned "by taking [a] short piece of cedar wood and splitting it down from one end, into thin strips. Cedar bark fiber is wound tightly around the other end to keep the whole together. The sections or splints are then separated by driving wedges in, so they are spread apart like fingers of the hand. Their points are then sharpened" (Waterman, 1973, 53). This tool worked as a rake that could be built in a few minutes, allowing a picker to whip the elderberry bush, detaching the berries, but not twigs or leaves. A mat was placed under the bush to collect the berries, which were then poured into a basket. A second type of berry picker was used for blueberries, which grow on a small bush close to the ground. This one, often made of cow horn, had shorter "fingers" that curved inward, following the contour of the bush, allowing for a quick and very efficient harvest.

Pacific Coast Native peoples hunted elk, deer, cougar, bear, ducks, geese, swans, pigeons, grouse, beaver, mountain goat, wolf, beaver, mountain lion, mink, land otter, and water fowl from their homelands into the foothills of the Cascade Mountains and up the slopes of Mount Tahoma (Rainier). Mountain goats were difficult to capture; consequently their horns, so difficult to obtain, were treasured. Horns were steamed soft and then bent to make bowls. Beaver teeth were used to carve designs into them. Mountain goats were caught with netted snares set on the rocky ridges of the mountains' lower slopes. The goats' wool was made into burial robes. Nets hung inches above water in foggy weather also were used to catch ducks. The ducks could not see the nets and consequently became snared.

Hunting required an eye to the weather and a sense of ready opportunity. South Puget Sound Salish hunters would wait for heavy snow in the mountains and foothills to drive deer to lower elevations, often to Puget Sound beaches, where they could be surrounded and killed. If a deer was spotted swimming to an island in the sound, "several canoes might put out in pursuit, the men pounding the animals across the head with their paddles to kill it" (Smith, 1940, 269). Strong social sanction prevented hunters from wasting meat. A lone traveler who had to kill a deer because no smaller game was available would feel compelled to stop and camp for several days to prepare the meat for the journey (rendering and drying it) so that nothing useful would be left behind.

Contemporary Forms

The soil of many inland prairies is black, deep, and productive to this day. Muckleshoot ancestors, among others, maintained their prairies by regular burning to remove trees and create forage for elk, deer, and horses, removing underbrush that inhibited hunting. Periodic burning also increased production of salmonberries, huckleberries, raspberries, soapberries, roots, and other berries, as well as other plants that were used as medicine, such as camas, a medicinal perennial herb native to the Pacific Northwest.

Deer and elk jerky were dried in strips. Huckleberries were dried in the sun on mats, as well as in a fire pit to keep bugs away. Camas also was baked in pits, then dried and sometimes pounded into powder for later use. Other prairie resources included skunk cabbage root, oak acorns, and hazelnuts. Cranberries were harvested from bogs dug by beavers; strawberries were gathered. Some European American immigrants were surprised to find Native people growing relatively large crops of potatoes when they arrived. Potatoes may have come to the area from aboriginal people to the south, or from the Hudson's Bay Company. Other vegetable roots or bulbs such as salmonberry sprouts, bitter roots, wapato, tiger lily, and fern were dug between early spring and late fall. During the summer and fall, berries such as red and blue elderberries, blackberries, salal berries, huckleberries, prairie berries, cranberries, wild strawberries, thimbleberries, and blackcaps were available. Huckleberry leaves were dried for tea.

The area has thick forests of fir and pine—Douglas fir, spruce, red cedar, yellow cedar, hemlock, and pine. Broadleaf trees mix at lower elevations, including maple, oak, dogwood, alder, aspen, birch, and madrona. Cedar has played an important role in traditional culture, providing housing for large longhouses, clothing, eating utensils, and canoes. Red cedar splits easily for planks. Soft yellow cedar and alder, which do not split easily, are better for bowls and dishes. Yew is flexible and it good for bows and spear fishing. The herbs of the forest shaped healing practices. Later, some of these practices were adopted by non-Indian naturopaths. For example, the bark of cascara trees, which grew throughout the Pacific Northwest, was a source of medicine used to treat diarrhea. Muckleshoots and Puyallups harvested cascara, dried it in the sun, and sold it to pharmacies.

Marian W. Smith, who wrote an extensive ethnography of the region, described the use of herbs and other naturally provided substances to deal with physical ailments. In her preface to *The Puyallup-Nisqually,* Smith (1940) defined her work as "applied to all Coast Salish of Southern Puget Sound" (p. xi). The fieldwork was done in 1935 and 1936 with the cooperation of some well-known anthropologists, including Ruth Benedict, Franz Boas, Erna Gunther, and Arthur C. Ballard. The work was funded by the Columbia University Council for Research in the Social Sciences and the Columbia University Anthropology Department and published in 1940 by Columbia University Press.

Hundreds of such remedies were used by the South Sound Salish, according to Smith. A few included use of a willow bark poultice that, heated and applied to a wound, would staunch bleeding from a wound and cleanse it. A tea of wild cherry bark was used to treat internal injuries. Baked skunk cabbage root was heated and used to draw out infections and poisons. The tea of the salal berry was good for coughs, and nettle-bark tea could blunt the symptoms of the common cold, as could tea brewed from tips of cedar, hemlock, and white fir branches while in bud.

Erza Meeker, an early European American immigrant to the area, admired the Salish ancestors' food crops in addition to salmon—dried camas and sunflower roots that he said were very nutritious and quite tasty. He also wrote approvingly of a berry, "kinnikinneck," or Indian tobacco, that was dried, roasted, and smoked, mixed half-and-half with tobacco, "when it makes very fine smoking . . . fragrant and very acceptable, [with an effect] like opium or ether. Some Indians I have seen using it would keel over in a trance." The kinnikinneck also could be eaten mixed with dried salmon eggs (Meeker, 1905, 174–175).

See Also PART 1: OVERVIEW: NATIONS, TRIBES, AND OTHER NATIVE GROUPS: Northwest Coast Culture Area; **PART 2: CULTURAL FORMS: FOOD:** Agriculture; Fishing Culture, Pacific Northwest; Food Sovereignty; Food Sovereignty: Local and Regional Examples; **TRANSPORTATION AND HOUSING:** Longhouses (Pacific Northwest)

Further Reading

Lane, Barbara. "Political and Economic Aspects of Indian-White Culture Contact in Western Washington in the Mid-Nineteenth Century." May 10, 1973. Typescript in Muckleshoot Indian Tribe Preservation Program Archives.

Meeker, Ezra. *Pioneer Reminiscences of Puget Sound: The Tragedy of Leschi.* New York: Lowman & Hanford, 1905.

Smith, Marian W. *The Puyallup-Nisqually.* Columbia University Contributions in Anthropology. Volume 32. New York: Columbia University Press, 1940.

Waterman, T. T. *Notes on the Ethnology of the Indians of Puget Sound.* Indian Notes and Monographs. Misc. Series No. 59. New York: Museum of the American Indian/Heye Foundation, 1973.

FOODS AND MEDICINES FROM NATIVE AMERICAN CULTURES

History and Origins

A large proportion of foods consumed by world peoples today originated with Native Americans. Some are very well known, such as corn, potatoes, many kinds of melons, turkey, peanuts, and chocolate. Others' origins have largely been lost to popular history. Consider "Indian" (East Indian) curry. The spices that comprise it actually began as a chili in what is now Brazil. They were transported to India by Portuguese seamen, then mixed with Asian spices to produce the mixture we know today.

The domesticated fowl that would come to be called "turkey" in English was first eaten by Native Americans in the Valley of Mexico, including the Aztecs, who introduced it to invading Spaniards. By the time the Pilgrims reached Plymouth Rock, Massachusetts, in 1620, turkeys had been bred in Spain and exported to England for almost a century. The passengers of the *Mayflower* had some turkeys on board their ship, so when they prepared for the first Thanksgiving, the English immigrants were familiar with the wild turkeys that were hunted by Native American peoples in eastern North America. Wild American turkeys seemed larger and better tasting to many colonists than their European-bred brethren. They also were easy to hunt. Thomas Morton said that a hunter in early 17th-century New England could shoot one turkey while others nearby looked on: "The one being killed, the other sit fast neverthelesse" (Cronon, 1983, 23). By the late 20th century, wild turkeys were scarce in much of New England.

Regional Variations

Native Americans gathered the seeds of corn when it was a wild grass and selected for the most productive, hardiest varieties. By the time European immigrants made landfall in North America, corn was more productive per acre than any cereal crop in the Old World. Corn, along with squashes, beans, fish, venison (deer meat), and various "fowls" (probably turkeys, ducks, and geese) were consumed during the first Anglo-American thanksgiving. The abundance was welcomed by the Pilgrims, who had arrived in the New World with English seeds, most of which did not sprout in American soil. They nearly starved during their first winter. William Bradford, governor of the small colony, wrote in his diary that Squanto, who was able to teach the immigrants how to survive in their own language, was "a special instrument sent of God for [our] good" (Case, 2002).

American Indian Herbal Remedies

The use of herbal medicines has been an important part of Native American cultures for many thousands of years. Following sustained contact with Europeans after 1492, several American Indian medicines came into use in several other cultures as well. By the late 20th century, more than 200 drugs first used by American Indians were listed in the *United States Pharmacopoeia*, an official listing of medicines and their uses. These include quinine, laxatives, muscle relaxants, and nasal remedies, as well as several dozen drugs and herbal medicines. To this day, scientists are discovering more beneficial drugs in plants once known only to Native Americans. One reason that many people are concerned at the demise of the Amazon rainforests is that such destruction could keep us from learning more about the Native American uses of plants there.

A Navajo medicine man collecting medicinal plants, smelling the plant as he says a ritual prayer. (Nathan Benn/Ottochrome/Corbis)

Examples of American Indian herbal remedies are plentiful. For example, some Native Americans used foxglove (*Digitalis purpurea*) to treat heart problems. They administered it with extreme care because high doses are required and the plant can be extremely toxic if it is used incorrectly. American Indian healers developed a sophisticated system of medical treatment compared to European medical doctors several centuries ago, who relied on bloodletting, blistering, religious penance, as well as concoctions of lead, arsenic, and cow dung to treat various diseases. In addition to performing surgery, American Indians from several areas understood the importance of keeping wounds sterile as they used botanical antiseptics. They made syringes from bird bones and animal bladders to administer plant medicines.

Native peoples in the Americas had developed so many botanical medications by the time of contact that the Spanish king Philip II sent physician Francisco Hernando to the Americas in 1570 to record Aztec medical knowledge and bring it back to Europe. As early as 1635, after less than a generation in America, English colonists were using herbal medicines introduced to them by the Native peoples. "A Relation of Maryland," written to give prospective immigrants information on the new colony, included this passage:

This Countrey affords naturally, many excellent things for Physicke and Surgery, the perfect use of which, the English cannot yet learne from the Natives: They have a roote which is an excellent preservative against Pyson [poison], called by the English the Snake roote. Other herbes and roo-tes they have wherewith they cure all manners of wounds; also Saxafras, Gummes, and Balsum. An Indian seeing one of the English, much trou-bled with the tooth-ake, fetched of the roote of a tree, and gave the party some of it to hold in his mouth, and it eased the pain presently. (Birchfield, 1997, 705–706)

By the 18th century, European American observers, many of them mission-aries, were compiling lists of Native herbal remedies, some of which were pub-lished in several European languages. One of these lists carried to Europe the knowledge that the bark of a particular tree that grows in North America could alleviate toothache. The Canada shrubby elder could be used to combat fevers and inflammations. The jalap root could be used as a laxative and also to relieve the pain of rheumatism; the ipecacuanha also functioned as an enematic, as well as an antidote to snakebite. Peter Kalm, the Swedish botanist, visited the Mid-dle Atlantic states between 1748 and 1750 to catalog Native medicinal herbs.

Captain John Smith learned through Pocahontas that her people applied a root that she called *wighsacan* to wounds for its healing power. John Lawson, visiting the Carolinas about 1700, observed that Natives there chewed a root (which he did not name) to soothe stomach ailments. European observers also wrote of Indians who committed suicide by eating certain roots and mush-rooms. William Penn wrote that a Delaware woman who had been betrayed by her husband "went out, plunk't a Root out of the Ground, and ate it, upon which she immediately died" (Birchfield, 1997, 706). Native peoples often warned Europeans which plants, if eaten, could make them ill, produce skin rashes, or kill them. In some cases, Native peoples also provided antidotes. The Delawares, for example, dealt with the rash produced by contact with poison sumac by preparing a tea from the inner bark of the sour gum tree, which gave off a distinctive odor that caused Native peoples to compare it to raw fish.

Some Native plant remedies became popular among Europeans based on the evidence obtained by observation, while others took Europe by storm on the basis of unsupported health claims. Use of sassafras root (the "saxafras" in the "Relation of Maryland," above) was noted as early as Shakespeare's time. The use of sassafras tea spread throughout Europe as a general health tonic, and a trading network grew up across the Atlantic specializing in its harvest, sale, and transport. At about the same time, all sorts of extravagant claims were being made for the tonic effects of tobacco that do not stand up to scientific scrutiny. Tobacco was said to aid digestion, cure toothaches, kill nits and lice, and even stop coughing. The advocates of tobacco seemed to draw their advice from Native peoples who often used tobacco as a ceremonial herb, and who only very rarely became addicted to nicotine.

Most Native American peoples used the by-products of animals, as well as plants, for medicinal and cosmetic purposes. English immigrants in Virginia and Massachusetts learned early that an emollient of bear grease allowed Native people to range in the woods wearing a minimum of clothing on hot summer days without being bitten by mosquitoes and other stinging insects. Goose grease and bear fat were widely used as hair dressings, and skunk oil was sometimes applied to the chest and throat to relieve the symptoms of colds, including chest congestion. The Delawares sometimes slowed the flow of blood from a cut by inserting spider webs, which probably helped with the clotting of blood.

Witch hazel is a commonly used Native botanical remedy that has been adopted generally by Euro-American society. Used as a first-aid treatment for insect bites and cuts, witch hazel is the distilled extract of the witch hazel bush combined with alcohol. The shrub grows commonly in the eastern United States; its leaves were boiled and applied to bites and cuts by many Native peoples in that area. The root and leaves of the wintergreen contain methyl salicylate, which is used today in creams and other forms to treat rheumatic pain, muscular aches, and similar ailments. Salicylic acid is the main active ingredient of aspirin, probably the most widely used relief for minor pain in the late 20th century. The inner bark of the white pine (the national symbol of the Iroquois Confederacy) today is used in cough syrups. Terpin hydrate, a prescription drug used to treat coughs and colds, is derived from the sap of pine trees (turpentine). The Indians also were the first people to utilize caffeine as a stimulant.

Tobacco was one of many herbal weapons in the arsenal of Native "medicine men," or shamans, across the continent. The role of the medicine man had no direct counterpart in Europe. The various Native names for the persons who performed these functions can be translated as shaman, juggler, conjurer, sorcerer, priest, and physician, as well as "medicine man." Even the translation of Native words that correspond to "medicine" in English can be tricky, because Western culture has no single term that incorporates all the aspects of the shaman's work. Whereas "medicine" in English connotes treatment of a disease with a drug or other specific remedy, a "medicine man" was a spiritualist, as well as a person who had learned the basics of physical medicine and herbal cures. Native shamans combined the art of mental suggestion with physical cures as well; the mental attitude of the "patient" was often considered as important as any physical cure. The casting of spells (and other practices of sorcery) had as much to do with a person's state of mind as with physical and biological reactions.

See Also PART 2: CULTURAL FORMS: FOOD: Agriculture; Spotlight: Examples of Foods Native to the Americas and Spotlight: Native American Vegetal Remedies Used Today; Food Sovereignty; Food Sovereignty: Local and Regional Examples; TRANSPORTATION AND HOUSING: Longhouses (Pacific Northwest)

Further Reading

Birchfield, D. L. *The Encyclopedia of North American Indians*. Vol. 5. New York: Marshall Cavendish, 1997.

Case, Nancy Humphrey. "Gifts from the Indians: Native Americans Not Only Provided New Kinds of Food and Recreation; They May Have Given the Founding Fathers Ideas on How to Form a Government." *Christian Science Monitor*, November 26, 2002. http://www.csmonitor.com. Accessed October 30, 2014.

Cronon, William. *Changes in the Land: Indians, Colonists, and the Ecology of New England*. New York: Hill and Wang, 1983.

Crosby, Alfred W. *The Columbian Exchange: Biological and Cultural Consequences of 1492*. New York: Greenwood Press, 1972.

Edwards, Everett E. "The Contributions of American Indians to Civilization." *Minnesota History* 15, no. 3 (1934): 255–272.

Forbes, Jack. *The Indian in America's Past*. New York: Prentice-Hall, 1964.

Frachtenberg, Leo J. "Our Indebtedness to the American Indian." *Wisconsin Archeologist* 14, no. 2 (1915): 64–69.

Keoke, Emory Dean, and Kay Marie Porterfield. *Encyclopedia of American Indian Contributions to the World*. New York: Facts on File, 2002.

Kraus, Michael. *The Atlantic Civilization: Eighteenth Century Origins*. New York: Russell & Russell, 1949.

Selsam, Millicent. *Plants That Heal*. New York: William Morrow, 1959.

Weatherford, Jack. *Indian Givers: How the Indians of the Americas Transformed the World*. New York: Fawcett Columbine, 1988.

Weatherford, Jack. *Native Roots: How the Indians Enriched America*. New York: Crown, 1991.

Spotlight

EXAMPLES OF FOODS NATIVE TO THE AMERICAS

Asparagus
Avocados
Beans, green and yellow
Blueberries
Cassava (tapioca)
Chewing gum (Chicle)

Chocolate (Cacao)

Corn

Corn products such as hominy, cornstarch, and cornmeal

Cranberries

Cucumbers

Currants

Leeks

Maple sugar and syrup

Mint and mint flavorings

Peanuts and peanut products

Pecans

Peppers, green and red

Popcorn

Potatoes and potato products

Sassafras tea

Squashes (including pumpkins, watermelon, yams, and cantaloupe)

Sunflower seeds

Turkey

Vanilla

Venison

Wild rice

Spotlight

NATIVE AMERICAN VEGETAL REMEDIES USED TODAY

Balm of Gilead: Mixed with cream to form a balm for sores.

Blackberry: Roots (as tea) said to cure dysentery.

Black haw: Liquid boiled from bark; relieves stomach and menstrual cramps.

Black walnut: Tea boiled from bark relieves severe colds.

Catnip: Tea from the leaves may quiet a restless baby.

Corn silk: As tea, to combat pain caused by kidney trouble.

Dogwood: Tea from the roots serves as a general tonic.

Elder: Tea made from flowers relieves colic in children.

Elm (American or white): Liquid from steeping the inner bark in water relieves symptoms of flu, such as coughs and chills. Elm is also used as a poultice for gun-shot wounds. (General Washington's army used it during the Revolutionary War.)

Fishweed (Jerusalem artichoke): A tea of its leaves may rid children of worms.

Flannel mullein: Heated leaves in a compress provide relief from rheumatic pains.

Hogweed (ragweed): The root is a strong laxative.

Hops: Leaves (in a tea) relieve symptoms of a cold, or (as a compress) relieve pain.

Jimson weed: Heated leaves relieve pain of burns; not to be taken internally.

Morning glory: A tea of the leaves relieves some types of stomach pain.

Peach: Crushed leaves used as a compress reduces swelling.

Peppermint: Boiled leaves sometimes relieve stomach pains.

Prickly ash: Tea made from the bark relieves symptoms of colds; the bark and root can be used to relieve toothache pain.

Sassafras: A tea may reduce high blood pressure.

Tobacco: A soft wad of chewed tobacco will reduce the pain of a bee sting.

Watermelon: Tea from boiled seeds may relieve the pain of kidney trouble.

White oak: Liquid steeped from bark helps heal cuts and scratches.

Wild grape: Juice conditions hair and scalp.

Wild strawberry: Crushed fruit applied to face may improve complexion.

Yarrow: Crushed roots boiled as tea reduces excessive menstrual flow.

FOOD SOVEREIGNTY

History and Origins

Native Americans are reclaiming their traditional diets, as well as reconstructing age-old agricultural systems. Often, the "food empowerment movement" is taking place collectively, in a conscious effort to bring the era of commodity cheese to a close. Along the way, Native peoples also are finding that maintaining sustainable traditional agriculture also requires fending off environmental challenges, from proposed mines to a galaxy of contaminants in country food and fish.

Remarked Kim Severson in the "Dining and Wine" section of the *New York Times*:

> One result is the start of a new sort of native culinary canon that rejects oily fry bread but embraces wild rice from Minnesota, salmon from Alaska and the Northwest, persimmons and papaws from the Southeast, corn from New York, bison from the Great Plains and dozens of squashes, beans, berries and melons. . . . Modern urban menus are beginning to feature three sisters soup, built from the classic Indian trilogy of beans, squash and corn.

At the Mitsitam Cafe, opened last year in the National Museum of the American Indian in Washington, cooks create dishes with roasted salmon, chilies and buffalo meat. (Severson, 2005)

Bushmeat, fish, and berries may have been the original low-carb diet. Generous portions of protein, low carbohydrates, and high fiber may be the latest dietary avant-garde trend, but there's nothing new here. The hunter-gatherer's diet was highly 21st-century politically correct—rich in polyunsaturated and monounsaturated fatty acids but relatively low in overall fat and very low in that dietary villain—saturated fat.

For people who lived without modern health and dental care, hunter-gatherers seemed to have been relatively healthy. The Weston A. Price Foundation noted "an almost complete absence of tooth decay and dental deformities among Native Americans who lived as their ancestors did. They had broad faces, straight teeth and fine physiques. This was true of the nomadic tribes living in the far northern territories of British Columbia and the Yukon" (Fallon and Enig, n.d.). Most of the diseases that have afflicted Native Americans set in after contact with Europeans. These included diabetes and alcoholism, as well as more devastating pathogens such as smallpox.

Major problems with internal organs, such as the gall bladder, kidney, stomach, and appendix, tend not to occur among people on a traditional Native diet. The same problems are very common, however, among the same peoples when they consume a diet of commodities. Traditional Native diets were fashioned from whatever nature offered in any particular locale. Most were heavy on bushmeat (including fish) and berries, as well as cultivated foods, including corn, beans, squash, and others. Range-fed meat often was much lower in fat than the feedlot products sold today. Pemmican (a variation of which is sold in some grocery stores today) combined meat with berries, crushed and dried for easy transport.

Regional Variations

Traditionally, Native food systems have been community-based, as people shared in clearing, planting, harvesting, and other endeavors. Today, the First Nations Development Institute has been applying this collective spirit on a continental level to rebuild Native American agricultural systems, using its Food Summits to convene people who will return home to improve local food production efforts. Native governments are among the largest agricultural landowners in the United States, but much of their land has been leased to non-Indians. The Indian Land Working Group, among other organizations, seeks to consolidate holdings lost to allotment and to increase the number of Native Americans making productive uses of this land in the market economy.

A food system redevelopment program has been revitalizing the production and distribution of traditional Tohono O'odham foods in an effort to combat the diabetes that is devastating its community. In 1960, no tribal member had ever suffered from the disease; by the year 2000, more than half of the population had type 2 diabetes, the highest rate in the world. The loss of a sustainable food system is the primary cause of the epidemic. Traditional Tohono O'odham foods have been shown to regulate blood sugar levels, thereby helping prevent and regulate diabetes.

Support has been expressed for efforts to integrate local agricultural efforts with the Food Distribution Program on Indian Reservations (FDPIR), heretofore best known for pumping reservation stomachs full of surplus commodity cheese. Native farmers have been asking why this federal program can't buy local produce, benefiting both producers and consumers. This is one of a number of proposals aimed at making the U.S. Department of Agriculture a partner in the development of Native food production systems.

Contemporary Forms and Nutritional Benefits of Traditional Foods

Traditional Native American diets have many nutritional advantages over a fast-food diet that has become overloaded with refined sugar and fats, and that is low in fiber and complex carbohydrates. Native peoples have come to realize that many diseases that plague them in today's world, such as type 2 diabetes, are diet-induced. The Diabetes Talking Circle in Winnebago, Nebraska, "provides a local forum for discussing issues related to diabetes and helps reduce fatalistic attitudes" (Dewees, 2003, 4).

Many traditional foods (examples are wild greens, berries, and several varieties of beans) are slow to digest and loaded with vitamins and fiber. Foods that digest slowly also impede release of glucose and insulin, which are a primary cause of diabetes. In contrast, foods heavy on refined sugar (such as soda pop, white bread, and potatoes), break down into sugar in the bloodstream quickly. A traditional diet also lowers cholesterol, reducing the incidence of heart disease, strokes, and some cancers, as well as high blood pressure and obesity, which are endemic on Indian reservations where commodity food has been a major part of people's diets. (Higher fiber foods, since they are slow to digest, help to control appetite.) Enrique Salmón writes in *Eating the Landscape: American Indian Stories of Food, Identity, and Resilience* (2012), "Cancer and ulcers are virtually unheard of for people who subsist primarily on traditional foods" (p. 79).

Traditional Mohawks and other Haudenosaunee (Iroquois) have such a high regard for berries that they are regarded as sacred; thanksgivings were given in their names, especially the wild strawberry, the first berry food to appear in the spring, which is eaten as a blood purifier. Elderberries, red raspberry, and tender sumac berry sprouts are also used for their blood-building properties. "Wild berries remind us of our childhood," wrote Mohawk Katsi Cook. "Indeed, they are a special gift of Creation to the children and to women. Over 250 species of berries and fruits—strawberry, red raspberry, currant, elderberry, juniper berry, cranberry, bearberry, to name a few—in Native America are gathered and utilized for their nutritional and medicinal value" (Cook, n.d.). Berries are eaten raw; crushed and mixed with water and maple syrup or honey for drinks; mixed with soups, bread, puddings, and meats; and dried for winter storage. The berries, leaves, and roots can be collected and used together or separately and drunk as a medicinal tea. Wild berries are very rich in vitamin C, a water-soluble nutrient that detoxifies the body, promotes healing, strengthens connective tissue, helps to absorb iron, and cooperates with the B vitamin complex in maintaining the endocrine system. A severe deficiency of vitamin C leads to scurvy, a disease that was common in Europe, where it was attributed to "bad air." Native peoples of North America had already recognized the dietary basis of the disease, and they knew how to prevent and cure it with a variety of medicines from natural sources. Cranberries are antiscorbutic, meaning that they are effective in preventing and treating scurvy. They can be used alone or in combination with other berries like sumac berry and other natural sources high in vitamin C like the fresh, new tips of evergreens.

Berries also benefit the urinary tract. They act as diuretics, promoting the flow of urine. They also acidify the urine to create a hostile environment for bacteria. Cranberry and bearberry have long been used in the treatment of cystitis (urinary bladder infection). Berries also have astringent properties, meaning that they cause contraction of tissue and arrest bleeding. In this capacity, they are proven remedies for diarrhea. Blackberry root in combination with wild strawberry leaves has long been known as an effective remedy for diarrhea.

"Still today," wrote Cook, "Indian women and children prize the various wild berries that grow in our territories and we will travel long distances and make camp and harvest those berries which aren't quite as near to home. We join our elders in their lament that gravel pits and concrete are causing the berry and other plants to turn their faces from the people and disappear" (Cook, n.d.).

Food sovereignty can use dried berries to tap old standards and provide an economic opportunity as well. An example is Karlene Hunter and Mark

Karlene Hunter and Mark Tilsen, owners of Native American Natural Foods, display Tanka Bars in Rapid City, South Dakota. The company, based on the Pine Ridge Indian Reservation, makes Tanka Bars from buffalo and cranberry. (AP Photo)

Tilsen's Native American Natural Foods, which has launched the Tanka line, some of which have been sold at Whole Foods, REI, and other retail stores across the United States. Their buffalo and cranberry Tanka Bar is based on an Oglala Lakota recipe called *wasna*, which was packed on buffalo hunts (often stored in buffalo horns) until the 19th century. "Diabetes and obesity are at record levels among my people," Hunter said. "And our leadership and health professionals are working hard to reverse those trends" (Hunter, 2013, 63). Hunter said that the buffalo raised for use in Native American Natural Foods products contain no antibiotics, hormones, preservatives, or other residual drugs.

The Native American Food Systems Project

The Native American Food Systems Project—a collaborative effort between the Northwest Indian Applied Research Institute, South Puget Intertribal Planning Agency, and Evergreen State College in Olympia, Washington—is designed to assist tribal communities in addressing serious nutrition and health problems. The project encourages Native peoples in the Puget Sound area to return to production and consumption of the healthy, traditional foods enjoyed by their ancestors, before the Food Distribution Program on Indian Reservations brought them surplus commodities, including those infamous bricks of government cheese. Native nutrition is familiar to many Native peoples in the Pacific Northwest, who are only two or three generations removed from diets based on game animals and fish, a time when obesity, diabetes, and heart disease, all common today, were rare.

The Native American Food Systems Project started with a Native American food production and marketing conference sponsored by the Northwest Indian Applied Research Institute during 1998. Nutritionists, health workers, elders, and other interested individuals congregated from several Western states to discuss everything from the ecological restoration of Native crops to greenhouse production on reservations. Alan Parker, executive director of the institute, hired Alysha Waters, an expert in the organic food industry, to direct the project and develop programs. An Anishinaabe of the Great Lakes area in Michigan, Waters said, "Cutting-edge research is indicating that because Native Americans' and other Indigenous people's diets were so rapidly switched to industrialized processed diets ... they have not had time to adapt. Traditional foods really need to come back into play to deal [with] some of that" (Montana, 2000).

Working with members of the Shoalwater Bay, Nisqually, Skokomish, Squaxin Island, and Chehalis peoples, Waters helped design program models for intergenerational gardens, foraging programs, health and nutrition education, support groups, medicinal plant reserves, ecological restoration, and the development of Native American food product lines. Nutritionists, gardeners, and marketing educators from Evergreen State College also provided assistance.

Carmen Kalama, community services manager for the South Puget Intertribal Planning Agency and a Nisqually tribal member, said that she is excited about the traditional food program and how it has helped her people culturally. "For a lot of us, just like in a lot of places, we don't know the language or we know very little of our traditions because they just haven't been carried on," Kalama said. "I would say the same thing for a lot of our traditional foods and plants. Growing your traditional foods and assisting your tribal members in incorporating those things back into their diet ... results in more healthy communities and it ... creates awareness in the youth" (Montana, 2000).

See Also PART 2: CULTURAL FORMS: FOOD: Food Sovereignty: Local and Regional Examples/Spotlight: Seed Recovery: The Iroquois White Corn Project and Spotlight: Frybread; Wild Rice

Further Reading

Cook, Katsi. "Using the Berry Plants for Nutrition and Medicine." *Indians.org*. http://www.indians.org/welker/berry.htm. Accessed May 10, 2014.

Dewees, Sarah. *Native Food Summit: November 15–17, Albuquerque, New Mexico. Time for Harvest: Renewing Native Food Systems. Summit Report*. Fredericksburg, VA: Native Assets Research Center, First Nations Development Institute, 2003.

Fallon, Sally, and Mary G. Enig. "Guts and Grease: The Diet of Native Americans." *The Weston A. Price Foundation*. http://www.westonaprice.org/traditional_diets/native_americans.html. Accessed May 7, 2014.

Hunter, Karlene. "Self-Determination: A Path to Health and Economic Opportunity." *Native Peoples* (May–June 2013): 63.

InterTribal Bison Cooperative. Home Page. 2004. http://www.intertribalbison.org/main.asp?id=6&archive=33. Accessed October 30, 2014.

Iroquois White Corn Project. April, 2004. http://www.pub.naz.edu:9000/~ethnobot/ebot2003/kevinwhite/cornproject/cornproject.htm. Accessed October 30, 2014.

Kummer, Corby. "Going with the Grain: True Wild Rice, for the Past Twenty Years Nearly Impossible to Find, Is Slowly Being Nurtured Back to Market." *The Atlantic Monthly*, May 2004, 145–148.

Montana, Cate. "Project Develops Native American Food Systems Models." *Indian Country Today*, August 30, 2000. http://www.indiancountry.com/?2482. Accessed October 30, 2014.

Salmón, Enrique. *Eating the Landscape: American Indian Stories of Food, Identity, and Resilience*. Tucson: University of Arizona Press, 2012.

Severson, Kim. "Native Foods Nourish Again." *New York Times*, November 23, 2005. http://www.nytimes.com/2005/11/23/dining/23nati.html. Accessed October 30, 2014.

FOOD SOVEREIGNTY: LOCAL AND REGIONAL EXAMPLES

The Pimas and Tohono O'odham (Papago) Rediscover Desert Fare

The Pimas and Tohono O'odham (Papago) of Arizona have been rediscovering the desert foods their people routinely ate as recently as the 1940s, extending their cultural roots along the way. This rediscovery has been prompted by the realization that the present-day diet of the North American mainstream is making many of them sick. Where once most of them were lean, now many weigh 200 to 300 pounds, fattened by carbohydrate-laden commodity foods.

As many as half of the Pimas and Tohono O'odham have been developing diabetes by the age of 35, an incidence 15 times higher than for the United States, on average. Before 1940, diabetes was nearly unknown among them.

Increasingly, they are returning to nature's table, where one tablespoon of buds from the cholla cactus contains as much calcium as eight ounces of milk. The buds also are rich in soluble fiber that helps regulate blood sugar. A return to such desert fare, along with traditional beans, corn, grains, greens, and other low-fat, high-fiber plant foods can normalize blood sugar, suppress between-meal hunger, and probably also aid in weight loss, while helping to alleviate high blood pressure and heart disease.

Along with the buds of the cholla, the Pimas and Tohono O'odham have been rediscovering the edible parts of such indigenous plants as mesquite and prickly pear cactus, as well as tepary beans, chia seeds, and acorns from live oaks. Elders recall these foods, which have been all but forgotten among younger people who eat mainly hamburgers, fries, soft drinks, and other fatty, sugary, overly refined fast and packaged foods.

As recently as the 1930s, Tohono O'odham farmers grew more than 1.5 million pounds of tepary beans a year. None of them had even so much as heard of diabetes. By the year 2000 the beans had become scarce, and more than half of the Tohono O'odham adults had diabetes, most of which was attributed to poor diet. Noland Johnson by 2005 was harvesting 14,000 pounds of tepary beans per year, selling them for about $2.50 a pound at small stores on the reservation. The beans look a little like flattened black-eyed peas. The white ones cook up creamy. The brown ones may be simmered like pinto beans.

Tepary beans also are rich in fiber and drought-resistant, the only cultivated beans with heat-resistant enzymes that can withstand the climate of the Sonoran Desert. Like mesquite pods, teparies are rich in protein, iron, and calcium. Amaranth, called "pigweed" by some gardeners, thrives in the desert, producing edible greens and seeds, both rich in calcium. The seeds are rich in high-quality protein. Protein-rich chia seeds come from a salvia plant that produces two crops a year. When mixed with water, the fiber in chia forms a gel that lowers cholesterol and stabilizes blood-sugar levels.

Home cooks pay as much as $9.50 a pound for teparies online. Big-city chefs are in love with the little beans, too, turning them into cassoulets, salads, or beds for braised local pork. Johnson began farming beans partly as a tribute to his grandfather, who died from complications related to diabetes. He always saves some beans for his grandmother, who likes to simmer the white ones with oxtail. "I see my grandmother telling her friends, 'Yeah, I can get some beans for you,'" Johnson said. "The elders, they're so glad to see them" (Severson, 2005).

Native peoples of the Southwest also have been rediscovering acorns from live oaks, which can be eaten whole or ground into meal to help maintain stable blood-sugar levels. While the sweet corn consumed by most Americans contains rapidly digested starches and sugars (which raise sugar levels in the blood) the hominy-type corn of the traditional Indian diet contains little sugar, and its starch is slowly digested. Commodity pinto beans that the federal government gives to the Indians (along with lard, refined wheat flour, sugar, coffee, and processed cereals) are far more rapidly digested than local tepary beans. Government food programs replaced the tepary bean, which is rich in fiber, protein, iron, and calcium, with the pinto bean. Mesquite, which occupies 70 million acres in the American Southwest, is considered a pesky weed by many Anglos, but it grows nutritious pods that have a natural caramel-like sweetness. Mesquite pods, which are 40 percent protein, also are good sources of calcium, manganese, iron, and zinc. Mesquite flour ground from the pods produces fructose, which can be processed without insulin, and soluble fibers, which are slowly absorbed, without a rapid rise in blood sugar.

Carolyn J. Niethammer has authored *American Indian Food and Lore* and *The Tumbleweed Gourmet*, a cookbook published by the University of Arizona Press. Gary Paul Nabhan, a professor at Northern Arizona University, directs Native Seeds/SEARCH (Southwestern Endangered Arid-lands Resource Clearing House), founded to preserve Native plants in the Southwest and northwestern Mexico, which is studying the value of Native desert foods for controlling diabetes among Indians and Hispanic Americans of the border region. The group, housed on the grounds of the Tucson Botanical Gardens, teaches health professionals about Native foods and promotes their use through school and community programs, seed distribution, and cooking instruction. In 2004, Nabhan started RAFT (Renewing America's Food Traditions), a coalition of seven nonprofit food, agricultural, and conservation organizations, which has published a "red list" of 700 endangered American foods, including heritage turkeys and Louisiana Creole cream cheese.

The Intertribal Bison Cooperative

The Intertribal Bison Cooperative (ITBC) dates from February 1991, when people who raise buffalo from 19 Native American nations met in the Black Hills with the common purpose of restoring bison to Indian nations in a manner that is compatible with Native spiritual and cultural beliefs and practices. The systematic raising of buffalo across the plains and prairies of North America has recovered since more than 60 million were slaughtered during the 19th century in an organized effort to cripple the independent Native economy that was based on them. The buffalo therefore have long been an important symbol of a broader Native resurgence, with important implications for sovereignty, self-sufficiency, and independence. Members of the cooperative understand that reintroduction of the buffalo to Native lands will help heal the spirits of Native people and the buffalo.

Although some Native peoples have been engaged in the production of buffalo for sale, subsistence, and cultural use, these activities until 1991 were conducted by each individual group with little or no collaboration. Congress appropriated funding for tribal bison programs in June 1991. The cooperative met again during December 1991 to discuss how these appropriations should be spent. At this meeting, plans were discussed to help existing bison herders expand and develop into successful, self-sufficient programs.

Fred DuBray has been executive director of the cooperative at its national office in Rapid City, South Dakota, since early in 2002. DuBray, an enrolled Cheyenne River Sioux, one of the founders of the cooperative, also has been executive director of Pte Hca Ka, Inc., the Cheyenne River Sioux bison program, the largest tribal bison operation in the United States.

By 2004, ITBC had a membership of 42 tribes with a collective herd of over 8,000 bison. The ITBC is a nonprofit organization that is committed to reestablishing buffalo herds on Indian lands in a manner that promotes cultural enhancement, spiritual revitalization, ecological restoration, and economic development.

The ITBC is governed by a board of directors comprised of one tribal representative from each member tribe. The role of the ITBC, as established by its membership, is to act as a facilitator in coordinating education and training programs, developing marketing strategies, coordinating the transfer of surplus buffalo from national parks to tribal lands, and providing technical assistance to its membership.

Traditional Foods for Elders at White Earth

On the White Earth Anishinaabe reservation in Minnesota, the White Earth Land Recovery Project (WELRP) maintains a program called Mino-Miijim, which delivers wild rice and other traditional foods, such as hominy and buffalo meat, to elderly people who are afflicted with type 2 diabetes. The program was initiated by Winona LaDuke (known nationally as Ralph Nader's vice presidential candidate on the Green Party ticket in 1996 and 2000) and Margaret Smith, a former teacher. The program is meant to substitute traditional foods for high-fat fast foods and government commodities that contribute to diabetes. "Oh," a tribal member exclaimed to one WELRP intern who accompanied Smith on her monthly delivery route, "Here come the good commodities" (Kummer, 2004, 148).

The White Earth Land Recovery Project also offers an Internet organic foods catalog (http://www.welrp.org/nativeharvest/itemjelly.html) containing wild rice, maple syrup, maple candy, maple butter, hominy, raspberries, plum jelly, strawberry jam, strawberry and raspberry teas, and buffalo sausage. Each product is explained in a Native cultural context.

A Community Garden

A community garden on the Muckleshoot reservation near Seattle is part of a broader effort to reclaim a traditional diet. The Muckleshoot Food Sovereignty Project, which was funded for two years by the U.S. Department of Agriculture and supported by Northwest Indian College's Traditional Plants and Foods Program, has identified more than 300 types of fish, shellfish, berries, and greens that people ate before the advent of government commodities programs that emphasized processed foods, such as the ubiquitous blocks of "commod cheese" that so many Native people came to know so well. A fatty, heavily processed diet has been linked to epidemic levels of diabetes, heart disease, and other problems among Native people, including Muckleshoots.

"The foods that were eaten here were a pillar of our culture," said Valerie Segrest, a Muckleshoot and Native nutrition educator at the college who heads the food sovereignty project at the college. Along the way, some traditional foods have taken contemporary twists, such as elk burgers and huckleberry smoothies, kelp pickles, rosehip jam, and nettle pesto. "We're sick of being sick," Segrest said. "We know that diabetes was nonexistent in our communities one hundred years ago, because we ate these [traditional] foods" (Minard, 2012, 8). Muckleshoot Tribal Schools hold regular "culture nights" for the community, including one on April 12, 2012, that emphasized traditional foods.

Further Reading

Cook, Katsi. "Using the Berry Plants for Nutrition and Medicine." *Indians.org.* http://www.indians.org/welker/berry.htm. Accessed May 10, 2014.

Dewees, Sarah. *Native Food Summit: November 15–17, Albuquerque, New Mexico. Time for Harvest: Renewing Native Food Systems. Summit Report.* Fredericksburg, VA: Native Assets Research Center, First Nations Development Institute, 2003.

Fallon, Sally, and Mary G. Enig. "Guts and Grease: The Diet of Native Americans." *The Weston A. Price Foundation.* http://www.westonaprice.org/traditional_diets/native_americans.html. Accessed May 7, 2014.

Kummer, Corby. "Going with the Grain: True Wild Rice, for the Past Twenty Years Nearly Impossible to Find, Is Slowly Being Nurtured Back to Market." *The Atlantic Monthly*, May 2004, 145–148.

Minard, Anne. "Food Empowerment: The Muckleshoot Tribe Reintroduces Traditional Fare." *Indian Country Today* in *Muckleshoot Monthly*, March 15, 2012, 8.

Montana, Cate. "Project Develops Native American Food Systems Models." *Indian Country Today*, August 30, 2000. http://www.indiancountry.com/?2482. Accessed October 30, 2014.

Severson, Kim. "Native Foods Nourish Again." *New York Times*, November 23, 2005. http://www.nytimes.com/2005/11/23/dining/23nati.html. Accessed October 30, 2014.

Spotlight

SEED RECOVERY: THE IROQUOIS WHITE CORN PROJECT

The Pinewoods Community Farming Project was created in 1997 as the brain-child of Professor John Mohawk at State University of New York at Buffalo. This "Ma and Pa" organization began with the hope that Native Americans once again would begin to use and appreciate the Iroquois white corn that for so long had been their traditional food. John Mohawk, who is Seneca, had long been an advocate of Iroquois white corn. This corn is renowned for its slow-released carbohydrates. These carbohydrates can be crucial in the fight against diabetes, a disease that has reached epidemic proportions in the Native American community. The project has specialized in recovering and using heirloom seed for various kinds of Iroquois corn.

The white corn project has grown quickly. The original restaurant situated in the Cattaraugus Reservation is still open. There the corn is hulled and milled after being collected by various Iroquois farmers. Mohawk realized that if the corn is healthy for Native Americans, there might also be a market among non-Native Americans. Not only have the health benefits warranted interest but also the earthy aroma and unusual flavor. In a society where we expect our corn to be unnaturally sweet, this corn has grown a sort of cult following. It has been such a sensation that the project has recently attained national coverage and praise on the pages of *Gourmet* magazine.

Iroquois white corn may be used in many ways. Two flours can be made from it, according to Mohawk. The corn flour's hulls are removed by roasting. Then the flour can be used as a healthy substitute for white and wheat bread. Tamales can be made from it, as can pancakes, stuffing, and muffins. Master chef Bobby Flay has recently added the products to his personal line. The corn can be used in essentially every dish as common sweet corn. It also adds a unique flavor that can bring new life to ordinary dishes.

The leaders of the project have not forgotten their goals at home, even while expanding nationally. At a Native American historical site, Ganondagan, New York, the project has supplied Iroquois white corn for festivals and pageants. By supplying the corn, they are teaching people what they are missing. Local growers are encouraged to share their knowledge of the crop. Currently, mainly men have showed interest in the project, but efforts have been made to include women.

The group operates a small restaurant in Gowanda, New York. Here diners may sample many of the ways that white corn can be prepared. The menu includes corn and bean soups and chili made with buffalo meat. Diners also may sample meals with all of the three components of the Iroquois diet represented, known as the "Three Sisters": beans, corn, and squash.

FRYBREAD

Native Americans today sometimes wax nostalgic about frybread and commodity cheese, two staples of Indian humor. According to an old reservation joke: "You could be Indian if you think that the four basic food groups are Spam, commodity cheese, frybread, and Pepsi." In fact, frybread is what creative minds and hungry stomachs came up with after the buffalo had been slaughtered, guns and horses had been seized, and all the residents of open-air concentration camps had to eat (and eat with) was a fire, a skillet, lard, and white flour, often of questionable quality. Frybread also was the Native introduction to a diet of "commods"—government-provided surplus food—and all the health problems associated with it, beginning with diabetes, which is still epidemic in Indian Country.

Further Reading

Ellis, Clyde, Luke Eric Lassiter, and Gary H. Dunham, eds. *Powwow*. Lincoln: University of Nebraska Press, 2005.

Hobsbawm, Eric. "Introduction: Inventing Traditions." In Eric Hobsbawm and Terence Ranger, eds. *The Invention of Tradition*. Cambridge: Cambridge University Press, 1983, 1–14.

Thomas, Robert K. "Pan-Indianism." *Midcontinent American Studies Journal* 6, no. 2 (1965): 75–83.

WILD RICE

History and Origins

Wild rice, the only grain indigenous to North America, has been harvested for thousands of years by Native peoples from the shores of shallow, glacial lakes in areas bordering on the Great Lakes eastward to Maine. Many of the wild rice beds have been lost to recreational development and dredging, so areas still harvested by Native peoples today center on Minnesota. Wild rice (called *manomin*, or "good berry" by the Ojibwe) is a major traditional food staple for Native peoples in areas where it is grown, and it is regarded as sacred. Many locations in Indiana, Illinois, Michigan, Manitoba, Ontario, Wisconsin, Minnesota, and

Saskatchewan are named in part after the Ojibwe name for wild rice, two examples being Menomonie and Minnesota. As a dried whole grain, wild rice is high in protein, lysine, and dietary fiber, as well as riboflavin, potassium, iron, thiamin, niacin, folate, magnesium, zinc, manganese, and phosphorus.

Regional Variations

The cultivation of wild rice has long been vital to the culture of the Ojibwe (Anishinaabe), especially in present-day Minnesota with its many lakes. Their oral history says they moved to Minnesota from the east to avoid death, and that a prophet told them to settle in a place where food—wild rice—grows over the water.

When reservations were created, the Native peoples requested land around lakes with wild rice beds. From antiquity, people have said prayers, then set out in canoes, two by two. One "pulls" (propels and steers) a canoe with an 18- to 20-foot pole as the other "knocks," bringing down the rice into the boat with a yard-long cedar stick. The canoe cannot be paddled because the lake's surface is thick with plants and fallen rice. Propelling the canoe requires quite a bit of physical strength.

Wild rice germinates in the muddy bottoms of lakes and streams during the spring, reaching the water's surface in June. By August and September, seed-bearing shoots have reached several feet in height, at which point the "rice" is "knocked" into canoes. The best years are dry—but not so droughty that lake bottoms cannot be navigated. The size of knockers are set by state and tribal statutes. In Minnesota, they must be one inch in diameter, not more than a pound in weight, and 30 inches in length. The plants are brushed to dislodge the grain.

After the harvest, the rice is packaged in gunnysacks and taken to a processor, where it is laid out to dry and then parched. Once Indians danced on the rice to shake off the shells; later, a "basher" was invented to do the work by machine. The hulled rice is then sorted by size. The harvest is always concluded with a feast. "We feast all of our harvests," said White Earth Anishinaabe Winona LaDuke. "We have a big thanksgiving feast for the first rice, and we have a big dance. We have a wild rice dance starting in August. We also have our ceremonies and our powwows" (LaDuke, 2008, 2087).

Contemporary Forms

The size of the wild harvest has been declining steadily. In 1968, the Minnesota Department of Natural Resources issued 16,000 licenses, but that number declined to less than 2,000 after 1996, plus as many as 3,000 Native people who do not require licenses to harvest on reservation waters. At one time college students harvested wild rice to pay their way through school, but "wild" rice farming has depressed what people get for the rice. During the 1950s and 1960s, 15 million pounds were harvested in a good year, 15 times what was being taken after 2000.

Minnesota declared wild rice its state grain in 1977, just as it was being raised more often on a mass-production model. Soon, however, most of the industry moved to California, where large companies raised it in paddies with copious application of herbicides and fertilizers for machine harvest. The resulting product is more like commercial white rice than the crunchy grain that Indians cull in the wild. "The domesticated paddy rice doesn't taste like a lake," LaDuke said. "It tastes like a paddy" (2008, 208). Some states (one is Minnesota) have laws that require the packaging to specify whether the wild rice has been paddy-raised ("cultivated") or harvested wild in the traditional Indian manner. Nevertheless, the cheaper paddy-grown rice damaged the livelihoods of the Anishinaabe, who long had lived off wild-rice exports.

Over the years, traditional methods of wild rice harvesting fell into disuse and consumption of processed commodity foods rose among the Ojibwe, resulting in an epidemic of diabetes. With diabetes rates reaching 40 percent of adults on the White Earth reservation, many people began returning to older foods, including wild rice.

Wild rice is facing a number of environmental threats. One is rising levels of sulfates, mercury, and phosphates in the water, all caused at least in part by rising mining activity. Another threat is climate change. Scientists also have been researching sulfate levels in more than 100 lakes across Minnesota, trying to determine at what level sulfates damage the wild rice crop, even as Native peoples take to their canoes for the age-old annual harvest. State agencies and mining companies have been battling over legal limits on sulfates in lake water. The limits affect levels of taconite mining, as well as exploitation of copper and nickel deposits that are among the world's largest. Some mining operations may not be able to meet a 10 parts per million limit on sulfate that the state deems safe for lake water. Wild rice is Minnesota's largest wild food crop. Wild rice's ability to utilize nitrogen, an essential nutrient, is impeded by high levels of sulfate. Bacteria transform aquatic nitrogen into toxic hydrogen sulfide in the sediment that nourishes the wild rice.

The stakes are high in Minnesota: "The $1.5 million study—Minnesota's largest involving wild rice—started slowly last year [2011], expanded this summer and will conclude after the 2013 growing season, when state funding is scheduled to run out. All of the research is getting input from a 32-person 'advisory committee' representing taconite companies, business groups, environmentalists, Indian resource agencies and research universities" (Myers, 2012). The researchers tested wild rice's reaction at 10 parts per million of sulfate, then at 50, 100, 150, and 300 parts per million. The researchers also spot-tested more than 150 Minnesota lakes for sulfate "hot spots."

Wild rice harvests also were reduced in 2012 by early spring warmth that caused plants to germinate too early, followed by early summer deluges, all signatures of climate change. Hand-harvested wild rice is more vulnerable to climate changes involving foods, winds, and other extremes than that which is raised on farms and harvested by machine. Much of the Native peoples' wild rice is hand-harvested. The hand-harvested rice has a taste and texture that the farmed variety often lacks. Flash floods such as those of June 2012 tend to uproot and drown truly wild rice. The crop losses in 2012 exceeded those of other bad years, such as 1999 and 2007. In 2012, several Native American wild rice harvests ended early.

See Also PART 2: CULTURAL FORMS: FOOD: Agriculture; Food Sovereignty: Local and Regional Examples

Further Reading

LaDuke, Winona. "Protecting the Culture and Genetics of Wild Rice." In Melissa Nelson, ed. *The Original Instructions: Indigenous Teachings for a Sustainable Future*. Rochester, VT: Bear, 2008, 206–214.

McAuliffe, Bill. "Summer Deluge Ravaged Hand-harvested Wild Rice." *Minneapolis Star Tribune*, September 7, 2012. http://www.startribune.com/local/169000086.html?refer=y. Accessed October 30, 2014.

Myers, John. "Who Cares about Wild Rice Study? Let's Start with the Mining Industry." *Duluth News-Tribune*, August 26, 2012. http://www.duluthnewstribune.com/event/article/id/241131/. Accessed October 30, 2014.

"Wild Rice Not Looking Good." Associated Press in *Janesville* (Wisconsin) *Gazette*, August 25, 2012. http://gazettextra.com/weblogs/latest-news/2012/aug/25/wild-rice-not-looking-good/. Accessed October 30, 2014.